Springer Series on

REHABILITATION

Volume 1 **The Psychology of Disability**
Carolyn L. Vash, Ph.D.

Volume 2 **Disabled People as Second-Class Citizens**
Myron G. Eisenberg, Ph.D., Cynthia Griggins, and Richard J. Duval, Editors

Volume 3 **Behavioral Approaches to Rehabilitation: Coping with Change**
Elaine Greif, Ph.D. and Ruth G. Matarazzo, Ph.D.

Volume 4 **Chronic Illness and Disability Through the Life Span: Effects on Self and Family**
Myron G. Eisenberg, Ph.D., LaFaye C. Sutkin, Ph.D., and Mary A. Jansen, Ph.D., Editors

Volume 5 **Handbook of Private Sector Rehabilitation**
Lewis J. Taylor, Ph.D., C.R.C., Marjorie Golter, M.S., C.R.C., Gary Golter, M.A., and Thomas E. Backer, Ph.D., Editors

Volume 6 **Applied Rehabilitation Counseling**
T. F. Riggar, Ed.D., Dennis R. Maki, Ph.D., and Arnold W. Wolf, Ph.D., C.R.C., Editors

T. F. Riggar, Ed.D., received his Ed.D. in Rehabilitation Counseling from the University of Northern Colorado and is a Professor in the Rehabilitation Administration and Services Unit, Rehabilitation Institute, Southern Illinois University at Carbondale. He has co-edited Special Issues for the *Journal of Applied Rehabilitation Counseling* and has been on the Editorial Advisory Board of eight other professional rehabilitation journals. He has produced a half-dozen books and over 40 professional articles in rehabilitation.

Dennis R. Maki, Ph.D., is an Associate Professor in the Division of Counselor Education, Rehabilitation Counseling Program, The University of Iowa. He is the Co-Editor of Special Issues for the *Journal of Applied Rehabilitation Counseling.* Dr. Maki received his Ph.D. in Rehabilitation Counseling Psychology from the University of Wisconsin-Madison.

Arnold W. Wolf, Ph.D., CRC, is Chief, Psychiatric Rehabilitation Services, City Hospital Center at Elmhurst, New York. He is an Adjunct Associate Professor of Psychology and Education at Columbia University, Teacher's College, Department of Social, Organizational and Counseling Psychology; an Adjunct Associate Professor of Education at New York University, SEHNAP, Department of Rehabilitation Counseling; and an Adjunct Associate Professor of Education at the Borough of Manhattan Community College, Department of Allied Health Sciences. He is the current editor of the *Journal of Applied Rehabilitation Counseling.*

Applied Rehabilitation Counseling

T. F. Riggar, Ed.D.
Dennis R. Maki, Ph.D.
Arnold W. Wolf, Ph.D., C.R.C.

Editors

SPRINGER PUBLISHING COMPANY
New York

Springer Publishing Company, Inc.
536 Broadway
New York, NY 10012

86 87 88 89 90 / 5 4 3 2 1

Library of Congress Cataloging-in-Publication Data

Applied rehabilitation counseling.

(Springer series on rehabilitation; v. 6)
Bibliography: p.
Includes index.
1. Rehabilitation counseling. 2. Rehabilitation—United States. I. Riggar, T. F. II. Maki, Dennis R. III. Wolf, Arnold W. IV. Series.
HD7255.5.A67 1986 362′.0425 86-21923
ISBN 0-8261-5371-2 (pbk.)

Printed in the United States of America

Contents

Contributors

Harry A. Allen is a Professor with the Rehabilitation Institute at Southern Illinois University. Dr. Allen has over 15 years experience as a therapist/counselor and rehabilitation educator.

Norman L. Berven is an Associate Professor in the Rehabilitation Counseling Program, Department of Studies in Behavioral Disabilities, University of Wisconsin-Madison.

Susanne M. Bruyere is currently a private consultant in rehabilitation practice and management in Ithaca, New York. She has a doctoral degree in Rehabilitation Counseling Psychology from the University of Wisconsin-Madison, and master's degrees in Rehabilitation Counseling, Adult Education, and Public Administration.

Rosanita Cespedes is the Director of the Center for Ethnic Student Affairs. She also has a clinical appointment in the Department of Educational Psychology, Rehabilitation and Community Counseling Program at the University of Utah.

David Clemmons, M.Ed., is a staff member at the Regional Epilepsy Center, Harborview Medical Center, University of Washington, Seattle.

Robert H. Couch is an Associate Professor and Head of Auburn University's Department of Rehabilitation and Special Education. Dr. Couch is a past president of the Vocational Evaluation and Work Adjustment Association (VEWAA), the Alabama Rehabilitation Association, and the Alabama VEWAA.

Marita Danek is employed in the Department of Counseling at Gallaudet College in Washington, D.C.

Fred Dickman is employed at the University of Southern Florida, Department of Rehabilitation Counseling, Tampa.

John Dolan, Rh.D. is an Assistant Professor in the Department of Rehabilitation Counseling, Louisiana State University-Medical Center, New Orleans.

Robert W. Flexer is an Associate Professor, Department of Special Education, at Kent State University, Kent, Ohio.

Robert T. Fraser, Ph.D., is a staff member at the Regional Epilepsy Center, Harborview Medical Center, University of Washington, Seattle.

Thomas C. Fuller is a Ph.D. candidate in Counseling Psychology in the School of Health Education, Counseling Psychology and Human Performance at Michigan State University. He received his M.A. in Clinical Mental Health Counseling at Western Michigan University.

Bruce Growick is the Coordinator of the Rehabilitation Counseling Program at the Ohio State University.

Rochelle V. Habeck is an Assistant Professor in Rehabilitation Counseling in the Division of Counseling Psychology, School of Health Education, Counseling Psychology and Human Performance at Michigan State University. She received her doctoral degree in Rehabilitation Counseling Psychology at the University of Wisconsin.

Geraldine Hansen is the Director of the Region V Rehabilitation Continuing Education Program (RCEP) located at Southern Illinois University-Carbondale. She received her doctorate in Rehabilitation Counseling from the University of Northern Colorado.

James T. Herbert, M.S., M.A., is completing doctoral studies in Rehabilitation Counseling Psychology at the University of Wisconsin-Madison. He has master's degrees in vocational rehabilitation and clinical psychology and is also a Certified Rehabilitation Counselor.

Ross K. Lynch, Ph.D., CRC, is President of Professional Rehabilitation Services, Ltd., Madison, Wisconsin. Dr. Lynch has several years experience as a rehabilitation counselor, educator, and researcher.

Ruth Torkelson Lynch is the Director of Vocational Services for the University of Wisconsin Hospital and Clinics Rehabilitation Center, Madison, Wisconsin. Dr. Lynch is also Clinical Assistant Professor in Rehabilitation Medicine with the University of Wisconsin Medical School.

Ralph E. Matkin, Rh.D., is owner of Vocational Management Systems, a consulting firm specializing in rehabilitation education and training, vocational analysis and research, and vocational expert testimony, located in Reseda, California. He is author of *Insurance Rehabilitation: Service Applications in Disability Compensation Systems.*

Jane E. Myers, Ph.D., Associate Professor, is Director of Rehabilitation Counselor Education at Ohio University in Athens.

Joseph N. Ososkie is presently Assistant Professor in Rehabilitation Counselor Education in the Department of Educational Psychology at the University of South Carolina.

Steven S. Ostby is an Assistant Professor in the Division of Rehabilitation Counseling, Department of Medical Allied Health Professions, School of Medicine, University of North Carolina at Chapel Hill.

Randall M. Parker is Professor and Associate Director, Rehabilitation Counseling Training Program, Department of Special Education, University of Texas at Austin.

Dean C. Patrick, Rh.D., is a Research Fellow at South Carolina State College. He received his doctorate at the Rehabilitation Institute, Southern Illinois University at Carbondale. Previously he worked as a rehabilitation counselor with the South Carolina Department of Vocational Rehabilitation.

Elizabeth A. Phillips is employed at the University of Southern Florida, Department of Rehabilitation Counseling, Tampa.

James M. Rice received his M.A. degree in Applied Behavior Analysis at Drake University and his Doctor of Rehabilitation (Rh.D.) degree at Southern Illinois University-Carbondale. He is currently an Assistant Professor in the Department of Psychology at Indiana University-Purdue University at Indianapolis.

Orlando A. Rivera is an Assistant Professor in the Department of Education Psychology and teaches in the Rehabilitation and Community Counseling Program. He is also an Associate Vice President for Academic Affairs at the University of Utah.

Warren R. Rule is a Professor in the Department of Rehabilitation Counseling at Virginia Commonwealth University. He received a Ph.D. from the University of South Carolina. Dr. Rule has published in the areas of rehabilitation counseling and psychology and has served in different capacities for Adlerian and rehabilitation publications.

Vincent A. Scalia, Ed.D., is Director of the Region VIII Rehabilitation Continuing Education Program and Associate Professor and Chair of the Department of Human Resources, Rehabilitation Counseling, at the University of Northern Colorado.

Patricia Schmitt is a graduate student in the Rehabilitation Counseling Program at the Ohio State University.

John D. See is an Associate Professor of the Stout Vocational Rehabilitation Institute, University of Wisconsin-Stout.

Kenneth R. Thomas is Professor and Chair, Department of Studies in Behavioral Disabilities, University of Wisconsin-Madison.

Shari Thurer is Assistant Professor of Rehabilitation Counseling at Boston University and a psychologist in private practice. She is currently enrolled in an advanced training program in psychoanalytic psychotherapy at the Boston Psychoanalytic Society and Institute.

Joseph O. Turpin is a doctoral candidate in Rehabilitation Counseling Psychology in the Department of Studies in Behavioral Disabilities at the University of Wisconsin-Madison.

Charles J. Vander Kolk, Ph.D., CRC, is the Chairperson, Rehabilitation Counseling Program, University of South Carolina, Columbia.

David Vandergoot is Research Coordinator with the Human Resources Center, Albertson, New York.

Barbara J. Witten, Ph.D., is Assistant Director of the Graduate Program in Rehabilitation Counseling at the University of Kentucky.

Richard R. Wolfe, Ph.D., is Professor of Rehabilitation Counseling and Coordinator of the Graduate Program in Rehabilitation Counseling at the University of Northern Colorado.

George Wright, Ph.D., CRC, is Professor of Rehabilitation Counseling Psychology at the University of Wisconsin-Madison and a consultant in personal injury insurance rehabilitation. Dr. Wright is current president of Rehabilitation Psychology Division 22 of the American Psychological Association, a former president of the American Rehabilitation Counseling Association, and has held offices in various other rehabilitation organizations.

Preface

The editors of this text met in 1982 to discuss the long-range needs of the *Journal of Applied Rehabilitation Counseling (JARC)*, the professional publication of the National Rehabilitation Counseling Association (NRCA). There arose out of that meeting the realization that three people could not explore the depths of that need on their own. This resulted in a decision to make an annual "call" for topics and papers to practitioners, educators, administrators, and students in rehabilitation counseling. Consequently a special annual issue of the journal was projected to explore one selected theme in depth. It would be published as the fall issue of *JARC*, or issue number 3 of each volume year.

The first special issue was published in the fall of 1983 under the title "Rehabilitation Counseling: State of the Art with Special Populations." It was received extremely well by the profession as determined by the numerous letters addressed to the editor of *JARC*. Many requests were received for additional copies of the issue for classroom or lecture purposes. Eventually, letters and telephone calls requested that the journal undertake publication of a text based upon this material.

The subsequent special issues for 1984 and 1985 were entitled "The Contemporary Practice of Rehabilitation Counseling" and "Rehabilitation Counseling: Orientations to Practice," respectively, with the thought of incorporating this material into the projected text. This could be used for a variety of courses in rehabilitation counseling graduate programs and simultaneously serve the practitioner who wished to remain current in applied practices.

Many individuals assisted in the development of this text at all levels from the inception of the concepts through the ranks of authors, manuscript reviewers, and NRCA leadership. The great bulk of the work, however, was accomplished by T. F. Riggar and Dennis Maki, who were responsible for the annual special issue, while I had the easier task of editing the regular issues of the journal. The team of Maki and Riggar had to select the theme and develop specific guidelines for each special issue. This was further influenced by the need to either call for papers or select appropriate authors and to make sure that each submitted manuscript fit the need of the special issue and the overall theme of the projected text: the applied aspects of rehabilitation counseling practice.

The chapters of this text are based upon and contain the material found in the three special issues mentioned. The text explores components of the contemporary practice of rehabilitation counseling, current orientations to rehabilitation counseling, and the relationships between practice and specific populations and disabilities. It is realized that the text does not exhaust each topic of discussion presented, and future special issues of *JARC* will explore areas not covered.

Arnold W. Wolf, Ph.D., CRC
Editor
Journal of Applied Rehabilitation Counseling
January 3, 1986

Acknowledgments

The National Rehabilitation Counseling Association, the NRCA Board of Directors, the Editorial Board of the *Journal of Applied Rehabilitation Counseling*, and the editors of this text would like to thank the authors who served for three special issues of *JARC*. The expertise and voluntary participation exhibited by these rehabilitation professionals made the special issues the dynamic and sought after publications they have become and have made this text a milestone in the field.

We would also like to thank Dr. Gary F. Austin, Director of the Rehabilitation Institute, and Dr. Seymour Bryson, College of Human Resources Dean, for their understanding of the time and effort involved in research, as well as the administration and management of the Word Processing Unit within the College upon which this text was prepared. Ms. Linda Patrick, who operates the Unit, was able to put up with poor direction, bad communication, and computer illiteracy on our part and still produce this quality project.

This work is dedicated to our families, Anila Mennon Singh, Gordon and Donna Smith, and to the memory of David Malikin, teacher, colleague, and friend.

We wish to thank Ms. Barbara Watkins, Vice President and Senior Editor, Springer Publishing Company, whose unenviable job it is to work with university professors; she taught us well.

Consulting Reviewers

Consulting Reviewers were selected by the co-editors of the special issues based on exceptional individual knowledge, experience, training, and background in rehabilitation. Without the voluntary assistance of such rehabilitation professionals throughout the country the task of reviewing appropriate manuscripts submitted for publication would be difficult.

Harold Adams
Division of Counselor Education
University of Iowa

John Banks
National Rehabilitation
Counseling Assn.
Alexandria, VA

Mario Barillas
Coordinator of Planning
Rehabilitation Education and
Services Branch
State of Iowa

Norman Berven
Dept. of Studies in Behavioral
Disabilities
University of Wisconsin-Madison

Donna Chandler
Rehabilitation Education and
Services Branch
Iowa City, Iowa

Nicholas Colangelo
Division of Counselor Education
University of Iowa

Cary Cox
Division of Rehabilitation
Services
Staff Development and Training
State of Georgia

William Criminado
Rehabilitation Institute
Southern Illinois University

Robert M. Davis
Dept. of Psychology
Purdue University at
Indianapolis

Henry DeVasher
Past President
National Rehabilitation
Counseling Assn.
Tuscaloosa, AL

John Dolan
Dept. of Rehabilitation
Counseling
LSU Medical Center

Timothy F. Field
Dept. of Counseling and Human
Development Services
University of Georgia

Jon Fortune
Vice President
Southwest Wyoming
Rehabilitation Center
Rock Springs, WY

Nadya Foyad
Dept. of Educational
Psychology
The University of
Wisconsin-Milwaukee

Saul Freedman
Director
National Consultants Dept.
American Foundation for the Blind, Inc.

Susan H. Godley
Jackson County Mental Health
Carbondale, IL

Rochelle V. Habeck
Dept. of Counseling, Educational Psychology and Special Education
Michigan State University

Marilyn Hafer
Rehabilitation Institute
Southern Illinois University

Geraldine Hansen
Director, Region V RCEP
Southern Illinois University

Mary A. Jansen
California School of Professional Psychology
Fresno, CA

Derrell Johnson
Division of Vocational Rehabilitation
Salt Lake City, UT

Michael Klein
Rehabilitation Counselor Education Program
University of Wisconsin-Milwaukee

Michael Kogutek
Private Practice
Orange, California

Richard H. LaFon
President
National Association of Rehabilitation Professionals in the Private Sector

Thomas R. Lehmann, M.D.
Dept. of Orthopedic Surgery
The University of Iowa

Jerome R. Lorenz
Rehabilitation Institute
Southern Illinois University

Ross Lynch
Professional Rehabilitation Services, Ltd.
Madison, Wisconsin

Sherry Lynch
Client Assistance Program
Kansas Dept. of Social and Rehabilitation Services

William E. Martin, Jr.
Dept. of Human Services
Univ. of Northern Colorado

Paul S. McCollum
Director
Graduate Program in Rehabilitation Counseling
University of Texas Health Science Center

Brian T. McMahon
Dept. of Human Services and Studies
Florida State University

Thomas Modahl
Dept. of Vocational Rehabilitation
University of Wisconsin-Stout

Jane E. Myers
Applied Behavioral Sciences and Educational Leadership
Ohio University

Michael Nelipovich
Dept. of Rehab and Special Education
University of Arkansas

Deborah A. Pape
Dept. of Educational Psychology
University of Wisconsin-Milwaukee

George Petrangelo
Dept. of Psychology
St. Cloud State University

Robert Pullo
Rehabilitation Counseling Program
Rhode Island College

Sherry Repscher
Utah State Director
Governor's Comm. on Employment of the Handicapped

James M. Rice
Dept. of Psychology, Purdue University at Indianapolis

Ralph R. Roberts
Rehabilitation Counseling Program
University of Iowa

Brockman Schumacher
Rehabilitation Institute
Southern Illinois University

Bettye Shofner
University of Arkansas
Hot Springs, Arkansas

Gary L. Sigmon
Psychology Department
Appalachian State University

Jerry L. Starkweather
Director
Rehabilitation Education and Services Branch
State of Iowa

Kenneth R. Thomas
Rehabilitation Psychology Program
University of Wisconsin-Madison

Richard W. Thoreson
Dept. of Educational and Counseling Psychology
University of Missouri-Columbia

Sharon Van Meter
Coordinator, Office of Disabled Student Services
Veterans Services
University of California-Santa Cruz

George N. Wright
Dept. of Studies in Behavioral Disabilities
University of Wisconsin-Madison

I

The Contemporary Practice of Rehabilitation Counseling

1 Foundations of Applied Rehabilitation Counseling

Dennis R. Maki

Rehabilitation counseling has evolved as a field largely in response to legislative mandates. Since the enactment of PL 83–565 in 1954, the emergence of the profession has witnessed advances in research, education, and the practice of rehabilitation counseling. The discipline has established professional organizations, professional journals, certification and accreditation procedures, codes of ethics, and a political lobby. The art and science of rehabilitation counseling continues to develop as research and practice enumerate principles for efficient and effective service delivery. The purpose of this volume is to present the current state of applied rehabilitation counseling.

The goal of rehabilitation counseling is to assist persons with disabilities to achieve functional independence and effective adjustment. Prior to describing the contemporary practice of rehabilitation counseling, orientations to practice, and applications to specific clientele, it is essential to discuss some fundamentals. Specifically, basic definitions, concepts, and tenets need be presented. The intention of this chapter is to provide an overview and introduction to rehabilitation counseling.

THE REHABILITATION CONCEPT

The rehabilitation concept is based on the fundamental belief in the worth and dignity of each person. The philosophy of rehabilitation services emphasizes the assets of each person. Bitter (1979) has enumerated three principles which provide a philosophic foundation for the practice of rehabilitation in the United States.

1. The philosophy advocates equality of opportunity for all persons. Thus, persons with disability are provided specialized services to prepare for employment and participation in the privileges and responsibilities of citizenship (Garrett, 1969).

2. Each person is holistic and cannot be divided into parts such as physical, social, mental, vocational, and economic. These aspects interact together to form the whole (Jacques, 1970).

3. Each individual is unique. Reaction to disability varies from person to person. Each person possesses unique assets, coping mechanisms, needs, and goals.

Rehabilitation represents the philosophy that whenever possible persons with a disability are to be integrated into the least restrictive environments. Thus, rehabilitation is a comprehensive, individualized process, prescriptive in nature, and directed toward the development or restoration of functional independence. Vocational rehabilitation defines functional independence in terms of economic self-sufficiency.

The following represent the key elements in understanding the concept of rehabilitation:

1. *It is comprehensive in scope.* The rehabilitation process is an orderly sequence of activities related to the total needs of the individual. Though comprehensive services will differ from client to client, there are certain basic dimensions relevant to understanding the total person. The most significant dimensions include the medical aspects, psychological factors, socio-cultural, as well as educational and vocational considerations. To understand the client or provide services relating to only one aspect of the person's functioning, without considering the other aspects and their interdependency would be ineffective and result in the failure of rehabilitation effort. Effective rehabilitation thus usually demands the coordinated efforts of a multidisciplinary team.

2. *It is an individualized process.* Each person is unique in skills, residual capacities, functional limitations, resources, and personality. The manifestations of disability present themselves differently to each individual, with varying meanings and implications. Rehabilitation is a process based upon the needs of a particular client. Rehabilitation counselors must continually be aware of the pitfalls of labeling and stereotyping. Nathanson (1979), noted that counseling professionals are not immune to bias or prejudice regarding disability and must be aware of their own attitudes and expectations. Successful rehabilitation is based on individualized rehabilitation plans developed with clients based on evaluation data.

3. *It is prescriptive in nature.* That is to say, a prescriptive course of action is developed for each individual. The type and amount of services provided are based on the needs and characteristics of the individual. Services are selected which will remove, reduce, or com-

pensate for the functional limitations of the individual in achieving the goals established in the individualized plan. Environmental modifications must be considered, as well as client development.

4. *It functions to develop or restore. Habilitation* is the term which denotes the development or acquisition of skills and functions previously not attained. This term is commonly used in reference to serving persons with disabilities, who, due to lack of training or experience, are now developing their functional independence. *Rehabilitation* refers to the restoration or reacquisition of skills and functions lost through injury, disease or trauma. The term *rehabilitation* is used here to generically describe either process resulting in functional independence.

5. *Its goal is functional independence.* Functional independence is the capacity to take care of one's own affairs to the extent that one is capable. This is a broad goal; subsumed under it are economic self-sufficiency as well as personal, social, and community living skills (Morris, 1973). It also reflects the individualized orientation in defining success and functioning. Functional independence considers the total individual in his or her environments.

THE REHABILITATION COUNSELOR

Rehabilitation counseling is a process involving a counselor and client to assist the client to understand existing problems and potentials, and to help the client make effective use of personal and environmental resources for their best possible vocational, personal, and social adjustment (Jacques, 1970). Maki, McCracken, Pape, and Scofield (1978) define the effective role of the rehabilitation counselor as one of problem-solver. The main characteristic subsumed in this role is the ability to perceive the problems of each client as they relate to vocational adjustment and to help plan appropriate intervention strategies. This professional role is composed of responsibilities and functions (Sinick, 1977). Specific functions are determined by the needs of a client, the nature and demands of the agency, and the requirements of the community.

Regardless of setting and specific clientele, the rehabilitation counselor must possess a core of competencies that correspond to the performance requirements of their position. George N. Wright (1980), building on the work of McGowen and Porter (1967), reported the following knowledge, skills, and duties of the rehabilitation counselor.

Necessary Knowledge

The rehabilitation counselor must acquire professional knowledge of:

1. Human behavior as it relates to personal, social, and vocational adjustment.
2. Significance of client skills, aptitudes, interests, and educational backgrounds.
3. The effects of disability on personality as related to personal and community adjustment.
4. Employment policies regarding persons with disabilities.
5. Local, state, and federal laws pertinent to rehabilitation.

Necessary Skills

The rehabilitation counselor must have ability to:

1. Establish and maintain a functional counseling relationship.
2. Apply human relations skills to not only clients but other key people in the agency and community for a more effective professional and personal life.
3. Realize the broad, pervasive effects of the environment in shaping human motivation.
4. Understand and accept human behavior as it relates to a specific client.
5. Relate varied professional competencies, including one's own, to the needs of the client as a person.
6. Assess the potential of the client in choosing a suitable objective and develop plans for achieving that objective.
7. Evaluate the personality dynamics, skills, aptitudes, interests, and capacities of the client throughout the rehabilitation processes.
8. Understand employment procedures in all fields and relate them to the needs of the client.
9. Understand community organization, including job structure, job requirements, and training facilities.
10. Work collaboratively with a rehabilitation team of professionals representing other disciplines and other agencies.
11. Develop and utilize community resources.
12. Function effectively in a public relations and advocacy role in order to improve community understanding of rehabilitation and persons with disability.

Necessary Duties

The rehabilitation counselor has a multiplicity of job responsibilities:

1. Collecting, analyzing, and evaluating relevant information about the client.
2. Securing a medical workup and diagnosis.
3. Determining client eligibility for agency services.
4. Obtaining necessary information about a client, including making provision for psychological, social, and vocational evaluations.
5. Integrating information into a comprehensive program of rehabilitation services through an individualized plan.
6. Arranging for purchased services such as physical or psychological restoration, personal adjustment, and/or vocational training, transportation, and maintenance.
7. Assisting the client to learn techniques for coping with life adjustment problems.
8. Developing job opportunities suitable for agency clientele.
9. Assisting clients in securing employment consistent with their capacities, personality, and preparation.
10. Following up the client after employment.

Whitehouse (1975) referred to the rehabilitation counselor as a "rehabilitation clinician," possessing a comprehensive knowledge base with multiple competencies, able to work with the whole person. He considered the rehabilitation clinician as a professional whose skills included those of guidance counselor, therapist, case manager, case coordinator, clinical life reviewer, psychometrician, educator, team member, social and family relator, placement counselor, community and client advocate, life engagement counselor, long-term conservator, and clinician. Rubin and Roessler (1983) note that much of the available research supports the validity of Whitehouse's (1975) position that the rehabilitation clinician is a professional who is able to serve persons with disability from a multifaceted but integrated service standpoint.

In summary, the *Occupational Outlook Handbook* (1985) describes the rehabilitation counselor's work as follows:

> *Rehabilitation counselors* assist physically, mentally, emotionally, or socially handicapped individuals to become self-sufficient and productive citizens. Rehabilitation counselors evaluate their clients' potential for employment and arrange for medical care, rehabilitation programs, occupational training,

and job placement. To do this, they learn about their clients by talking with them, evaluating school and medical reports, and consulting with family members. They also confer with physicians, psychologists, and occupational therapists about the types of work their clients could perform. They then recommend an appropriate rehabilitation program and specialized training to help the individual with disability become more independent and more employable. Since employment success is an important goal of rehabilitation counseling, counselors keep in touch with employers about job openings and the training required. (p. 108)

THE REHABILITATION CLIENT

As persons with disability are served by rehabilitation counselors, it is important to understand basic concepts relating to our clients. To begin with, distinctions must be made between the terms *disability, functional limitations,* and *handicaps.*

A *disability* is defined as "a condition of impairment, physical or mental, having an objective aspect that can usually be described by a physician. It is essentially a medical thing" (Hamilton, 1950, p. 17).

A *handicap* is defined as "the culminative result of the obstacles which disability interposes between the individual and his maximum functional level. The handicap is the measure of the loss of the individual's capacity, wherever evident. It is an individual thing composed of the barriers which the handicapped person must surmount in order to obtain the fullest physical, mental, social, vocational, and economic usefulness of which he is capable" (Hamilton, 1950, p. 17). Handicap is not a medical condition. It is recognized that the severity of disability correlates with the severity of handicap. However, two persons may possess the identical medical diagnosis; both have a disability, but both are not necessarily handicapped.

In determining the handicapping effect of disability for an individual, an analysis of the following factors is necessary:

1. *Medical:* What limitations are imposed by the disability itself?
2. *Psychological:* What limitations are imposed on the individual by the individual as a result of the disability?
3. *Socio-cultural:* What limitations are imposed by societal forces, particularly those in the immediate environment (i.e., family, peers, community)?
4. *Educational:* What limitations are imposed educationally as a result of the disability?

5. *Vocational:* What limitations are imposed by the world of work as a result of the disability?

In considering the effect of the disabling condition on the functioning of the individual, as well as the environmental variables operative in the situation, it is possible to assess the degree and types of handicap(s) impinging on the individual.

It is important to note that the medical profession differs from rehabilitation in its use of these terms. The term *impairment* is used in reference to the medical condition, while disability refers to what the rehabilitation professional would call the handicap.

The concept which has the most relevance to the rehabilitation counselor working with persons with disability is that of functional limitations. *Functional limitation* is the inability to perform a role or task or activities required or expected within one's social and physical environment. Functional limitations operationally define the impact of disability and represent the intervening physical and/or behavioral variables/obstacles considered in describing the nature and extent of handicap. The following factors are based on the work of Wright (1980) and consider specific limitations which disability may impose.

1. *Sensory impairment* refers to reduction in or incapacity to receive environmental stimuli in the visual, auditory, olfactory, tactile, or taste domains.
2. *Communication difficulty* refers to reduced or incapacity to receive, process, and/or transmit messages, either verbally or nonverbally, to or from other persons in the environment.
3. *Atypical appearance* refers to physical or behavioral cues emitted by an individual which may be interpreted as significantly different from environmental normative standards to attract the attention of other persons in the environment.
4. *Emotional/behavioral considerations* refer to those interpersonal, intrapersonal, or physical manifestations of affective and/or cognitive processes which interfere with an individual's ability to effectively function within his/her environment.
5. *Unapparent limitation* refers to those situations where although disability is present, no cues are overtly transmitted to others in the environment. Thus, the disability is invisible and the person is considered to be able-bodied by the general public.
6. *Cognitive/learning difficulty* refers to an impaired ability to obtain, process, or retain information potentially impacting on the individual's ability to attend, conceptualize, abstract, judge, problem-solve, or gain from interaction with the environment.

7. *Substance dependency* refers to the physical or psychological need for and use/misuse of chemical agents over a period of time either on a prescribed or self-regulated basis.

8. *Pain sensitivity/intolerance* refers to those situations where the physical or psychological sensation of pain exceeds the individual's threshold of tolerance impacting on their life-style and ability to concentrate, learn, effectively interact, or physically maneuver within the environment.

9. *Consciousness* refers to an inability to maintain a condition of mental awareness of the environment at any given point in time.

10. *Debilitation* refers to a progressive, though usually gradual deterioration of physical, emotional, or intellectual capacities.

11. *Motion deficit* refers to partial or total restrictions in movement or coordination in the limbs or trunk of the body impacting on the individual's ability to maneuver within and to manipulate his/her environment.

12. *Mobility* refers to an impaired ability or the inability of an individual to independently move between points in his/her environment as a result of physical, psychological, sensory, or environmental factors.

13. *Restricted environment* refers to the situation in which an individual is unable to interact within the total context of the environment as a result of physical barriers, when factors may be present which cause or exacerbate the disabling condition, when the individual would be a threat to self or others if permitted to interact, or if a controlled environment is required in the treatment of the disabling condition.

14. *Uncertain prognosis* refers to the inability to predict with any degree of certainty the duration, severity, and/or probable final status of a disease or mental disorder.

15. *Special considerations* refers to those unique implications of a situation which if unattended to would result in less than optimal rehabilitation outcomes for any given individual.

The translation of the impact of disability through an analysis of the functional limitations imposed provides the rehabilitation counselor with an effective and efficient problem-solving format. It is important to stress that while the identification of functional limitations is a necessary first step, it is the identification of residual capacities and transferable skills which form the basis of rehabilitation planning and placement activities.

In closing this section, it is important to mention the language we use in describing our clients. Avoid using adjectives as nouns. That is, referring to a client as retarded is inappropriate in contemporary rehabilitation practice. It is preferable to put the person before the disability. Therefore, reference would be made to a person with mental retardation. Persons with disability is to be used rather than disabled persons. Able-bodied is the preferred term for describing persons without disabilities. Avoid the use of the term "normal" in this regard. As professionals working with persons with disabilities, it is essential we communicate clearly in functional terms and reflect a regard and dignity toward our clients.

SUMMARY

The process and practice of rehabilitation counseling is dynamic and evolutional. Since the beginnings of our profession, changing social and political trends have impacted on the clientele served, the counselor's functions and responsibilities, the organization of service delivery, and the definition of appropriate outcomes. Research and education have also impacted on these same factors, thus also influencing contemporary practice. We continue to emerge and diversify, yet hold constant our primary mission of facilitating the independence of persons with disability.

With a foundation of understanding the rehabilitation concept, counselor, and client, the section which follows describes the contemporary practice of rehabilitation counseling. To emphasize the key aspects of the practice, the topics include assessment, counseling, adjustment service, placement, case management, and administration. However, as education and research are integrally related to contemporary practice, these aspects are included as well. Finally, a discussion of employment trends is presented.

2 Professional Perspectives and Planning

George N. Wright

By every indication there is now more than ever before opportunity to vastly expand utilization of rehabilitation counseling as a mature profession. Reasons for an optimistic view will be given along with some of the problems that are surfacing and solution strategies. A format based on issues will provide background information and positive and negative considerations along with suggestions for planning future action and perspectives.

Summarizing us favorably, a stock market analyst might issue this report:

> Rehabilitation Counseling, Inc., is a growing corporation by business standards. Its product continues to be highly profitable; both cost-benefit and effectiveness attract public investors with firm support. Such success is in part attributable to its unique technology derived from a substantial research investment since 1954 when preparations for the firm were initiated. Moreover, this is an organization with outstanding leadership and a well-trained, industrious work force; yet despite excellent productivity its wage rates are comparatively low—particularly in some of its shops and in many states. However, its new and rapidly expanding branches in the private insurance field are making large dollar profits through billable hours, and this competitive surge in demand for qualified workers can be expected to impact upon salary levels throughout this industry. In summary, we are optimistic about the company as a whole as compared to others in the field of high technology. It combines the investment attractions of being a well-established, low-risk, and diversified firm with high annual yields. With future planning this group has an enormous growth potential in other and expanding markets for long-term capital gain and opportunity for new acquisitions, mergers and mutually beneficial collaboration agreements with others in rehabilitation fields.

Insiders, while optimistic in their overall analyses of perspectives of the profession of rehabilitation counseling, should be aware of potential barriers to growth and development. Rather than citing excerpts for the enormous body of relevant literature, the reader is referred to the nearly 1,000 bibliographic references of the author's 1980 book, *Total Rehabilitation,* published by Little, Brown, and to a 1984 list of 200 relevant documents compiled by the author with Marita Danek for a National Council on Rehabilitation Education (NCRE) research grant application available from the National Rehabilitation Information Center (NARIC).

Strategic planning is needed by rehabilitationists in the same way that American businesses examine and shape their futures. It involves identifying our mission, assessing our resources and opportunities for growth and development as well as potential obstacles, and then setting goals and objectives. Our profession's mission statement should define our purposes and roles (i.e., we are in the business of . . .). Objectives that we set forth should be achievable in a reasonable time (e.g., five to ten years) and consistent with our mission's long-term goals. A strategic plan must have the input and support of every leadership group in order to ensure communications and commitment by all rehabilitationists. Moreover, such planning requires mechanisms for continuing program evaluation, modification, and implementation. This chapter will look at foundations and strategies for a professional plan incorporating the entire field of extra-medical rehabilitation.

COUNSELOR OR REHABILITATOR

Counseling is an essential function of the rehabilitationist but not the only important tool of our extra-medical team. In addition to "counseling," other areas of psychology include "measurement" (psychometrics), "somatopsychology," "social," "industrial" (personnel), "occupational" (vocational), "health," and "clinical" psychology. One of the unique aspects of our profession is that it utilizes these many sources of psychology as its parent science. We should not be separated from psychology professionally, conceptually, educationally, or organizationally by the artificial distinction of "guidance and human development" from "counseling psychology." Our professional identification as "rehabilitation counseling psychologist" accommodates the broad competency bases we require for our clientele. Even the psychology title is important to our future.

Until the 1940s the public rehabilitation counselor was referred to as "field worker" or "agent"—even on federal forms. At the time very few state rehabilitation workers had appropriate preparation for counseling or their other job tasks. Nevertheless, state rehabilitation administrators back then decided to adopt the title "counselor" as more prestigious and warranting a higher salary scale. Their decision helped to shape the role perception and qualifications conceptions (preparation requirements) for the new profession of rehabilitation counseling. Otherwise, the professionalization process might well have adopted the social work model as public vocational rehabilitation agencies did in Canada and many other countries. In fact, an aborted attempt was made in many state rehabilitation agencies in the late 1940s with the employment of master's degree level "social work consultants." Of course, the real assurance of rehabilitation counseling as a profession came with the 1954 Act which provided federal grant support for specific preprofessional training for rehabilitation (mostly to new rehabilitation counseling education programs in universities) and for research and demonstrations (mostly to develop the technology of the rehabilitation counselor as the basic professional worker). These new training grants were made initially to school guidance departments; consequently, few rehabilitation professors had relevant experience.

The "rehabilitation counselor or coordinator" issue of the 1960s was warmed over (from a concept originally proposed in 1926) to promote the "guidance counselor educator" interpretation of appropriate activity of the counselor in rehabilitation—that "counseling is their *only* professional function" and things like job placement and the like do not require advance preparation. Now a far better understanding shows us that while specialization (such as job development and placement) is needed, all rehabilitationists should be qualified through preprofessional and continuing education under a broad umbrella of psychological knowledge and skills which includes, but is by no means limited to, counseling.

This background may explain in part our role identity problem—rehabilitation counseling psychologist or guidance counselor in rehabilitation. The solution to the dilemma may be for us collectively to rise above the political basis of the argument. We have a well-developed professional identification that need not be subsumed. Consequently, our "Strategic Plan" should start with articulation of our unique goals and qualifications as specialists in the rehabilitation of clients who have a handicap to life adjustment.

PROFESSIONAL PREPARATION

Preprofessional and continuing education for expected competencies is required by all respected professions for the right to practice. The competency basis of our curricula reflect various functions which serve client needs. In rehabilitation counseling, criteria for preprofessional master's degree education and university program accreditation is provided by the Council on Rehabilitation Education (CORE); evaluations of competencies standards for the "right" to practice are provided by the Commission on Rehabilitation Counselor Certification (CRCC). Both CORE and CRCC, compatible organizations established in the 1970s to assure practitioner qualifications, have as their ultimate goal the improvement of service delivery to clients. State licensure for rehabilitation counselors is now at issue and will require leadership for proper planning and operation nationally. Similarly our profession continues to develope and inculcate in students and practitioners codes of ethical conduct. Credentialing in all of these forms derives from prescribed standards covering what the professional practitioner needs to know and do for clients.

A standardized curriculum for the professional master's degree in rehabilitation counseling was planned in a historic workshop after federal training grants were authorized in 1954. Sponsored by the National Rehabilitation Association (NRA) and the National Vocational Guidance Association (NVGA), this meeting of national authorities on rehabilitation and graduate counselor education provided the initial guidelines to curriculum planning for university grantees. Even before this, NRA had a committee charged with course content for rehabilitation counselor education. The July 1955 NRA-NVGA Charlottesville course suggestions are still followed although there are differences in emphasis. Also, new curriculum content must be continually added with changes in roles, functions, clientele, and settings of rehabilitation practice; new courses include independent living, behavioral modification, proprietary and forensic practice, preventive rehabilitation, and employee assistance programming and substance abuse. The author has also suggested standard post-master's education with instruction for specialization according to disability, role and function, or site.

Rehabilitation counseling education matured magnificently in the 1960s with assistance by the so-called Joint Liaison Committee representing all rehabilitation counselor educators and state administrators. They met annually with federal grant assistance for curriculum planning with in-depth focus each year on unique instructional content and methods for a specific course (e.g., medical aspects). This opportunity for counselor educators to learn about the real world of rehabilitation employment helped shape practical curriculum based upon client needs. At that time few rehabilitation educators had worked in this field; subsequently, through doctoral degree programs in rehabilitation counselor education, professors and researchers with rehabilitation experience and explicit education have been made available. The compilation and dissemination of practitioner relevant information has flourished through federally sponsored conferences and published proceedings since 1947, called "Guidance Training and Placements Workshops" until 1962, then "Institutes on Rehabilitation Services," and now "Institutes on Rehabilitation Issues."

Unfortunately, the other specializations in rehabilitation have not shared the benefit of extensive educational planning accorded over the years to rehabilitation counseling which identified client service needs, requisite professional competencies, and required instructional content. Nor has there been sufficient professional planning for the establishment of training grant categories creating such specializations or their relationships with rehabilitation counseling education and practice. All of this has compounded problems in the allocation of training grants by category.

Finally, continuing education is recognized as essential for qualified practitioners. Originally outservice training of employed rehabilitation counselors was largely done through extra grants to local university rehabilitation programs; now Regional Rehabilitation Continuing Education Programs supplement state rehabilitation in-service training. Needed is an investigation of strategies most effective for enhancing competencies for all employed rehabilitation practitioners with adequate funding and training resources.

UNIFYING THE PROFESSION

Rehabilitationists suffer fragmentation as no other profession—particularly in specialization by function (counseling, assessment, adjustment, placement, and administration). Contrast this with social work which retains a single professional identification despite multifaceted specializations (e.g., medical, child, school, public welfare, psychiatric social work). We could benefit from the model of the medical profession for which there is a uniform initial preparation (the M.D. degree with internship for general practice) optionally followed by further training for specialization and additional credentialing (various board memberships). Unanimity perhaps could never be accomplished through professional merger; however, it is possible to obtain unanimous consent by practitioner representation from the various specializations formally agreeing to an overall plan-of-service strategies. Willingness to do this will require primary devotion to clientele rather that turf interest.

Specialization in rehabilitation counseling—as the author initially pointed out in 1980 in *Total Rehabilitation*—may have several dimensions: by employment setting (e.g., public or voluntary agency, facility, or proprietary business); by type of client handicap (e.g., retardation, blindness, cultural disadvantage); or by function (e.g., vocational or personal adjustment counseling, client vocational assessment, job placement). Still another specialization is by role, where the goal of service may be other than traditional vocational and personal adjustment; examples are in employee assistance programs, health maintenance organizations, and forensic (legal aspects) practice as a vocational and psychosocial expert on the impact of personal injury cases.

Perceiving ourselves as practitioners of various areas of psychology uniquely adapted to rehabilitation service can help to overcome a narrow and shortsighted professional self-image (e.g., "counselors who happen to be in rehabilitation"). It is time to join the forces of only somewhat different (extra-medical) rehabilitation professionals without basic distinction of identification because of variations in title, work setting, association membership, and specialization. Overcoming divisive influences could be the major benefit of strategic planning such as proposed here.

PROFESSIONAL ASSOCIATIONS AND IDENTIFICATIONS

While federal training funds have been and still are critical for the future of rehabilitation service, this federal program may have inadvertently facilitated the fragmentation of our profession. After a number of years of successful rehabilitation counselor education projects, new categories of training grants were established in areas previously assumed to be a part of rehabilitation counselor functions (e.g., vocational evaluation and assessment, job placement and development, work adjustment). These new specializations led to separate professional identification, and so new associations were organized long after state agency and other practitioners were professionally affiliated in one or both of the two established rehabilitation counseling associations.

The American Rehabilitation Counseling Association (ARCA) and the National Rehabilitation Counseling Association (NRCA) were both established at about the same time (1956–57) but with different constituencies, purposes, and parents. The specializations for job development and placement, work evaluation and adjustment, and administration now have their own divisions of the National Rehabilitation Association. And yet out of division can come growth—not through competition but with collaboration among special competencies. For example, NRCA and ARCA both bring great strength to the profession in part because they have the force of different parent associations. For years, the leadership of these two groups have talked of merger; but a single rehabilitation counseling organization may never be possible because of the legal and many other problems connected with the dissolution of a division of a larger association. However, they can and should cooperate with perhaps separate spheres of responsibilities defined for each of these many rehabilitation groups. This, too, can best be accomplished through a master plan.

There is danger of still further splitting of this profession as our colleagues go into new types of employment. An illustrative group is rehabilitation professionals in the private sector, associating rehabilitation counselors, nurses, and others in insurance rehabilitation through the organization of a separate group. A still more serious threat to professional unity is the recent split in the credentialing (accreditation, licensure, and certification) mechanisms. These problems can be avoided only through professional planning by the concerned parties.

In a sense, the demonstrated effectiveness of rehabilitation counseling is our greatest danger because of ensuing growth and applications. But the expansion of employment opportunities into new sectors—with better remuneration levels—is also a dynamic strength. This will help us to expand our numbers so that we are not overshadowed by older and larger professions. Thus, planned development and professional status is facilitated by our multifaceted growth, and this can and should promote collaboration as a form of unification.

REHABILITATION RESEARCH AND TECHNOLOGY

The largest single force for professional cohesiveness is a common body of knowledge. Largely due to federal research grants over the last 30 years, we have accumulated a substantial research-based technology. In the hands of trained rehabilitation workers, these advances have made it feasible now to rehabilitate individuals handicapped by a wide range of severe disabilities, cases whose application would have been turned down before.

While the past and future of rehabilitation practice depends upon this research, funding levels may be endangered. Prior to the formation of the National Institute of Handicapped Research (NIHR) in the new U.S. Department of Education, *all* funds were designated for rehabilitation as then administered by the Rehabilitation Services Administration (RSA) of the old U.S. Department of Health, Education and Welfare (HEW). It is important that this source for rehabilitation know-how not be siphoned off by special education. A similar situation was encountered in the HEW Social and Rehabilitation Services Administration when the formerly autonomous RSA was merged with Social Work which did not have a significant federal research program and coveted these funds. This is a current political problem for all rehabilitation practitioners and as such requires the political force of a unified voice.

Under the director, the NIHR program improved greatly through the reintroduction of substantial field-initiated projects and research fellowships for rehabilitationists. In the early years (after 1954) rehabilitation funds were targeted for many different research and demonstration projects. A 1968 review of 98 final reports by qualified university and other researchers showed the great value of field-initiated research in producing a new knowledge for use by practitioners.

This profession's research objective is to direct federal funds into projects which will increase knowledge about the life adjustment impact of permanent impairments and improve rehabilitation procedures (e.g., adjustment, assessment, counseling, placement) for residual limitations. The NARIC Rehabilitation Review Series (begun in 1983) funded by NIHR and cosponsored by NCRE is providing the basis for identifying useful research. Written by rehabilitationists these documents provide guidelines for needed future research based upon analyses of comprehensive (annotated) reviews of the literature on subjects of concern to rehabilitation practitioners.

The growth and improvement of our profession depends upon applied research, situational observations, and demonstrations that will improve practice. Still, even with useful studies, there is a time gap before they are implemented despite the fact that rehabilitation has long benefited from a model federal program of research utilization. Clearly, the best single source of disseminating this useful research information is through preservice and other training programs. But the content and effectiveness of research and training requires comprehensive, fact-based planning that leads to better client service.

ORGANIZING FOR STRATEGIC PLANNING

Just as insiders of a corporation may identify strengths and dangers better than an outside analyst, so too can we in rehabilitation see our own problems. But in light of these problems, we can also be optimistic about the future of professional rehabilitation technology because we know how effective it is and how much it is improving. Realistic optimism, however, requires solid evaluation and unified planning.

What we must recognize and deal with is the natural tendency to split up after growth and diversification. Such division can be healthy if there is working collaboration in the best interest of client needs. A new mechanism could be established to design and implement strategies for intraprofessional/association cooperation; suggested is a new superstructure of leadership organized as an "Academy of Rehabilitation Professionals." Other organizations bring together diverse leadership through cooperation in an "academy" of professional organizations, and this can accomplish a merger of goals and relationships for rehabilitationists.

Proactive responding for future perspectives suggest (a) establishment of an "Academy of Rehabilitation Professionals" with broad representation through the various credentialing and professional organizations; and (b) development and implementation by the Academy of a 10-year strategic plan for all professional rehabilitationists covering their collective mission, general goals, and explicit objectives. Strategic planning would presuppose perspectives on contemporary practice including analysis of background, problems and solutions organized (as above) according to various professional roles and specilizations; the different professional identifications and membership associations; a multifaceted professional technology; and the various kinds, levels, and methods of professional education. The chapters in this section on these and related subjects which follow provide still further perspectives on important issues for collaborative long-term planning.

3 Assessment Practices in Rehabilitation Counseling

Norman L. Berven

Assessment practices in rehabilitation counseling include all activities designed to (a) describe an individual and his or her functioning and needs; (b) specify the outcomes to be achieved through the rehabilitation process; and (c) identify the interventions and services required to achieve those outcomes (Vocational Evaluation and Work Adjustment Association (VEWAA), 1975). Assessment goes beyond merely describing an individual to also translating that description into a service plan. The success of the entire rehabilitation process in implementing plans that will maximize the likelihood of desired outcomes depends on a thorough and systematic assessment, which serves as the basis for differential treatment.

The purpose of this chapter is to discuss the process and practices of assessment in rehabilitation counseling, including sources of assessment data, the interpretation and synthesis of data, and the translation of data into case service decisions and determinations. In addition, future perspectives are considered in terms of developments in technology and needed research.

ASSESSMENT PROCESS AND PRACTICES

The assessment process begins as soon as the first information is received regarding an individual to be served, whether that information comes through a letter from a referral source, through a phone call from the individual, or through an initial interview. From the time of that first information, the rehabilitation counselor begins to form impressions about what sort of person this is, what his or her needs might be, and what actions might have to taken to meet those needs. As more and more information is obtained, it is interpreted and synthesized with data already gathered to provide an increasingly sophisticated picture or image of the client. The counselor uses this picture to predict how the client might behave in different situations and respond to different interventions. These predictions, in turn, facilitate the decisions which must be made to effectively serve the client and meet his or her needs.

Sources of Assessment Data

A variety of assessment data is typically utilized in rehabilitation counseling, gathered through a wide variety of sources. Assessment data include both quantitative scores obtained through standardized tests and related instruments and qualitative data obtained through interviews and observations. Sources of data include clients themselves, others who know or have worked with the client, and physicians and other professionals who may be called upon to provide evaluations of client potential and functioning. Some of the data-gathering procedures are identical to those used in other counseling specialities, while others have been specially developed to meet the needs of individuals with disabilities.

The interview as an assessment tool. The interview is probably the most widely used assessment tool in rehabilitation counseling. It is often the first point of contact between the rehabilitation counselor and the client and serves to initiate the assessment process. The interview provides a rich source of client self-report data, as well as an opportunity to observe the client during the interaction. Also, unlike standardized tests and inventories, the interview is not restricted to prespecified questions and directions of inquiry. The counselor is able to move the data-gathering process in whatever directions are judged to be most productive. On the other hand, there are many potential sources of error in assessment data gathered through interviews (Sundberg, 1977). These sources of error include subjectivity on the part of the counselor, intentional or unintentional distortions in client self-report, the bias which can be produced in client responses by the manner in which questions are asked, and the effects which the counselor-client relationship can have on openness and honesty in client communication. In addition, observations made of the client during the interview may be situation-specific, limiting generalizability to other types of situations.

It would seem likely that the usefulness of the interview as an assessment tool could be enhanced through more comprehensive and systematic interview procedures. Several authors have attempted to provide comprehensive listings of assessment questions or areas to explore through the initial interview which have relevance to rehabilitation planning (e.g., Esser, 1980; Farley & Rubin, 1982; Rubin & Roessler, 1983). In addition, training packages and modules have been developed to train counselors in effective initial interview skills (e.g., Pape & Berven, 1983; Rubin & Farley, 1980; Sturm, Otto, & Bakeman, 1972).

Tests and inventories. Psychological and vocational tests and inventories are also widely used in rehabilitation counseling. They may be categorized as tests of "maximum" performance and tests of "typical" performance (Cronbach, 1970; Maki, McCracken, Pape, & Scofield, 1979). Tests of maximum performance are relevant to predicting the behavior of an individual when performing at his or her best and can be further divided into tests of ability or aptitude and tests of current skills or achievement. Tests of ability include intelligence tests, multiple aptitude batteries, and tests of specific aptitudes, and are relevant to determining potential to master certain skills if given appropriate opportunities. Tests of current skills focus primarily on academic skills, such as reading and mathematics, and are relevant to determining *current skill mastery.* Tests of typical performance are relevant to determining how an individual may be expected to typically behave in different situations. They can be further divided into vocational inventories, focusing on vocational interests, attitudes, and values and designed to predict job satisfaction and likely job tenure; and personality inventories and projective tests. Berven (1980) provides a more extensive discussion of the various categories of tests and inventories and their potential uses in rehabilitation counseling.

The number of tests and inventories available for use is almost overwhelming. In addition, tests with the same apparent purpose may differ substantially in the nature of their content, and the empirical documentation regarding their reliability and validity may vary greatly. Botterbusch (1976, 1978) has provided reviews on some of the most commonly used instruments in rehabilitation counseling. Other documents provide general discussions of the advantages and disadvantages of tests and inventories when used in rehabilitation settings and special problems associated with disability in interpreting test scores (Berven, 1980; Neff, 1966, 1977; Sherman & Robinson, 1982).

Simulated and real work. The use of simulated or real work as an assessment tool has long been one of the most widely used approaches to vocational assessment in rehabilitation counseling. At least three different methods using simulated or real work may be differentiated (Neff, 1966, 1977; VEWAA, 1975). *Work Samples* use simulations of tasks actually performed in occupations or clusters of occupations.

Work samples are administered using standardiized procedures, performance is scored, and scores are compared to a norm group or to industrial standards established through engineering studies, such as Methods-Time-Measurement (MTM) or Modular Arranged Predetermined Time Standards (MODAPTS). A number of commercially available work sample systems are frequently used, and local rehabilitation facilities sometimes develop their own work samples based on jobs in the local labor market.

In contrast to work samples, *situational assessment* uses simulations of entire work environments rather than specific occupational tasks. Situational assessment is conducted in rehabilitation facilities where real work, often industrial subcontracts, is performed, piece-rate wages are paid, and the demands of real work are approximated as closely as possible. Where work samples seek to assess ability or skill in performing a specific occupational task, situational assessment focuses on the general behavior and skills important to work in virtually any occupation, such as attendance, punctuality, productivity, and interpersonal relations on the job.

Finally, *job tryouts* or on-the-job evaluations utilize actual community job sites. A client is placed in a job tryout for a limited period of time so that performance can be observed, and a determination can be made regarding the suitability of the job for the client.

Neff (1966, 1977) discusses some of the advantages and disadvantages of the various assessment methods using simulated and real work. In addition, Botterbusch (1982) provides reviews of commercially available work sample systems, and several documents provide reviews of rating scales which can facilitate behavioral observations, particularly in situational assessment (Esser, 1975; Harrison, Garnett, & Watson, 1981; Walls, Werner, & Bacon, 1976).

Functional assessment scales. Functional assessment may be defined as any systematic approach to describing an individual's functioning in terms of skill ("can do" behaviors), current behavior ("does do" behaviors), or both (Brown, Gordon, & Diller, 1983). The items in functional assessment scales are composed of comprehensive listings of client functional areas, so that each can be systematically rated, evaluated, or described. Some scales produce summary scores and score profiles, while others rely on checklists and narrative descriptions of individual functional areas. In most cases, multiple data sources are used (e.g., interviews, client self-report, direct observation, and reports from other professionals), and the scales can assist the counselor in organizing information from multiple sources to comprehensively identify client assets and limitations in terms of functional areas.

A number of different functional assessment scales have been introduced, the majority within the last 5 to 10 years. Reviews of different scales are provided in several documents (Brown et al., 1983; Harrison et al., 1981; Indices, Inc., 1978; Perdue & Minton, 1983; Roessler & Bolton, 1983). Two of the most widely known scales are the Functional Assessment Inventory (Crewe & Athelstan, 1981; Crewe, Athelstan, & Meadows, 1975) and the Rehabilitation Indicators (Brown, Diller, Fordyce, Jacobs, & Gordon, 1980; Diller et al., 1983).

Interpretation and Synthesis of Assessment Data

As assessment data are gathered, the meaning of the data must be determined, any inconsistencies with other available data must be resolved, and all of the assessment data gathered must be organized and synthesized into a consistent picture of the individual. This process of making sense out of diverse bits of information in order to understand individuals and their needs is much like the process researchers must go through in finding the order underlying the observed complexities in their data (Sundbery & Tyler, 1962).

Clinical interpretation and synthesis. Several authors have described the process of interpreting assessment data. Different levels of interpretation have been described, each characterized by different degrees of inference (Sundberg, 1977; Sundberg & Tyler, 1962). At the lowest level of inference, assessment data can be viewed as a sample of behavior in its own right, giving full consideration to the situational context in which the behavior occurred. At the next higher level of inference, pieces of assessment data are interrelated in search of consistencies and generalizations. At the next higher level of inference, a hypothetical construct (e.g., depression, motivation) may be applied to explain the descriptive generalization. In making such interpretations, it is important to remember that inferences are sometimes far removed from the facts of the situation and, consequently, interpretations must be made with caution, remaining tentative and open to change as new data emerge.

Organization of assessment data can be very important when clients present diverse and complex rehabilitation needs. One useful approach is to organize all assessment data under three categories—assets, limitations, and preferences. Assets include all characteristics of the client and his or her surrounding situation which may facilitate the accomplishment of rehabilitation goals, while limitations are those characteristics which may pose barriers. Preferences represent the individual's likes and dislikes, interests, and needs, which are significant in developing rehabilitation plans which will result in outcomes satisfying to the individual. As assessment data are interpreted and synthesized, increasingly sophisticated statements can be formulated regarding assets, limitations, and preference, which can facilitate subsequent planning.

In a classic study, McArthur (1954) found that the most important factor in determining the accuracy of clinical predictions was whether the clinician systematically constructed a "model" or conceptualization of a client and then used that model as a basis for predictions. Goldman (1971) has provided a description of this "model building" process. The process begins with *inductive* reasoning, in which inferences are drawn regarding individual pieces of data. The inferences from the different data are compared with one another, so that inconsistencies can be resolved through revisions in inferences. Inferences are continually tested against new data, moving on to broader hypotheses that integrate multiple inferences. These hypotheses are tested through a process of *deductive* reasoning to see if the hypotheses are consistent with the new data, and if they are not, the hypotheses are revised. In this manner a comprehensive, integrated "theory of the person" is developed, which can be used to predict how the individual would likely behave in other situations.

Some research has been conducted in related professions, examining processes followed in interpreting and synthesizing assessment data. Clinicians are asked to think aloud as they are confronted with tasks in clinical judgment so that the cognitive processes followed can be examined. Research with physicians has suggested that they formulate a small number of clinical hypotheses very early in the diagnostic process and that these hypotheses tend to be resistant to change, even when new contradictory evidence emerges (Elstein, Sprafka, & Shulman, 1978; Schiffman, Cohen, Nowick, & Selinger, 1978). Butcher and Scofield (1984) examined the clinical judgment and problem solving processess used by a sample of mental health counselors. They also found that the counselors tended to reach conclusions very quickly, prior to thoroughly examining all available data and considering other rival hypotheses. To the extent that rehabilitation counselors follow similar procedures in interpreting and synthesizing assessment data, their success in developing effective treatment and service plans may be diminished.

Statistical interpretation and synthesis. The discussion thus far has concerned "clinical" approaches to interpreting and synthesizing assessment data. "Statistical" or mechanical models provide an alternative approach. Statistical models utilize specified assessment data as input (e.g., test scores, biographical data, ratings on functional assessment scales) and statistically combine the data to yield probability statements regarding subsequent outcomes (e.g., probability of successful closure, expected performance in school or training, probability of success in a particular ocupation or in a particular type of living environment, or the expected effects of particular type of treatment or service). An example is provided by the McCarron-Dial Work Evaluation System, which utilizes client scores on the evaluation task along with other selected data and yields probability statements regarding likely success in different types of work environments and living environments (McCarron & Dial, 1976). Research in psychology has consistently found statistical prediction to be superior to clinical prediction (Meehl, 1954; Sawyer, 1966; Wiggins, 1973). Bolton (1979) has reviewed statistical prediction studies and has found that chance is consistently exceeded in predicting rehabilitation outcomes. Further, Bolton, Butler, and Wright (1968) have found statistical prediction superior to clinical prediction of rehabilitation outcomes. Most of the research on statistical prediction models has focused on predicting general rehabilitation outcomes (e.g., probability of successful employment). For the vast majority of assessment problems, statistical prediction models have not been developed. Cook (1980) has discussed the advantages of statistical vs. clinical prediction and has advocated wider use of statistical models. Cook has gone on to suggest that "cumulative indexing," which allows "experts" to identify and even weight variables they judge to be related to a particular outcome, prior to deriving statistical equations, as a method to enhance predictive accuracy.

Making Clinical Decisions and Determinations

The final aspect of assessment involves the translation of assessment data into clinical decisions and determinations. The most common decisions and determinations in rehabilitation counseling include selection for service, establishment of vocational objectives, decisions regarding case service plans, and disability determinations.

Selection for service. As discussed by Wright (1980), all rehabilitation agencies have criteria established for determining who will be served. Some of these criteria may be relatively objective and easily determined, such as the presence of a medically diagnosed disability or financial need. Others rely on more subjective determinations. Perhaps the most universal criterion concerns the perceived benefits which are likely to occur if treatment or services are provided, and whether these likely benefits are sufficient to justify whatever time, effort, and expense would be required. Such determinations require that the working image or model of the individual be projected into the future to determine the likely outcomes of the rehabilitation process, the extent to which those outcomes would be judged "successful," and the cost associated with the services which would be required to achieve those outcomes. These determinations are highly subjective and are based in part on the experience of the rehabilitation counselor with other clients judged to be similar to the individual being assessed, and the outcomes achieved with those clients. A decision regarding selection for service then requires that a value judgment be added to this determination concerning whether it is "worthwhile" to proceed with provision of treatment or service.

In state vocational rehabilitation agencies, individuals who are eligible for rehabilitation services must have a "physical or mental disability," which is a "substantial handicap to employment," and there must be a "reasonable expectation" that the provision of rehabilitation services will benefit the individual in terms of "employability." The presence of a "physical or mental disability" is relatively objective and generally diagnosed by a physician or other professional. The existence of a "substantial handicap to employment" is determined by identifying occupations consistent with the individual's abilities, projecting the image or working model of the individual into the environments corresponding to those occupations, and judging the impact that the disability would have on functioning. The "reasonable expectation" criterion requires a determination of the likely benefits of service provision, as previously discussed. Much of the research on statistical prediction in rehabilitation is relevant to predictions of success in state vocational rehabilitation agency settings and thus to eligibility determination. As discussed by Cook (1980), statistical predictions of rehabilitation success have been consistently found to exceed chance and to be superior to clinical predictions, but they are seldom used in rehabilitation counseling practice.

Establishing vocational objectives. To establish a vocational objective, the working model or image of the individual must be projected into work environments associated with different occupations in order to deduce likely functioning and, consequently, likely satisfactoriness and satisfaction (Lofquist & Dawis, 1969). To the extent that the assets, limitations, and preferences of the individual have been identified in developing the working image or model of the individual, the process will be facilitated. A suitable vocational objective will capitalize upon the assets of the individual, will minimize the effects of any limitations, and will be consistent with preferences. Assets and limitations must be considered as they are likely to exist following intervention; in addition, as an individual's likely functioning in a particular work environment is deduced from the working image or model of the individual, other assets or limitations may be identified which are relatively specific to that work environment. Information about the ability requirements and sources of satisfaction provided by different work environments can be found in various printed sources of occupational information and through job analysis. Similar procedures may be followed in establishing other types of objectives to be pursued through rehabilitation counseling (e.g., suitable living environments which are consistent with the assets, limitations, and preferences of the individual).

Case service plans. The individual's limitations which have been previously identified provide the basis for developing case service plans. As the working image or model of the individual is projected into the environment corresponding to the vocational or other type of objective, the impact of various limitations on functioning in that environment can be deduced. Similarly, their impact can be determined on *obtaining employment* in that occupation and in functioning successfully in whatever environments might be required in *preparing for employment* in that occupation. Those limitations which are deduced as posing barriers to accomplishment of the objective are then targeted for intervention. Limitations targeted might include skills deficits (e.g., academic skills, social skills, specific vocational skills, independent travel skills, test-taking skills), inconsistencies between behavior and environmental expections (e.g., punctuality, mannerisms, accuracy or speed of production), lack of credentials (e.g., diplomas, degrees, licenses), or a wide variety of other limitations which may pose barriers (e.g., limitations in self-confidence, social support network, finances, and transportation).

For each targeted limitation one or more interventions must be identified. Some interventions would be counseling or other strategies implemented directly by the rehabilitation counselor; other agencies or professionals would be called upon to provide other interventions. The technique of "brainstorming," which involves the identification of *all* possible alternatives while temporarily suspending any judgment about their appropriateness, can assist in identifying a comprehensive list of alternative interventions. The preferred intervention can then be identified by evaluating each alternative in terms of cost (e.g., monetary expense, time, effort) and likely outcome of implementing the intervention; again, the likely outcome is determined by projecting the working image or model of the individual into the intervention situation and deducing the likely effects.

Disability determinations. Increasingly, rehabilitation counselors are being called upon to provide expert opinion regarding the vocational implications of disability in workers' compensation, personal injury, and Social Security hearings (Andersen, 1979). Lynch (1983) has conceptualized vocational expert testimony as including both employability opinions and placeability opinions. Employability opinions require the identification of occupations that are compatible with the client's residual capacities. This involves procedures similar to those described above for establishing vocational objectives, in which the working image or model of the individual is projected into work environments associated with different occupations to deduce likely functioning. Placeability opinions concern the likelihood of actually obtaining employment in various occupations. To determine placeability, the working image or model of the individual is projected into the hiring process to deduce the likelihood of a favorable hiring decision. In addition, the availability and competition for jobs in a geographically defined labor market must be determined.

The determination required of a vocational expert varies depending upon the type of proceeding (Field & Sink, 1981; Lynch, 1983). In Social Security proceedings, determinations must be made as to whether or not the client is prevented by disability from engaging in substantial and gainful activity in jobs which are available in significant numbers in the *national* economy. In workers' compensation and personal injury proceedings, a determination must be made regarding the *loss of earning capacity* resulting from a disability; this requires a comparison of earnings in jobs available to the client in the *local* labor market prior to the onset of the disability with earnings from those available following onset. Field and Sink (1981) have described the Vocational Diagnosis and Assessment of Residual Employability (VDARE) system, which provides a step-by-step systematic procedure to facilitate such determinations.

FUTURE PERSPECTIVES

Technological Developments

In recent years there has been a tremendous growth in assessment technology, particularly in the variety of data-gathering devices available (Berven, 1983). For example, 15 of the 17 commercially available vocational assessment systems reviewed by Botterbusch (1982) have been introduced since 1970. Functional assessment scales represent an even more recent development in assessment technology. Consequently, the rehabilitation counselor has a much wider variety of instruments from which to choose than was true only a few years ago. By the same token, it has become increasingly difficult for counselors to remain current in their knowledge of assessment devices, and they may be frequently confronted with scores from unfamiliar instruments and systems. If counselors are to make proper use of assessment data and avoid deferring completely to other professionals in interpreting scores, they will have to maintain access to sources of information on new tests and systems and be diligent in consulting those sources of information when needed. There is every reason to believe that this growth in available instrumentation will continue.

A recent development which can be expected to accelerate in future years is the application of computer technology in assessment. As discussed by Sampson (1983a, b), computers have two basic applications in assessment. One is in computer-assisted interviewing, where computers can be used to collect information directly from a client regarding demographic characteristics and the nature of problems being brought to the counselor. The other is in computer-assisted assessment, where computers can administer tests and inventories and related instruments and also perform the routine clerical and computational tasks required in scoring and reporting results. One important advantage of computer-assisted administration is the possibility of "adaptive" testing, where a test or inventory can be "adapted" to the needs of a particular individual, avoiding the administration of unnecessary items and concentrating on those pools of items most relevant to the individual (Space, 1981; Vale, 1981). In addition, computer capabilities can make it easier to adapt administration procedures to meet the special needs of individuals with visual, auditory, and physical disabilities (Sampson, 1983a). Computer-assisted vocational assessment systems are currently being marketed to rehabilitation agencies (e.g., the MESA and APTICOM systems), and it appears that they are being purchased in rapidly increasing numbers.

Needed Research

Although the range of available instrumentation for assessment in rehabilitation counseling has increased dramatically in recent years, there is little empirical support for many of the instruments and systems commonly used (see Berven, 1983). For example, of the 17 vocational assessment systems reviewed by Botterbusch (1982), 8 are indicated as having no validity data whatsoever to support their use, and of those remaining, many have very limited support. Thus, although these systems are widely used in assessment in rehabilitation settings, rehabilitation counselors often have little or no assurance that performance on the assessment tasks has *any* relation whatsoever to vocational potential. Similar statements could be made regarding all categories of data-gathering devices commonly used in assessment in rehabilitation counseling.

Standardized tests and inventories which have been developed for general populations may have more extensive documentation regarding reliability and validity; however, there is typically little known about the impact on reliability and validity of scores when standardized administration procedures have been altered due to functional limitations associated with disability (Sherman & Robinson, 1982). Rehabilitation counselors need to be discriminating consumers of assessment data, determining the purposes for which particular scores are valid and avoiding overinterpretation of assessment data. Otherwise, inappropriate goals may be set with clients, opportunities may be unnecessarily denied, and service plans may fail to adequately address rehabilitation needs. In addition, research should be encouraged to build sound empirical support for all instruments and systems commonly used in assessment.

Research is also needed on the interview as an assessment device. Little research has been conducted in rehabilitation counseling to determine the reliability and validity of assessment interviews in accurately identifying client assets and limitations. The interview is probably the most widely used assessment device in rehabilitation counseling, and it is also probably the least studied. Research is needed both to examine the measurement characteristics of the interview and to develop systematic procedures to enhance its reliability and validity.

Another area of needed research concerns the processes by which rehabilitation counselors interpret and synthesize assessment data and translate the data into treatment and case service decisions. Little is known about these clinical problem-solving processes and the factors which influence them. Much could be learned from studying the clinical problem-solving processes utilized by rehabilitation counselors who demonstrate outstanding skills in clinical judgment and decision-making. The understanding gained could lead to more effective training procedures to facilitate the skills of counselors in performing assessment functions. Standardized case management simulations provide a methodology for studying clinical problem solving processes

(Berven & Scofield, 1980a, b; Butcher, Scofield, & Baker, 1984, 1985; Currie, 1977), and Butcher and Scofield (1984) have demonstrated how this methodology can be applied to gain a qualitative understanding of those processes. In addition, Coker, Currie, Menz, Andrew, and Dunn (1976), have used the same methodology to examine various factors in influencing the problem-solving process. Finally, as discussed by Cook (1980), research is needed to expand and refine statistical prediction methodology and achieve an integration with clinical prediction methods.

Given the importance of assessment to the overall success of the rehabilitation process, high priority should be given to research on assessment practices. The research which has been done has focused on data-gathering procedures and, more specifically, on tests and inventories, work samples, and rating scales. Little if any research has been conducted on interpretation and synthesis of assessment data or on the translation of data into service plans. In fact, these latter two aspects of assessment are often ignored or poorly elaborated in conceptualizations of the assessment process. Developing a better understanding of the clinical problem-solving process is a highly important aspect of building more effective assessment capability.

4 Counseling Interventions

Kenneth R. Thomas
Randall M. Parker

In its endeavor to gain professional status, rehabilitation counseling has attempted to focus on and develop its unique aspects. Rehabilitation counseling has been portrayed as a new and unique ameliorative treatment; it is not "just plain old" counseling but a highly differentiated modality called Rehabilitation Counseling. This assertion was proudly stated by American Rehabilitation Counseling Association President-elect Kenneth W. Reagles (1980): "We are no longer counselors doing rehabilitation or rehabilitationists who counsel, but rehabilitation counselors doing rehabilitation counseling" (p. 8).

The events and attitudes contributing to this distinction between counseling and rehabilitation counseling have been developing for some time now and are identified, discussed, and critiqued in a recent paper by Thomas and Parker (1981). They include the following: (a) the development of a separate accreditation mechanism for rehabilitation counselor education programs; (b) the development of a separate certification mechanism for rehabilitation counselors; (c) the acceleration of research and scholarship in content areas directly relevant to the practice of rehabilitation counseling; and (d) the general feeling that the roles, functions, and clients of rehabilitation counselors differ sufficiently from those of other counselors to warrant separate professional status.

While it is not the purpose of this chapter to discuss the merits and limitations of these events and attitudes, their cumulative effect has been to weaken the relationship between rehabilitation counseling and the broader field of counseling and to alter perceptions of the rehabilitation counseling process. Specifically, there has been a deemphasis on the rehabilitation counselor's face-to-face relationship counseling function and an increase in the emphasis given to other counselor functions and competencies such as job placement and vocational assessment.

EROSION OF COUNSELING IN THE REHABILITATION PROCESS

At a time when the importance and unique contributions of the rehabilitation counseling process are being asserted, it is ironic that the counseling function is being insidiously eroded both conceptually and operationally. It has been a generally accepted truism that *counseling* is at the core of rehabilitation counseling. Without getting into the problems of definition, *counseling* at a minimum usually involves face-to-face contact between counselor and client(s) in which the counselor interacts with the whole person (client) at all levels: affective, cognitive, and behavioral. It is also possible to further specify the term "counseling" by listing what activities are not included under the rubric of counseling.

1. The rehabilitation counselor (RC) elicits and collects client information, but the RC is not primarily an *interviewer.*
2. The RC may provide information and occasionally advise clients on decisions, but the RC is not an *advisor.*
3. The RC engages in client evaluation but is not primarily an *evaluator.*
4. The RC keeps thorough client contact and other agency records but is not primarily a *caseworker.*
5. The RC intercedes on the client's behalf when individuals, groups, or bureaucracies discriminate against the client, but the RC is not primarily a client *advocate* or *ombudsman.*
6. The RC engages in job development and job placement but is not a *job placement specialist.*

In short, the RC engages in many activities and functions which do not define this professional as a counselor. The critical activities that define the rehabilitation counselor as a counselor include vocational, educational, personal, social, and adjustment counseling.

After reviewing the recent literature, one gains the impression that counseling (variously defined) remains as the single most important facet of rehabilitation counseling. For example, Porter, Rubin, and Sink (1979) found that the theory and practice of counseling and interviewing was identified most frequently by a cross section of rehabilitation professionals as essential among 13 basic rehabilitation counseling competencies. Harrison and Lee (1979) reported that counseling process competencies were most frequently rated higher in importance than other competencies. McFarlane and Sullivan (1979) surveyed rehabilitation counselors in Region IX and found that training in *individual counseling techniques* was singled out as having the highest priority in meeting both professional and agency responsibilities.

In spite of its perceived importance, counseling over the past decade has consumed less and less time in the rehabilitation counselor's day-to-day functioning. Muthard and Salomone (1969) found that rehabilitation counselors spent more time in counseling, 33.6%, than in any other function. Ten years later Rubin and Emener (1979) discovered that rehabilitation counselors were spending less time counseling (20.65%) in spite of their stated desire to almost double the actual amount of time counseling. Fraser and Clowers (1978) similarly found that rehabilitation counselors spend 20.2% of their time in counseling and planning with clients. Emener and Rubin (1980) concluded that in part the role strain generated by the frustrated desires of rehabilitation counselors to spend more time in affective counseling was leading to a 20 to 25% burnout rate. Finally, in Rubin and others' (1984) recent study of roles and functions of "certified" rehabilitation counselors, vocational counseling and assessment and affective counseling accounted for less factor variance in a counselor job task analysis than job placement and development and case management.

These findings suggest that the RC is faced with a curious dilemma. Something peculiar is happening on the RC's way to professional status—counseling is being taken out of rehabilitation counseling. The core of rehabilitation counseling—its heart and soul—is being insidiously eroded.

Fortunately, it is still the excitement of helping disabled clients in a counseling relationship which attracts the overwhelming majority of students to the field, courses in counseling theories and techniques remain the most popular in the graduate curriculum (e.g., see Rasch, Hollingsworth, Saxon, & Thomas, 1984), and the study and practice of counseling is still the royal, if not only road to generally recognized professionalism. In fact, in our opinion, if someone doesn't put the counseling back in rehabilitation counseling—and soon—the field is destined to lose its most competent and qualified students and practitioners and will eventually become a nebulous federation of vocational evaluators, job placement specialists, case managers, and "rehabilitation insurance specialists."

The purpose of this chapter is to discuss that aspect of rehabilitation counseling which we consider to be its most necessary and important ingredient, namely, counseling. Major sections will be presented on basic considerations (including the counseling relationship and other factors), career counseling, and psychosocial adjustment counseling.

BASIC CONSIDERATIONS

The Counseling Relationship

Many authors have commented on the importance of the counseling relationship to the success of counseling (Alexander, 1963; Benjamin, 1981; Carkhuff & Berenson, 1977; Fiedler, 1950; Goldstein, 1973; Krumboltz, 1966; Orlinsky & Howard, 1978; Parloff, 1961; Rogers, 1957, 1975). Generally, the development of a good counseling relationship requires that the counselor possess three qualities: (a) genuineness, (b) unconditional positive regard, and (c) empathy (Rogers, 1957). Carkhuff and Berenson (1977) added a fourth quality which they called concreteness.

While only some of the more extreme (and naive) person-centered theorists would contend that a good counseling relationship is both necessary and sufficient to effect positive client outcomes, virtually of all of the psychodynamic (Alexander, 1963; Alexander & French, 1946; Bordin, 1955; Rank, 1945; Thorne, 1968), trait-factor (Williamson, 1965), behavioral (Dollard & Miller, 1950; Goldstein, 1973; Krumboltz, 1966), and existential (Frankl, 1955; Gendlin, 1973; May, 1967) theorists regard the counselor/therapist-client/patient relationship to be a critical aspect of effective counseling. Thus, it is considered of paramount importance that rehabilitation counselors possess the ability to develop facilitative relationships with their clients and that rehabilitation counselor education programs, regardless of emphasis or specialization, formally promote the development of such skills on the part of their students.

Transference/Countertransference

Another aspect of the counseling relationship which is considered critical is the counselor's recognition that our interactions with others, including clients, are often primarily structured on the basis of how we have previously interacted with significant others in our lives (Alexander, 1963; Wolf, 1963). This aspect of the counseling relationship has been unduly neglected in recent years due to the influence of person-centered theory and the recent emphasis on behavioral and cognitive approaches. However, examples of transference (i.e., the client acting toward the counselor as if he or she were a parent, sibling, or other significant person) and countertransference (i.e., the counselor acting toward the client as if he or she were an offspring, sibling, spouse, old friend, or parent) abound in counseling practice (e.g., see Watkins, 1983). In fact, many psychoanalysts consider virtually *all* of our interactions with others to be transference of one type or another.

A common misconception is that unless one is practicing psychoanalysis or psychoanalytic counseling or psychotherapy, transference and countertransference situations are to be avoided at all costs. However, one need only consider the support and encouragement which a warm, facilitative female counselor can give to an individual who is insecure and distrustful of others due to an unsatisfactory mother-son or mother-daughter relationship to see that the consequences of transference-countertransference need not necessarily be negative. Therefore, it is important that counselors recognize the potential effects of these phenomena (both positive and negative) and conduct their practice accordingly.

Empathy

The *sine qua non* of the counseling relationship is empathy, i.e., the ability to accurately perceive the client's internal frame of reference, including all of the feelings and meanings experienced by the client, without losing objectivity (Rogers, 1959). Without accurate empathy, there is little chance that the counselor will ever really understand what the client actually wants, needs, or is trying to say.

The importance of having accurate empathy in rehabilitation settings was empathically punctuated in a study by Tichenor, Thomas, and Kravetz (1975), where it was found that counselors frequently perceived the client's handicapping problem differently than the client and that discrepancies between the counselor's and client's perceptions of the problems often resulted in the counselor viewing the client as being *unmotivated.* If rehabilitation counselors are really in the business of helping people, it is absolutely essential that they seek to see and understand the world from the client's point of view.

Reinforcement

Like it or not, reinforcement is here to stay. Even an analysis of a Carl Rogers interview revealed that his expressions of counselor empathy, warmth, and directiveness seemed to be contingent on those responses of his client that would be consistent with Rogers' theory of client progress (Truax, 1966). Moreover, several authors have proposed or demonstrated that reinforcement can be used to assist clients in their vocational exploration and decision-making activities (Kravetz & Thomas, 1978; Krumboltz & Schroeder, 1965; Krumboltz & Sheppard, 1969; Ryan & Krumboltz, 1964).

Essentially, the problem for the rehabilitation counselor is this: How can I use reinforcement in a way which helps my clients without imposing my values or objectives on them? Unfortunately, there is no easy answer to this question; however, probably the best response is that reinforcement should be intentionally used only when it promotes the attainment of skills and behaviors which clients need to meet *their own objectives* (e.g., finding a job, making a vocational decision, feeling better about themselves, or making friends). Reinforcement should be viewed as a useful counseling tool, but it is important that it be used systematically rather than randomly. Also, it is important that counselors seek to become familiar with the behavioral literature and that they continually assess how they might better use their own behaviors and the reinforcers in the client's environment to help the client meet his or her needs. The question is really not whether to use reinforcement or not (you will anyhow); the question is how to use it in the most effective way possible to help clients meet their objectives.

Group Techniques

Utilization of group counseling methods in conjunction with individual, one-to-one methods offers many advantages over the use of individual methods alone (Thomas & Butler, 1981). However, despite these advantages, group work is surely one of the most underutilized intervention strategies in the rehabilitation counselor's armamentarium. A primary reason for this underutilization is that counselors frequently equate the use of groups with the human potential or "encounter group" movement rather than viewing the group as a milieu in which many purposeful and directed affective, social, and cognitive learnings can take place.

Some of the more salient counseling activities which can be conducted in groups are (a) the provision of occupational information; (b) the learning of new and more productive ways of relating to others; (c) the provision of information on how to apply for jobs and interact with employers and co-workers, and the opportunity to practice and receive feedback on the skills gained; (d) the opportunity to take risks in a supportive environment and to gain a sense of trust in other persons; and (e) the opportunity to improve self-esteem and self-awareness through the gaining of new skills, new friends, and the learning that one's insecurities in approaching career planning and other problems of daily living are not maliciously unique.

In rehabilitation settings, probably the most visible use of groups relates to the formation of job clubs (Azrin & Besalel, 1980; Azrin & Phillip, 1979); however, as noted above, groups can be used for many purposes regardless of whether the objectives are vocational adjustment, job placement, acceptance of disability, or general personal and social adjustment. The fact that they are so blatantly underutilized is really quite unfortunate.

CAREER COUNSELING

The first and perhaps the most important step in becoming an effective vocational or career counselor is to develop a theoretical frame of reference from which to view how people make occupational choices and develop vocationally. Of the major career development and occupational choice theories, only Super's (1957) refer explicitly to the special career problems encountered by individuals with handicapping conditions. However, despite their infrequent reference to the conditions of disability and several limitations when applied to handicapped populations (Conte, 1983; Schlenoff, 1975), virtually all of the major career development and occupational choice theories offer something to counselors in rehabilitation settings. Roe's theory (Roe, 1957), for example, with its emphasis on the importance of the parent-child relationship, stimulates discussion of the potential effects of child-rearing practices on later work behavior of congenitally disabled children (e.g., see Britton & Thomas, 1973).

An important application of the developmental theories (Ginzberg, Ginsberg, Axelrad, & Herma, 1951; Super, 1957; Tiedeman & O'Hara, 1963) is that they provide frameworks for viewing the stages and tasks necessary for "normal" career development and decision making. As such, these theories can be used to identify problems in development or redevelopment and to establish specific strategies for implementing the career development process. Two concepts resulting from the work of Super and his associates which are particularly useful to counselors who work with handicapped individuals are the importance placed on developing a sense of *planfulness* (Super & Overstreet, 1960) and the concept of *multipotentiality* (Super, 1953). Due to socioeconomic and other variables, individuals with handicapping conditions may be especially likely to place an inordinate amount of emphasis on "chance" factors in career and other life choices. The concept of multipotentiality is helpful to both the counselor and client because of the tendency to pigeonhole persons with specific disabilities into particular occupations (e.g., recommending that blind persons become piano tuners).

While Holland's (1966; 1973) vocational choice theory, with its emphasis on personality types, creates some conceptual problems for counselors attempting to facilitate the career development of adventitously disabled persons (e.g., the theory does not explain the potential effects of traumatic injury on personality), fewer problems are created in the case of persons with a congenital disability. Moreover, those psychometric instruments (for example, the Vocational Preference Inventory and the Self-Directed Search) typically associated with Holland's theory offer assistance to a wide range of clients. Finally, counselors can use Holland's descriptions of the six work environments to provide very general information on the relationships among different types of occupations.

Although there have been others (e.g., Hershenson, 1974; McMahon, 1979a; Osipow, 1976), the most extensive effort to investigate the vocational behavior of individuals with handicapping conditions was conducted by Lofquist and his associates at the University of Minnesota. Specifically, over a period of several years, Lofquist and others formulated and tested what is commonly referred to as the Minnesota Theory of Work Adjustment (Lofquist & Dawis, 1969, 1972). A significant advantage of the Minnesota Theory over other vocational theories is that terms such as needs, abilities, ability requirements, and reinforcer systems have been operationally defined, and specific psychometric instruments have been developed or are available to measure them. Among these instruments are the Strong-Campbell Interest Inventory, the Minnesota Importance Questionnaire, the Minnesota Job Description Questionnaire, and the General Aptitude Test Battery. By using the various psychometric instruments available, counselors are assisted in helping clients to identify the kinds of job requirements and reinforcers most suited to their abilities, and needs (Lofquist & Dawis, 1972).

The literature on the effects of career counseling and other career interventions have recently been reviewed by Holland, Magoon, and Spokane (1981). Among their many findings Holland and his colleagues discovered four common elements in various interventions that appeared to account for positive results:

> (a) Exposure to occupational information; (b) Cognitive rehearsal of vocational aspirations; (c) Acquisition of some cognitive structure for organizing information about self, occupations, and their relations; and (d) Social

support or reinforcement from counselor or workshop members. (p. 285)

It is important to note that the last three elements would be likely to occur only within the context of a counseling relationship. We now turn to a form of counseling that relies even more heavily, perhaps, for its effectiveness on the client-counselor relationship—psychosocial, or personal adjustment, counseling.

PSYCHOSOCIAL COUNSELING

The term psychosocial counseling derives from the definition of *handicap* that suggests that a handicap is the result of the imposition of psychosocial barriers by individuals or groups in the environment. As a consequence of these impositions an individual with a handicap may develop a negative self-image. The internalization of demeaning social influences may lead to psychosocial difficulties. It is therefore, quite logical for rehabilitation counselors to focus their efforts on the removal or amelioration of these psychosocial problems through counseling—psychosocial counseling.

Psychosocial counseling may be viewed as fostering both the client's realistic, positive self-evaluation and assertive, effective transactions with significant others in the community. Specifically, psychosocial counseling assists the client to

1. Accurately and rationally assess and understand the nature, extent, and effects of the disability on functioning.
2. Actively explore the emotional ramifications of the disability on the client's self-concept.
3. Clearly identify the effects, or lack of effects, the disability may have upon the client's developmental processes.
4. Effectively cope with the ill-founded beliefs, attitudes, and values promoted by society that encourage the formation of psychosocial barriers by the client and the community.
5. Thoroughly consider all relevant psychosocial, educational, vocational, and social variables in an attempt to reach the client's highest level of potential functioning.

Psychosocial counseling is client-centered in the broadest sense. The primary ingredient of the process that is catalyzed by the counselor is the formation of an effective counseling relationship. The process of psychosocial counseling continues to support and further build the counseling relationship. The process may be conceptualized along lines similar to those presented by Patterson (1974) and Carkhuff and Berenson (1977). It begins with a responsive phase in which the counselor fosters client self-exploration and self-understanding. Next, the counselor facilitates an initiative and action phase by assisting the client to make decisions and plans and to take actions which will lead to the client's rehabilitation. Many other elements may enter this process, but a thorough detailing of them is beyond the scope of this article. The interested reader may refer to Patterson and Carkhuff and Berenson for further information.

Supervisors and administrators of rehabilitation agencies, facilities, and programs may bristle at the notion that their rehabilitation counselors should do psychosocial counseling. This negative attitude, when it exists, reflects a basic misunderstanding of the core of rehabilitation—counseling. In fact, many rehabilitation counselors themselves fail to appreciate the need for psychosocial counseling. There are three primary reasons why this service should be available to clients:

1. Without the basic relationship promoted through psychosocial counseling many other rehabilitation services will be relatively ineffective or doomed to failure. This assertion has been documented in many ways, but most recently by the empirical demonstrations of increased effectiveness of medical services and reduced costs of the services when accompanied by counseling and psychotherapy (see Kiesler, Cummings, & Vanden Bos, 1979).
2. Rehabilitation counselors are trained in their master's programs to do psychosocial counseling. As previously indicated, they tend to perceive this counseling as an integral part of their professional role.
3. There are few, if any, other trained professionals who can effectively provide psychosocial counseling services to clients with disabling conditions.

The literature on the outcomes of counseling and psychotherapy, including Kiesler et al. (1979) cited above, is extensive. The most statistically sophisticated effort to review and summarize the findings of the outcome studies on counseling and psychotherapy was undertaken by Smith, Glass, and Miller (1980). Using a meta-analysis methodology, these investigators were able to statistically combine the effects of 475 controlled outcome studies. Their findings indicate that "an applicant for therapy who is not better off than average . . . in psychosocial well-being . . . after treatment . . . is better off than 80 percent of those who need *[sic]* therapy but remain untreated" (p. 124). This finding is relevant to the whole range of psychological treatment from psychosocial counseling to in-depth psychotherapy.

The need for effective counseling services in rehabilitation settings is clear, whether the counseling focuses on career or psychosocial issues. Further erosion of counseling in the rehabilitation process will lead to the deterioration of the professional status of the rehabilitation counselor and, more importantly, to the dilution of the positive impact of rehabilitation services on rehabilitation clients. A renewed commitment must be made to counseling by the rehabilitation counseling profession.

5 Basic Approaches to Adjustment Services in Rehabilitation

Robert H. Couch

In 18th-century England, Henry Danette experienced frustration in his early attempts to provide vocational training for the blind. Danette discovered that "those long inured by habits of idleness and dissipation soon become disgusted with useful industry" (Obermann, 1965, p. 68). This observation prompted Danette to add classes in work habits and attitudes to his workshop program (Obermann, 1965). Rehabilitation counselors of today know of Danette's frustration. Too often their handicapped clients have exhibited life problems for which there were no readily available medical or paramedical cures nor a vocational training program addressing these critical client needs. Yet these problems in attitude, motivation, coping, and community survival have continually presented real obstacles to the vocational rehabilitation of many severely disabled clients. The search for answers to these primary questions in vocational, personal, and social adjustment has continued unabated.

In the intervening years since Danette's encounter with adjustment needs of disabled individuals, the search has led rehabilitation professionals to advancements along a variety of fronts. Even though the final answers have not been found, four basic approaches to adjustment services appear to have emerged. Although not mutually exclusive, these four approaches, when viewed separately, may shed some light on the current state of adjustment services and its practice in rehabilitation for both the rehabilitation counselor and rehabilitation facility personnel (Couch, in Coffey & Ellien, 1979).

THE WORK ACCLIMATION APPROACH

The work acclimation approach most likely evolved when sheltered workshops began to discover or perhaps sell vocational rehabilitation and other agencies on the idea that work in itself was therapeutic.

In varying degrees and at all levels of sophistication, this is one of the most popular approaches in use today. Hard-pressed rehabilitation facility directors, coping with economic recession and funding cutbacks, appear to have discovered more and more therapeutic value in income-producing real work and less in other, more costly approaches to adjustment. The national Easter Seal Society has led a move to change the name of traditional workshops or work-oriented rehabilitation facilities to "work centers." At the lowest and least sophisticated level of this approach, the simple provision of any available type of work activity is espoused as, and may well be, an adjustment service program. Individuals gain work experience, exposure, and work hardening by practicing work in a work center. In this approach, the principle of behavior generalization may apply (Wainwright & Couch, 1978). This psychological principle holds that the greater degree to which a given environment resembles a future environment, the more likely an individual would behave in the same manner in a future environmental setting. If real work environments are available in rehabilitation facilities, clients who experientially learn to function in the work center should be acclimated to function in similar outside work settings. Gellman (1961), Oseas (1963), Gellman and Friedman (1965), and Hallenbeck and Campbell (1966) advanced this early conceptual model. More recently, at Cornell University, Gregory, Whitlow, Levin, and Wasmuth (1982) identified several work-adjustment techniques that epitomize the work acclimation approach to adjustment. Among the techniques found almost exclusively in work centers were pay incentives, peer and supervisory work pressure, production rate feedback, production line pressures and pacing equipment, lead workers, time studies, and status-promotion incentives.

The rehabilitation practitioner in the facility-based work acclimation program may serve as workshop foreman or supervisor and provide vocational role models in the work setting. As activity counselors, they formulate hypotheses based upon observed vocational behaviors and demonstrated attitudes and integrate other necessary treatment/training procedures into the *real work* program. Community-based work programs, like vocational education's cooperative diversified-education school programs and on-the-job training for rehabilitation clients, are other examples of the work acclimation approach.

PROBLEM-SOLVING APPROACH TO ADJUSTMENT SERVICES

In the problem-solving approach the client's adjustment problems are delineated in evaluation, baseline measures of the problem are recorded, and adjustment services consist of any and all treatment/training modalities necessary to ameliorate the problem to the extent that the client can function vocationally. This holistic approach causes some problems. Any and all treatment modalities could include the totality of human services knowledge, i.e., medicine, psychology, counseling, human factors engineering, etc. More than a decade ago, the *Tenth Institute* (1972) did attempt to delimit adjustment services by suggesting in its definition that the scope was determined by the treatment/training procedures used (work and work-related activities). None of the adjustment curriculum studies to date, however, appear to accept this limited function of adjustment services (Baker & Mercer, 1973; Coffey, 1978; Coffey & Ellien, 1979; Means & Akridge, 1978; Pruitt, 1973). It is difficult to separate an individual's parts from his total being. Carter (1978) emphatically asserted that even medical adjustment cannot be isolated from psychological and other adjustment parameters as all are inseparably intertwined. Given the impossibility of mastery of all related fields of knowledge in vocational, personal and social adjustment, those espousing the problem-solving approach are faced with somehow "roping off" and delimiting the area that encompasses adjustment services or committing themselves fully to a realistic team approach encompassing many other professional disciplines.

Perhaps the best current delimitation of the problem-solving approach is found in behavioral counseling and behavior modification techniques that can be applied by both the field counselor and rehabilitation facility personnel. Applied behavior analysis and systematic reinforcement procedures have been repeatedly demonstrated as effective in numerous rehabilitation settings (Couch & Allen, 1973; Esser & Botterbusch, 1975). Even though behavior modification offers an excellent example of the problem-solving approach, this approach is not limited to contingency management techniques. It is much broader in scope. Maki, McCracken, Pape, and Scofield (1978) have offered a theoretical model for the problem-solving approach in all rehabilitation activities, and Sawyer (1983) used functional analysis to identify specific client problems needing accountable solutions in rehabilitation facilities. This approach, therefore, appears to be a way of thinking as opposed to a set of techniques. It readily lends itself to utilization of techniques generally identified with other approaches.

DEVELOPMENTAL APPROACH

A more recent approach could be called appropriately the developmental model of adjustment services. Means and Akridge (1978) defined adjustment services in this framework as "the body of knowledge and skills which are primary to effective, self directed functioning in all areas of human endeavor and directed toward achieving continuation of life, creative growth, personal freedom, individual pleasure and meaning, and social harmony" (p. 25). A well-defined, structured curriculum to achieve fulfillment of this definition, Personal Achievement Skills Training (PAST), has been developed at the Arkansas Rehabilitation Research and Training Center. In the PAST System, skills needed by the adjustment specialist include counseling, philosophy, communications, English, and rehabilitation. Presented in a small group format, the PAST Sequential Training Package consists of a series of structured skill-building activities in communication, goal setting and achieving, problem solving, and valuing. The overall goal is personal growth (Means & Roessler, 1976).

The philosophical stance in the developmental approach views the rehabilitation adjustment client as a capable, problem-solving individual, fully qualified to accept responsibility for his/her life and determine its direction (Anderson, 1976). In a developmental adjustment program, the client is taught self-responsibility, self-potency, beliefs, values, and skills that will enable him/her to solve problems, maintain a sense of worth, and grow as a person (Akridge & Means, 1982; Cosgrove, 1977; Means & Akridge, 1978). Teaching clients problems-solving skills, assertion, and transactional analysis techniques would be included in this holistic approach as would individual and group counseling (Andrews, 1981; DeLoach & Greer, 1981).

EDUCATIONAL APPROACH

Taking a slightly different slant, other adjustment programs focus on skill deficits. Job readiness classes concentrate on good work habits, grooming techniques, and job interviewing skills. Remedial education programs may lead to General Education Development (GED) certificates and driver education programs lead to licensed drivers. Activities-of-daily-living programs help the newly physically disabled and the mentally disabled to care for themselves and survive in the community. Specific task training or vocational skill training is another feature of the educational approach which presupposes that lack of skill is the primary reason the disabled individual cannot function adequately. Cooperative programs with special education often and appropriately adhere primarily to this approach and counselor innovations have offered community resources for special training of their clients.

Support for this didactic approach is widespread, and examples of its use and effectiveness abound. The Greenleigh Study of Sheltered Workshops (1976) found that job readiness training was among the most important variables in whether or not workshop clients were placed in competitive employment. Job readiness and other prevocational skills are taught in a variety of ways and address a host of concerns. Godley (1979), for instance, taught interview skills; Schloss and Schloss (1982) focused on social skills; and Greenstein and Baum (1981) illustrated the involvement of the placement specialist and employers in teaching on-the-job adjustment for visually impaired clients. Crimando and Sawyer (1983) has discussed the use of microcomputers for individual instruction and related adjustment activities. These are but a few examples of the educational approach to adjustment services in rehabilitation.

DISCUSSION

In the actual practice of adjustment, a combination of the four approaches is usually found. Emphasis is generally given to one or two approaches based upon the preference of program leaders, level of training of the adjustment specialist, available resources, and the realities of the setting. The rehabilitation counselor, given sufficient time, can implement several approaches to adjustment. The counselor can easily provide individual and group counseling, job readiness classes, and on-the-job training. Further, innovative rehabilitation counselors can create their own community adjustment programs by forging an adjustment staff from related community professionals and agencies. Welfare social workers, special education teachers, mental health professionals, public health nurses, employment service counselors, and their respective agencies offer tremendous manpower and other resources for adjustment services. Business and industry have been used by other creative counselors to create community adjustment programs. Some projects with industry have work-adjustment components. More frequently, however, busy rehabilitation counselors need the assistance of rehabilitation facility adjustment programs in meeting the special adjustment needs of their more severely disabled clients.

Each of the basic approaches to adjustment services has its own set of strengths and limitations. Real work settings can provide a realistic training ground that helps to prepare the individual with work experience. Yet most real work settings are limited in the number and variety of available work tasks and work environments. A work setting featuring packaging, simple assembly, or reclamation of donated goods may not remotely resemble a job environment in high-tech industries, clerical, sales, or service establishments. Further, facility personnel trained primarily for human service professions may be novices in the world of business. Few have training in contract procurement; prime manufacturing, marketing, production practices; and fiscal management. As a consequence, these facility professionals may be unable to create a real work environment necessary for the benefits available in the work acclimation approach.

Similarly, the problem-solving, developmental, and education approaches have been demonstrated effective. But the skill level of adjustment practitioners again becomes an issue. Few service areas have the wide variety and skill diversity that is found among current practitioners of work adjustment. It is not uncommon to discover a high school graduate, with little or no special training, serving as the workshop supervisor and providing the vast majority of client contact time in facility adjustment programs. These individuals are often ill equipped to provide training or vocational skills needed in the education approach and the counseling, therapy, and personal growth experiences of the developmental approach. The ideal adjustment specialist, equipped with the skills of an industrial engineer, business manager, teacher, trades and industrial instructor, and counseling psychologist, does not exist. Few vocationally oriented rehabilitation facilities have been able to afford a team composed of professionals from each of the needed disciplines. Yet evidence exists that rehabilitation clients have a better chance for successful rehabilitation in rehabilitation facilities where there are more professional service programs, more professionals, and lower professional-to-client ratios (Greenleigh, 1976). There is also growing evidence demonstrating further developments in, and success with, each of the adjustment approaches described herein. Innovations in the various approaches have been reported with increasing frequency.

Despite the encouraging developments within each basic approach, professional adjustment services in rehabilitation are still in the embryonic stages and are only beginning to be defined specifically (Coffey

& Ellien, 1979). Yet adjustment service, when practiced at its best, has the potential for becoming one of the most important services in the rehabilitation professional's arsenal for serving severely disabled people. Each current approach needs refinement, and new approaches must be found to solve, circumvent, and minimize obstacles to the rehabilitation of individuals with disabilities.

6 Placement Practices in Vocational Rehabilitation

David Vandergoot

Authors of two important literature reviews have pointed out the failure of the rehabilitation community to put placement practices to empirical test (Dunn, 1974; Zadny & James, 1976). This review of some of the more timely literature relating to placement will highlight how the rehabilitation community has progressed in its conceptual and practical handling of placement. A summary of relevant developments will be provided. However, of more importance will be the illustrations of how placement has been defined over the years and the suggestions regarding who should do it and how it should be done. It is not possible to provide detailed descriptions of placement services and techniques. A chart is provided so that the interested reader can easily determine which references deserve further inspection.

HISTORICAL DEVELOPMENT

Providing employment for people with disabilities has been the mission of vocational rehabilitation since federal legislation initiated it over 60 years ago. Yet it has only been within the last 10 years that texts have tried to accumulate knowledge of placement concepts and practice (Geist & Calzaretta, 1982; Graves & Brown, 1976; Vandergoot & Worrall, 1979). At the same time, universities with federal support have been developing specialized curricula for instruction in placement. Excellent literature and research reviews have also been produced in this past decade (Dunn, 1974, 1981a; Fraser, 1978; Melia, 1984; Zadny & James, 1976). This scholarly work represents the maturing of the profession of rehabilitation counseling.

Fraser (1978) found that the scope of research has expanded beyond client-oriented techniques to include evaluating employer contact practices and searching for correlates of placement among counselor characteristics and agency factors. This shows that we recognize that there is a complex array of variables involved in the entire placement process.

Similarly, Melia (1984) shows this maturing process is continuing. Earlier research focused mainly on demonstrations of specific services directed at disability groups. Now we have more descriptive studies suggesting how placement actually happens. Empirical studies have experimentally evaluated the impact of specific techniques on outcomes.

Another positive sign is that we are borrowing more frequently from other fields of study to help us understand the mechanics of finding and keeping employment. Labor market studies from the fields of economics and sociology have been particularly useful (Dunn, 1981; Vandergoot & Worrall, 1979).

In spite of these advances, there are still problems with placement. Zadny and James (1979b) surveyed counselors to find out what these were. Employers, clients, and agency administrative requirements took most of the blame. Employers fail to develop openings or resist hiring when there are. Clients lack marketable skills and motivation. Agencies do not provide rewards for achieving placement results. In a more recent overview of barriers, May and Vieceli (1983) repeat many of these themes but include the counselor in the brow-beating also. They point out that counselors have negative attitudes toward placement, would rather spend time counseling, and do not have the necessary skills and knowledge.

Complaints about employers and clients persist without good evidence. Fechter and Thorpe (1977), in a study designed to determine why people with disabilities do not compete favorably in the labor market, suggest that although employer discrimination may be involved, other factors include limited productive capacities and decisions not to work on the part of persons with disabilities. Many clients may not have the education and skills to compete for the better jobs, and they may have incentives to remain out of the labor force. Dunn (1981a) and Berkowitz (1981) highlight these last two points in much more detail. However, evidence about clients suggest that they come to rehabilitation primarily because they want to work (Gregg, Miller, & Roberts, 1976) and that a majority of clients place themselves (Fraser, 1978).

Counselors may not be able to identify when clients are work-ready (Kneipp, Vandergoot, & Lawrence, 1980); may not adequately perceive clients' vocational needs (McGraw & Bitter, 1974) nor their handicapping conditions (Tichenor, Thomas, & Kravetz, 1975). Also, Crystal (1981) found that counselors would provide placement service to clients who had difficulty accepting the implications of their disability and who were actually expected to remain unrehabilitated. It seems as if counselors see placement as a part of the service process and not as an outcome of services. This use of placement contradicts our oft-quoted pledge to employers to provide them only with prescreened, ready-to-hire job applicants.

Why does this confusion about placement exist? It is not because there has never been a sense of direction. In the 1960s, Ortale (undated) urged that all services facilitate placement. He reasoned that if there is not a clear relationship between a service and placement, it may not be justifiable. He felt rehabilitation counselors will not achieve professional status in the eyes of the clients, employers, and the community without this. Likewise, in the early 1970s, Morgan (1980) called for counselors to see placement as the outcome that gave them their central purpose. In his view, work is the essential element that allows a person with a disability to achieve a sense of self-worth. Morgan challenged professionals to know their clients' values, needs, and hopes and to know employers and labor markets equally well.

Before a discussion of placement concepts and practices, it is useful to review the definitions of placement that have been offered in the recent past. These include selective and client-centered placement.

Selective Placement

This originated in the employment service and refers to the assessment of the capabilities, needs, and other relevant characteristics of clients and matching these to a compatible job. Geist and Calzaretta (1982) add, "[Selective placement] involves matching the client with a job, while the counselor acts as a resource person, agent and advocate in obtaining the job leads, making the employer contacts, and even accompanying the client to the interview" (p. 14).

Client-Centered Placement

Salamone (1971) rejected selective placement and recommended client-centered placement in which the client assumes responsibility, secures job leads, contacts employers, and self-places. The counselor teaches the client job-seeking skills and provides encouragement and support. Geist and Calzaretta (1982) clarify by adding "[Client-centered placement] requires frequent client-counselor meetings, an involvement of the counselor while helping the client plan strategy for his job search, and an intense, genuine working relationship between the counselor and the client" (p. 14).

Zadny and James (1976) say placement refers to "the steps taken in preparation to secure satisfactory employment as rehabilitation comes to a close" (p. 9). They acknowledge that "placement is a continuing concern throughout the rehabilitation process, even though the type and level of related activities varies considerably at different points" (p. 9).

Vandergoot and Worrall (1979) in an attempt to separate goal from process defined placement as "the crucial event in the rehabilitation process; it indicates that a client has accepted a job offer. . . . placement is the goal of rehabilitation, all other rehabilitation activities can be related to it" (p. 7).

Dunn (1981a) attempted to find a balance between process and outcome. His frame of reference for placement is "getting a job," which "refers to the time period and activities that take place between two major decision points or events: the decision to actively search for employment in the labor market and the decision to accept a job offer" (p. 115).

Obviously, we have not yet agreed on what placement really is. Is it a service? Is it an outcome? Is it the entire rehabilitation process or only a part of it? If it is only a part, which part?

PARTICIPANTS IN THE PRACTICE OF PLACEMENT

The definitions do suggest that the principal actors are counselors, clients, and employers. How these actors interact is less clear. One can imagine different roles for counselors and clients depending on whether one follows the client-centered or selective placement definition. In fact, these definitions seem to have become surrogates for expressions of rehabilitation philosophy (Salamone & Usdane, 1977; Usdane & Salamone, 1977). The definitions would be better used to guide selection of techniques that can be individually tailored to the needs and capacities of clients. This is the role of a rehabilitation professional, but which professional is to do this is another point of debate. McDonald (1974) feels the counselor should coordinate the entire process and be a resource to clients and employers. Minton (1977) and Walls (1983) support this view and further emphasize that employers are clients as well as persons with disabilities. Usdane (1974) recommended that a placement worker be provided to help overly burdened rehabilitation counselors. He felt the counselor should still have placement duties but did not clarify how the two should work together. He recommended that master's degree programs be set up to train placement specialists. This suggestion has been implemented by several universities. Hutchinson and Cogan (1974) called for a Rehabilitation Manpower Specialist and spelled out a job description. How this role relates to the counselor role is not clear. Schlenoff (1978) said a placement specialist is crucial but did not provide rationale or the functions that attend this role. Flannagan (1977) returned the honor to counselors but said they must become thoroughly familiar with employers and their firms and be willing to work with clients during their job search.

Veglahn (1976) cited evidence that this mutual job search effort is beneficial beyond what either party can do on their own. Granovetter (1979), based upon his analysis of how information exchanges influence labor market decisions made by applicants and employers, suggested that the most appropriate role for a rehabilitation counselor is as an information broker between clients and employers. Granovetter recommended that the counselor be a direct channel to both parties. In this way the information needs of both would be served. Also, due to how information is best exchanged, third parties, such as placement specialists, may only create a barrier or filter, thus limiting the credibility of information in the eyes of employers and clients. According to this, the ideal role for the rehabilitation counselor would be to handle the entire process of preparing clients and employers to deal with each other.

Recently, several writers have called for a compromise (Garvin, 1983; Vandergoot, 1982). A new professional is called for who will provide specialized services to employers to promote rehabilitation and open jobs for people with disabilities in general. This specialist would obtain labor market information which will be used by counselors and clients to plan preparation activities and the job search. Counselors would remain responsible for the entire rehabilitation process until a client is successfully employed. Ideally, the new specialist will open doors and provide assistance, thus eliminating some of the burden and trial-and-error while not interfering with the counselor's role to serve both client and employer in the labor market.

CONTEMPORARY SERVICES RELEVANT TO PLACEMENT

Table 6.1 lists how others have described placement services and includes the references where more detailed descriptions can be found.

It is believed that those responsible for placement need to attend to many if not all of these services. If more than one professional is involved, close collaboration will be needed. Not all the writers used the same terms, so the classifications are somewhat arbitrary. Also, the sequence of services is intended to convey a typical approach to service delivery which is also not consistently found in the references. This chart may give the impression of agreement which does not really exist in the literature. However, every effort was made to be as objective as possible in classifying similarly described services within the terms selected.

The first six services, from counseling through placement planning, are primarily done with a client. The remaining services are primarily done on the client's behalf, usually involving employers, except for, perhaps, career planning, which may involve collaboration with both. These seem to be the activities that are fairly frequently mentioned as important ones for accomplishing placement. One assumption is that placement, or employment, is the goal. There are no assumptions made regarding whether a particular professional or a client should have primary responsibility for a task. The impression is that someone should do a majority of these activities if employment is to be achieved.

The chart suggests that more recent analyses of placement functions involve an increasing array of services. Perhaps achieving placements is more complex than previously recognized or placements now require more effort. Also recommended are more services that require contact with the work environment, thus providing more direct links for clients to labor markets.

Service categories consistently recommended over the years include work-readiness assessment, labor market information, job-seeking skills, job development, referral to employers, and coordination with other resources. Relatively little attention is given to counseling. There is also a recent concern for longer-range outcomes as evidenced by the increasing call for follow-up and career planning services.

Unfortunately, there is little research available documenting the effectiveness of many of these services. The impact of counseling is being seriously questioned in rehabilitation (Thomas & Butler, 1981) and in psychology as a whole (Garfield, 1981). Also, as mentioned earlier, research has shown counselors have difficulty identifying needs of clients and their work readiness. However, there are positive signs. Zadny and James (1979a) found a correlation between counselors' knowledge of labor market information and their placement rates. A similar relationship existed between placement plans and successful closures. The effectiveness of a variety of job-seeking skills techniques

Table 6.1

	Bridges (1946)	Meadow (1964)	Ninth Institute (1971)	Flannagan (1974;1977)	Dunn (1974)	Hutchinson & Cogan (1974)	Zadny & James (1976)	Minton (1977)	Vandergoot & Worrall (1979)	Dunn (1981a)
1. Counseling	X		X		X				X	X
2. Work Readiness Assessment	X	X	X	X	X	X	X	X	X	X
3. Labor market information		X	X	X	X	X		X	X	X
4. Transferability of skills	X									X
5. Job-seeking skills		X	X	X	X		X	X	X	X
6. Placement planning			X						X	X
7. Job development				X	X	X	X	X	X	X
8. Job analysis	X		X				X	X	X	X
9. Referral to employers for specific jobs	X			X		X	X	X	X	X
10. Job modification/ accommodation			X		X		X	X	X	X
11. Follow-up	X		X		X	X	X	X	X	
12. Career planning								X	X	
13. Coordination with other resources		X	X		X	X			X	X

Reprinted from p. 24; Cooper, P.G., & Davis, S. (1979). Case flow modeling: A program management innovation for planning services to the severely disabled. *Journal of Rehabilitation Administration,3* (1), 22–30.

has been documented (Azrin, Flores, & Kaplan, 1975; Keith, Engelkes, & Winborn, 1977; McClure, 1972). Job development techniques have been researched to some extent. Mailing approaches have limited success and may be useful only for screening out employers (Cates, 1981; Roessler & Hiett, 1983; Vandergoot, 1976). Employers with whom rehabilitation has established a successful relationship may be useful recruiters of other employers (Vandergoot, Swirsky, & Rice, 1982). An innovative study in the 1960s suggested that referral to employers worked equally well whether it was done directly by counselors or given as a job lead to clients (Mooney, 1966). A project reported by Mallik and Yuspeh (1979) indicated that job modification/ accomodation was successful in placing 79 of 116 clients originally considered too disabled to achieve employment. Post-employment services, or follow-up, have been associated with helping clients solve work adjustment problems, thereby maintaining successful placement (U.S. Department of Health, Education, and Welfare, 1980). Little information is available in rehabilitation research literature to shed light on the impact of transferability of skills, job analysis, career planning, and coordination activities.

SUMMARY AND DISCUSSION

Progress has been slowed over the years by not keeping a clear vision of employment as the goal of vocational rehabilitation. As a relatively time-limited service, rehabilitation can contribute much to a person's life by giving him or her an edge in the labor market and work force. This is not to say that other aspects of achievement are not important. If we really believe people with disabilities are much like the rest of us, except for a physical or mental impairment, we should not assume we need to help them with more than vocational concerns if our main task is rehabilitation. We might better direct some of our energies toward helping educational and medical systems and other community resources accommodate their services to people with disabilities just as we do with employers. We should not have to create new specialized services within rehabilitation until a special need becomes apparent which cannot be served by existing agencies. Diffusing our goals could lead to reduced effectiveness and hence less social support. This may be happening already.

Our graduate level curricula needs to have a sharper employment orientation. What we teach ought to have relevance for practice. However, we do not know too much about how specific practices contribute to outcomes. This, of course, has implications for research. We need to develop better models that link outcomes to how practices are offered to clients, by whom, and under what circumstances (Paul, 1967). Our research also needs to investigate the sociological processes of how labor market information is best accessed and how worker integration can be enhanced after placement. Such findings could add much to the more prevalent clinical models we now borrow from medicine and psychology.

Until we do understand more about placement, it does not appear wise to establish a professional certification or academic degree for any specialist with a separate placement mandate. We should avoid institutionalizing placement as somehow separate from vocational rehabilitation.

In early and recent role and function studies and also in studies identifying relevant competencies for rehabilitation professionals (Fraser & Clowers, 1978; Harrison & Lee, 1979; Muthard & Salamone, 1969; Porter, Rubin, & Sink, 1979; Zadny & James, 1977) placement is classified as a service category. In study after study counselors report that less than 10% of their time is spent on placement. However, it is also typical to find placement described as the goal of the entire process. It does not appear conceptually sound to have the same term apply to a part of a process and also to the goal of the process. It is not surprising there is much debate on what placement is, how it should be done, who should do it, and how it should be taught. It seems much more valid to accept placement as the outcome of the service process (after all, that is why clients come to the system) and to concentrate on linking the array of possible services, activities, and techniques in the rehabilitation tool kit to placement outcomes. Everything that professionals do should be justified in terms of placement, not just 10% of time and effort.

7 Case Management and Administration

T. F. Riggar and Dean Patrick

For rehabilitation counselors to successfully rehabilitate the handicapped involves not only the mastery of skills and functions examined previously in this chapter but requires that these activities be carried out in an efficacious manner. No matter the degree of competence that goes into any particular step in the rehabilitation process it is imperative upon counselors to coordinate all of their own activities as well as the supplemental tasks performed by other professionals who may be involved in working with the handicapped client. Due to the wide variety and diversity of opportunities, potentialities, and settings it is difficult to clearly outline a single specific format or paradigm which may be followed by each rehabilitation counselor in every agency, organization, or facility. Hence, the intent herein will be to define what is meant by case management and case load management as well as show their utility from several different orientations and to examine how these processes may be carried out in various settings.

DEFINITION

Case management, or the case load manager, has been known by a number of different names—resource manager, resource collaborator, service coordinator, etc. (Evans, 1984). Whatever the title, case management requires coordination by the rehabilitation counselor of the various activities with which the handicapped client is involved to achieve appropriate, desired outcomes. Several definitions will serve to examine this process by the counselor. As we will see, these or similar terms may also be defined as including more than just the rehabilitation counselor and the immediately associated professionals.

> . . . the process of ensuring that clients move sequentially through the appropriate statuses without undue delay. (Thompson, Kite, & Bruyere, 1979, p. 3)

> . . . the counselor's managerial activities that facilitate the movement of each rehabilitant through the service process. (Wright, 1980, p. 170)

These definitions outline the functions of the rehabilitation counselor working with a single client proceeding through the rehabilitation process. The next step is to examine the relationship of the rehabilitation counselor to groups of clients, in fact, an entire case load which makes up the employment parameters of most rehabilitation counselors.

> Caseload management includes the systematic use of management tools, guidelines, and staff in order to make maximum use of funds in achieving organizational goals and for maintaining the planned distribution, quality, and quantity of the individual caseloads. . . . (Gaines, 1979, p. 113)

> Case load management refers to the responsibility of the counselor for the progress of the whole group of clients who constitute the counselor's caseload. (Wright, 1980, p. 170)

> Being certain that all work is being processed efficiently and appropriately is the major task of workload management. This processing includes all the work done on a case, including that done by supervisors and secretaries. (Willey, 1978, p. 156)

We have seen from the above definitions that neither case management nor case load management, frequently confused, have standard, set definitions of what skills comprise case load and case management (Pape, 1983), or in fact the "how-to" of the most efficient and effective means by which to implement professional rehabilitation counselor management techniques to aid the disabled. Despite these and other definitions, "caseload management is conceptualized, defined, and practiced in a variety of ways" (Gaines, 1979, p. 112). The same is true of case management in that the specific rehabilitation counselor relates directly to a specific client, and perceptions of the counselors effectiveness will depend, in large part, on quality and quantity of closures (Crisler & Barney, 1976).

Further on, both case and case load management will be examined from various perspectives particularly as they relate to a number of rehabilitation counselor employment settings. A prime generator of the need to develop efficacious management techniques (in addition to increased accountability) is simply that "to keep pace with the increasing demands, the counselor needs to become a more competent administrator of his work and better organized in managing a caseload" (Willey, 1978, p. 156).

HISTORICAL PERSPECTIVE

Although the rehabilitation counseling profession can be said to have its formal legislative establishment with the Smith-Fess Act of 1920, which initiated the civilian federal-state rehabilitation program (Roessler & Rubin, 1982), the true evolution of case and case load management may be said to start with the Vocational Rehabilitation Act Amendments of 1954 (Public Law 565). This legislation provided grants to higher education programs for education and training of rehabilitation personnel in college and university settings. As a result of this law thousands of individuals sought and obtained federally fiscally supported master's degrees in rehabilitation counseling. With the initiation of such advanced training the National Council on Rehabilitation Education (NCRE) now numbers in its 1984 Membership Directory 74 programs throughout the United States that provide higher education in the field of rehabilitation. This huge influx of counselors has resulted in at least 20,000 persons employed in rehabilitation counseling throughout the country (Feinberg & McFarlane, 1979; Schumacher, 1977). This number may not, of course, account for all of those individuals who received specialty training and degrees in vocational evaluation, work adjustment, job development and placement, rehabilitation administration/facility management, etc. Nor may the total account for the large percentage of rehabilitation counselors and other rehabilitation direct-service providers who become administrators and supervisors shortly after they receive their master's degrees (Riggar & Matkin, 1984). (For further information concerning employment trends see Chapter 10.)

The next significant historical perspective influencing case and case load management must be said to be the Rehabilitation Act of 1973. Two portions of the Act directly affect both types of management we have defined. They include the Individualized Written Rehabilitation Program (IWRP) and the State Program Evaluation (PE).

For the first time all federal-state rehabilitation counselors employed by state agencies were required to develop an individualized written rehabilitation plan with each client served. This program, and its subsequent written plan, must be developed *with* the client and not *for* the client. Prior to 1973 a wide variety of plans, programs, and reporting devices had existed throughout the country. Although not specifically drawn as a "must use" form, the Act provided that the IWRP shall involve the client and be developed by both client and counselor. Specifically, the plan/program must include documentation of "terms, conditions, rights and remedies under which services are provided" (Wright, 1980, p. 150). In addition to vocational goals, subobjectives (the steps to the goal), counseling, education/training, work adjustment, job placement, etc., criteria must be jointly developed, implemented, and evaluated. This report provides a sequential, documented process to follow as services are provided for the client. The culmination of the plan/program allows a confluence of all client-counselor interactions and enables a framework, a system guide, showing direction toward successful rehabilitation on a one-to-one, or case management approach basis.

The second section of the 1973 Act, state program evaluation, holds that state agencies must provide certain information to the federal funding source. These data, which include information about percentages served, effectiveness (timeliness and quality), outcome (placement and follow-up), and client satisfaction can only come from the development of evaluation systems at the state level into which counselors must input data concerning all of their clients, i.e., case load. For the PE system to work it must establish steps, procedures, and standards to allow the necessary comparisons to determine quality and quantity. It is this system, coupled with the IWRP, which provides the structural guidelines (not the actual techniques) by which rehabilitation counselors may focus their case load management.

Thus, the last historical perspective considered, the Rehabilitation Act of 1973, brings together mandated systems which may, at the least, serve as a guide to the counselor when they consider implementation of a systematic process by which the disabled may be rehabilitated. As we will see, these demands for planning and accountability result in considerable paperwork. In fact, Truitt and Vandergrift (1980) find that "the bureaucratic administration responds to the request for accountability by requiring its work force to provide evidence, most often in the form of detailed reports" (pp. 65–66).

PARTICIPANTS

Primary responsibility for both case and case load management rests with the rehabilitation counselor. In some circumstances and with all continuing management objectives the responsibility for accomplishment rests with organization administrators and supervisors. Wright (1980) cites the Third Institute on Rehabilitation Services (Muthard, 1965): "control the distribution, quality, quantity, and cost of the aspects of case work activities in order to accomplish the program goals of the agency" (p. 12). Wright indicates that the responsibility for this performance is "at all levels—administrator, supervisor, counselor, and other staff levels" (p. 172).

The recording, report writing, clerical work, and overall planning activities performed by rehabilitation counselors to guarantee goal attainment generally takes between 30 and 50% of their total work time (Rubin & Roessler, 1983). This rather considerable amount of time is often an unpleasant surprise to many new counselors. Sussman (cited in Truitt & Vandergrift, 1980) indicates that the rehabilitation system is sometimes "seen as de-professionalizing to recent graduates entering the field with the classic complaint being one of too much paperwork" (p. 67). With a goal of serving the greatest number of clients in the most cost-effective manner constantly considering quality, much of the "paperwork" is an absolute necessity for work planning, decision making, case selection priorities, and evaluation.

Notwithstanding the legislative and practical necessity of recording, report writing, clerical work, planning, and evaluation by both rehabilitation counselors and administrators/supervisors, the toll these functions takes on rehabilitation professionals is often considerable. Riggar, Godley, and Hafer (1984) documented the existence and relative levels of both job satisfaction and burnout in rehabilitation personnel. While burnout and reduced levels of job satisfaction may not be obverse sides of the same coin, burnout and job satisfaction are significantly inversely related. Not uniquely, factors such as high levels of satisfaction with working conditions; interest in, liking for, and emotional involvement in the job; and physical and mental exertion are predictive of membership in the administrator group rather than direct-service provision. Simply stated, rehabilitation counselors tend to be more burned out and less job satisfied than their bosses.

As we will see, the management techniques of case and case load management are extremely varied, depending principally on employment settings. To standardize and regularize the rehabilitation process, even within a single agency, facility, or organization, will take a concerted effort, particularly on the part of rehabilitation administrators, to reduce whatever burden may exist for rehabilitation counselors.

CONTEMPORARY PRACTICE

The public (federal-state) rehabilitation case management process is categorized in a number of steps, each of which has its own nationally recognized status code. Each and every handicapped client entering the system becomes a case client for a specific rehabilitation counselor, and proceeds through these stages. The data, pooled for each rehabilitation counselor's entire case load, allow for more effective planning, programming, and subsequent overall statewide service evaluation. Cooper and Davis (1979) have provided an excellent description of the 15 statuses through which monitoring of case movement is conducted.

Table 7.1. Case Movement Statuses

Pre-service statuses	
00	Referral status—rehabilitation services has name, address and minimal information about a potential applicant
02	Application status—the client has signed an application for services
06	Extended evaluation
10	Individualized written rehabilitation program development
12	Individualized written rehabilitation program completed
Service statuses	
14	Counseling and guidance only
16	Physical restoration
18	Training
20	Ready for employment—planned services such as counseling, physical restoration and training have been completed
22	In employment
24	Service interrupted—services are interrupted while client is in one of the other service statuses
Closure statuses	
08	Closed ineligible—client declared ineligible for services from status 00, 02, or 06
26	Closed rehabilitated
28	Closed not rehabilitated from a service status
30	Closed not rehabilitated from status 10 or 12

Reprinted from P. G. Cooper & S. Davis. (1979). Case flow modeling: A program management innovation for planning services to the severely disabled. *Journal of Rehabilitation Administration, 3*(1), p. 24. Used by permission.

We may see from Table 7.1 how such a case movement device would serve as an overall guide for client case management. Although surely the largest single employer of rehabilitation counseling graduates, the federal-state rehabilitation system is by no means the only employer. There is some evidence (Riggar & Matkin, 1984) that the fastest-growing employer is the private sector of rehabilitation. Known also as private-for-profit, industrially injured rehabilitation, or insurance rehabilitation, this portion of the national rehabilitation movement has a somewhat separate case and case load management paradigm.

Registered nurses (RN) were the first professional group to become involved in injured worker or insurance rehabilitation. Because of their medically oriented training they were able to interact with the disabled, particularly the injured worker, at an earlier time than is normally the case with rehabilitation counselor involvement. A unique feature of private sector rehabilitation is that "the injured worker's rehabilitation case manager is usually a claims adjuster or a compensation clerk" (Hanna, Mullinax, & Sadler, 1983, p. 75). A current concern is that certain case services such as counseling, vocational evaluation, work adjustment, job development and placement, etc. are beyond the purview of nurses.

Case management in insurance sector rehabilitation, also known as disability management, medical care coordination or medical management (Matkin & Wallace, 1985) is generally divided into four stages:

1. Medical care costs and disability.
2. Case selection by the insurer.
3. Initial evaluation.
4. Planning and developing rehabilitation goals.

Keeping in mind that insurance companies seek to determine what will constitute a rehabilitation case with potential for successful completion or outcome insurance claims representatives generally consider certain issues with reference to coverage and liability (Matkin & Wallace, 1985):

1. What is the insurer's potential exposure in the case?
2. In first-party cases, would involvement by a rehabilitation professional reduce the exposure?
3. Could the involvement by a rehabilitation professional reduce the value of a personal injury liability claim and decrease the

insurance company's exposure and/or possible award in excess of the policy limits?
4. Could information about potential wage loss or future projected medical expenses assist in the development of an individually designed annuity settlement?
5. Is this a second-injury case? If so, what is the extent of liability to the current insurer for the second injury?

When insurance companies consider monetary expense and projected length of disability, the known and proven cost-effective and cost-beneficial factors of the rehabilitation process most often become paramount. In most private sector cases an initial evaluation is conducted to provide case-specific information, then insurance company approval, proceeding to a case management/rehabilitation counseling process similar to that seen in Table 7.1.

Yet another orientation to case management may be seen with physical rehabilitation settings. Evans (1984) cites the resource management role as being necessary "because of the special needs of persons with multiple problems, often requiring a multitude of opinions and services" (p. 16). The role performance descriptions include

1. Social needs assessment.
2. Hospital discharge or community care activity planning.
3. Brokering services of health care professionals and advocacy on behalf of clients.
4. Facilitating referrals.
5. Community resource development.

This type of collaborative helping process is partially inherent in the other models described as well. Its uniqueness here is that collaborative interaction helps reduce unintended consequences.

The three case management models described and examined here are but a small portion of the procedural models that exist. In reality each organization possesses its own process modified to account for a wide variety of variables, i.e., time, cost, counselor expertise, type of client, outcomes intended, etc. Once the rehabilitation counselor has learned the singular, one-to-one case management process, the case load management techniques come into play to provide the same kind of quality service for quantity performance.

Case load management is often dependent on the organizational management system developed to support counselor performance. Germane bureaucratic activities may include

1. Development of policies and procedures.
2. Development and implementation of fiscal and reporting mechanisms.
3. Implementation of controls in both the client services and counselor performance areas.
4. Staff development activities (Gaines, 1979, p. 112).

These and similar developmental and organizational activities by rehabilitation administrators clearly assist the rehabilitation counselor in appropriate case load management. Competent administrators are aware that although more case-service monies are needed "beyond a certain point, adding counselors is preferable to increasing existing budgets" (Schneider & Dunaway, 1977, p. 17).

TECHNIQUES

Once the rehabilitation counselor has a grasp of the rehabilitation process it is evident that distinct phases are involved—evaluation, planning, treatment, and termination (Roessler & Rubin, 1982). More specifically, they include

1. Intake interviewing.
2. Eligibility determination.
3. Development of the rehabilitation plan.
4. Arranging and purchasing rehabilitation services.
5. Monitoring and problem solving.
6. Placement and follow-up (Greenwood, 1982, pp. 160–161).

On a day-to-day basis techniques are available to learn how to become more case- and case load–efficient (Henke, Connolly, & Cox, 1975). By learning how to evaluate one's own efforts one can not only improve performance but enhance professional capacities to aid handicapped clients. Basically these techniques, to become more effective and efficient, are subsumed into three categories (Wright, 1980): (a) managing time, (b) elements of work, and (c) work simplification.

The first approach simply reflects good time-management skills for which numerous books and articles are available. Task identification, rearrangement, element reduction, and delegation compose the elements of work which can be controlled. Work simplification is used by many rehabilitation counselors to aid clients more easily to learn a job, and the same principles apply to the more complex counseling task.

To examine case and case load management in any greater depth is obviously beyond any single article. Resources are available at the end of the chapter for those wishing a more complete examination of these management functions. Performing in such a management role frequently leads rehabilitation counselors and other rehabilitation personnel rather quickly into upper level administration and supervision. A recent study reported in the *Journal of Applied Rehabilitation Counseling* (Riggar & Matkin, 1984) found that about 50% of rehabilitation counselor education (RCE) graduates advance to managerial positions, on the average, within 14.25 months following graduation for many, despite having no previous work experience in administrative or supervisory capacities. The total is 74.2% at 3 years after graduation. The study suggests learning precisely what constitutes various rehabilitation personnel job functions and employer expectations of master's level RCE graduates.

We have seen then that although management functions are crucial to the average rehabilitation counselor, the factors concerning specifics may be infinitely variable. Fortunately, a number of approaches are available to make case and case load management more relevant to rehabilitation counselors in the future.

DISCUSSION

Both peer counselors and supervisors appear to agree that rehabilitation counselor effectiveness is dependent on the number of plans and closures (Crisler & Barney, 1976). With such perceptual expectations Truitt and Vandergrift (1980) recommend three logical prerequisites that would improve casework quality. The first of these is that most rehabilitation counselors must accept that they are employed in a legislative bureaucracy which carries with it certain accountability standards. The next item is that those in power, top-level administrators, must set standardized, firm criteria for both casework quality and accountability requirements. Next, these standards must be clearly and unequivocally communicated to the personnel who are expected to perform and conform. The last point is that at all stages those who are going to implement and be responsible for these activities be consulted prior to standard and criteria establishment. Once these steps have been taken, case and case load management will be reduced to skills that can be examined, researched, identified, and taught. We must always remember that our primary purpose is to aid and rehabilitate the handicapped. Appropriate professional systems and techniques surely provide this assistance in the most efficacious manner.

RESOURCES

Several references are particularly important for rehabilitation counselors and others who seek more information about case and case load management:

The Advanced Facilitative Case Management
Training Package Series. (1981).
Arkansas Rehabilitation Research and Training Center,
University of Arkansas
Fayetteville, AR 72701

Deborah A. Pape. (1983). *Case Management Techniques.* #13.
Rehabilitation Research Review.
National Rehabilitation Information Center
4407 Eighth St., N.E.
The Catholic University of America
Washington, DC 20017

Richard T. Roessler and Stanford E. Rubin. (1982).
Case Management and Rehabilitation Counseling
PRO-ED
5341 Industrial Oak Blvd.
Austin, TX 78735

Ralph E. Matkin. (1985).
Insurance Rehabilitation: Service applications in disability compensation systems.
PRO-ED
Austin, TX 78735

8 Rehabilitation Counselor Education

Vincent A. Scalia
Richard R. Wolfe

Rehabilitation as a definable body of knowledge and practices entered the field of human services 60-plus years ago. Early practitioners had the general goal of returning the disabled individual to functioning as effectively as possible toward the goal of becoming self-supporting.

In the ensuing 60 years, the country's rapid technological and medical advancements made working with the disabled more complex. Not only do the disabled populations served by vocational rehabilitation require specialized services, but the combined effect of these advancements mandated the development of more highly trained rehabilitation counselors.

The professional rehabilitation counselor is finally coming of age. The professional rehabilitation counselor is responsible for aiding disabled individuals, appraising their abilities and interests, understanding their needs, adjusting to their handicaps, and obtaining employment consistent with their capacities and capabilities. "Professional" is the key word. "Professional" indicates the counselor is performing a needed function, knowledgeable and skillful, trained, ethical, and involved in continuing education to keep abreast of the most recent advancements in service delivery. The professional counselor must possess special knowledges and skills. These knowledges and skills are acquired through specialized training and continuing education.

A complementary relationship among research, pre-service training, continuing education, and service has gradually developed since rehabilitation education was authorized by Congress in 1954. The result has been an impressive network of pre-service and continuing education programs based in colleges and universities throughout the nation.

Rehabilitation counselor education as described in this article is limited to the pre-service education (university degree program) and continuing education—the continuing education provided through the various Regional Rehabilitation Continuing Education Programs. No attempt is made to focus upon the agency in-service training programs or the short-term training programs once funded through federal resources. These areas may be mentioned as they aid in developing the rehabilitation counselor education theme.

HISTORICAL PERSPECTIVE

Although states had concern about trained personnel to provide services, the Rehabilitation Act of 1920 provided no federal funds to meet this need. Through the VR Amendment Act of 1943 (PL 78–113) administrators of state programs were authorized to train or pay for training of personnel. No specific federal dollars were funded for this purpose. As the rehabilitation program grew, it became evident that qualified personnel were needed if the program were to reach its potential.

Through the VR Amendment Act of 1954 (PL 83–565) federal monies were made available for training. Funding included, but was not limited to, training grants for physicians, nurses, occupational therapists, physical therapists, and rehabilitation counselors. As of August 15, 1955, about a year after the 1954 Amendment was signed into law, 91 teaching institutions had arranged their curricula and had received grants to help expand their teaching programs in rehabilitation. To aid students, 104 traineeship grants were made available to institutions, aiding nearly 600 students in physical therapy, occupational therapy, rehabilitation counseling, social work, and other fields closely allied to vocational rehabilitation (Switzer, 1956).

Patterson, introducing Part III of his *Readings in Rehabilitation Counseling* (1960) discussed the concept of the counselor as a generalist or jack-of-all-trades. His contention was that this approach leads to a training program which is broad-based but one with little depth and no core.

Hahn (1954) suggested dividing skill materials into four broad areas, which he labeled *psychology, social casework, medicine,* and *contributing areas.* He suggested 40 to 50% of the training in the psychology area, 30 to 40% in social casework, as much as 10% in medicine, and 5 to 10% from the contributing area. (This contributing area included tests and measurements, occupational information, etc.)

Levine and Pence (1953) discussed the action of the Education and Research Committee of the San Francisco Chapter of the National

Rehabilitation Association. The curriculum recommended covered a 2-academic-year preparation, to be presented at the graduate level and to terminate in a master's degree in Rehabilitation Counseling. This program was seen as one that could be built upon an undergraduate major in any of the social sciences fields. In this proposal, the student would have 1 didactic academic year and 1 clinical internship year—3 months each in three different agencies — for the second year. Topical headings for the didactic part of the program included rehabilitation counseling; medical survey of rehabilitation aspects in illness and injury; psychodynamics of personal, social, and occupational adjustment; communication organizations; assessment of individual differences—a survey of psychological testing; legal, financial, and administrative aspects of rehabilitation including public assistance and welfare legislation, social casework, and vocational and occupational counseling.

Cantrell (1958) researched what state rehabilitation counselors and privately employed rehabilitation counselors as well as the Veterans Administration's rehabilitation psychologist believed to be the important knowledges and skills. In rank order, those topical areas identified included counseling and interviewing, professional activities of the counselor, field work and supervised practice, psychological and related areas, testing, occupational information, casework, rehabilitation, social, community and related areas, research and statistics.

Patterson (1960) discussed the interdisciplinary nature of rehabilitation counselor training. In his summary he stated that the training is basically psychological, and the rehabilitation counselor is fundamentally a psychological/vocational counselor working with handicapped clients.

Patterson (1969) presented "The University as a Producer of Rehabilitation Counselors" to the Joint Liaison Committee of the Council of State Directors of Vocational Rehabilitation and Rehabilitation Counselor Educators (JLC) in 1967. He stated this was essentially the same topic discussed between those two groups (directors and educators) some 10 years earlier. Patterson cautioned that all suggestions for change should not be blindly accepted, that we should think twice before abandoning current practice for untried innovations. Patterson gave three principles which he felt should be understood by both the counselor educators and employers of counselors.

1. A first and basic principle of professional education is that such education is *directed toward preparation for a profession.*
2. A second principle is that it is *theoretically oriented.*

3. A third principle of professional education is that it is oriented toward *preparing persons not simply for the present, or for an existing profession, but for the future.*

In a policy statement, American Rehabilitation Counseling Association, August 1968 (cited in Moses & Patterson, 1971) it is stated that the objective of graduate education is to prepare the individual for entering upon a lifelong profession, not for a specific job or position (p. 91). To be included in the curricular content, according to the policy statement, are an understanding of the philosophy, the theory, and the psychological, sociological, and economic principles that constitute the foundations of counseling; a 2-year course of study; curriculum elements which are shared with all counselors; curriculum elements specific to rehabilitation counseling; supervised experiences; and an internship.

The Preamble to the Ethical Standards of the American Personnel and Guidance Association (1961) (cited in Moses & Patterson, 1971) focuses upon the marks of a profession and a professional organization. Highly emphasized in this preamble is the need for knowledge and skills and how these knowledges and skills might be gained. It is important that we as educators review our philosophical beliefs.

The Joint Liaison Committee (JLC) cited above was instrumental in developing some guidelines to be used in rehabilitation counselor training programs. Although these documents are now relatively old, much of what is seen in our current rehabilitation counselor education curricula can be traced to these philosophical positions. A series of pamphlets entitled Studies in Rehabilitation Counselor Training were produced and/or commissioned through the JLC. Seven publications in this series include

No. 1. *Guidelines for Supervised Clinical Practice*
No. 2. *Experience of State Agencies in Hiring VRA Trainees*
No. 3. *Agency-University Communication, Coordination and Co-operation in Rehabilitation Education*
No. 4. *Medical Information in the Rehabilitation Counseling Curriculum*
No. 5. *Communication Dissemination and Utilization of Rehabilitation Research Information*
No. 6. *The Rehabilitation Counselor Rating Scale*
No. 7. *The Utilization of Support Personnel in Rehabilitation Counseling.*

As one reviews these documents, the joint effort of college/university educators and state rehabilitation administrators in solving mutual problems and impacting on curriculum is evident.

CONTEMPORARY PRACTICE

Pre-Service Education

A study of the Region IX Task Force on Graduate Preparation in Rehabilitation Counseling was published in October 1973. This task force was chaired by F. R. McFarlane, and the report was compiled and edited by McFarlane, Hillis, Johnson, and Meadows (McFarlane, 1973).

The objective of the study was twofold: (a) to assess and report the present functioning of graduate education in rehabilitation counseling in Region IX, and (b) to identify and develop a model and recommendations which could be used by graduate programs in rehabilitation counseling. Included in the present curriculum were principles of rehabilitation, organization of rehabilitation services, medical aspects of disabilities, psychological and social aspects of disability, psychosocial and medical aspects of disability, career and life-style development, appraisal in school/agency counseling, evaluation in rehabilitation, transitional work programs in rehabilitation counseling, clinical procedures in rehabilitation counseling, counseling practicum, internship and rehabilitation counseling.

The task force developed a curriculum model. The elements of the model included education in supervisory and administrative skills; ability to effectively use local community resources; understanding of the medical/psychological/societal aspects of all major disabilities; in-depth command of techniques of individual and group counseling; ability to analyze past, present, future trends in the profession; ability to assess human behavior, study career development process, psychology of the work-factors influencing adjustment to specific work settings; ability to engage in program development, and consultation skills.

Wrenn and Darley (cited in Patterson, 1969) discussed the movement of rehabilitation counseling toward becoming a profession. In their discussion they compared the progress of rehabilitation toward accepted criteria. The criteria of a profession, as described by Wrenn and Darley includes the following:

1. The performance of a socially needed function.

2. The definition of job titles and functions.
3. Existence of a body of knowledge and skills.
4. Application of standards of training.
5. The self-imposition of standards of admission to practice and of professional performance.
6. Development of a professional consciousness and professional groups.
7. Development of a Code of Ethics.
8. Legal recognition—by certification or licensing of practitioners.

The goal of rehabilitation leaders has been to establish rehabilitation as a profession. That goal has now been attained.

The Council on Rehabilitation Education, the accrediting body for master's degree programs in rehabilitation counseling has designated a required curriculum content for graduate study. The stated goal of the curriculum is "to provide for obtaining essential knowledge, skills and attitudes necessary to function effectively as a professional rehabilitation counselor" (p. 3). The curricular areas of study include (a) history, philosophy, and legislation related to rehabilitation; (b) organizational structure of the vocational rehabilitation system; (c) counseling theories, issues, and practices (individual and group); (d) case management process; (e) theories, methods, and practices of career vocational development; (f) medical aspects of disability; (g) psychological aspects of disability; (h) planning client vocational rehabilitation services; (i) utilizing occupational information; (j) knowledge of community resources; (k) understanding requirements and characteristics of a variety of jobs; (l) vocational placements; (m) rehabilitation research; (n) trends, issues, legal, ethical tenets of practice; (o) supervised clinical experience.

In a recent (undated) memorandum, the Board for Rehabilitation Certification issued guidelines for criteria for CRC eligibility effective July 1, 1985. Subject areas which were included encompass those requirements for college/university accreditation, and also reflect the current needs of the field. These were categorized into five rehabilitation counseling job functioning areas: (a) job development and placement; (b) case management; (c) professional development and administrative planning; (d) vocational counseling and assessment; (e) affective counseling.

In this review of the progression of rehabilitation counselor education, it is evident that the didactic material deemed critical for rehabilitation counselors has not significantly changed from the 1953 recommendations of the San Francisco Chapter of National Rehabilitational Association. There have been significant changes in technology and in delivery systems, but the basic curricular core remains intact. This reinforces the concept that rehabilitation is a profession. Certification of rehabilitation counselor standards reflect both the body of knowledge and the current state of the art.

Through the supervision of interns and interactions with agency personnel, rehabilitation programs are aware of current needs, and these are incorporated into the various courses in the curriculum. The core, however, remains intact.

Rehabilitation education programs have incorporated more emphasis on vocational evaluation, job development, and job placement into the curriculum. Independent living rehabilitation, private for-profit rehabilitation, workers' compensation rehabilitation, and legal aspects are just a few of the concerns of the practitioner that have been addressed in the curriculum. Some universities have developed complete master's degrees in special unique areas, i.e., vocational evaluation, job placement, administration, etc. Other programs have included the concepts in existing master's degree programs. Recent studies (Matkin, 1983; Rubin et al., 1984) consistently confirm the efficacy of the basic core curriculum. Additional research indicates that counselors, vocational evaluators, and work adjustment personnel bring a common knowledge base to the rehabilitation process (McFarlane & DiPaola, 1979), and that many counselors rise quickly to administrative roles (Matkin, Sawyer, Lorenz, & Rubin, 1982; Riggar & Matkin, 1984), basing their performance on their counseling education.

Curricular offerings are reviewed and modified on a regular, continuing basis, yet the long-term rehabilitation training programs (pre-service programs) cannot respond to the immediate needs and concerns of all agencies, organizations, and facilities. In the past much of this attention to the mission and goals of the agency was accomplished through short-term training and/or in-service training. Rehabilitation education staff of the various rehabilitation counselor programs were called upon to aid in the delivery of the training.

Nature and Limitations of Pre-Service Education

Pre-service education is limited to preparing individuals for professional counseling activities which must be performed. Pre-service education emphasizes basic theory and general principles of practice. It is directed toward preparation for a profession, not for a specific job. There is a general perception among many educators that rehabilitation counselor training be directed specifically or wholly toward preparing counselors to work in state agencies. Traditionally, state agencies have been a large employer of rehabilitation counselors. However, they are not the only employer of rehabilitation counselors nor, for many programs, the largest employer of graduates. Thus, the profession of rehabilitation counseling goes beyond a particular setting. The preparation, then, through pre-service education emphasizes the development of understanding and the acquisition of some general principles which will guide a rehabilitation counselor in general practice and not a given setting. Since rehabilitation counseling is practiced in many different settings, it is not possible for pre-service training programs to prepare people specifically or completely for any particular setting. Pre-service education offers training in a theoretical base. Once in practice, rehabilitation counselors will have ample opportunity to learn from experience. The short time of a counselor's professional life in pre-service education may be the only opportunity to obtain a theoretical foundation for practice.

Finally pre-service is viewed as a beginning, not an end, of professional training. It is designed to orient the new counselor to the present condition and prepare the counselor for the future and change.

Continuing Education

The primary emphasis on rehabilitation training during the 1950s and the 1960s was in pre-service education. The general objective of pre-service education was then, and remains today, to prepare counselors for the duties and responsibilities of the profession. As a profession, rehabilitation counseling is not static but rather a rapidly changing and developing field, and a truly professional rehabilitation counselor must be prepared to change. The very nature of a profession dictates that professional education must continue during a person's entire professional life. A profession, then, carries the responsibility for supplementing and extending the preparation obtained in the pre-service (academic) setting.

In 1974 the Regional Rehabilitation Continuing Education Programs (RRCEPs) were established by the Rehabilitation Services Administration (RSA) as primary resources for continuing education of rehabilitation personnel in public and private rehabilitation agencies and facilities. the RRCEPs were developed as a means to complement existing RSA training efforts (pre-service, short-term) with an emphasis on multi-state recurrent training needs of rehabilitation personnel at all levels. Predominantly training was directed toward rehabilitation counselors. The emphasis on "multi-state recurrent training needs" differentiated this training effort from other continuing education efforts, such as the state agency in-service program and RSAs short-term training program. The four goals established for the RRCEPs by the RSA are

1. To deliver continuing education programming to rehabilitation personnel.
2. To provide assistance in post-employment training program development within rehabilitation agencies.
3. To coordinate continuing education resources and serve as a resource center for a variety of training materials and information data.
4. To develop continuing education instructional content for meeting identified manpower training needs.

The training provided by RRCEPs is based on a broad, integrated sequence of training activities and focuses on meeting recurrent training needs common throughout a multi-state geographic area. There are 11 RRCEPs, with at least one in every federal region. Each RRCEP determines, in collaboration with its advisory board, the content and manner in which the RSA objectives will be met.

The continuing education efforts provided by RRCEP are financed with federal funds through RSA. The major thrust of the continuing education efforts is directed at state vocational rehabilitation agencies and rehabilitation facilities. The general approach of the continuing education efforts is toward the specific aspects of functioning in a particular setting.

RRCEPs provide continuing education from a framework of Human Resources Development (HRD) (Nadler, 1979). The HRD model incorporates training, education, and developmental activities. Training is defined as that set of activities which is geared to increasing skill in one's present job. As such, training activities are skills-based and job/role-centered. Education can be defined as that set of activities which is geared toward informing and enlarging the individual's repertoire responses in a given situation. Education activities are designed to enhance the responses the individual can bring to bear when faced with any issue or problem. Developmental activities can be defined as that set of learning activities which help prepare individuals for an uncertain future. They are often process-centered and designed to bring about a change over long periods of time.

Pre-service education is directed at training individuals for the field of vocational rehabilitation. Continuing education is directed at training rehabilitation counselors for a specific job or position. Pre-service education is more than the inculcation of skills and techniques. It is more than imparting information and knowledge. Pre-service education aims at developing the student to think critically, analyze, synthesize, and exercise judgment. Continuing education takes the counselor in the work setting and provides the means, or upgrades the ability of that person, to function effectively in his/her specific job. Pre-service education addresses identified shortages of rehabilitation personnel, while continuing education serves to upgrade knowledges and skills of current personnel.

The professionalization of rehabilitation is dependent to a large degree on the availability and maintenance of competent professionals. Rehabilitation education (pre-service) and continuing education meet all the criteria to identify rehabilitation counseling as a profession. Rehabilitation education and continuing education are the underpinnings of the profession. As the two areas become more sophisticated and grow, so will the profession of rehabilitation counseling. Rehabilitation education and continuing education taken together create a synergistic product, professional rehabilitation counselors, and demonstrate that the whole is greater than the sum of its parts.

9 Research Utilization in Rehabilitation Counseling Practice

Geraldine Hansen

The goal of rehabilitation research is to eliminate barriers disabled persons experience in achieving their life goals through the methods and resources of science and technology (Fenderson, 1984). Since rehabilitation practitioners and administrators are primarily responsible for the delivery of services, it is logical that their efforts would be the target of research-based ideas and innovations. Yet the uncertainty of the impact of research findings on professional practice exists. The purpose of this chapter is to discuss research and program evaluation in rehabilitation, both its utilization and impacts. Due to the requirements of brevity, the chapter will be limited to a discussion of the role of research for the practitioner and administrator.

In the absence of research, professionals must fall back on the accumulated wisdom of the field based on custom and past usage. That is not entirely inappropriate as people learn through their experiences. Gordon (1979) states that experience is simply a less systematic method of empirical research. However, reliance on experience does not move the profession forward because experience is conservative. Bolton (1974) indicates that practical experience provides considerable subjective evidence regarding more or less effective methods and approaches to serving clients. Research, on the other hand, is an objective attainment of knowledge based on replicable methods. It is this objectivity that will guide the profession beyond knowledge to action.

Research in rehabilitation has been the subject of substantial criticism. Such criticism identifies three main shortcomings: (a) limited relevance of rehabilitation research to practice; (b) an inadequacy with respect to its basic approaches; and (c) its ability to bring about an integrated body of knowledge that contributes to the development of rehabilitation theory. Efforts to develop useful research in rehabilitation are similar to those in most other human service programs;

however, the efforts still fall short of what is desired and needed to maximize effective programs and services.

PROGRAM EVALUATION

Another type of research is evaluative research, or what is commonly known as program evaluation. Program evaluation and research are means of providing information for decision making. Organizations are created to solve problems, and administrators deal with many problems in planning, organizing, and managing such organizations. Over the years, the need for using research and evaluation data in managing vocational rehabilitation services has increased.

The 1960s witnessed significant growth in the vocational rehabilitation program, with an emphasis on comprehensive statewide planning projects. These projects often demonstrated the lack of objective data on which to base planning. A federally instituted reporting system for states greatly advanced the capacity for evaluation and monitoring of rehabilitation services to clients. Early in 1970 the Rehabilitation Services Administration created the annual Program and Financial Plan, which required agency administrators to project services to clients and integrate these data with budgetary projections.

The greatest impetus for accountability resulted from the Rehabilitation Act of 1973, requiring state rehabilitation programs to establish procedures for measuring and evaluating program effectiveness. Current regulation in program evaluation has designated four areas for state agency study: (a) needs of handicapped persons within the state; (b) the state's need for rehabilitation facilities; (c) characteristics of ineligible applicants; and (d) estimates of population in need of rehabilitation services. Such requirements demonstrate that rehabilitation program accountability has been externally driven.

Program evaluation, a relatively new development in human service programs, has experienced problems similar to other types of research in that the practice of evaluation and the incorporation of findings into organizational policy decisions have proved difficult. Struthers (1982) identifies several reasons why evaluation findings are not fully utilized; for example, data are not provided to managers in a timely manner; management based on data is impractical as management is essentially political; many vocational rehabilitation managers do not use evaluation/research findings; researchers and evaluators do not provide the crucial data needed; and the gap between broad policy decisions and objective data is too large.

RESEARCH UTILIZATION

The ultimate fruition of research is the useful application of findings to help persons with handicaps. There is mutual interest among researchers, practitioners, and policymakers in making research more useful.

National promotion of research and development grant programs dates back to 1954. Included in the research was an effort to convey findings to professionals so that the information would be evident in their practice. In 1969, a comprehensive utilization program was established to help professionals and organizations adopt new ideas and modify service components. Some of the developments under this thrust included the following:

1. Research BRIEFs (Bring Research into Effective Focus) were published containing a summary of usable research results for busy rehabilitation practitioners and administrators.
2. Research utilization laboratories were established at Chicago Jewish Vocational Services and the International Center for the Disabled to study and enhance the utilization of research results.
3. Rehabilitation Research and Training Centers were established to conduct applied research in the areas of medical, vocational, mental retardation, and deafness, and translate results into training programs for rehabilitation practitioners in a variety of settings.
4. Regional research institutes were created to conduct programmatic research on designated topics of broad interest (counselor functioning, the culturally disadvantaged client, etc.) and disseminate their findings nationally.

Research contributions to the enhancement of the rehabilitation practitioner's professional therapeutic skills date back to the sixties, when Truax and Carkhuff (1967) developed the thesis wherein support personnel could apply principles of the helping professional in therapeutic settings.

At the same time Truax and Carkhuff were conducting research, studies were undertaken in understanding the work environment and work personality (Lofquist, Dawis, & Hendel, 1971) at the University of Minnesota.

Other major contributions have emerged since then to advance rehabilitation in areas such as mental illness, low back pain, assessment scales, family adjustment and participation in an individual's rehabilitation process, diagnostic strategies for persons with learning disabilities, and improved techniques with the geriatric population.

The National Institute of Handicapped Research (NIHR) has continued formal programmatic research in medical, psychosocial, technologic, and special population areas by expanding the number of Research and Training Centers (R&TC) to 33 and establishing Rehabilitation Engineering Centers (REC). Research and demonstration projects, research fellowships, and field-initiated rehabilitation research grants are also among the scope of research activities that NIHR encompasses. Such a vast scope of research impacts disabled populations served, the service delivery strategies provided by rehabilitation practitioners, and program outcome criteria used to determine program effectiveness.

Although many research efforts are federally supported grants and projects, non-funded research is ever present and conducted by rehabilitation professionals, rehabilitation organizations, and universities. Within the past few years, the National Rehabilitation Information Center (NARIC) and the National Council on Rehabilitation Education (NCRE) have initiated a cooperative project to review and disseminate research results. *Rehabilitation Research Reviews* are state-of-the-art reviews of the research literature on a variety of rehabilitation topics. However, recent reviews (Crimando & Godley, 1984; Pape, 1983; Scofield, 1983) in the areas of case management techniques, rehabilitation education and training, and technology in placement note that much of the literature reviewed did not consist of empirical research but rather discussion.

As society moves into the age of information, accessibility to information is vital. For a rehabilitation professional, information systems will prove invaluable to enhancing services to disabled persons. Table 9.1 lists several resource centers, in addition to the R&TCs, RECs, etc., previously noted, that provide a wide variety of rehabilitation-related information on research, adaptive devices, curricula, products, etc.

In addition to these resource centers, which provide research and other information to improve the quality of life for disabled persons, commercially developed computerized data bases have emerged; for example, computerized job-matching systems, psychological testing, and vocational assessment. When professionals engage in vocational assessment, decision making, and placement, computers support their work by alleviating the time-consuming task of independently collecting, organizing, and compiling information. Innovative and tech-

Table 9.1. Resource Centers for Rehabilitation

National Referral Center for Science & Technology
Science & Technology Division
Library of Congress
Washington, DC 20540
(202) 426-5000

National Spinal Cord Injury Data Research Center
Good Samaritan Hospital
1130 E. McDowell Rd., A6
Phoenix, AZ 85006
(602) 257-2000

University Center for International Rehabilitation (UCIR)
Erickson Hall
Michigan State Univ.
East Lansing, MI 48824
(517) 355-1824

National Clearinghouse for Mental Health Information
National Institute of
Mental Health
5600 Fishers Lane
Rockville, MD 20857
(301) 443-4517

National Rehabilitation Information Center
4407 Eighth St., N.E.
Catholic Univ. of America
Washington, DC 20017
(202) 635-5822

Oklahoma Clearinghouse of Rehabilitation Training Materials
Oklahoma State University
115 Old USDA Bldg.
Stillwater, OK 74074
(405) 624-7650

Accent on Information
P.O. Box 700
Bloomington, IL 61701
(309) 378-2961

Clearinghouse on the Handicapped
Rm. 3631, Switzer Bldg.
330 C St., SW
Washington, DC 20202
(202) 472-3796

Impart
Texas Rehabilitation Commission
118 E. Riverside Dr.
Austin, TX 78704
(512) 447-0100

Materials Development Center (MDC)
Stout Vocational Rehabilitation Institute
University of Wisconsin-Stout
Menomonie, WI 47551
(715) 232-1342

Veterans Administration
Office of Technology Transfer
252 Seventh Ave.
New York, NY 10001
(212) 620-6659

National Library of Medicine
8600 Rockville Pike
Bethesda, MD 20014
(301) 656-4000

Institute for Information Studies
200 Little Falls St., 104
Falls Church, VA 22046
(703) 533-0383

nological techniques have increased the usage and acceptance of this knowledge that was based on major research efforts.

THE ROLE OF RESEARCH FOR THE PRACTITIONER

When research is mentioned to rehabilitation service providers, a groan, frown, questionable expression, or combination thereof results. Soloff (1972) states that "the results of research do not automatically become disseminated to potential users. Moreover, even if the efforts are carried out well, usage is not guaranteed" (p. 66). Thus, getting more research used by more professionals is a complex task requiring understanding beyond the know-how required for successful dissemination of knowledge.

Bolton (1974) identifies three barriers to the utilization of research: (a) failure to include practitioner in the planning of projects; (b) research reports which are not written for practitioners; and (c) the natural tendency of individuals and organizations to resist change.

Many speculate that research findings are not sought out nor widely accepted by practitioners because of the lack of communication between practitioners and researchers. This problem is purported to cause the time lag between research reports and use of the findings (Human Interaction Research, 1976). The difficulties in communication arise out of the different orientations of researchers and practitioners. While researchers tend to focus on statistical analysis and are interested in group trends and significance, practitioners look for information that can be applied to specific clients, wherein their clinical skills can be manifested.

Whether or not the best and most relevant research reaches the practitioner depends on the effectiveness of the communication links. Therefore, the usual prescription for improving the use of research is to improve the means of communication. A program, Dialog With Researchers, created by the George Washington University Rehabilitation Research and Training Center, focuses on the communication between researchers and rehabilitation professionals on findings from research projects. This form of dialogue provides an opportunity to discuss the projects whereby practitioners learn about research in areas that may affect their work, and researchers receive feedback about the utilization potential of their findings.

While the role of research has increased the professionalism of rehabilitation practitioners, Emener (1981) and Bolton (1980) postulate that knowledge and skill in research would complement a counselor's clinical judgment. Yet the counselor education programs do not systematically prepare future practitioners to be research consumers.

Much research has been accumulated regarding rehabilitation practitioner competencies in meeting client needs. These empirically derived competencies have been the basis for curriculum development for in-service training and continuing education, certification, and licensure in rehabilitation counseling and work adjustment.

A major aspect of research that supports professionals in rehabilitation has been the efforts to provide empirically based studies to identify and establish rehabilitation as a profession. These professional members include counselors, vocational evaluators, adjustment counselors, job developers/placement specialists, etc. Without an empirical evidentiary foundation, the professions in rehabilitation would continue to lack creditability when compared with other professions of equal stature.

THE ROLE OF RESEARCH FOR THE REHABILITATION ADMINISTRATOR

Rehabilitation administrators, like rehabilitation researchers, must respond to policy, priorities accountability, and utilization in ultimately improving services to disabled clients.

As discussed earlier, the administrator is often supported by a standardized management information system and program evaluation studies. These provide a framework for the administrator to engage in systematic planning. As Struthers (1982) notes, few rehabilitation administrators use research findings or program analyses for assessing organizational decisions and policies.

It has often been said that scholarly inquiry, better known as research, is a luxury seldom afforded to administrators yet is needed to keep abreast of change. Thus, administrators tend to be reactive rather than proactive. As discussed earlier, a reactive stance suggests an inclination to focus on "experience" rather than moving ahead. Oftentimes, "experience" represents a lower risk for the administrator involved in decisions which blend politics and pragmatism. As Kallsen (1982) said at a regional meeting of state rehabilitation program evaluators: "Your conclusions and recommendations must be based on hard evidence, not politics or persuasion. You are paid to look for truth, uncover it, and let that evidence help chart the strong direction for an agency" (p. 2).

Struthers (1982) discusses the reasons for limited utilization of empirical information in agency decision making as "a) the information is not suitable for use; b) the intended user will not use information as a natural tendency to resist change in management styles; and c) the process for utilizing data is not clear and managers need methods for applying new information to agency problems" (p. 173).

The University of Michigan Rehabilitation Research Institute proposed a model for using program data in the planning and implementation of state agency program initiatives. The model identified a process consisting of policy development, needs assessment, resource assessment, managerial objectives, implementation, and evaluation. Each step in the process consists of inputs, outcomes, and sources of data to support the outcomes. The input requires a variety of organizational personnel to communicate with one another, and this triggers the collaborative efforts for dialogue and ownership in the development of solutions.

The rehabilitation movement has been able to substantiate its accomplishments by describing its clientele, services, outcomes, and cost benefits. In a day when technological advances are increasing our ability to access information, continued study of program improvement will be essential to justify our future.

SUMMARY AND CONCLUSION

Research does have a vital role to play for the practitioner, administrator, and other rehabilitation professionals, but barriers of communication, attitude, and perspective prevent a more dynamic utilization. Efforts to increase rehabilitation research interaction and integration have primarily been federally supported and, thus, thwarted as government policy has changed with various administrations.

If a photographer were to capture on film the status of research in rehabilitation today and 10 years from now, a comparison of the photos would look identical, only with more brilliance contained in the later picture. The attitudes and activities necessary to enhance research relevance and use among practitioners and administrators will probably not have developed much more than already exists. Why such a bleak outlook? Recognition of research as the best hope of improving rehabilitation services to disabled individuals does not exist to a significant degree among key rehabilitation decision makers. In the opinion of this writer, it is not anticipated that there will be any traumatic event to dislodge this widespread perception. Then what movement and direction can be anticipated in the coming decade? The following developments in rehabilitation research are anticipated:

1. The population of persons with disabilities will continue to increase (i.e., elderly, head-injured, developmentally disabled). Thus, improvements in assessment strategies, service delivery strategies, and employment alternatives are important and will require study (Fenderson, 1984).

2. Asch (1984) suggests that research will explore whether existing psychological theories and research methods can account for experiences of people with disabilities. This includes research of the experiences of people with disabilities on gender and race.

3. Attitudes and behaviors toward the disabled that limit their opportunities will continue to be studied. This includes the values of appearance and independence that underlie these actions and the power that accompanies discrimination (Asch, 1984).

4. Rehabilitation administrators will be required to forge beyond their current information systems to innovative research studies to justify their program's value and future. More sophisticated methodologies will be applied, and different data collection techniques will become evident as human service agencies join together. Concern will increase about assessing what independent variables make the most difference in our consumers' lives.

5. Computer technologies will advance the practitioners' and administrators' means of accessing information relative to management of disabled individuals. Thus, researchers will need to direct their utilization schemes through the application of high technology. While computers have enabled the automation of information systems, future technological developments will enhance everyone's access to more and varied types of administrative and direct service uses.

6. Research will remain the steadfast foundation upon which emerging rehabilitation disciplines will look toward for substantiation of their professional status. While there is a paucity of empirical information for determining rehabilitation personnel needs by discipline, region, or type of training, this will change for the positive.

Research is critical to the progressive development of rehabilitation. In order for us to move beyond our current concepts, theories, and knowledge, we need to examine existing barriers and limitations in an effort to remove them.

10 Employment Trends for Rehabilitation Counselors

Ross K. Lynch
James T. Herbert

Concurrent topics that have explored contemporary practice of rehabilitation counseling as examined in this section attest to the multiplicity of skills which counselors possess. Certainly, the role and function studies (e.g., Muthard & Salomone, 1969; Rubin, et al., 1984) provide empirical evidence to the diversity of counselor skills, which result in numerous career opportunities. Although these studies suggest that rehabilitation counselors essentially perform case management, counseling, placement, administrative, and professional development functions, it has been increasingly apparent that counselors can apply such skills in many nontraditional settings. The professional literature has documented the utilization of rehabilitation counselor skills in several nontraditional work settings including the court system (Evans, 1983; Lynch, 1983), diagnostic and treatment clinics (Reagles, 1983), educational settings (Riggar & Riggar, 1978), insurance companies (Rasch, 1985), major corporations (Ashton, 1979), various industrial settings (Shrey, 1979, 1982), and private rehabilitation practice (McMahon, Matkin, Growick, Mahaffey, & Gianforte, 1983). It would appear that the employment potential for rehabilitation counselors desiring to enter these settings presents unique opportunities and challenges.

Although employment opportunities for rehabilitation counselors desiring to enter the state and federal systems have decreased, opportunities to work in nontraditional work settings have resulted in a dramatic increase. For example, Crisler and Fowler (1981) found a significant change in employment trends when comparing employment outcome of a rehabilitation counselor training program to an earlier survey of graduates from the same program (Crisler & Eaton, 1975). While a significant decrease in graduates employed by state/federal vocational rehabilitation (VR) agencies was reported, a substantial increase in graduates entering closely related rehabilitation agencies (e.g., private nonprofit rehabilitation facilities and mental health programs) was also found. Crisler and Fowler (1981) attributed this shift to the decrease in available jobs within the public sector as well as the higher salaries established in other employment settings.

Anderson and Parente (1982), in attempting to forecast the future of rehabilitation counseling, asked counselors to make predictions concerning the profession. Relevant to this discussion, rehabilitation counselors believed an increased growth in job opportunities, especially those developed in the private sector, would result. Associated with this development was the need for rehabilitation specialization in particular disabilities. Similar conclusions regarding specialization within the general domain of professional counseling as well as increased employment opportunities in business, industry, and private settings were echoed by Daniel and Weikel (1983). Taken collectively, these studies suggest that while budget cuts in state and federal programs continue, counselors perceive an optimistic future that may result in greater specificity as defined by work setting or clientele.

Recent research reviews (Mitchell & Sink, 1983; Wright, 1983) and other articles previously cited have examined isolated topics concerning emerging career opportunities and related training needs. The primary purpose of this chapter is to identify and briefly examine nontraditional career opportunities available to rehabilitation counselors.

EMERGING EMPLOYMENT TRENDS

In the past, rehabilitation counselors trained at the master's level typically pursued one of three career settings: state/federal systems and private nonprofit agencies, to obtain work; or universities, to gain further education in order to teach (Dohanian, 1981). These conventional career pursuits represented the dominant work opportunities at that time. However, with the emergence of available funding from various private-for-profit, nonprofit, and public sources, new markets have developed resulting in a rapid proliferation of potential career options for rehabilitation counselors. While an earlier review by Feinberg and McFarland (1979) outlined some of these trends, recent developments have resulted in further expansion. Consider the following:

School Systems

The Office of Special Education and Rehabilitation Services has established a national priority on improving the transition from school to work for all individuals with disabilities. Current estimates (Will, 1984) indicate that 250,000 to 300,000 students leave special education each year and that many others graduate from regular programming, but because of a disability, require specialized services to obtain employment. As discussed by Will, "Approximately one school generation after guaranteeing the right to a free appropriate public education for all children with handicaps [PL 94–142], it is appropriate that the federal government address the transition of persons with disabilities from school to working life" (p. 1). Rehabilitation counseling can take a major role in this process.

In addition to the above, in October 1983, the Job Training Partnership Act (JTPA) [PL 97–300] replaced the Comprehensive Employment and Training Act (CETA) as the major federal employment and training legislation. Under JTPA, funding ($3.7 billion for 1983–84) issued by the federal government (Department of Labor) is given to each state. Seventy percent of the funds must be used for job training in the private sector. Ten percent of such funds can be used for handicapped and other hard-to-serve populations. With strong advocacy by rehabilitation counselors as well as special and vocational educators, significant training activities can be made available to handicapped individuals (Tindall, Gugerty, & Dougherty, 1984). Both increased emphasis and funding for special needs students will result in increased employment opportunities for rehabilitation counselors in school systems.

Hospitals

Research (Jellinek & Harvey, 1982) has demonstrated that hospital-based vocational rehabilitation programs significantly enhance the probability of vocational rehabilitation among patients in medical settings. Recognition of the benefit of such services has resulted in a greater number of VR staff in hospitals. The Joint Commission on Accreditation of Hospitals (1983) notes, "Vocational counseling, education, work evaluation, training, and placement assistance shall be provided as required" (p. 167). The Commission also stipulates that direction and supervision of such services "shall be provided by a qualified vocational counselor or vocational evaluator" (p. 167). Moreover, accreditation requires that "each staff counselor and evaluator, shall be a graduate of a vocational rehabilitation program at the graduate level" (p. 167). As a result of such recent provisions, a significant increase in the number of VR counselors employed in hospital settings is predicted.

Multidisciplinary Clinics

Many allied health professionals, rehabilitation counselors included, are combining their services in multidisciplinary clinics (Reagles, 1983). In this manner, rehabilitation counseling may combine psychology, social work, nursing, and several other human services providers to offer a well-rounded, multi-faceted treatment and counseling center. Due to the number of services offered, a broad referral base can be developed, resources pooled, grants pursued, and costs shared. Such a clinic model is becoming an increasingly attractive employment setting to rehabilitation counselors.

Private Practice/Consultant

In recent years, numerous rehabilitation counselors have entered private practice (McMahon et al., 1983). Such individuals are self-employed, offer a variety of services (although many specialize), and receive referrals from numerous sources (e.g., attorneys, insurance carriers, government agencies, and physicians). Services that private rehabilitation practitioners offer typically include one or several of the following: rehabilitation counseling, vocational and psychological assessment, development of retraining programs, consultation and/or expert testimony as to residual earning capacity, job site analysis, job modification, job development, job placement assistance, career guidance and planning, affirmative action consultation (e.g., identification of workers with handicaps, recruitment of qualified handicapped applicants, reasonable accommodation, architectural barrier removal, and training), retirement counseling, personal adjustment counseling, as well as offering various seminar, workshop, and research services on rehabilitation-related topics. Future years will witness a significant increase in the number of rehabilitation professionals functioning as private practitioners and/or consultants.

Private Rehabilitation Companies/In-House Insurance Rehabilitation Programs

Industry Week estimated that the for-profit rehabilitation business "has grown from nothing in 1970 to nearly 1,000 companies and total annual revenues approaching $250 million" (Lauterbach, 1982,

p. 53). Matkin (1982b) reported that approximately 5,300 practitioners work for private-for-profit rehabilitation companies. Of those, nearly one-third were graduates of rehabilitation counselor education programs. Additionally, recent research indicates increasing employment opportunities for rehabilitation counseling graduates in the private sector (e.g., Geist & McMahon, 1981; Gutowski, 1979; Lynch & Martin, 1982; The Urban Institute, 1980). Moreover, due to the large number of workers' compensation, long-term disability, bodily injury liability, and automobile no-fault claims, many insurance companies have created in-house rehabilitation programs to monitor and/or coordinate rehabilitation services or, in some cases, act as direct service providers to injured individuals. The employment opportunities for rehabilitation counselors are expected to continue in both private rehabilitation companies and insurance companies.

Outplacement Counseling Services

The experience of losing a job is increasingly common. In 1979 an estimated 15,000 to 20,000 executives earning salaries in the $40,000 to $100,000 range were terminated for their jobs (Finley & Lee, 1981). Economic pressures, technological displacements, corporate reorganizations, and mergers combine to create a fluid and unpredictable employment situation (Fasel, 1983). As pointed out by Drucker (1980), when early retirement, retraining, or transfer are not feasible, termination has been the result. As terminations at the executive level increase, the number of providers of outplacement services also increase. Typically, outplacement services include identification of transferable skills, job search techniques, interview preparation, clerical assistance, and emotional support to recently terminated workers (Harrick, Hansel, & Schutzius, 1982). Such services may also involve consultation and training of the manager who will do the firing, assistance to the terminated individual in informing the spouse, and psychological evaluation and personal counseling (Meyer, 1977). Employers have found that outplacement assistance reduces organization costs (e.g., severance pay, unemployment benefits); reduces fear, resentment, and loss of productivity by fellow workers; enhances the organization's public image, and decreases the risk of litigation by the terminated employee (Davenport, 1984; Driessenack, 1978; Henriksen, 1982; Papalia & Kaminski, 1981). It is estimated that 75% of the 1,500 largest corporations provide outplacement services to executives, the bulk of which is provided by external sources (Silverman & Sass, 1982). Additionally, the use of outplacement services is expected to increase during the next decade (Henriksen, 1982;

Morin & Yorks, 1982). Outplacement counseling provides a fertile area for employment opportunities among rehabilitation counselors.

Employee Assistance Programs

Pelletier (1983) contends that on any given day, there are over 1 million workers who call in sick. Accordingly, 80% of such absences are stress-related. Within the executive level, the cost of stress during 1980 has been estimated at $10–20 billion. That figure represents only clearly measurable items, such as workdays lost, hospitalization, out-patient care, and deaths. In an effort to control such costs, Employee Assistance Programs (EAPs) assist employees with stress and other personal problems in order to enhance personal health and, at the same time, improve job performance. In this manner, rather than replacing troubled employees, by providing rehabilitation services, business and industry can realize substantial economic savings (Busch, 1981). While the early focus of EAPs was closely aligned to alcohol treatment, current programs provide assistance in many other areas related to job performance (Toomer, 1982). EAP consultants may train company supervisors to note decreased job performance (possibly indicative of psychological and/or physical problems), perform initial assessments, provide therapeutic counseling, or facilitate referral to an appropriate provider. Such services have been shown to have a beneficial effect upon absenteeism, workmanship, attitude, supervisory time, medical costs, safety, and job performance (Roman, 1981; Roth, 1981). Recent studies have indicated that 57% of "Fortune 500" companies have implemented EAPs and that there are 5,500 programs operating throughout the country (Tuthill, 1982). The bulk of such services is provided by independent consulting firms, in addition to private hospitals, community mental health centers, or family service agencies. Employment possibilities for rehabilitation counselors in the area of employee assistance programs is very encouraging.

SUMMARY AND CONCLUSION

The nontraditional employment settings identified in this chapter represent career alternatives but serve only as a guide. Perhaps it may be overly simplistic to suggest that the employment potential of rehabilitation counselors is limited by the person's willingness to examine new career choices. Obviously, the potential job seeker must have sufficient skills to support work competence and, where deficiencies exist, subsequent training may be required. However, complete retraining to meet new employment challenges is not required. Nevertheless, in terms of educational preparation, the potential rehabilitation counselor may need to supplement coursework from a variety of disciplines such as business, industrial/organizational psychology, law, medicine, pharmacology, or personnel administration. Practica and internships to develop applied skill proficiency also represent key elements to professional practice. Again, the degree and nature of coursework and field experience will depend upon the desired job/career goal. Proposed curricula and training models to meet specific employment opportunities that have been proposed (e.g., Lynch & Martin, 1982; Matkin, 1980, 1983; McMahon, 1979a) certainly merit careful consideration.

It is also important to recognize that skill proficiency as a result of rehabilitation counselor education and supplemental coursework represents only the first hurdle in securing employment in emerging new areas. Counselors should also be prepared to deal with the potential biases and skepticism of persons who have the responsibility in the hiring decision. In essence, why should a rehabilitation counselor be hired to work in any employment setting other than traditional vocational rehabilitation? Counselors desiring to enter new employment fields must have the marketing strategies to address employer concerns. This task should not be something new since a critical function in rehabilitation counselor performance requires assisting others in addressing hiring concerns of employers. In any event, career opportunities for rehabilitation counselors are dramatically expanding into many diverse and nontraditional settings. Such expansion requires that professional preparation keep pace with changing labor markets. In this manner, rehabilitation counselors will have the knowledge and skills necessary to successfully compete in nontraditional settings and, through successful performance, will lay the groundwork for future generations.

II

Various Orientations to Rehabilitation Counseling

The goal of rehabilitation counseling is to assist persons with disabilities to achieve functional independence and effective adjustment. The orientation to practice held by rehabilitation counselors is premised on beliefs regarding the nature of persons, the impact of disability, and those strategies which most effectively achieve our goals. Such orientations are the result of experience and training. Each approach offers different perspectives for defining client issues and effective methods of intervention. To date, research has not demonstrated the viability or efficacy of one orientation over another. However, it is unlikely that rehabilitation counselors can effectively or confidently participate in the counseling process without an orientation with which they feel comfortable. That is, the approach selected must be compatible with their personal philosophy and be operational within the constraints of their setting. It is, therefore, essential that rehabilitation counselors conscientiously understand their orientation to practice and its impact on their role and function.

The purpose of this section is to provide information describing the perspectives exposed by some of the major counseling orientations. Specifically, we have asked persons with known experience and expertise to discuss various theories of counseling as they apply to working with persons with disabilities. That is not to say that counseling with these clients is different than counseling with able-bodied persons. However, the applications of these approaches to the unique needs of our clientele is the focus of this section. It should also be noted that the focus here is on individual and not group counseling.

The authors were given the following outline for consideration in articulating their perspective. The outline was intended to promote a degree of uniformity across the various orientations to practice. We encourage you to consider it as you read the articles and articulate your personal orientation.

1. *Introduction*
   A. Define the perspective, its key terms and basic concepts.
   B. Enumerate how the perspective is similar to or different from other perspectives.
   C. Discuss the impact of disability and the concept of rehabilitation counseling from the perspective.
2. *Evolution*
   A. Describe the historical evolution of the perspective. Briefly outline the origin and development of this approach, identifying key personnel and factors influencing its growth and current status.
   B. In a parallel way trace the historical evolution of the perspective in rehabilitation counseling.
3. *Assumptions*
   A. Describe the basic assumptions and core constructs underlying this perspective considering a person with disability.
   B. Discuss the role of development over the life span as it relates to the age of disablement and subsequent adjustment.
   C. In terms of the perspective, how would a psychologically healthy person with disability be defined? In a similar sense, how would the person who is not psychologically healthy be described?
   D. Cite the necessary conditions for client change.
4. *Applications*
   A. Identify those clients, disabling conditions, and/or concerns for which this approach is appropriate. Likewise, state when it is counterindicated.
   B. In what terms are the goals and objectives for counseling a person with disability defined? Examples may be helpful.
   C. Describe the relationship between the rehabilitation counselor and the client from this perspective. Highlight the role and responsibilities of each.
   D. If there is a prescribed sequence of activities which the counselor follows/enacts in working with a client, please describe it.

E. List and briefly describe the approach's major therapeutic techniques or strategies. Examples of their applications to counseling persons with disability would be helpful.

F. Describe how progress toward the client's goals is determined. How do the counselor and client know when termination is appropriate?

5. *Research*
   A. Briefly overview the extent and type of available research concerning the process and outcome of this approach.
   B. What are the research needs of this approach?
6. *Resources*
   A. List major references and resources for the reader interested in further information.

With this perspective in mind, we hope you find the information within this section helpful in more clearly understanding the various orientations available to the rehabilitation counselor. We also hope to provoke you to more clearly and conscientiously understand your personal orientation to your work.

11 A Psychodynamic Perspective

Shari Thurer

The psychodynamic perspective would seem to be out of favor in rehabilitation counseling circles these days. An informal review of recent rehabilitation literature reveals views of psychodynamic therapy* ranging from ambivalence to outright antipathy.

> With the exception of Bordin (1955) psychoanalytic theorists offer little to the counselor who is primarily involved in the resolution of vocational or educational problems. (Thomas & Butler, 1981, p. 236)

> For many years, rehabilitation relied mainly on professionals' clinical observations for understanding what was going on and what to do with respect to the psychosocial adjustment of people with disabilities. We followed Freud's model of *subjectively* analyzing . . . of interpreting it from a mental set of pathology, too. People with disabilities were sometimes reduced to stereotypes. . . . In the 1950's some began to question the correctness and usefulness of the 'clinical folklore' which had developed this way. (Hahn, 1984, p. 1)

> The use of psychoanalytic theory in rehabilitation efforts becomes possible only with the translation of the previous motivational problems into mental health problems. . . . Problem patients become sick patients, that is, people with sick minds . . . any type of denial is viewed as a maladaptive defense mechanism. (Duval, 1982, p. 179)

> According to some psychoanalytically inspired views . . . loss is intrapsychic; it is caused by events occurring within the mental life of the patient. . . . However, intrapsychic theory [of pain and suffering] must be evaluated in light of the fact that it rests primarily on clinical observations rather than experimental evidence and contains considerable speculation. Indeed, many psychoanalytic theorists do not regard controlled experimentation as a valid source of data about human suffering. . . . Another difficulty with

* Psychodynamic psychotherapy refers to the expanding array of approaches to psychotherapy derived from psychoanalysis. It, therefore, is usually synonymous with psychoanalytic psychotherapy, but psychodynamic therapy may also include forms of treatment less rigidly tied to classical psychoanalytic principles and techniques.

> such theories is that they offer little immediate assistance to members of most professions. (Shontz, 1975, p. 92)

These comments are just a few in the growing litany of criticisms of psychodynamic therapy—that it is oblivious to humanistic concerns in its focus on illness; that it minimizes the present in its absorption with the past; that it minimizes self-responsibility in its search for unconscious motives and determinants; and that it is authoritarian and judgmental (Appelbaum, 1982). Psychodynamic therapy has been accused of being overly deterministic (and therefore pessimistic), antiwoman, wildly impractical, elitist, too concerned with sex, and irrevocably tied to the medical model and diagnosis, of perpetuating the status quo, of encouraging individuals to conform to a "sick" society, and of being oblivious to consciousness in its focus on the unconscious. Also, there seems to be a prevailing notion that psychodynamic therapy does not work.

Despite their current popularity, these criticisms are based largely on half-truths or misunderstandings of psychodynamic thinking and practice. Rehabilitation counselors seem to have only the haziest and most simplistic ideas about psychodynamic theory. This is not surprising when one peruses rehabilitation or counseling theories texts (e.g., Bitter, 1979; Carkhuff & Berenson, 1967; Thomas & Butler, 1981; Wright, 1980). These books typically present psychodynamic theory in a highly schematized, superficial manner, heavily weighted toward pre-1920 thinking (i.e., metapsychology). Moreover, every counseling theory in vogue, no matter how dubious, is accorded equal space, as if they are somehow of equivalent importance, homogeneous. This blurs the historical fact that many recent formulations and techniques are derivatives of psychodynamic therapy, mere reworkings of old ideas, and that the theory pervades contemporary thought. Psychodynamic concepts address themselves to the very nature of humanity and basic motivation. These concerns are central to writers, artists, anthropologists, historians, teachers, investigative reporters, and parents—indeed, to 20th century man and woman (Orne, 1975). Despite this, one recent text (Baruth & Huber, 1985) does not discuss the psychodynamic perspective at all!

In addition to misapprehending the theory, many rehabilitation counselors have distorted ideas about what actually goes on in a psychodynamic therapist's office. Counselors sometimes conjure up cartoon-like images of bearded male "shrinks" smoking cigars, spouting irrelevances about one's id, as a patient lies nearby, unhelped. Rehabilitation counselors fail to understand that psychodynamic therapy is not tied to a Procrustean bed of fixed technique that is incapable of being adapted to a patient's specific needs. There is not *one* psychodynamic technique. Janet Malcolm's acclaimed book (1981) documents some of the highly charged controversies within the psychoanalytic community and should destroy any notions of conformity in theory and practice.

Contrary to the popular wisdom, rehabilitation counseling, as currently practiced, *embodies* a psychodynamic perspective. Moreover, the specific ways rehabilitation counselors' techniques differ from those of psychodynamic therapists are far from clear. This chapter attempts to comprehend the therapeutic influence of the psychodynamic perspective on both rehabilitation theory and practice.

OVERVIEW OF PSYCHODYNAMIC THEORY AND THERAPY

The psychodynamic (or psychoanalytic, or insight-oriented, or in-depth) forms of therapy have evolved in a more or less direct line from classical analysis, the procedures of which were described by Sigmund Freud in his publications on technique between 1911 and 1915. Classical analysis in the pure form is rarely practiced today, and is becoming rarer. Only 10% of the nation's psychiatrists are psychoanalysts, and in 1976 they averaged only 2.7 patients under treatment, down from 6.2 a decade earlier (*Time*, 1979). Relatively few of these psychoanalysts would describe themselves as being of the unswervingly classical, Freudian sort. On the other hand, psychoanalysis' derivative—psychodynamic therapy—is still flourishing, though this orientation is growing at a declining rate.

Psychodynamic therapy, as originally conceived, assumes that people have innate drives (sex and aggression) that conflict with both the external requirements of society and the internal needs and internalized standards of the individual. Conflict is part of our psychic structure (id vs. ego vs. superego), part of the human condition. People's unacceptable drives are forced out of conscious awareness (i.e., repressed) by defense mechanisms, but they continue, unconsciously, to press for expression. Defense mechanisms are imperfect. Psychopathology is partially conceptualized in terms of the efficiency and adaptive value of these defense mechanisms. When they are inadequate, symptoms result. Symptoms, then, are not random events but are meaningful expressions of underlying conflicts over needs and drives.

From a psychodynamic perspective, an infant matures into an adult according to a predictable pattern, passing through a succession of relatively consistent phases with specific tasks and characteristic maneuvers for solving these tasks (Baker, 1985). Freud wrote about psychosexual stages, but later theorists added interpersonal (object relations), cognitive, psychosocial, and moral development states. A person's normal development may be interrupted by early life experiences that either intolerably deprive or, in contrast, overgratify the child's innate drives. In these instances, a child may become fixated in a particular phase, or may regress to patterns of behavior characteristic of an earlier stage. In either event, the child's development may be blocked. These blockages are another way psychodynamic therapists conceptualize psychopathology.

Traditionally psychodynamic treatment involves making the unconscious conscious. During this process, people are helped to understand the meaning of their symptoms and hence of their underlying conflicts and their destructive developmental experiences. This growing awareness leads to psychological growth and elimination of specific symptoms.

In classical psychoanalysis, the two basic strategical operations employed to achieve this goal of insight are the analyses of resistances and of transference (Nemiah, 1975). The former refers to examining the gamut of feelings and behaviors used (ironically) by the patient to avoid facing unpleasant unconscious material. The latter refers to the examination of the relationship the patient attemps to establish with the therapist. It is assumed that the patient "invents" the therapist according to the early blueprints, i.e., that the relationship mirrors the patient's conflicted childhood relationships. Among the various techniques used to facilitate the therapeutic process are free association, a neutral therapeutic stance, the interpretation of dreams, appropriate inquiry into feelings and thoughts associated with various experiences, and the analysis of the discrepancies between what individuals do and the reasons they provide for their behavior (Orne, 1975).

Although classical psychoanalysis continues to be employed in clinical practice, a number of theoretical modifications have occurred since the days of Freud's dominance in the field. Baker (1985) has summarized these recent alterations in theory nicely. First, there has been a shift to an emphasis on the ego as the psychological arena in which many significant psychological activities occur, including memory, perception, impulse control, interpersonal relationships, and identity formation. Consequently, "ego analysis" now takes precedence over "id analysis." A second major trend has been to emphasize the role of very early developmental experiences. Freud had focused on the Oedipal conflict and resulting neurotic disorders. But more modern theorists such as Mahler (1968), Kernberg (1975), and Kohut (1971) are paying close attention to developmental factors influential in the earliest years of life and the resulting character pathology. A third trend (closely related to the second) has been the growth of attempts to apply psychodynamic technique to clinical populations not directly considered by Freud, for example children, psychotics, individuals with various forms of character disorders (e.g., borderline and narcissistic personalities), and medical populations. A fourth trend has been an emphasis on interpersonal factors, termed "object relations." What was formerly understood in exclusively psychosexual terms is now additionally explained in a psychosocial context. Hence, classical issues of orality are currently being discussed in terms of attachment, dependency, and the development of trust. An additional trend has emphasized the nature of personality organization rather than the specific dynamic conflicts underlying a neurosis.

These conceptual alterations have resulted in a considerable modification of technique. It should be noted that even contemporaries of Freud [e.g., Otto Rank and Sandor Ferenczi (Marmor, 1979)] advocated variations in technique, but such modifications did not seem to permeate the rank-and-file until recent times. Today, most psychodynamic psychotherapists practice an eclectic form of treatment, tailoring technique to patient.[1] In particular, modern psychodynamic therapy is characterized by increased activity and directiveness of the therapist, who frequently is more gratifying to his or her patient than could be expected within the context of classical psychoanalysis. Therapists will give advice, exhort, and provide structure and support. There is a decreased emphasis on uncovering and genetic interpretations, with a greater focus on contemporary events and the resolution of specific problems. Interpretations are more often framed in a psychosocial (ego) rather than psychosexual (id) vocabulary. There is considerable emphasis on pre-Oedipal experiences; patients' difficulties are often described in terms of basic problems with separation, attachment, and individuation. These approaches tend to place greater technical focus on the utilization of the real and non-transferential aspects of the therapy relationship. A full-fledged regression within the transference is not encouraged. (Hence, the patient sits face-to-face with the therapist.) There is a focus on the support of useful defenses, enhanced adaptation, and adjustment.

[1] Let me emphasize that a number of psychoanalysts perform classical psychoanalysis exclusively, but many, if not most, perform psychodynamic psychotherapy as well. The bulk of psychodynamic therapy, however, is practiced by non-analysts who comprise the overwhelming majority of psychotherapists. This latter group presumably never practices classical psychoanalysis as they have not been trained or certified to do so.

Therapeutic goals for therapy have become more modest. Psychodynamic therapists may now focus on limited and delineated aspects of character structure and development as they relate to the presenting problem, instead of attempting to reconstruct personality. There may be a significant decrease in the frequency of therapy sessions to once or twice a week, and a briefer course of treatment. Treatment has become applicable to a broad range of individuals with a variety of complaints.

Note that current-day psychodynamic practice, with its expanded repertoire of techniques, belies many of the criticisms leveled at psychoanalysis. As psychodynamic psychotherapists have begun taking into account the social and cultural context in which the patient lives, have shortened the course of treatment, and have become more active and flexible, they hardly may be accused of being impractical, authoritarian, or elitist. Psychodynamic therapy is not insufficiently humanistic. After all, it advocates self-understanding; its data are introspections! (Appelbaum, 1982). Psychodynamic therapy is not overly deterministic. As men or women gain insight, they may change (sublimate). Modern psychoanalysts do not limit themselves to facile explanations such as penis envy and female masochism. At a 1983 Boston conference, Karl Menninger, a patriarch in the field of psychoanalysis, argued against nuclear weapons—hardly the stance of one who wished to perpetuate the norm. Moreover, data from research (e.g., Frank, 1979; Horowitz, 1976; Luborsky, Singer, & Luborsky, 1975) tend to support the conclusion that psychodynamic psychotherapy is a valuable form of treatment that has proven to be successful and effective in the therapy of many different types of patients.

PSYCHODYNAMIC THEORY AND REHABILITATION COUNSELING

Perhaps unbeknownst to themselves, many rehabilitation counselors actually view their clients from a psychodynamic perspective. Psychodynamic ideology has become a part of their contemporary web of beliefs. It provides an unacknowledged but very real framework for understanding clients. For instance, rehabilitation counselors may readily point out that some clients tend to somatize, that is, they respond to stress by becoming physically ill. Other clients may fail to become rehabilitated because of secondary gain. Such notions are essentially psychodynamic; they assume that dynamic forces outside their clients' awareness underlie their clients' behaviors.

Psychodynamic theory has contributed to the elucidation of the dynamics of the counselor-client relationship and the processes of communication between counselor and client. While rehabilitation counselors rarely speak of this relationship in terms of transference/counter-transference, nevertheless they usually take it seriously, as something that affects outcome. Consider how ineffective counselors would be in the treatment of their clients if they were unable to recognize and respond appropriately to the hidden messages and double messages ever present in human communication. From psychodynamic theory we have learned the meaning of mannerism of speech, slips of the tongue, errors, omissions, distortions, out-of-context associations, asides, metaphors, dreams, fantasies, jokes, parables and anecdotes, gestures, postures, facial expressions, and symptomatic acts (Engel, 1975).

Psychodynamic theory enables counselors to understand the unique, subjective meaning of a disability to an individual. Is a cancer patient's attention-seeking behavior a desperate cry for help or simply testing? If it is testing, what does it mean? Psychodynamic theory provides a starting point for speculations that may lead to an explanation. Is the patient manipulative because of a deep-seated fear of loss of control, perhaps because he has to defeat the counselor, even if it means defeating himself in the long run? Without theory, these behaviors are merely chaotic. With a psychodynamic theoretical framework, the counselor may get closer to the patient's actual experience. Psychodynamic theory enhances empathy. It enables the counselor to understand why an obsessive-compulsive patient who loses sphincter control becomes depressed, while another patient with strong dependence needs thrives.

Additionally, psychodynamic theory provides a developmental perspective. With it, counselors have a context for explaining why an adolescent female burn patient may engage in promiscuous acting out, while a burned middle-aged woman may withdraw, or a latency-age girl will be compliant.

Psychodynamic theorists have microscopically analyzed the processes of mourning and bereavement. Though Freud (1949) and Lindemann (1945) are rarely cited in rehabilitation texts, they were among the first writers to examine loss and grief, which may be understood in terms of object relations theory. Kubler-Ross (1969) and others have made a valuable contribution to the understanding of grieving patients, but their writings are essentially descriptive. Psychodynamic theories, on the other hand, have attempted to explain why patients respond the way they do. Certainly these concepts are important for rehabilitation counselors, who must help clients adjust to losses of physical functioning and to associated symbolic losses.

The failure to credit sources for many ideas in rehabilitation betrays a sloppiness in scholarship. A thorough and systematic teaching of psychodynamic principles, properly labeled as such, would not only rectify a lack of academic integrity, but would enhance counselors' effectiveness in working with clients.

PSYCHODYNAMIC TECHNIQUE AND REHABILITATION COUNSELING

Certainly classical psychoanalysis differs widely from rehabilitation counseling as practiced in a public vocational rehabilitation agency. The former is highly reflective and verbal, and seeks personality reconstruction or at least the remediation of symptoms via insight. The latter, of course, is active, skill-oriented, primarily educational, and seeks adjustment rather than cure. But classical psychoanalysis has evolved, in part, into psychodynamic psychotherapy, and psychodynamic psychotherapy has broadened its scope. Psychodynamic psychotherapy is continually modifying its techniques and goals and expanding its population to include, for example, medical patients, so that at present it is becoming more congruent with rehabilitation counseling.

We can note this congruence by reviewing Marmor's (1979) synthesis of common denominators in all psychodynamic psychotherapies. These common denominators include (a) a release of tension (catharsis) in a setting of hope and expectation of help; (b) a constructive patient-therapist relationship (therapeutic alliance) based on both unconscious factors (transference factors) as well as the real qualities that both patient and therapist bring to their transactions; (c) cognitive learning based on interpretations (insight); (d) operant conditioning based on overt and/or covert indications of approval or disapproval from the therapist that move the patient in the direction of mental health (an additional facet of this operant conditioning is the existence of corrective emotional experiences in which the therapist reacts differently and more constructively to the patient than did significant authority figures in the patient's past); (e) identification with the therapist in which the patient, usually unconsciously, models himself/herself after the therapist, incorporating some of the latter's value systems and/or behavioral patterns; (f) elements of suggestion and persuasion, either covert or overt, which are present in all psychotherapies; and (g) some aspects of practice and rehearsal of new adaptive techniques and their generalization, sometimes called "working through" or "reality testing," all in a setting of consistent emotional support from the empathic therapist.

When we consider these seven denominators in light of rehabilitation counseling, we see that they, along with vocational counseling and placement, are the techniques of rehabilitation counseling. Rehabilitation counselors provide settings of hope, establish rapport with clients, plan and teach skills, use behavioral techniques, provide support, act as role models, make suggestions, rehearse new behaviors with clients, all in an empathic environment. To be sure, some of Marmor's vocabulary may seem odd in rehabilitation circles, but the strategies and concepts are familiar. Although the terminology may differ, there is significant overlap of the techniques of psychodynamic psychotherapy and rehabilitation counseling.

This overlap, however, does not imply an identical approach. Psychodynamic psychotherapists would seem to employ the techniques of rehabilitation counselors with appropriate clients (namely, those clients who seek adjustment, or who are unwilling or unable to undergo a more introspective kind of therapy), yet they do so from a different vantage point than rehabilitation counselors. Presumably, they choose these techniques from among a whole array of more classical interventions. Their choice is based on a specific set of reasons, matching patient to treatment strategy (based on psychodynamic theory); and they formulate explanations as to why various techniques work (also based on psychodynamic theory).

Rehabilitation counselors, in contrast, employ these techniques more naively, more as a matter of course. Their perspective is somewhat limited. They may do what they do well—improve clients' psychosocial functioning—but they may fail to know why. They are like motorists who do not understand the mechanics of an automobile engine, but who are skilled drivers nevertheless. Perhaps this lack of deeper understanding is not a serious deficit, but it limits creativity and innovation, and would tend to promote rigid, stereotypic thinking and behavior. A thorough, systematic familiarity with the principles of psychodynamic psychotherapy would help rehabilitation counselors not only more fully understand their clients, but would help them understand the dynamics of their interventions. This does not imply that rehabilitation counselors should be doing classical psychoanalysis with their rehabilitation clients.[2] Indeed, clients do not come to rehabilitation counselors for that purpose (Diller, 1959). But a psychodynamic perspective would provide counselors with an in-depth, multidimensional view of both their clients and their own counseling

[2] Disabled individuals, however, should not be automatically excluded from undergoing psychoanalysis, merely because they are disabled. Some make excellent candidates for psychoanalysis (Castelnuovo-Tedesco, 1981).

techniques. It would enhance their understanding, and perhaps even provide a tool for inventing new interventions.

In short, the psychodynamic perspective pervades rehabilitation theory and practice. Psychodynamic theory provides a framework for understanding the response to disability. Psychodynamic techniques have become so modified over time that many of them are identical to strategies used by rehabilitation counselors. To those rehabilitation counselors who are detractors of the psychodynamic perspective, I can only say, "We have met the enemy; and they are us!"

12 An Adlerian Perspective

Warren R. Rule

From a rehabilitation counseling perspective, perhaps the most useful Adlerian contribution is the potent concept of "life-style." This term, coined by Alfred Adler more than 50 years ago, meant something considerably different from the many contemporary connotations related to one's career, fun pursuits, appearance, or awareness of the vogue.

Adler's use of the term (and its use in this chapter) was considerably more oriented to the true uniqueness of the individual as a person. Briefly stated, he viewed this "life-style" as the overall mental pattern that influences feelings and behavior. From a rehabilitation perspective, an awareness of a client's life-style pattern can be very helpful to both the client and the counselor. This is particularly helpful if they are attempting to understand the implications of a congenital or acquired disability within the context of the client's unique expectations of self, others, and life.

EVOLUTION

Alfred Adler was born in Vienna in 1870. After practicing medicine for several years, he became associated with Sigmund Freud and his explorations. However, Adler's developing ideas were becoming increasingly dissimilar to Freud's (especially regarding Freud's conviction that the sexual instinct was omnipotent), and they parted ways. He continued to develop his own approach and was influenced by other perspectives (e.g., Vaihinger's philosophy of "As If," Smut's approach to holism and evolution) and by his experiences as a physician in the Austrian army during World War I. Prior to coming to the United States, he was a pioneer in establishing a network of family guidance clinics. In this country, he continued to have an impact through his teaching, writing, and lecturing until his death in 1937. Some of his students have established institutes and professional journals for the purpose of continuing the application and investigation of Adler's ideas (see Resources section at end of chapter). For a number of years, Adler's ideas were sometimes overshadowed by those of Freud. Even today, some individuals in the helping professions naively regard the two as similar. However, as Ford and Urban (1963) observed in their comparative review of systems of psychotherapy:

> In contrast to Sigmund Freud, Adler developed a point of view that sought to study behavior from the vantage point of the subjective rather than objective observer; emphasized the goal-directed rather than the drive-impelled causation of behavior; stressed the unity and integration of behavior rather than the conflict of disparate elements; proposed the use of molar and holistic concepts rather than restricted units of analysis; held an ideographic rather than a nomothetic purpose in studying behavior; and, in short, differed from Freud in the most fundamental and basic fashions possible. (p. 303)

Adler's approach, which he termed "Individual Psychology" to emphasize the indivisible nature of the individual, would primarily be aligned with the humanistic psychology movement (Ansbacher & Ansbacher, 1956). In addition, Adler has been described as being "the psychological theorist who most closely approximated an application of systems concepts to the individual level" (Amerikaner, 1981, p. 33).

The ideas of Adler are receiving considerable attention, as evidenced by increasing numbers of Adlerian-oriented practitioners, writings, research, training opportunities, and societies. In addition, many eminent pioneers in the counseling and helping professions have studied under Adler or have been strongly influenced by his thinking (e.g., Rollo May, Victor Frankl, Eric Berne, Albert Ellis). So Adler's influence has been receiving justified recognition; however, misunderstanding of some of Adler's concepts—even in the field of rehabilitation counseling—continue to persist.

The most frequent misunderstandings in rehabilitation appear to be the result of either an oversimplification or a misrepresentation of some of Adler's ideas. Much of this probably stems from an overemphasis of his earlier writings. Adler developed, early in his career, a theory of behavior based upon organ inferiority, which preceded the crystalization of his life-style concept. This theory, as well as related ones (e.g., compensation, inferiority), have attracted particular attention in the field of rehabilitation and, indeed, are helpful concepts for the rehabilitation practitioner. However, often overlooked is the fact that in the subsequent quarter century, Adler continued to develop, change, and refine his approach. A number of individuals attempting to apply Adler's ideas to the field of rehabilitation have focused on the original, less-developed concepts, which appear, because of their labels at the time, to be the most related to rehabilitation. Unfortunately, then, generalizations were made from the outdated, limited perspective to the overall current worth of the Adlerian life-style approach to rehabilitation.

Adler's later-refined concept of the life-style, to be discussed further in the next section, is a more well-rounded approach to understanding human nature. His subsequent thinking reflects a shift from an organic to a sociopsychological explanation of behavior, a refinement of inferiority and compensation, a heightened emphasis on the creativity of the individual, and an even sharper focus on the personal attitude toward disability and the goals to which a disability can be directed.

ASSUMPTIONS AND CHARACTERISTICS

The term *life-style,* originated by Adler, was regarded as essentially an individual's holistic pattern of beliefs and goals that the person uses for interacting with others and for measuring self-worth. A broad definition is "that unity in each individual, in his thinking, feeling, acting, in his so-called conscious and unconscious, in every expression of his personality" (Ansbacher & Ansbacher, 1956, p. 175). Adler liked the analogy that music cannot be fully appreciated by studying each note itself—one needs to have the context of the other notes in order to express the melody.

The life-style is pervasively at work in everyone's daily life. The life-style expresses itself (often at a vaguely conscious level of awareness) in our jobs, in our selection of and interaction with our friends, in our love relationships, in the purchases we make, in what we regard as our successes and failures, and in the perspective we hold on the implications of a disability.

This mental pattern is useful to the individual because it *works* according to the subjective perspective of the person. Just as blinders on horses serve the purpose of focusing—and limiting—their perspective and of getting them through confusing and potentially harmful traffic, so do our selective perceptions and goals serve the purpose of getting us through and reacting to the psychologically threatening hazards of life.

Due to the consistency of the cognitive nature of the life-style, it can be very helpful to the individual to have an awareness of one's unique life-style pattern when facing decisions or facing problems.

This is significant because this unique pattern of thinking, the life-style, with its built-in blinders and tunnel vision, leads us both to our successes and our failures. Thus, the life-style, the time-tested pattern of basic attitudes and expectations, becomes most obvious when the individual is experiencing stress—the pattern that has worked before is suddenly no longer effective. Awareness of this phenomenon has helpful implications for rehabilitation counselors; first, however, more discussion needs to be given to specific characteristics of the life-style.

Significant Characteristics

Adler concluded that the interpretation of early childhood events has a large bearing on how each person develops in later life. These early years certainly do not totally determine a person's life-style. Instead, he asserted that each individual creatively uses heredity and environment to mold a unique life-style.

The focus in Adler's approach is on social living. In each of us there exists the desire to belong and to have a place of significance in the eyes of others. Each person strives for a place of "somebodyness" differently. This "somebodyness" is largely, although not totally, related to the conclusions drawn in early childhood about self, others, and life. He believed that an individual's personal difficulties occur in an interpersonal context, that personal problems are basically social problems.

Adler was convinced that everything we do is goal-oriented. Expressed another way, all behavior, including our emotions, is a function of our ideas, both conscious and dimly conscious, about consequences to be obtained in the future. Behaviors that apparently cannot be explained become more understood as the goal or purpose comes to light. Much of the time we are not aware of our unique self-concerned goals that are related to our (previously discussed) innate desire to enhance ourselves within a social context. "How is this person striving to be known by others?" is a handy question for the rehabilitation practitioner to keep in mind. The counseling focus, then, should be on the subjective or internal frame of reference which influences one's behavior more than "reality" does, i.e., the interpretation of "reality" is the key focus.

The creativity of the individual is continually present as the person moves through life. Usually, a range of behavioral patterns is available to the individual for any given life-style conclusion. The Adlerian life-style approach asserts that people can indeed change in major ways, in both fundamental thinking as well as behaving, although changing the basic life-style itself is quite difficult. However, sometimes these changes, even seemingly major ones, may really be variations on the same life-style theme. Expressed another way, sometimes the individual's characteristic *sensitive position*, or cognitive reactivity, on a life-style conclusion, attitude, or notion may actually be the common thread that continues to run through the "changes," usually behavioral, that a person seems to have made.

Such creative behavioral implementations may exist over the life span, in response to changing circumstances in the social environment. For example, Mosak (1958) discussed a variety of behavioral implementations a person may choose (depending on a host of related life's circumstances) who has taken a sensitive position on the life-style conclusion that "life is dangerous":

> Such a person, behaviorally, may see danger where none exists. He may exaggerate the dangers of life. He may retreat from these perceived dangers with anxious or phobic behavior. Or he may call upon certain defense mechanisms to cope with the omnipotent threat. In the compulsive individual, for example, one observes reliance upon ritual and feelings of omnipotence and the necessity to control as response to danger. Many compulsives are preoccupied with death because this is the greatest threat—the one force which cannot be controlled. Hypochondriacs may develop into towers of strength or become dependent upon or identify with "strong" people or groups in order to minimize the dangers of life. Still others may actually court or provoke personal disaster in order to confirm their basic attitude. Some flirt with danger in order to prove that they possess a charmed life. While these reactions do not exhaust the repertoire available to people who feel that life is dangerous, they do serve to exemplify the variety of reactions which are possible within a single dimension of an individual's perceptual frame of reference. (p. 306)

Regarding individual creativity, Adlerians hold that the person is the product of both individual "laws" and general "laws." Expressed another way, the person is the product of individual laws which the self created and of general laws that apply to all people or specified groups of individuals, e.g., birth order positions, certain physical characteristics, etc.

In terms of a person with a disability, Adler believed that the creativity of the individual is foremost and that conceptual frameworks and stereotypes which predict rigid, deterministic reactions to disability were useless. If disabled from childhood, the individual's disability was likely a factor in the formation of the life-style; if disabled later in life, the person's life-style will influence the individual's adjustment to disability and view of the situation.

Adler was particularly interested in what the individual contributed subjectively—through the life-style "filter"—to the situation, not in simplistic cause-and-effect relationships. Adler observed that quite a number of possible responses exist for the disabled individual: despair leading to retreat; courageous compensation; a protective, hesitating attitude, etc. Dreikurs (1967), one of Adler's students, stated that the despairing response may mean retreat into a disability, the courageous response converts the disability into a blessing, and the somewhat neurotic response may mean "How much better would I do if I had not had this disability!" (p. 174). Generally speaking, he further concluded that "inferiority" tends to be somewhat of an objective assessment or comparison; "inferiority feelings" have existed in everyone at various times and influence future and compensatory development; and "inferiority complex" seems to be a fatalistic reaction to a difficult situation without attempting to improve it.

Comparisons

The Adlerian life-style approach shares quite a number of main assumptions and characteristics with many of the other major counseling approaches. Like the Gestaltists, Adlerians believe that the life-style is holistic and cannot be dissected without sacrificing understanding. The Rational-Emotive approach and the Adlerian life-style perspective both focus on irrational or biased thought processes that undergird emotions and behavior. Like the Client- or Person-Centered Approach, Adlerians ultimately respect personal meaning and the internal frame of reference. Similar to the behavioral perspective, the life-style approach highlights the usefulness or consequences of behavior. Akin to the psychoanalytic perspective, Adlerians are concerned with the implications of one's early past, although considerably differently. From an existential vantage point, the life-style approach is concerned with the individual being and meaning. The Adlerian concept of social interest, or empathic awareness and action related to human innerconnectedness, relates to interpersonal and life-style dynamics, a focus of Transactional Analysis. Significantly, Adler regarded the helping process as essentially educational in nature, a mainstay of the Psychoeducational perspective. In view of the foregoing parallels, it is not surprising that the Adlerian life-style approach has been described by some professionals as a uniquely useful *eclectic* perspective.

APPLICATIONS

In considering the usefulness of the Adlerian life-style approach as a rehabilitation method, it is important to keep in mind that this perspective, particularly life-style self-awareness, is just as applicable to disabled groups as the able-bodied. Reviews (Dunham & Dunham, 1978; English, 1974) of relevant investigations related to personality and disability have concluded that very few, if any, personality differences exist between persons with disabilities and the normal population. Life-style analysis would appear to have as much merit for use in rehabilitation settings as in the other helping services. Once a measure of life-style understanding is achieved between the practitioner and the client, exploration can be given to the exceedingly important issue of the relationship between the client's life-style and disability. The emphasis would be on how the client's life-style notions and goals are contributing to—or undermining—the rehabilitation process. Generally, the Adlerian life-style counseling process can be viewed as having four phases: relationship, life-style investigation, life-style interpretation, and reorientation.

Relationship

Relationship conditions continue throughout the entire process; however, this initial phase emphasizes the relationship factors of respect, trust, and genuineness.

This phase also serves a number of other purposes: (a) the rehabilitation worker gains insight into the client's internal frame of reference; (b) the client can explore the implications of disability; (c) specific information can be exchanged, such as medical, procedural, work history, and so on; (d) the rehabilitation practitioner has the opportunity to gauge how appropriate the life-style approach is for the client (it may be counter-indicated for someone of quite low mental functioning if the expectation is for insight on the client's part to lead to change; yet increased counselor awareness of the client's life-style may be helpful in terms of selecting other counseling strategies or in considering changes in the client's environment).

Life-style Investigation

Before gathering information on the client's early childhood (to be discussed subsequently), the rehabilitation practitioner usually asks questions about how the client's life-style is functioning in the present, particularly in the three tasks of life. Adler believed that everyone takes a position, probably with varying degrees of success or failure, on each of three areas of social living: friendship, work (or school), and love. The assumption is that the individual life-style, including its unique strengths, weaknesses, blind spots, functions as a coping device in all areas of life. This information may provide a fuller picture of how the client's chosen life-style is contributing holistically to disability-related as well as other presenting problems.

Another technique used during this phase is "The Question." This simply involves asking the client what would be different if one were well (or able-bodied) or if the problem did not exist. The reply to this question can sometimes indicate for what purpose the client is experiencing unusual difficulties, against what threat or demand the person is defending oneself by having such difficulty accepting or adjusting to this disability, or against whom or what the symptoms are directed.

There are a number of ways by which the counselor can learn more about an individual's life-style. Some sources are broad; others are narrow. Some draw from readily available information; others require gathering additional information. Lombardi (1973) discusses eight different avenues that yield information about the consistent and patterned life-style:

1. Case history data—knowing about subject.
2. Psychological interviewing—talking to subject.
3. Expressive behavior—observing subject.
4. Psychological testing—measuring subject.
5. Family constellation—social influence on subject.
6. Early recollections—subject's meaning in life.
7. Grouping—interacting with subject.
8. Symptomatic behavior—subject's telltale signs. (p. 6)

Often the practitioner must settle for less than all of the above information. In fact, one of the most widely used procedures for learning about a person's life-style entails using a life-style assessment form. Several versions exist; one of the more popular is a form, or variations thereof, developed by Dreikurs (1967). These forms provide a structure for obtaining patterns from a client's remembered childhood. Specific areas of questioning include concept of self and family constellation, especially age differences, ordering of sexes, alliance groups, and siblings' development. Furthermore, questions are asked regarding parental influences and expectations, family atmosphere and values, peers, and—very importantly—specific early recollections. In sum, questions are mainly centered around the client's first social group, the family, that contributed to the biased slice of life that was the *only* slice of life that the child had available to draw conclusions from about self, others, and life.

Very significantly, the life-style approach asserts that memory, especially very early memory, is selective. Adlerians (e.g., Dreikurs, 1967) claim that people operate on an economy principle by selectively using their memories in accordance with their (often dimly conscious) goals. Thus, a person's memories of the early childhood years seem to serve as anchoring orientation points, reflecting the most useful conclusions, expectations, and goals that crystalized during the formative period. In a sense, the counselor is reconstructing significant aspects of the client's early environment. Once accomplished, the practitioner can look for themes or patterns in the remembered early environment which, due to the selectivity-of-memory phenomenon, reflects the dimly conscious expectations and goals that the person is *presently* using to move through life.

Emphasis is given in the life-style approach to family constellation from a sociopsychological perspective. Essentially, according to Shulman (1973), there are 5 basic positions: only, eldest, second, middle, and youngest child. Each one has several very modest probabilities of birth order characteristics attached to it. Other life-style information is used to round out these tentative hypotheses. For example, firstborns might strive to be high achievers, to be on top, or be very mindful of being "dethroned"; only-borns tend to view others as curiosities and can be very sensitive to what the authorities or "big" and accomplished people think; youngest-borns sometimes try to be charmers, be the lovable boss, or display incompetence or neediness in order to put others in their service.

Along with family constellation variables and related family information, a person's specific early recollections and dreams round out the structured life-style analysis. From the thousands upon thousands of experiences in which the individual has been involved as a child, only those specific recollections are remembered that coincide with one's present outlook (i.e., the selectivity-of-memory phenomenon is in operation). Generally, a person can remember at least six specific incidents, however *seemingly* insignificant, that occurred in early childhood. Each recollection reflects a current expectation and supplements or rounds out the outlook reflected by the other early memories. Significantly, the Adlerian approach focuses on the interpersonal movement in each early recollection, not on hidden, symbolic meanings.

Next, the counselor studies the client's responses to the interview. The practitioner is, in a sense, putting together a jigsaw puzzle or cognitive map that takes the form of lifestyle patterns. Basically, the practitioner's conceptual framework is as follows: if this person has drawn these conclusions about self, others, and life, then what kind of unique, overriding goals would the individual have chosen as a guide in striving to be a coping, significant person?

Mosak (1977) has provided examples of different life-style themes, although he emphasized that predictions cannot be made as to what behavior will coincide with a particular life-style. Moreover, he cautioned that any typology, which should be limited to didactic purposes, violates the uniqueness of the person. Examples of these patterns are getting, controlling, driving, being central or the best, always being right, pleasing, being against, being admired for moral superiority, being a martyr, being an excitement seeker, being victimized. Each of these terms, it may be noted, denotes the powerful determination to enhance the self. Understandably, each theme can work to one's advantage or disadvantage, depending especially on other factors, such as the behavior and the environmental context.

Life-style Interpretation

After the rehabilitation counselor has tentatively identified the person's life-style patterns, expectations, or goals, these are shared with the client in a spirit of respect and exploration (e.g., "Could it be that . . . "; "A guess I have is . . . "). Several frameworks exist for presenting life-style information (e.g., Mosak, 1954, 1972a; Rule, 1982).

The emphasis is on encouraging the client to take responsibility for identifying linkages between the life-style information and daily living, especially on implications for the client's disability, such as life-style blinders. In a sense the past is used to understand the present better; however, the client is not allowed the luxury of hiding behind the past—current responsibility for self, along with new awareness, is emphasized. Highlighting strengths of the life-style is important in fostering a positive attitude toward the life-style counseling process, particularly as the counselor and client move into the next and final phase.

Reorientation

This phase emphasizes change. Now that both counselor and client have achieved insight into the daily implementation of the client's life-style, a springboard for agreed-upon change has been created.

In addition to identifying the ultimately self-defeating features of the life-style and establishing goals and homework strategies for overcoming them, a broader educational perspective often can be utilized. This might include exploring the interrelatedness between thinking, feeling, and doing, especially how thoughts are usually at the root of emotions which energize behavior; encouraging the client to believe in a significance of self that is not a function of comparisons with others or self-ranking; fostering an increased other-directedness, i.e., empathy or social interest, toward other individuals.

Along a similar vein, the rehabilitation counselor would be well-served to remember the goal-directedness of behavior. "Causes" or "whys" imply past unchangeable reasons; "goals" indicate future-oriented, changeable targets. Perhaps the client may want to learn new behaviors (or emotions) to implement more effectively the long-standing life-style goals. Possibly the client may need assistance in modifying the frequency or felt intensity of a life-style goal. It may be that life-style awareness can provide insight into the client's unproductive use of mood-altering chemicals, i.e., the goals being met in a euphoric state of mind. Maybe life-style barriers to acceptance or adjustment to disability need to be worked on, such as comparison-related vulnerabilities stemming from inferiority feelings, "near-normalcy," dependency, social consequences of loss of liberty. Further readings on life-style and adjustment to a variety of major disabilities can be found in Rule (1984).

It is important for the practitioner to remember that the client is doing the best and most useful thing—within the blinders of his life-style—that the individual can do at the time. This realization results in a somewhat different meaning given to the term *resistance* as compared to other conceptual frameworks. Resistance is essentially, as Dreikurs (1967) contended, a discrepancy between the goals of the client and those of the practitioner. Then, accepting the client's goals "as they are" has special meaning.

Behind what may be labeled resistance by the counselor may be client goals that are essentially self-protective devices against perceived dangers. Shulman (1973) provides some examples of these perceived dangers: being ridiculed, submitting to order, not getting necessary help, incurring disapproval, having to face responsibility, being taken advantage of, having to face unpleasant consequences. Individual life-style information may shed light on the likelihood of whichever of these may be in operation. In addition, some considerations for dealing with what may be labeled client "negativism" can be found in Shulman (1972, 1977) and Rule (1977).

The creativity of the unique individual life-style is ever present, and a host of methods for struggling against symptoms in order to maintain face (Mosak, 1977a, b; Shulman, 1973) varies from life-style to life-style. Illustrating how symptoms can be safeguards for self-esteem, Shulman (1973) cites possible purposes (secondary gains) for suffering: as justification ("I have a right to my own way. Look how much I suffer when I don't get it"); as manipulation ("If you don't do what I want, I'll die and then you'll be sorry"); as self-glorification ("The amount of my suffering proves my nobility").

The facilitative use of humor in conveying life-style awareness and in reminding the individual of lifestyle goals cannot be underestimated. This may be accomplished by fables, parables, metaphors, cartoons, audio-recordings, photographs, and so on. Humor, like all Adlerian tactics and strategies, is handled in a spirit of true encouragement (not necessarily praise), which conveys worth, acceptance, and uniqueness of the client.

In summary, the application of the life-style counseling process involves the realms of feeling, thinking, and acting. A useful metaphor is that the interaction of relationship factors (feeling-oriented) is the key that opens the door to the dark room; the life-style self-understanding (thinking-oriented) creates light in the room; and the reorientation methods (action-oriented) rearrange the room and polish the furniture according to the wishes of the individual.

RESEARCH

The issue of research, including process, outcome, reliability, and validity studies on the life-style approach is not to be taken lightly. Discussion of these may be found in sources such as Allen (1971), Kern, Matheny, and Patterson (1978), and Mosak (1979). Approximately 1,000 studies have been done on variables related to birth order; many of the significant findings have been discussed by Forer (1979) and Sutton-Smith and Rosenberg (1970). Quite a number of studies from an Adlerian perspective have been completed on early recollections; the bulk of these are discussed by Mosak (1958, 1984), Olson (1979), and Taylor (1975). A comprehensive bibliography by Mosak and Mosak (1975) is a helpful reference for many life-style–related studies. Statistical research is capable of making a contribution in the study of nomothetic, or general, laws as related to the Adlerian life-style approach; however, the ideographic laws, or individual guidelines that the person created, often dimly consciously, for moving through life are considerably more difficult to study with statistical methods.

From a broader perspective, we as rehabilitation practitioners may be deluding ourselves if we believe that, in counseling, objective considerations can be the total masters of subjective ones. Accordingly, life-style self-awareness can be personally helpful to both the client *and* the counselor. A complete awareness on the counselor's part of all the research studies ever done in the entire field of counseling will not prevent the counselor's own subjective life-style from oozing through the mask of objectivity into the counseling process.

RESOURCES

Information on resources and ongoing training throughout the world can be obtained from North American Society of Adlerian Psychology, 159 North Dearborn Street, Chicago, IL 60601. Membership in this organization consists of individuals from a variety of backgrounds who are interested in the applications of Adlerian psychology. This society publishes the quarterly *Individual Psychology: The Journal of Adlerian Theory, Research, & Practice.* This journal, as well as the Alfred Adler Institute (159 North Dearborn Street, Chicago, IL 60601), can provide much information on Adlerian family counseling, a major contribution which is outside the scope of this article. Below is a list of suggested readings on the life-style perspective:

Ansbacher, H. L., & Ansbacher, R. R. (Eds.). (1956). *The individual psychology of Alfred Adler.* New York: Basic Books.

Dreikurs, R. (1967). *Psychodynamics, psychotherapy, and counseling.* Chicago: Alfred Adler Institute.

Mosak, H. H. (1977). *On purpose.* Chicago: Alfred Adler Institute.

Mosak, H. H. (1984). *Adlerian psychotherapy.* In R. J. Corsini (Ed.), *Current psychotherapies* (3rd ed.). Itasca, IL: Peacock.

Rule, W. R. (Ed.). (1984). *Lifestyle counseling for adjustment to disability.* Rockville, MD: Aspen Systems.

Shulman, B. H. (1973). *Contributions to individual psychology.* Chicago: Alfred Adler Institute.

Sweeney, T. J. (1981). *Adlerian concepts: Proven concepts and strategies* (2nd ed.). Muncie, IN: Accelerated Development Press.

13 An Existentialist Approach to Rehabilitation Counseling *

Susanne M. Bruyere

The role and function of the vocational rehabilitation counselor (VRC) has long been one of the issues which has turned up in endless debate among leaders in the field of rehabilitation counseling. Is the VRC a counselor/therapist or a manager/coordinator of services? Who determines the *goal* of the vocational rehabilitation (VR) process—the counselor, the agency, the client, or all three? And this debate often leads to discussion of the *purpose* of VR services. Should the services offered by VR agencies be exclusively focused on a return to remunerative employment (in the case of a traumatic injury) or should we be focusing more broadly on rehabilitation as the provision of services that enhance the total welfare of the individual, with equal emphasis on psychosocial and personal well-being and the long-range life satisfaction of the client?

In practice, the response of the field of VR counseling has been a range of roles and purposes which fall between the apparently polar positions presented above. But the debate has continued to go on, and the purpose of this chapter is to present the hypothesis that this may be due to the fact that we (in rehabilitation) have not clearly articulated the philosophical base from which we practice our profession. It is the proposition of this author that existentialism offers a philosophical stance that is consistent with the basic tenets of rehabilitation counseling and rehabilitation psychology. In the existentialist perspective, the counselor views the client as in control of and

*The author would like to thank the following individuals who generously contributed their time and energy in reviewing this manuscript: Steen Halling, Director, Program in Existential-Phenomenological Psychology, Seattle University; Thomas Longin, Provost, Ithaca College; and Dennis Maki, Associate Professor of Rehabilitation Counselor Education, University of Iowa. And a special word of thanks to Dr. Rollo May, whose writings have inspired many to attempt to live lives of existential authenticity.

responsible for his/her own existence or destiny. The existential belief in self-determinism is compatible with the thrust of our profession (of rehabilitation) to restore individuals to a position of independent functioning.

This chapter provides an overview of existentialism as a philosophy and as an approach to counseling practice. The key concepts and historical evolution of existentialism are presented, as well as a parallel to the tenets and evolution of the field of vocational rehabilitation. Application of an existentialist perspective to rehabilitation counseling practice is presented across the goals and objectives of counseling, the client-counselor relationship, therapeutic approach, and research. Conclusions about the implications of this approach for us as practicing professionals are discussed.

EXISTENTIALISM: KEY CONCEPTS AND HISTORICAL EVOLUTION

Existentialism, referred to as both a philosophy and a way to deal with clients in therapeutic intervention, "involves centering on the existing person and emphasizes the human being as he is emerging, becoming" (May, 1961, p. 11–12). The word *existence* comes from the Latin root *exsistere,* meaning literally "to stand out, to emerge" (May, Angel, & Ellenberger, 1958, p. 12). Existentialism, rather than attempting to describe the person from outside observation, has had as its focus the attempt to expand our understanding of human nature by probing deeply into the recesses of the inner, subjective reality of the individual, to discover how individuals experience their reality and give unique meaning to their lives.

When writing about the basic tenets of existentialism, many writers preface their discussions with statements about the difficulty of attempting to define it succinctly. Existentialism is not a discrete philosophical system or set of psycho-therapeutic principles. The existential approach calls for divergent methods to understand people, rather than espousing a single set of assumptions or approaches. It is a way of viewing individuals in relationship to their unique being-in-the-world, while at the same time focusing on problems common to all human beings by virtue of their human condition. Kohn (1984) identifies some of the key questions which human beings grapple with and existentialism attempts to address: "Why was I born if it wasn't forever? What will serve as meaning for me? What does it mean to choose? What am I to make of the fact that I am?"

The question "why" is seen as an expression of the human need to find meaning in existence. Ruffin (1984) concludes that meaning is a most important problem that must be addressed by counselors. Albert Camus is quoted as saying that "the meaning of life is the most urgent of questions" (Ruffin, p. 40). Viktor Frankl (1963) suggested that the human being is dominated by a deep-seated striving and struggle for a higher and ultimate meaning in life, rather than a striving for pleasure or power.

Some authors (Barrett, 1958) trace the beginnings of existential thought back to Socrates. Most contemporary writers, however, place the seeds of existentialism in the middle of the 19th century with the writings of the Danish philosopher Soren Kierkegaard (1813–1855). The focus of Kierkegaard's work was man and his conflicts. He viewed the human being as constantly seeking the infinite, yet realizing existence as temporal and finite. The conflict between these two opposing forces, according to Kierkegaard, toward eternity and toward temporality, stirs in humankind torment, anguish, and dread.

Misiak and Sexton (1966) place the crystallization of existentialism as a philosophical movement between the two World Wars in Continental Europe. The principal founders of the movement were the German philosophers Martin Heidegger and Karl Jaspers. In France, notable representatives of this philosophy have been Gabriel Marcel, Jean-Paul Sartre, Maurice Merleau-Ponty, Paul Ricoeur, and Simone de Beauvoir. On the American scene, existentialism appeared initially in the 1940s with Paul Tillich. It was not until the late 1950s that the word *existential* became familiar to a wider circle of American psychologists. In 1958, Rollo May edited *Existence*, credited with being the first presentation of existential thought for psychiatrists and psychologists in the United States.

From the existentialist perspective, the purpose of counseling is to restore in clients the sense of freedom and personal responsibility that will enable these individuals to discover for themselves the meaning of their personal existence and to encourage them to put it to full realization. At the core of existentialism is the premise that the *meaning of life* is the most urgent question with which human beings struggle, and that the striving for a higher and ultimate meaning in each person's own unique experience of existence is the driving force of human nature.

For the existentialist, the anguish—yet potential glory—of humankind is that we are ultimately *free* to choose our existence. There is no predetermined human nature that defines us, but rather we define what our nature will be by our *intention* and by the activities to which we choose to commit our life energy in the context of the particular circumstances in which we live our lives. *Existential anxiety* comes upon recognition of this ultimate responsibility. We can choose to despair at the prospect of a meaningless existence that ultimately ends in death (nothingness) or we can choose to create meaning in our lives in spite of, or perhaps because of, the inpediments which may cloud that possibility.

These constructs, in the existentialist way of viewing life, apply to all individuals regardless of where they have come from, or the particular problem or impediment which they are attempting to rise above. An existentialist approach to counseling centers on assisting individuals to remove the resistances that prevent them from *transcending* their past, their problems, or their impediments, in order to move into the future and become all that they can be.

PARALLELS TO REHABILITATION

Parallel Historical Evolution

The development and awareness of the existentialist way of viewing the human being has paralleled the growth and development of the profession of rehabilitation counseling. Sensitivity to the unique concerns of the disabled was becoming manifest in Europe in the late 1800s, as the early roots of existentialism were planted on the continent. A belief in the worth and dignity of each human being was demonstrated by the rise in services and institutions to care for those with physical or emotional disablement.

The growth of existentialism and the vocational rehabilitation profession paralleled each other because they grew out of the same historical roots. "The existential attitude was a response to the critical conditions of the mid-nineteenth century. It arose through the independent thinking of many minds in a spontaneous answer to the loss of a personal center" (Kemp, 1971, pp. 2–3). Existentialism was a reaction to the demands of a developing industrial society, where the index of a person's worth had become what she/he was able to produce and the paycheck she/he could bring home. Those interested in protecting and promoting the cause of the disabled were spurred by this same index of worth to create a profession of service providers who could help those with disabilities to hold their own with their able-bodied peers, getting the assistance they needed to be competitive in the labor market.

By the time existentialism was introduced to helping professionals in the United States by Rollo May and others, the profession of vocational rehabilitation counseling had already gone through a series of changes. From the earlier, post–World War I emphasis on returning disabled veterans to work, our services had expanded to a view which, although still vocational in focus, included much more attention to the development of the total person. Counselor training became greatly influenced by the "third force" orientation in American psychology—a name applied collectively or respectively to humanistic, phenomenological, and existential psychological orientations. The distinguishing common feature of all three is the emphasis on the functioning and experience of the whole human being. This influence brought to the rehabilitation counseling field reinforcement for the concepts of the worth of the individual and the full development of human potential, as well as the individual's ability to rise above adversity.

Compatible Philosophical Tenets

Three philosophical tenets of an existential approach to client intervention will be used to illustrate compatibility with rehabilitation counseling: the role of the client's background in development, perspective on psychological health, and the conditions for client change. Existentialists feel that by *emphasizing* the past as determining the present or future, or other "forces" (such as the "unconscious") which may be seen as having "placed" clients where they are, we are teaching clients that they are the products of both inner and outer forces which are outside their control. To the existentialist counselor, it is necessary to know the counselee's history and environment in terms of the meaning which these have for that particular individual. The present can best be understood as the intersection of previous choices, but we need not be confined by these. We rather can choose to give them the meaning we want, and build upon them to move ourselves forward into the future. It is the role of the counselor to help clients view their past as something they can draw from but are not necessarily bound to, and that they are free to transcend and move beyond the possible difficulties or transgressions in their past.

For the existentialist, psychological health is manifest when the individual is exerting his/her freedom to create a unique existence that provides meaning for that individual's life, moving him/her toward fulfillment of personal potential. May (1967) holds that "the various categories of illness themselves can be understood only as distortions in the (person's) realization of his human nature, as blockages in his endeavors to actualize aspects of this nature" (p. 115). For the existential counselor, then, a psychologically incapacitated or weakened person is one who succumbs to neurotic anxiety, taking a position of retrenchment in the face of the freedom to create his/her own existence. The "healthy" individual, rather, "has the courage to confront and move through the threatening experiences of isolation and anxiety which are 'normal'—cannot be avoided if one is to fulfill one's possibilities in the achieving of selfhood" (May, 1967, p. 69).

Some of the necessary conditions or characteristics seen as conducive for client change in the existentialist perspective are capacity to confront death, a need to fulfill one's being, and courage and commitment to change. The core premise, in existential thought, is that an authentic and full existence can only be gained when the individual is willing to confront his/her own mortality. May (1967) sees this as a prerequisite to growth and to self-consciousness, and also discusses the capacity to abandon oneself, giving up present security in favor of wider experiences as a necessary part of this change process. And "the urge and movement for (this) change and fulfillment . . . comes out of the patient's own being and his need to fulfill that being" (p. 127). May also presents the importance of *courage,* which enables us to rise above current adversity and past history and to transcend difficulties, moving on to new possibilities. By assuming responsibility both for *what* we have done and for *our response* to our circumstances, it becomes possible for us to see alternatives in the present and to choose how we want to live in the future.

APPLICATION OF AN EXISTENTIALIST APPROACH TO REHABILITATION COUNSELING PRACTICE

Goals and Objectives of Counseling

The goals of counseling in the existentialist view deal with life meaning, with existential anxiety, and with assuming responsibility for one's own existence. Ruffin (1984) says that "the goals of therapy should not be to help the individual find meaning. Rather, it should be to help individuals accept the responsibility to face meaninglessness, and through their creativity to bring order out of chaos" (p. 42). May et al. (1958) expand this further, in the humanistic–existential perspective, in saying that "the purpose [of counseling] is that he [the client] become aware of his existence fully, which includes becoming aware of his potentialities and becoming able to act on the basis of them" (p. 85).

In an existential approach to a helping relationship, the goal of therapy is *not* to free the client from anxiety but to free the client from *neurotic* anxiety so that she/he may meet normal anxiety more constructively, and to remove the blocks which keep him/her from being whole (Kemp, 1971; Koestenbaum, 1977; May, 1967). Nor is the goal to release the client from symptoms or help him/her to adjust and adapt into certain mores. Rather, the goal of therapy is to foster self-awareness, enabling individuals to integrate divided parts of their personality and to begin to assume responsibility for their own being-in-the-world and the meaning of personal events in relation to it.

Client-Counselor Relationship

Overs and Trotter (1969) point out the importance of the *quality* of the client-counselor relationship and its potential to teach the client about relationships in general. Some of the core qualities of the client-counselor relationship in the existentialist perspective are counselor authenticity and willingness to change, mutuality and mutual freedom, and an emphasis on understanding the client in his/her own world.

Counselor authenticity is the counselor's openness to come to grips with his/her own existential anxiety and willingness to share of self in the client-counselor interaction. Ruffin (1984) points out that it is "important that counselors courageously confront their own feelings of meaninglessness before beginning such a journey with another" (p. 42). May (1967) emphasizes the counselor's need for self-awareness or "self-relatedness," pointing out that a "lack of or distorted awareness of one's self blocks one's awareness of others; and the more clarified one's capacity is to see himself as subject, the more he can know other selves" (p. 195).

Kemp (1971) and Carpenter, Fishel, George, and Gould (1977) discuss the importance of a helping person being authentic or "translucent" in the therapeutic intervention. By that is meant that, different from other counseling approaches where there is more of a "helper" and "helpee" relationship, in the existential approach both client and counselor must change, and this change is brought about by an authentic and honest interaction.

Existentialist counseling is further distinguished from other approaches in the heavy emphasis upon knowing the person-in-their-world. Binswanger was one existential thinker/practitioner who felt that too much importance had been placed in psychology and psychiatry on the way in which people have deviated from a so-called "norm," usually assessed through testing. Instead, Binswanger emphasizes the importance of understanding clients in their own world. Kemp (1971) also emphasized that counselors need to know about the counselee in his/her totality in order to grasp his/her being; this, he maintains, is different than knowing *about* the counselee, which may be the counselor's way of defending him/herself against anxiety.

The quest for mutual growth and mutual freedom may be a characteristic different from other approaches in that there is a strong push for the independence of clients and their personal responsibility for their lives as they are now and for change in their lives. This belief in client responsibility for self is grounded in a helping relationship where the counselor offers an unconditional acceptance to clients which enables them to experience their own being more fully, and conveys to clients the belief that they are the way they are for a good reason and that there is an underlying meaning to their existence (Kemp, 1971).

Therapeutic Approach

The existential therapist does not stress technique. It is felt that the major block to human understanding in Western culture is the overemphasis on technique, which can result in the client being treated as an object (Overs & Trotter, 1969). In May's words:

> One of our serious dangers in America is the tendency to believe that technique in itself changes people, that anyone can change if only he finds the right method. This faith often times may serve as a substitute for courage inwardly to confront one's own existence in its tragic as well as joyous possibilities. *To do* is often easier, and may allay anxiety more quickly, than *to be* (May, 1967, p. 132).

The existential counselor's primary goal, then, is to understand the counselee as a person, a being, and as being-in-the-world. This does not mean that the counselor discounts the utility of all technique, but rather that technique takes its place in a larger perspective. This perspective proposes that the goal of the intervention is to help the counselee recognize and experience his/her own existence (Kemp, 1971). To accomplish this, the existential counselor is concerned about preserving the genuineness of the therapeutic situation and is careful to avoid using techniques which would block the reality of the situation (Overs & Trotter, 1969).

In examining the question of technique and the timing and evaluation of progress in therapy from the existentialist perspective, it is helpful to review the possible responses the client can have to the feelings of meaninglessness on which the existential counselor focuses. Ruffin (1984) identifies three alternative responses to feelings of meaninglessness, two of which seem to have negative consequences for the client. One alternative is for clients to attempt to shrink back and constrict their awareness, thereby avoiding the anxiety. The consequence of this avoidance can be an alienation for one's self and a forfeiting of one's authenticity (Bugenthal, 1965). The second alternative is despair, whereby individuals are so overcome by feelings of emptiness and meaninglessness that they succumb to severe apathy or a self-destructive life-style. Ruffin draws on Paul Tillich in suggesting a positive third alternative: courage. Courage is necessary not to remove the anxiety, but to take responsibility for our lives, and to exercise choices essential for personal meaning. From this range of possible client responses, progress in therapy can be measured by the degree to which the client moves toward a position of responsibility for self and courageously assumes the freedom she/he has to create meaning in his/her individual life.

RESEARCH

Taylor (1980), in an unpublished doctoral dissertation, concluded from a study of the tenets of rehabilitation psychology that we (in rehabilitation) sorely lack an identifiable and comprehensive philosophical base from which to practice counseling. He proposed that a humanistic-existential approach "speaks directly and persuasively to many issues especially significant to the rehabilitation psychologist, such as: the nature of the body experience, acceptance of loss, the nature of the helper-client relationship, an experience of the person as he exists in the context of the world" (p. 13).

A review of psychology-related literature from 1973 to date on existentialism as applied to rehabilitation offers very little in the way of meaningful research information on this approach. Sterman (1983), in an unpublished doctoral dissertation, applied an existential perspective to an investigation of life meaningfulness for individuals with a chemical dependency. Results of that study indicated that chemically dependent individuals had less general life purpose than non-chemically-dependent individuals.

Several other authors discuss the relationship between stress and disease, inferring that health problems are often symptoms of more basic philosophic conditions (Koestenbaum, 1977; Kohn, 1984). Kohn introduces the work of Suzanne Kobasa, who is described as attempting to take existential concepts and turn them into empirical constructs by doing a longitudinal evaluation on change, stress resistance, and illness. Both Kobasa and Koestenbaum point to the entire field of psychosomatic medicine as relevant to further research confirming the significant impact which individuals' perception of their world has on both their emotional and physical well-being.

CONCLUSIONS

Rehabilitation counseling as a helping profession has been caught up in ongoing debate about the role and function of the counselor and the goals of service provision. This problem stems in part from response to changing federal and state priorities, reflecting the significant role which political and economic factors often play in definition of our purpose. It is the proposal of this author, however, that part of this identity and purpose confusion is based on a lack of common philosophical stance for which we practice our profession.

Existentialism as both a philosophy and an approach to counseling is consistent with and can contribute to the professional practice of vocational rehabilitation counseling. Existentialism preserves the place of each individual in determining how she/he will live his/her life. Emphasis is placed more on the quality of the counselor-client relationship, rather than on any particular counseling technique. This is advantageous in that it calls for the counselor to model authenticity in his/her own life and in interaction with the client, yet allows latitude for counselors to draw upon the techniques which they may find useful from other approaches.

The whole area of psychomatic medicine points to the significant role which a person's will to live and overall life meaningfulness can play in both onset of and recovery from an illness or traumatic injury. We in rehabilitation counseling would be remiss if we did not actively engage the person's will in their rehabilitation process. As counselors, we should explore with clients meaning in life for them, so we are better able to set with clients both vocational and larger life goals consistent with this meaning. To do so better assures the ultimate value of rehabilitation services in the life of a given client.

14 A Person-Centered Perspective

John D. See

Carl Rogers is the undisputed standard-bearer of the person-centered approach. His original and often radical ideas have sparked controversy for over four decades. Although in his eighties, Rogers is still extremely active at the Center for Studies of the Person, which he helped establish in La Jolla, California. Currently one of his main concerns is world peace. He has recently extended the use of person-centered principles to include group work with people of differing ideologies.

It was he who had the audacity in the early 1940s to tell the psychotherapy community that man was basically good and could be trusted to lead his own life (Rogers, 1942). This was, of course, anathema to the then prevalent Freudian view of therapy as the process of helping people control the destructive forces of the unconscious. In addition to this more optimistic view of human nature, he had the genius to formulate a totally new treatment approach that was based more on the personality of the therapist than on techniques or formal training in psychology. In 1957 he announced that the "facilitative conditions" of empathy, positive regard, and genuineness were necessary and sufficient for therapy to take place (Rogers, 1957). This revolutionary idea meant that the medium as well as the essence of therapy was the *relationship* between the therapist and client.

Not only were these new formulations striking in their simplicity, elegance, and departure from the norm, but to make things even more remarkable, this humanist was also a tenacious researcher. Throughout the years he has revised his theories on the basis of the accumulating raw data. According to Grummon (1979) this research orientation has resulted in the largest empirical data base of any counseling theory, with the possible exception of behavior modification. In his recent book, *The Therapeutic Relationship: Foundations for an Eclectic Psychotherapy*, C. H. Patterson (1985) states:

> Considering the obstacles to research on the relationship between therapist variables and therapy outcomes, the magnitude of the evidence is nothing short of amazing. It might be ventured that there are few things in the field of psychology for which the evidence is so strong. The evidence for the necessity, if not the sufficiency, of the therapist conditions of accurate empathy, respect or warmth, and therapeutic genuineness is incontrovertible. (p. 244)

MAIN CONCEPTS OF PERSON-CENTERED PERSPECTIVE

What is person-centered counseling? Here is how Rogers explains it (*A Way of Being,* 1980):

> What do I mean by a person-centered approach? It expresses the primary theme of my whole professional life, as that theme has become clarified through experience, interaction with others, and research. I smile as I think of the various labels I have given to this theme during the course of my career—nondirective counseling, client-centered therapy, student-centered teaching, group-centered leadership. Because the fields of application have grown in number and variety, the label 'person-centered approach' seems the most descriptive.
>
> The central hypothesis of this approach can be briefly stated. (See Rogers, 1959, for a complete statement.) Individuals have within themselves vast resources for self-understanding and for altering their self-concepts, basic attitudes, and self-directed behavior; these resources can be tapped if a definable climate of facilitative psychological attitudes can be provided.
>
> There are three conditions that must be present in order for a climate to be growth-promoting. These conditions apply whether we are speaking of the relationship between therapist and client, parent and child, leader and group, teacher and student, or administrator and staff. The conditions apply, in fact, in any situation in which the development of the person is a goal. I have described these conditions in previous writings; I present here a brief summary from the point of view of psychotherapy, but the description applies to all of the foregoing relationships.
>
> The first element could be called genuineness, realness, or congruence. The more the therapist is himself or herself in the relationship, putting up no professional front or personal facade, the greater is the likelihood that the client will change and grow in a constructive manner. This means that the therapist is openly being the feelings and attitudes that are flowing within at the moment. The term "transparent" catches the flavor of this condition: the therapist makes himself or herself transparent to the client; the client can see right through what the therapist *is* in the relationship; the client experiences no holding back on the therapist. As for the therapist, what he or she is experiencing is available to awareness, can be lived in

the relationship, and can be communicated, if appropriate. Thus, there is a close matching, or congruence, between what is being experienced at the gut level, what is present in awareness, and what is expressed to the client.

The second attitude of importance in creating a climate for change is acceptance, or caring, or prizing—what I called "unconditional positive regard." When the therapist is experiencing a positive, acceptant attitude toward whatever the client *is* at that moment, therapeutic movement or change is more likely to occur. The therapist is willing for the client to be whatever immediate feeling is going on—confusion, resentment, fear, anger, courage, love, or pride. Such caring on the part of the therapist is nonpossessive. The therapist prizes the client in a total rather than a conditional way.

The third facilitative aspect of the relationship is empathic understanding. This means that the therapist senses accurately the feelings and personal meanings that the client is experiencing and communicates this understanding to the client. When functioning best, the therapist is so much inside the private world of the other that he or she can clarify not only the meanings of which the client is aware but even those just below the level of awareness.

This kind of sensitive, active listening is exceedingly rare in our lives. We think we listen, but very rarely do we listen with real understanding, true empathy. Yet listening, of this very special kind, is one of the most potent forces for change that I know.

How does this climate which I have just described bring about change? Briefly, as persons are accepted and prized, they tend to develop a more caring attitude toward themselves. As persons are empathically heard, it becomes possible for them to listen more accurately to the flow of inner experiencings. But as a person understands and prizes self, the self becomes more congruent with the experiencings. The person thus becomes more real, more genuine. These tendencies, the reciprocal of the therapist's attitudes, enable the person to become a more effective growth-enhancer for himself or herself. There is a greater freedom to be the true, whole person. (p. 114)*

It is clear from the above quote that Rogers intends his theory to have universal application. It applies as much to the relationships between rehabilitation counselors and their disabled clients as it does to relationships between parents and children or between teachers and students. Whatever the situation, the goal of therapy is self-actualization, and the means to that end are the facilitative conditions.

* From C.R. Rogers, *A Way of Being*, p. 114. Copyright © 1980 by the Houghton Mifflin Company, Boston. Used by permission.

The remainder of this section will briefly describe some additional working principles of the person-centered approach.

Actualizing Tendency

According to Rogers there is a natural urge within all of us to develop in a positive direction. However, before this natural urge (or actualizing tendency, as it is called) can operate, it must be liberated by a loving and permissive environment. This process of self-actualization is characterized by creativity, growth, socialization, and independence.

Self-Concept

According to Rogers the central personality construct consists of the picture we have of ourselves. It is the perceptual gestalt or sum total of all of the thoughts, feelings, and values we have of ourselves and of our relationships to the things and people within our world. It is material that is conscious or available to consciousness. It is more or less what we would say about ourselves if we could write a candid and exhaustive autobiography; it is who we think we are. This self-concept determines to a large extent how we behave.

Organismic Valuing Process

The infant evaluates experiences and behaviors according to how they make her feel. If the behavior produces good feelings it is because it furthers the needs of the actualizing tendency. The infant does not need to be told what is right or wrong; she automatically senses it in an intuitive way. Both good and bad experiences become part of the person's self-concept and are accurately symbolized in awareness. Because adults lose much of this natural and wholesome reactivity to the world, the task of therapy is to help the adult relearn how to listen to these organismic messages from within. To the extent the adult can recapture this childlike ability to trust feelings, she becomes more autonomous, more alive, and more congruent.

Need for Positive Regard

Sometime during the early stages of development, a powerful secondary need emerges which can work for or against the organismic valuing process. This is the need for love, or positive regard, from others. When parents and significant others provide unconditional love, the infant is free to develop according to the actualizing tendency and will learn of her potential by directly experiencing the world. Because humans are instinctively good and act in ways that enhance the organism, this self-directed search for identity can be trusted to result in a well-developed and congruent personality.

Things go badly for the developing individual when the love provided by significant others is dependent on how she behaves. Conditional love cripples her development because she now must listen to others rather than to herself. When she conforms in order to get love, she is living according to values introjected by others, or what Rogers calls the conditions of worth. This emotional blackmail results in individuals who deny their own actualizing tendency and relinquish their right to discover their own unique individuality. In the extreme, they become conforming, other-directed, authoritarian types with rigid self-concepts.

Inner Conflict and Anxiety

Inner conflict results when the individual is torn between doing what comes naturally and doing what others expect. When the individual accepts the values of others in order to gain positive regard, those values are internalized and become part of the personality. Then, if the individual behaves or thinks in ways that go against those introjected values, the self-concept is violated and the person loses self-esteem and suffers anxiety. The mother who spanked him 30 years ago for masturbatory activity has long been gone from this world, and yet the adult-child still gets nervous when he thinks of sex.

We defend against anxiety and threats to our self-esteem by developing a more rigid self-concept that will be less open to new and possibly disturbing experiences. We begin to distort reality through the use of defense mechanisms such as denial, projection, reaction formations, etc. By putting tight reins on our emotions, we can live out our lives in this stable but unfulfilled state.

In order for therapy to be effective, there must be a weakening of these defenses to the point where the individual can sense the incongruence between the self-concept and the experiencing self. It is this identity crisis and the ensuing anxiety that motivates the person to seek help and engage in self-exploration.

TREATMENT APPROACH

In the person-centered approach, treatment *is* the relationship between the counselor and the client. If that relationship is characterized by the following conditions, then constructive personality change will take place (Rogers, 1957):

1. Two persons are in psychological contact.
2. The client is in a state of incongruence, being vulnerable or anxious.
3. The therapist is congruent or integrated in the relationship.
4. The therapist experiences unconditional positive regard for the client.
5. The therapist experiences an empathic understanding of the client's internal frame of reference and endeavors to communicate this experience to the client.
6. The communication to the client of the therapist's empathic understanding and unconditional positive regard is to a minimal degree achieved.

Over the years the person-centered approach has de-emphasized the use of techniques. Reflection of feelings is still an accepted way to show empathy, but it is only a means to that end; and unless it is done with great skill and sensitivity, it is likely to be counterproductive. An excellent how-to-do-it text devoted to teaching empathic listening is *Counseling and Therapy Skills* by David Martin (1983).

SUPPORTIVE RESEARCH

Probably the most disturbing research in the history of psychotherapy was that of Eysenck (1960) and Levitt (1963), which revealed that clients receiving therapy fared no better than did untreated controls. It was Rogers and his associates (Rogers, Gendlin, Keisler, & Truax, 1967; Truax & Carkhuff, 1967) who provided one of the most convincing rebuttals to Eysenck and Levitt reviews. They found that there was greater client outcome variance in treatment groups than in control groups. This meant that while some clients improved through therapy, others deteriorated as a result of therapy. These extremes averaged out in the statistical analysis, causing the treatment group to appear the same as the control group. This revelation led to the popular dictum that therapy is "for better or worse." They also found that a major determinant in the client outcome variation was the interpersonal skill level of the therapist. In other words, clients treated by therapists demonstrating high levels of the facilitative conditions tended to improve, while the clients of low-functioning therapists remained neutral or deteriorated. Hundreds of subsequent studies have substantiated these early findings on the importance of the facilitative conditions. Needless to say, there were other studies that did not support this position; indeed, there is still controversy about the interpretation of this vast and complex data base. After his recent review of the literature, C. H. Patterson (1985) concluded:

> These conditions, then, must be part of any eclectic system of psychotherapy, since they are the very foundation on which any such system must be built. They cannot be ignored, dismissed, or relegated to a background position, as some writers have done. The evidence for their effectiveness . . . is too strong, and there is little or no evidence for the effectiveness of any other methods or techniques. (p. vi)

The following is an abbreviation of Grummon's (1979) sample of outcome research that seems to be associated with client-centered counseling:

1. There is an improvement in psychological adjustment as shown on personality tests.
2. There is less physiological tension and greater adaptive capacity in response to frustration.
3. There is a decrease in psychological tension.
4. There is a decrease in defensiveness.
5. There is a greater degree of correspondence between the client's description of her self-picture and her description of her wanted or ideal self.
6. Friends tend to rate the client's behavior as more emotionally mature.
7. There is an improvement in overall adjustment in the vocational training setting.
8. Client-centered play methods with elementary school children may result in accelerated reading improvement.
9. Successful clients evidence strong gains in creativeness.
10. A study on hospitalized schizophrenics revealed ambiguous findings. In many areas there was no difference between treatment and control groups, although treatment groups showed slightly better rates of release from the hospital and improvement in personal and interpersonal functioning.
11. There was a lower incidence of success among clients who accept little self-responsibility for their problems, and who see the source of their problems as residing outside themselves.

Some very impressive research regarding the person-centered approach comes not from the counseling field but from the education field. Aspy and Roebuck (1974) rated 550 elementary and secondary-level teachers on the facilitative conditions and then correlated these ratings with a large number of student performance criteria. The findings are quite remarkable. The students of high-functioning teachers showed greater gains in academic work as well as in a number of non-academic areas: creative problem solving, positive self-concepts, fewer discipline problems, lower absence rates, and even increased IQ scores. This monumental study of teaching has clear implications for rehabilitation counseling because of the many similarities between the two professions.

In a nationwide study of practicing rehabilitation counselors, the staff of the Arkansas Rehabilitation Research and Training Center investigated the relationship of the facilitative conditions to rehabilitation client gain (Bozarth & Rubin, 1978). This 5-year study of 160 rehabilitation counselors and 1,000 clients concluded, among other things, that "the counselors were at least as high on levels of empathy, respect, and genuineness dimensions as many other professional groups, including experienced psychotherapists in private practice" (p. 178). With reference to client gain they found that "the higher levels of the interpersonal skills, even though falling on the operational scale definition of minimally facilitative, tended to be related to higher vocational gain at closure, higher monthly earnings at follow-up, positive psychological change 10 months or more following intake, and greater job satisfaction at follow up" (p. 178).

CONTRASTS BETWEEN THE PERSON-CENTERED APPROACH AND OTHER APPROACHES

While an extensive comparison of the various counseling theories goes beyond this chapter, a brief statement will be made regarding some of the more obvious distinctions.

The greatest similarities exist between the insight therapies: person-centered, existential, and gestalt. These three insight therapies view man as being alienated from himself because of stultifying life experiences. All three see his salvation as stemming from his ability to courageously confront the deeper recesses of the self and find personal meaning within. These insight approaches usually consider behavior change per se to be somewhat prosaic; behavior takes care of itself if therapy is successful. All three theories see psychological change as something that occurs during the existential moment when the implied meaning of experience becomes known. This psychological change is produced by the intense personal relationship with the therapist.

These insight approaches are most effective with clients possessing high verbal skills and a slightly neurotic dissatisfaction with life. None of the insight approaches are especially appropriate for rehabilitation clients who know themselves well and are only seeking practical assistance; however, the same might be said of all other therapeutic counseling approaches.

One of the most provocative conflicts within the counseling field is between the person-centered theorists and the learning theorists. The Rogerians believe that psychological growth (improved self-concept) will automatically result in improved behavior. The Skinnerians just as emphatically state that the only legitimate focus of therapy is the behavior itself; once an individual learns to behave more appropriately, positive feelings will follow.

Person-centered theorists assert that when the behavior modification people are successful it is because they are unwittingly providing the facilitative conditions. It is the quality of the counselor-client relationship that produces the positive change in clients, not the mechanical application of learning theory principles. The learning theorists respond that person-centered counselors are effective only because the facilitative conditions happen to be very powerful reinforcers and that person-centered counselors use them much more selectively than they realize or admit.

Because the rehabilitation counselor's job is to provide client services, it might be well to sidestep this theoretical debate and simply remember that both of these polar positions have generated considerable empirical support over the years. Enlightened pragmatism dictates that rehabilitation counselors use whatever approach best helps clients reach their vocational goals.

LIMITATIONS OF THE PERSON-CENTERED PERSPECTIVE FOR REHABILITATION COUNSELORS

The person-centered counseling perspective in its "classical" form possesses nearly insurmountable obstacles for the rehabilitation counselor. The term *classical* refers to depth therapy which is guided by Rogers' formulations on personality development and is totally nondirective. This classical approach is as distinctive for what it prohibits as it is for what it prescribes:

1. The classical model does not set goals, aside from self-actualization; yet the rehabilitation counselor is required by law to develop Individual Written Rehabilitation Programs (IWRPs).

2. The classical model does not believe in diagnosing; yet the rehabilitation counselor is committed to using medical, psychological, and vocational evaluations.
3. The classical model does not give advice; yet one of the rehabilitation counselor's most distinctive assets is knowledge of occupational information and the world of work.
4. The classical model is relatively unconcerned with the external environment; yet the rehabilitation counselor is in constant interaction with the real world and spends considerable time coordinating community resources and delivering concrete services to the client.
5. The classical model is most effective with anxious and verbal clients; yet many rehabilitation clients do not fit this description.
6. The classical model is process-oriented; yet rehabilitation counselors are accountable for end results.
7. The classical model calls for personality restructuring; yet the physically disabled are often as psychologically sound as the non-disabled and do not necessarily need reorganization of the self-concept.
8. The classical model does not focus on client behavior; yet client skill development, education, and action are the life blood of rehabilitation.

The above limitations point out some of the role discrepancies between rehabilitation counselors and insight therapists. There is also evidence (Rubin & Roessler, 1978) that rehabilitation counselors spend a relatively small percentage of their time (approximately 10%) in what might be considered therapeutic counseling.

APPLICATIONS OF THE PERSON-CENTERED PERSPECTIVE FOR REHABILITATION PERSONNEL

A number of authorities have stressed the importance of the facilitative conditions in rehabilitation counseling. A task force of rehabilitation specialists (Porter, Rubin, & Sink, 1979) reported that one of the essential job competencies of both rehabilitation counselors and vocational evaluators is the ability to demonstrate the facilitative conditions. At the conclusion of the Counselor-Client Interaction Project (Bozarth & Rubin, 1978) the staff of the Arkansas Rehabilitation Research and Training Center recommended that "counselors might be amenable to increasing their levels of interpersonal skills by intensive, concentrated training, which should pay dividends in the form of increased client benefits on multiple criteria" (p. 179). Rubin and Roessler (1978) state, "For rehabilitation, the most significant approaches are the insight and behavioral" (p. 100). They go on to state, "Although empathy, respect, and genuineness, for example, are necessary conditions for effective counseling (Rogers, 1957), in and of themselves they are not sufficient conditions. Rehabilitation counseling also calls for specific action on the part of counselor and client to accomplish the rehabilitation plan" (p. 101).

The justification for training rehabilitation counselors and vocational evaluators in the use of facilitative conditions is not to turn them into psychotherapists, but rather to provide them with the interpersonal skills that will allow them to be more effective helpers in all that they do. These growth-producing human qualities are not the property of a school of thought or theoretical orientation. They belong to everyone in varying degrees and are operative in such widely divergent areas of human interaction as parent-child (Gordon, 1970), counselor-client (Carkhuff, 1969), teacher-student (Aspy & Roebuck, 1977), employer-employee (Carkhuff, 1983), and rehabilitation counselor-client (Bozarth & Rubin, 1978).

Being respectful, understanding, and honest with clients is not a technique. It is "a way of being" that contributes to a wholesome growth environment. Viewed in this way, the facilitative relationship is a necessary non-specific treatment factor that applies equally to all clients and provides the foundation for the delivery of other more individualized services.

When rehabilitation personnel are called upon to function as therapeutic counselors, the facilitative conditions will play a more central role and should be viewed as specific treatment factors. It becomes problematic, however, trying to judge which clients will benefit from this more intensive treatment and which counselors are qualified to provide it.

TRAINING OF REHABILITATION PERSONNEL

There is considerable evidence that short-term training can increase the levels of the facilitative conditions of trainees. Scofield (1983) in his literature review of rehabilitation education and training, states, "A review of the studies contained in this category of documents supports one generalization regarding the application of training methods. That is, both facilitative interpersonal skills and rehabilitation-related attitudes can be improved through the various systematic training procedures reported in the literature" (p. 3). Rogers (1980) reports that Aspy and Roebuck were able to produce substantial increases in the functioning levels of their teachers in as little as 15 hours. Mitchell, Bozarth, & Krauft, (1977) report that on the dimension of empathy, some trainees show improvement with as little as 6 hours of training, although most require considerably more time. Thomas and Butler (1981) state that because client-centered counseling emphasizes the personal attributes of the counselor rather than formal training in psychotherapy, it is "within bounds for the majority of rehabilitation counselors" (p. 239).

It is noteworthy that there is disagreement regarding the existing interpersonal skill level of rehabilitation personnel. While Bozarth and Rubin (1978) report that practicing rehabilitation counselors are functioning slightly above the minimally facilitative levels on the Carkhuff scales, Anthony (1978) found that beginning and advanced rehabilitation graduate students, as well as rehabilitation educators and rehabilitation counselors, were all functioning below the minimally facilitative levels on the Carkhuff scales. The Carkhuff (1969) scales are operationalized rating forms used to measure the facilitative conditions. A rating of 3 on these 5-point scales is usually considered the minimum level which can promote client gain.

There are a variety of ways to teach the facilitative conditions, but it is generally accepted that there should be some combination of didactic and experiential learning. Reading and hearing about the facilitative conditions is not enough. They must be experienced directly by the counselor trainee.

The original writings of Rogers are especially suitable for the student interested in gaining a fuller appreciation of this system of thought. *A Way of Being* (Rogers, 1980) and *On Becoming a Person* (Rogers, 1961) are both highly recommended. These original works possess a harmony and wisdom that many students will find quite compelling. He inspires us and ennobles our profession by showing how deeply connected our work is to the human condition. In addition to Rogers' own works there are numerous other authors who give excellent accounts of Rogerian principles: C. H. Patterson (1985), Martin (1983), and Grummon (1979), to mention a few.

Common teaching strategies include the use of role-playing, modeling, feedback and critique of videotaped counseling sessions, supervised practicum with real clients, and the use of scales such as those developed by Carkhuff and Truax (Carkhuff, 1969) to measure the trainees' functioning level and to teach discrimination.

One eclectic training approach that may be relevant for the rehabilitation counselor is that of Robert Carkhuff. Carkhuff and his associates have been developing and refining a generic helping model for some two decades. According to Carkhuff (1980) the helper skills of responding and initiating promote the helpee outcomes of exploration, self-understanding, and action. Empathy, positive regard, and genuineness have been modified and factored into this broad helping formula. Some recent books by this group that may be helpful to rehabilitation personnel are: *The Skills of Helping* (Carkhuff & Anthony, 1979), *The Art of Helping* (Carkhuff, Pierce, & Cannon, 1980), and *Psychiatric Rehabilitation Practice Series* (Books 1–6) (Anthony et al., 1980).

The Arkansas Rehabilitation Research and Training Center has developed training packages which incorporate the facilitative conditions: *Interpersonal Skill Training: Basic Helping Skills for Rehabilitation Workers* (Akridge, Means, Milligen, & Farley, 1978) and *Facilitative Case Management* (Rubin et al., 1974). These packages include operationalized rating forms for the facilitative conditions which may be especially helpful for beginning counselors.

No discussion of the person-centered perspective is complete without mentioning one serious caveat: Counselor educators themselves must be high in the facilitative conditions if they are to successfully teach these skills to counselor trainees (Carkhuff, 1969; Rogers, 1980).

CONCLUSION

The inescapable conclusion of this chapter is that rehabilitation professionals need to study themselves just as seriously as they study their clients. This self-examination is demanded by the overwhelming evidence that helpers demonstrating higher levels of the facilitative conditions tend to be more effective on the job, while those demonstrating lower levels are less effective and indeed may cause client deterioration. Short-term training has proven useful in upgrading these interpersonal skills.

15 A Gestalt Perspective

Harry A. Allen

DEFINITION

Gestalt therapy is an ahistoric, experimental, noninterpretive, phenomenological, existentially based form of therapy which focuses upon the person's present behavior (Kempler, 1973; Simkin, 1979). The term *Gestalt* is a German word meaning the forming of a meaningful whole or organized configuration. Fritz Perls, the founder of Gestalt therapy, used the word to mean a unique kind of perceptual patterning that individuals form to meet their needs. Perls (1973) suggested that persons become maladjusted because they are fragmented and cannot discriminate which objects from the environment will satisfy their needs. The role of therapy then is to help the person reclaim these fragmented parts and reintegrate them into a whole self. Thus, Gestalt therapy emphasizes self-awareness, self-integration, self-responsibility, and self-fulfillment (Coven, 1977).

Several concepts are important to the understanding of Gestalt therapy: awareness, the now orientation, responsibility, contact and withdrawal, polarity, figure-ground, and the I–Thou relationship (Corey, 1982; Gilliland, James, Roberts, & Bowman, 1984; Simkin, 1979).

Awareness is the primary therapeutic tool in Gestalt therapy. Simkin (1979) defines this as being in touch with one's own existence. What persons are aware of is what exists for them. This is their reality. As such "there is no right or wrong reality. What is, is. . . . [Thus] we are our awareness rather than have awareness" (Simpkin, 1979, p. 274). Awareness alone is curative (Corey, 1982; Yontef, 1971). When clients have the tools of awareness they are capable of personality change.

The *now orientation* focuses experience on the present moment. For Perls (1969), now is the only time that exists. The past is gone, the future is not yet here; thus, only the present moment is significant. As such, Gestalt therapy focuses upon the present moment of the person. Any issues of the past or the future are restated in the *now*. The Gestalt therapist actively confronts persons when they attempt to escape the present by running to the past or future.

Responsibility, particularly self-responsibility, is stressed in Gestalt theory. At one level, responsibility means that individuals determine their own life patterns. Thus, in therapy, persons are asked to *own* their projections instead of blaming others for their thoughts, feelings, behaviors, etc. On another level responsibility means the ability to respond ("response-ability") (Perls, 1973). Thus, in Gestalt therapy, persons are expected to take ownership of their life by accepting and integrating their feelings, thoughts, etc., and by taking the power to act on their own behalf.

Contact and *withdrawal* are concepts which focus upon how persons are able to fulfill their own needs. The Gestalt model assumes that persons are motivated by a continued striving for homeostasis and that the process of overcoming disequilibrium is a matter of organismic self-regulation (Perls, 1973). Thus, persons are understood to have an instinctual drive toward homeostasis; this urge is the basic force toward growth. Further, the individual must be understood as a whole and one who responds in a holistic fashion. When an imbalance occurs within the system (which is an ongoing flux between equilibrium and disequilibrium), the person must make contact with the environment. Contact with the environment is made through seven contact functions. These are looking, listening, touching, talking, smelling, moving, and tasting. The person is taught in therapy to use these functions to become aware of the impact of contact and withdrawal, for it is through these functions that gestalts are formed and completed.

Polarities arise when there is interference with the organismic self-regulation. The splits that develop within self take on the character of discordant poles (e.g., the victim vs. the oppressor, top dog vs. underdog, etc.). Such polarization serves to further block the person's level of awareness and thus is directly confronted by the Gestalt therapist. The task of integrating the polarities is accomplished by focusing awareness upon the two parts of self so that they may be fully experienced (Simkin, 1979).

Figure-ground is a basic concept within Gestalt theory. Gestalt therapists regard motor behavior and perceptual qualities of the individual experience to be organized by the person's most urgent organismic need. In the functional individual a meaningful perceptual pattern (a good gestalt) is formed with the person's dominant need being the figure. The person satisfies his need by making contact with the environment through some sensorimotor behavior. When the need is met, the gestalt it organized is completed, and the figure flows back into the background allowing the person to move to meeting his next need (forming a new *gestalten*). When this gestalt arousal and absorption process is disrupted, when needs are not recognized or expressed, they are not met. These unmet needs form incomplete gestaltens which demand energy and attention and interfere with the formation of new gestaltens. In Gestalt therapy, the incomplete gestaltens are referred to as "unfinished business." Such "unfinished business" involves unexpressed feelings such as resentment, rage, fear, guilt, grief, abandonment, etc. The feelings, though unexpressed, are still associated with specific memories and/or fantasies. Though they remain in a background, they demand personal energy to be maintained; the energy absorber can result in symptomatology. The therapist's task focuses upon helping the person become aware of the unfinished business. Through awareness, contact can be made and the gestalten completed (Yontef, 1971).

The *I–Thou* nature of the counselor-client relationship is the "sine qua non" of Gestalt therapy. Personal change occurs literally through the process of the I–Thou relationship. The counselor and client are involved in a dynamic two-way encounter. "The therapist is like a composing *maestro* facing an accomplished musician. . . . Together they are a creative process and the goal is the concerted behavior of each" (Kempler, 1973, p. 266).

In summary, the Gestalt approach is an experimental, here-and-now form of therapy which involves the active interaction of the counselor and client. The major goal is to facilitate awareness, which on the experiential level, is curative.

COMPARISON WITH OTHER MODELS

As Yontef (1971) notes, the theorized distinctions between behavioral approaches, psychoanalytic approaches, and Gestalt therapy are obvious. Yontef also claims that there are similarities among many recent forms of therapy as proposed by Carl Rogers, Eric Berne, Virginia Satir, Viktor Frankl, William Glasser, Albert Ellis, and Gestalt therapy. Notably, each of these schools places emphasis on the I–Thou nature of the counseling relationship, and all claim to be holistic, interactional, and to some degree existential. All have a tendency for the counselor/therapist to be more active than the psychodynamically orientated therapist. All of the recent forms use groups as well as individual modalities (Yontef, 1971, p. 73). However, Gestalt, as Simkin (1979) notes, places emphasis on the awareness process rather than on the content and attends to the obvious rather than searching for the underlying or hidden meanings. Further, Gestalt therapy emphasizes assuming responsibility for one's own behavior, thoughts, and feelings rather than placing the blame for present circumstances upon others in the past. In Gestalt, the person always responds in the present tense of *now.* Actual present-moment experience of a situation as done in Gestalt does not depend upon history nor interpretation, it is self-explanatory; and Gestalt uses games and experiments to increase the client's awareness.

GESTALT THERAPY AND THE IMPACT OF DISABILITY

Perls, and the major writers in the Gestalt approach, have not addressed specifically the impact of a physical disability and its implication for counseling. There are probably a number of reasons for this, the major being that the presence or absence of a physical disability would probably be of little concern for the Gestalt therapist. As Jung (1978) states:

> A major attraction of Gestalt Therapy is its adherence to a humanistic and holistic doctrine. In moving away from a medical model focused upon pathology with its concomitant adjustment oriented interventions. Gestalt is directed toward the individual's development as a whole emphasizing his positive qualities and potential. The outlook is one of optimism. The more limited goal of social adjustment is transcended by a striving toward growth and self realization. (p. 26)

Both Jung (1978) and Coven (1977, 1979) note that Gestalt therapy and techniques have relevance in working with a person who has experienced a disability. This author's own work in the area of invisible disabilities (Allen & Falvo, 1983; Falvo, Allen, & Maki, 1982) leads him to strongly agree that Gestalt therapy can be of great benefit in helping a disabled person deal with the experience of loss and the psychosocial correlates of a disability. The Gestalt emphases on self-awareness, self-completion, self-integration, and self-responsibility seem potent in the rehabilitation arena.

HISTORY AND EVOLUTION

The founder and best known practitioner of Gestalt therapy is Frederick S. (Fritz) Perls (1893–1970). According to Kogan (1976) there were a number of influences that shaped the nature of Gestalt therapy. Perls was impacted by some of the most important theorists in the fields of existential philosophy, gestalt psychology, and psychoanalysis of the early 20th century. Between World Wars I and II, Perls' teachers were Sigmund Freud, Wilhelm Reich, Sigmund Friedlander, Adhemar Gleb, Kurt Goldstein, and his wife, Laura (Presnec) Perls. Others who influenced his thought were Karen Horney, Max Wiethеimer, Wolfgang Kohler, Kurt Lewis, I. A. Richards, and J. C. Smuts (Kogan, 1976).

Perls studied and practiced psychoanalysis between 1924 and 1936. This became the anvil upon which Gestalt was pounded out. Freud, Horney, and Reich were all influential in the final shape of Gestalt therapy. Goldstein's theory of holism, with its emphasis on figure-and-ground formation as a major organizing function of the organism, became a major premise in Gestalt therapy. Friedlander's concepts of creative indifference and differential thinking led Perls to the concepts of "working toward awareness and integration of Polarities" (Gilliland et al., 1984, p. 94). Many of Perls' ideas are closely related to principles of general semantics. His work was strongly influenced by the work of semanticists I. A. Richards and A. Korzybski. Perls' wife, Laura, with whom he worked for 25 years, is credited by Kogan (1976) as having great impact upon the formation and development of Gestalt therapy. Fritz and Laura moved to South Africa in the mid-1930s to escape Hitler's Germany. Here they established a training school for psychoanalysts (1934 to 1942), and it was also here that the final break with psychoanalysis was made.

From 1947 until his death in 1970 Perls lived in America. This was the garden in which Gestalt therapy was grown and nourished. He and Laura founded, with Paul Goodman, the first Gestalt Institute in New York City in 1951. The human potential movement in America became a fertile soil in which Perls' seeds could flourish. However, Gestalt therapy was relatively unknown in America until 1963 when Perls went to the Esalen Institute. It was during his 6-year tenure at Esalen that Gestalt therapy gained a foothold in American thought. Since Perls' death in 1970 the Gestalt therapy movement has continued to grow through Fritz's students. Therapists continue to be trained in major Gestalt centers in San Francisco, Cleveland, New York, Los Angeles, and San Diego.

Interestingly, while many of the techniques of Gestalt have direct implications for rehabilitation counseling there is little in the literature about its use in the field. Connolly (1974) explored the use of Gestalt techniques in human relations training with rehabilitation clients. Coven (1977, 1979) has suggested ways in which Gestalt procedures may be used with rehabilitation clients and may also influence agency service and delivery systems. He suggests that the Gestalt approach can facilitate a holistic approach to rehabilitation counseling. Jung

(1978) has attempted to translate the components of Gestalt therapy into practice in a rehabilitation context. The present author is aware that Gestalt techniques are practiced in the field and indeed have been taught within the classrooms of several Rehabilitation Counseling Training Programs, but the literature to support its effectiveness both as a training and treatment modality is lacking.

ASSUMPTIONS

The basic constructs of Gestalt therapy that have particular relevance for rehabilitation are stated well by Passons (1975, p. 14):

1. A person is a whole. He is (rather than has) a body, motions, thoughts, sensations and percepts. All of these function interrelatedly.
2. A person is a part of his environment and cannot be understood outside of it.
3. A person is proactive rather than reactive. One determines his own responses to external and internal stimuli.
4. A person is capable of being aware of his sensations, thoughts, emotions, and perceptions.
5. A person through self-awareness is capable of choice and is thus responsible for his covert and overt behavior.
6. A person possesses the ability and resources to live effectively and to restore himself through his own assets. He can govern his own life effectively.
7. A person can only experience himself in the present. The past and future can be experienced only in the now through remembering and anticipating.
8. A person is neither intrinsically good nor bad. Perls does not present a developmental theory of personality as do Freud and Rogers. Rather the person is always in a dynamic balance motivated by the continual striving for homeostasis.

Gestalt therapy makes no assumptions about the impact that a disability might have upon a person. As Gestalt therapy is ahistorical, it makes no assumption about the role of development over the life span as it relates to the area of disablement and subsequent adjustment. The healthy person (physically disabled or not) is seen as the individual who has the capacity to assume personal responsibility and live fully as an integrated individual.

APPLICATIONS

The Nature of Therapy

Persons come to a Gestalt therapist because they are "stuck." Their needs are not being met, and they find life incomplete and often painful. The goals of Gestalt therapy are to help the person deal with his "impasse" (stuckness). Perls suggests that the impasse exists because the person does not fully want to work through it. Even though such impasses involve unsatisfied needs or unfinished business, clients believe that they do not have the power to resolve them and thus keep themselves away from full awareness of themselves and their environment. They have disowned a portion of themselves and their own "responsibility." The goals of therapy then are to teach persons to assume responsibility for themselves and to achieve integration of their lives.

The way we become healthy is by being aware. This awareness is the core of the therapeutic relationship and is born out of an I–Thou encounter between client and counselor. Thus, the counselor's role is to stay aware of the client and to interact with clients so that they may learn. A major technique used in counseling is the use of experimental, at times provoking games that force the client to confront the areas he avoids and resists. The counselor, rather than providing answers or insights, seeks to force the client to work through his impasse. This is often done first by structuring the situation so that the impasse comes into the open, then frustrating the client by refusing to give what is sought, and at the same time demanding that the person work in the now and continue to confront the stuck place. The experimental games the counselor uses are designed to foster the clients' self-awareness, increase their awareness of their impasse, and then help them reintegrate themselves. As George and Cristiani (1981) note, "the last step is the most crucial, for if individuals are stripped of all their defenses and given no new ways of behavior, they will be even more vulnerable to the outside than they were prior to counseling" (p. 78).

Techniques

The techniques used in Gestalt therapy are probably infinite in number. For each technique is an experimental game which the therapist may develop and suit to the particular situation.

Levitsky and Perls (1970, pp. 144–149) have provided a brief description of a number of games. Presented here is a brief overview of several that can be used both in individual and group therapy:

1. *The game of dialogue:* As has been previously noted, problems often arise because of internal conflicts (i.e., polarizations). One way to help the person confront these conflicts is through the use of the "empty chair" technique. In this technique the person carries on a dialogue with a rejected part of self. This dialogue allows both examination of the conflict and reintegration of the warring sides of self.

For the rehabilitation client there may be many such internal conflicts: (a) the able vs. disabled parts of self, (b) the dependent vs. independent sides, (c) the autonomous side vs. the residential side, (d) the parent inside vs. the child inside.

2. *The unfinished business game:* When "unfinished business" is identified, the client is asked to complete it. There are a number of techniques to aid this completion. One is the use of fantasy. For example, in the unresolved grief associated with a loss, the person might be asked to fantasize a lost limb and then to say goodbye to that part of self. This allows the grief to be externalized, and the disavowed feeling to be dealt with. As loss is of primary importance in rehabilitation this technique is most potent for the practitioner.

3. *"I take responsibility":* In this game the counselor asks the client to make a statement(s) of actions and then say "and I take responsibility for it." Some examples are "I feel helpless and I take responsibility for it." "Now I'm gritting my teeth and I take responsibility for it." This requires the person to re-own their thoughts, feelings, and actions. While the technique at first may appear superficial and mechanical, it can yield potent results for the rehabilitation client.

4. *The exaggeration game:* There are many times when the client's unwitting movements or gestures appear to be significant communications (e.g., clenched fist, trembling voice, etc.). The person is asked to exaggerate the movement, gesture, or posture. Repeatedly exaggerating the behavior intensifies the feeling associated with it and makes the inner meaning clear.

5. *"Can you stay with that feeling?":* This technique is used at key moments when the client expresses a feeling or attitude from which he wishes to escape. The counselor focuses upon the feeling and does not allow the client to flee from the unpleasant sensation. This allows the person to confront his fears in the present moment and move beyond them.

Levitsky and Perls (1970, pp. 141–144) suggest that there are certain general principles that are used regardless of the game played. Two of these have been previously noted (i.e., staying in the now and the I–Thou nature of the counseling relationship). Others are:

1. *Personalizing pronouns:* The client is encouraged to take responsibility by using *I, me, my* rather than *it* or *you.* "It–you" talk allows the person to distance himself from the experiences; "I" talk brings him back in contact. For example, note the differences between "It is hot" as compared to "I am hot."

2. *Awareness of present experiences:* This technique invites the person to examine the present moment and his experience of it. Simple and direct questions are used to focus the client on the present moment (e.g., "What are you aware of now?") or requesting the person to complete the phrase "Now I'm aware of . . ."

3. *Converting questions to statements:* Having the person make statements out of his questions can help him re-own his belief system and be responsible for it. For example, note the differences between "Do you really like me?" vs. "I don't think you like me."

As previously noted, the games and techniques used in Gestalt therapy are infinite in number. The only limit is the skill and creativity of the counselor.

Structure of the Interview

Gestalt therapy does not lend itself to examination of structure as do some other counseling models. Each session in Gestalt therapy is an existential encounter in which both the counselor and client "are engaged in calculated risks (experiments) involving a willingness to explore heretofore unknown or forbidden territories" (Simkin, 1979). The person who is working with a Gestalt therapist is aware, at some level, of a state of disbalance. Counseling provides them with a variety of experiments to heighten their awareness, bring polarities into focus, work through feelings, and reach closure (Gilliland et al., 1984). As such, the client initiates the process and determines for himself the time that integration and closure has been reached.

Limitations

Gestalt therapy has been used with a variety of persons in a variety of settings. The techniques, however, should not be used with persons who lack impulse control, who are given to acting out, or who are grossly sociopathic (Shephard, 1970, p. 235). Generally the limitations of Gestalt therapy, as of any other therapy, are more reflective of the skill, training, and experience of the therapist than the population being served. In terms of the physically disabled client the techniques and philosophy of Gestalt therapy seem to have much to offer (Coven, 1977, 1979; Jung, 1978).

RESEARCH AND EVALUATION

The systematic empirical research supporting the efficacy of Gestalt therapy is severely limited. As Simkin (1979) says, "As a group, Gestalt therapists are singularly unimpressed with formal psychodiagnostic evaluation specifically and research methodology in general" (p. 288).

This analysis is borne out particularly in the field of rehabilitation. While Simkin notes that Gestalt therapy has been effectively used with a wide range of somatic complaints (e.g., migraine, ulcerative colitis, spastic neck and back pain), the evidence appears to be anecdotal. Thus, although Coven (1977, 1979) and Jung (1978) are strongly supportive of the use of Gestalt therapy in rehabilitation, little if any research has been reported as to its use in the field. Perhaps this reflects both the disinclination of Gestalt therapists to research the outcomes and the general lack of systematic research in rehabilitation in regard to counseling processes and outcomes.

CONCLUSIONS

Gestalt therapy focuses upon the client's self-integration, self-responsibility, and maximization of the person's capacities. It is an action-oriented form of therapy which places great emphasis upon the counselor/client interaction. The process of Gestalt therapy is similar to the person's basic growth tendency. The therapist helps individuals become aware of their emergent need, facilitates contact so that the need may be met, and then moves to closure.

If the premise is accepted that the goal of rehabilitation is to facilitate the client's movement to his fullest level of functioning, then the Gestalt approach must be taken seriously as an avenue in rehabilitation counseling. Gestalt therapy provides the counselor with tools to allow persons to move toward fuller levels of growth and independence. This encompasses the essence of rehabilitation.

16 A Behavioral Perspective

James M. Rice

In order to provide a reasonable description of the behavioral approach to rehabilitation counseling, a definition of this area and some historical information are required. The terms "behavior modification", "applied behavior analysis", "behavior therapy", and "behaviorism" are all related terms that are often used interchangeably, much to the chagrin of many behavioral psychologists. *Behaviorism* is usually defined as the philosophy of the science of behavior (Skinner, 1969). *Applied behavior analysis* is the application of operant conditioning principles to significant social problems. *Behavior therapy* is the application of behavioral strategies to clinical problems such as anxiety, phobias, and depression. *Behavior modification* is perhaps the most general term, usually defined as the systematic application of behavioral strategies to alter or change behavior. A new term, *cognitive behavior modification,* incorporates both behavior therapy and cognitive therapy in the treatment of clinical problems.

The most confusing distinction appears to be between behavior therapy and applied behavior analysis. Applied behavior analysis is the application of operant conditioning principles originally developed by Thorndike at the beginning of this century (Kazdin, 1978) and further developed by Skinner and many others. Briefly, operant conditioning states that most behavior is learned as a result of the consequences that follow that behavior. A stimulus that follows the behavior and increases the frequency of that response is called a reinforcer, while a stimulus that decreases the frequency of the response is a punisher. Behaviorists emphasize the concept of a *contingency.* If a certain response is consistently (but not necessarily always) reinforced, then this behavior will be acquired and maintained at a level greater than if reinforcement was absent. Applied behavior analysts attempt to analyze these contingencies and to introduce new contingencies of reinforcement in order to promote adaptive, socially significant changes in behavior.

An example of applied behavior analysis in rehabilitation is the use of contingency management in the sheltered workshop. Zimmerman,

Stuckey, Garlick, and Miller (1969) provided verbal praise and token points (which were used to purchase tangible reinforcers) and compared productivity levels to baseline (no treatment) and noncontingent reinforcement (i.e., points were given out regardless of work performance). Zimmerman et al. (1969) found that productivity was much greater when contingent points were provided. Self-monitoring of the client's work performance, which may serve as feedback or to prompt continued work, has also been examined and found to increase vocational performance (Rudrud, Rice, Robertson, & Olson, 1984; Zohn & Bornstein, 1980).

Behavior therapy has its historical roots in classical conditioning, which was discovered by Pavlov. In classical conditioning, an unconditioned (unlearned) response always follows an unconditioned stimulus. For example, stimulation of the patella tendon produces a knee-jerk response. If a previously neutral stimulus is now paired with this unconditional stimulus, after a number of pairings this new stimulus will now elicit the knee-jerk response. This new response can also be unlearned (extinguished) by no longer pairing the unconditioned stimulus with the formerly neutral stimulus.

Early pioneers in behavior therapy (e.g., Joseph Wolpe) believed that many clinical problems were classically conditioned. An excellent example of this is the behavioral treatment of phobias. Using this model, the client with, for example, acrophobia (fear of heights), was once in a situation where fear and anxiety were paired with a neutral stimulus, being up on a ladder or on top of a building. The phobia, while irrational, is maintained because the client avoids the phobic stimulus; hence, extinction of the phobia cannot occur. In behavior therapy, the client is asked to develop a fear hierarchy (Lutzker & Martin, 1981), for example, a list of 20 situations that are rank-ordered from least frightening to most frightening. The client is then placed in a very relaxed state and asked to visualize the *least* frightening situation. This state of relaxation is incompatible with feelings of fear and anxiety, and therefore the phobic reaction is avoided. Ultimately, the client can visualize the phobic stimulus with no anxiety. The therapist then proceeds to have the client visualize the next situation on the hierarchy. This continues until the client can visualize all 20 situations without anxiety. At this point, the client can often approach the phobic stimulus and is "cured."

Part of the confusion with these terms is the mixture of both operant conditioning and classical conditioning techniques in both behavior therapy and applied behavior analysis. In addition, a new term, cognitive behavior modification, stresses the importance of cognitive variables as mediating variables in human behavior. These procedures are beginning to be used in rehabilitation (Crimando, Sawyer, & Poppen, 1984), and the reader desiring further information on this approach should consult Meichenbaum (1977) and Foreyt and Rathjen (1978) for a more in-depth description of cognitive behavior modification and therapy.

The emphasis with this perspective is on *behavior*, and on understanding the role of the environment in producing, maintaining, and decreasing human behavior. The environment consists of both the physical and the social environment. The mind, emotional states, and cognitive variables, while their existence is not questioned, are not used by behaviorists to explain behavior (adherents to cognitive behavior modification are an exception to this). Mentalistic explanations are rejected as being unnecessary. According to behaviorists, they are explanatory fictions (Skinner, 1953) which are convenient to use since mentalistic explanations are impossible to disprove. In addition, traditional developmental theories are also rejected by behaviorists. They do not deny the validity of the descriptions but suggest that environmental contingencies account for the acquisition of the specific behaviors, and not the maturation of the individual or the passage of time. Consequently, the use of developmental metaphors to explain or describe behavior—for example, "growth"—is also rejected.

Since overt behavior is the primary focus of this perspective, it is easy to understand that the behavioral approach also attempts to be objective, data-oriented, and evaluative in nature. Behaviorists attempt to define operationally the relevant behaviors and collect data on the frequency, duration, and/or magnitude of these behaviors. The success or failure of a certain therapy or treatment can be readily evaluated from these data. This objectivity and scientific attitude is fairly unique in a therapeutic discipline that is surrounded by subjective evaluation and "clinical judgment." Behavioral approaches do utilize subjective evaluations, but do so in combination with objective efforts. According to behaviorists, both are required to comprehensively evaluate the impact and applied significance of the problem (Kazdin, 1977; Wolf, 1978).

While the differences between the behavioral approaches are readily apparent, it is important to mention also the similarities in this approach to more traditional humanistic/existential approaches. All of these approaches strive to assist the disabled individual, and to maximize the individual's opportunity for medical, psychosocial, and vocational adjustment. In addition, the behavioral approach usually focuses on changing the behavior of the *individual*, and examining the individual's behavior with respect to his social/physical environment. This emphasis on the individual is shared by all or most of the perspectives in rehabilitation counseling. While the methods in this approach differ substantially from other perspectives, the goals of the approach and its emphasis on the individual represent common interests of all therapeutic perspectives.

Before proceeding to a specific discussion on the applications of behavioral strategies to rehabilitation counseling, a behavior analysis of disability and rehabilitation should be briefly mentioned. The onset of a disability produces limitations; that is, loss. As previously mentioned, reinforcers are contingent upon behavior. The *loss* in a disability is the loss of function, that is, the inability to behave and be subsequently reinforced. These reinforcers are often very subtle but tremendously significant. The blinded individual is denied the opportunity to see (a behavior) a sunset or his loved ones. The paraplegic individual can never walk as he did previously. From a behavioral perspective, disability onset usually produces up to three major obstacles for a comprehensive rehabilitation. They are

1. The need to acquire new behaviors as a result of disability onset; this may include, for example, new methods of ambulation, toileting and grooming, communication, and transportation.
2. The need to re-acquire old behaviors that were lost as a result of disability onset; for example, the stroke patient may need to relearn how to speak because of the expressive aphasia produced by the disability.
3. The need to eliminate aberrant behaviors produced by disability onset; for example, some individuals with closed head injuries often display highly aggressive behaviors that are unacceptable in society and preclude the individual's successful reintegration into the community.

Consequently, rehabilitation is conceptualized as being a problem of educational management (Michael, 1970). Certain behaviors need to be acquired, others re-acquired, and still others need to be decreased or eliminated. (Note: These issues are relevant to individuals who have become adventitiously disabled. Congenitally disabled individuals cannot re-acquire behaviors they have never possessed; however, they do have, in many cases, major deficiencies in their behavioral repertoire and often require additional interventions for inappropriate or maladaptive behaviors.)

Behaviorists also realize that disability onset also produces a number of profound emotional changes. Michael (1970) describes the effect of disability onset as an "emotional catastrophe" (p. 59) and suggests that initially after onset many individuals will not respond to any therapeutic intervention. The loss of reinforcers may be quite traumatic, since the disabled individual is able to understand the implications of the disability almost immediately. The rehabilitation issues of importance here appear to be essentially motivational in nature; that is, how can the individual be motivated to acquire and maintain the behaviors he will need for a successful rehabilitation? Behaviorists view acceptance and self-esteem as the products of increased function and autonomy rather than as cognitive variables required to ensure the rehabilitation process. Again, the critical difference is that the behavioral perspective focuses on changing behaviors that increase vocational potential, ADL skills, as well as the cognitive/affective variables (self-esteem, acceptance, self-confidence), while traditional approaches focus more heavily on the cognitive/affective issues as a prelude to the acquisition of new behaviors. Behavioral rehabilitation counseling can be viewed then as functional, focusing on behavior change and the concomitant changes in emotional and cognitive variables. [Note: An excellent examination of motivational issues in rehabilitation can be obtained by reading Goldiamond (1976).]

BEHAVIORAL APPLICATIONS IN REHABILITATION COUNSELING

The focus of any therapy is to help, to provide needed assistance, guidance, and understanding. Critics of behavioral approaches often point to the limitations of these techniques to rehabilitation counseling, with an emphasis on the word *counseling.* Since rehabilitation counseling has evolved as a verbal, insight-oriented therapy, behavioral techniques are not well suited for this approach. Rehabilitation counseling is essentially verbal because it developed from a humanistic/existential framework. There is no requirement that rehabilitation counseling be only verbal, and in fact rehabilitation counselors emphasize behavioral goals as well as adjustment of issues [cf. Slaney (1977) for a discussion of rehabilitation counseling and "real" therapy].

Behavioral strategies are perhaps an ideal approach to rehabilitation counseling, since they permit the verbal component for the necessary emotional support but also stress the importance of functional skills. This approach also permits the objective evaluation of client outcomes, and the collection of subjective data that is critical in determining the social or clinical significance of the services.

Before proceeding to a more detailed description of applications of behavioral principles in rehabilitation counseling, a brief overview of behavioral counseling is needed. In the mid-1960s, John D. Krumboltz shocked the field of counseling by stating that behavioral strategies should be emphasized. He stated that goals should be specified, target behaviors defined, and progress toward these goals continually assessed. Counseling is defined by Krumboltz (1965) as "whatever ethical activities a counselor undertakes in an effort to help the client engage in those types of behavior which will lead to a resolution of the client's problems" (p. 384). The significance in this definition, as pointed out by Krumboltz (1965), is the emphasis is on the *outcome* of therapy, not the adherence to a specific process. The behavioral counselor (and the rehabilitation counselor, for that matter) is a behavior therapist and an applied behavior analyst. There are numerous articles and a few textbooks on behavioral counseling, and this area continues to develop, although slower than in the previous two decades. The clients seen in the studies published by behavioral counselors have included children, couples with marital problems, and individuals seen in mental health centers. Rehabilitation clients have, for the most part, been excluded from this behavioral counseling literature.

In a brief review of the last 8 to 10 years of three major rehabilitation journals *(Journal of Applied Rehabilitation Counseling, Rehabilitation Counseling Bulletin,* and *Journal of Rehabilitation),* over 40 articles were found that used either a behavioral component or behavioral strategies exclusively. It is both impractical and beyond the scope of this chapter to provide the reader with a comprehensive review of this research literature. Instead three representative research areas will be reviewed.

Certainly the most well-known behavioral strategy in the field of rehabilitation is the Job Club. Nathan H. Azrin and his colleagues have produced a wealth of information on the Job Club and its effectiveness when compared to traditional placement models (Azrin & Besalel, 1980; Azrin, Flores, & Kaplan, 1975; Azrin & Phillip, 1979). The Job Club provides a very systematic approach to job finding. Clients participating in the Job Club spend the entire day searching for job leads, making up job résumés, attending interviews, soliciting job information from friends and relatives, and looking through help-wanted advertisements. Under the supervision of a trained Job Club counselor, clients essentially learn how to place themselves into competitive employment.

The results of this approach have been excellent. Most Job Club studies, even studies using handicapped clients, report job placement rates near 90% (Azrin et al., 1975; Azrin & Phillip, 1980). This compares quite favorably to placement rates of 50 to 60% for traditional placement services. Other more recent studies using strategies similar to the Job Club (Jacobs, Kardashian, Kreinbring, Powder, & Simpson, 1985; Mathews & Fawcett, 1985) have produced comparable results.

Another area where behavioral strategies have been used in rehabilitation counseling is the use of self-management strategies such as deep muscle relaxation. Relaxation strategies include progressive muscle relaxation (Jacobson, 1938) autogenic (self) instructions (Schultz & Luthe, 1969), and biofeedback training (Yates, 1980). For example, the disabled client is asked to tense and relax the various muscle groups of the body. In addition, the client is asked to breathe deeply and is sometimes asked to visualize pleasant scenes (e.g., the beach, the mountains, and so on).

The published research in this area with disabled individuals has focused on individuals with chronic pain (usually low back pain or cancer pain). For example, Dolan, Allen, and Sawyer (1982) outline the basic technique for achieving deep muscle relaxation for patients who suffer from cancer pain. Redd, Anderson, and Minagawa (1982) and Burrish and Lyles (1979) presented results from studies to ameliorate the anticipatory response in cancer chemotherapy. In their studies, they used either progressive relaxation techniques or hypnosis to relax the patient. As a result of these procedures, cancer patients were able to avoid the severe nausea that often occurs prior to receiving chemotherapy, and in some cases the severity of post-chemotherapy nausea and vomiting was diminished.

The final area where behavioral strategies continue to be used is in the sheltered workshop. Usually, the studies in this area emphasize the acquisition of a vocational skill, inceasing the clients' work productivity, or decreasing maladaptive behaviors. The goal of these studies is essentially the same: to increase the probability of employment outside the sheltered workshop. The rehabilitation research literature is replete with these studies (cf. Lutzker, Martin, & Rice, 1981, for a more thorough treatment of this area), and only one example will be provided.

Hourcade and Parette (1985) attempted to determine if verbal prompts, physical guidance (i.e., physically guiding the client through the prescribed task), or both produced the quickest acquisition of a three-piece assembly task. The clients were severely retarded adults. The results of this study indicated that all three procedures produced acquisition of the task, but no single method was more effective than another.

The fact that behavioral strategies have been used successfully with rehabilitation clients does not suggest that further improvement cannot be made. In fact, this area has a number of problems, which should be briefly addressed.

Most of the research studies in behavioral rehabilitation counseling, with the exception of a few studies using stroke or chronic pain patients, have focused on mentally handicapped populations. Obviously, these clients can benefit from behavioral programming. However, this does not preclude the application of this technology to other disability groups as well. In addition, researchers in this area need to pay more attention to the maintenance of the treatment gains and the generalization of these gains to the client's natural environment. Too often rehabilitation professionals assume that the behavior changes that result from treatment will automatically be maintained in the client's home. Often, this is not the case. Consequently, training may need to occur in the environment where the behavior is expected to occur (Stokes & Baer, 1977).

Finally, rehabilitation counselors using behavioral strategies must continually strive to evaluate the client's progress toward his goals. The magnitude of the behavior change must be socially or clinically significant (Kazdin, 1977; Wolf, 1978), and reliance on statistical significance alone is insufficient (Rubin & Rice, 1986).

CONCLUSION

There is no easy way to summarize this broad topic area. Behavioral strategies have been used successfully for many different types of problems faced by rehabilitation clients. This chapter has attempted to briefly explain the basis for these principles, provide a behavior analysis of the rehabilitation process, provide examples of behavioral rehabilitation counseling, and point to both the strengths and weakness of the research in this area.

Individuals interested in learning more about this topic would benefit from reading textbooks on basic learning (Catania, 1984), applied behavior analysis (Kazdin, 1980; Lutzker & Martin, 1981), and behavior therapy (Walker, Hedberg, Clement, & Wright, 1981). In addition, interested individuals are encouraged to examine the professional journals that publish behavioral research. A representative sample of these journals include: *Behavior Modification, Behavioural Psychotherapy, Behavior Therapy, Behaviour Research and Therapy, Journal of Applied Behavior Analysis, Journal of Behavioral Medicine,* and the *Journal of Behavior Therapy and Experimental Psychiatry.*

A final word on behavioral strategies in rehabilitation. In a recent issue of *Journal of Applied Rehabilitation Counseling,* Thomas and

Parker (1984) discussed various counseling interventions. Of behavioral approaches they said: "The question is really not whether to use reinforcement or not (you will anyhow); the question is how to use it in the most effective way possible to help clients meet their objectives" (p. 17). By understanding the basic principles, background, and current use of behavioral techniques, that goal—to help clients achieve their objectives—is more likely to be within the grasp of the rehabilitation counselor.

17 A Rational–Emotive Perspective

Steven S. Ostby

"[Humans] are not disturbed by things but by the views which they take of them."
Epictetus, *The Enchiridon*, 1st century, A.D.

This quote by Epictetus is representative of the philosophical basis of Rational-Emotive Therapy (RET), developed by Albert Ellis. Ellis' first formal presentation of RET was at the American Psychological Association's annual meeting in 1956. Since that time, Ellis and his colleagues at the Institute for Advanced Study in Rational Psychotherapy have continued to develop RET theory and its applications.

BASIC CONCEPTS

A major concept within RET theory is the interaction between human thoughts, emotions and behaviors (Ellis, 1962, 1973, 1977a, 1979d). Simply stated, individuals' thoughts influence their emotions and behaviors; their emotions will impact on their thoughts and actions; and their actions will affect/effect how people think and feel. Further, RET theory holds that humans do not respond directly, either emotionally or behaviorally, to their life experiences. Instead, they precipitate or cause their reactions by how they view or interpret their experience (Ellis, 1979d).

Ellis' famous A-B-C model explains how people's interpretation or evaluation of an event determines their emotional and behavioral response. Beginning with A (an activating experience or activating event) something real occurs within the person's environment, such as experiencing a loss or acquiring a disability.

C represents consequence, and involves the person's emotional or behavioral response to A. For example, a person may experience a disability or disabling event (e.g., sensory impairment, physical impairment) (A) and consequently (C) feel depressed (e.g., loss of appetite, sleep disturbance, withdrawal). Ellis states that most persons erroneously believe that it is the event (A) that makes them feel and act depressed (C). However, according to RET theory it is the person's belief system (B) or view about what has occurred (A) that determines (C) emotion and behavior (Ellis, 1973, 1977a, 1979d).

Further, Ellis (1979a) posits that our belief system (B) consists of both rational and irrational beliefs. When humans experience a dislikable or disagreeable event (such as disability or loss of a loved one), their rational beliefs may take the form of wishes, preferences, wants, and the like. For example, the person may think: "I don't want to have a disability," "I wish I didn't experience this loss," "I don't like having this happen and having others treat me differently." RET views these rational beliefs as leading to appropriate consequences (e.g. regret, disappointment, sorrow, grief) when an experience is unfortunate. If individuals continue to use their rational beliefs, they may be able to engage in behaviors that will minimize or modify the noxious experience (A); or if the situation is permanent, to continue to live with it, without continuing emotional crisis or upheaval.

Problems occur, however, when the person's *irrational beliefs* emerge. Irrational beliefs are commonly absolutist and include *must* and *should* statements. Irrational beliefs regarding disability may include: "This *must* not happen to me, and I *shouldn't* have to experience this," "How *awful* that this happened, I *must* not be like this," "I *can't stand* this," "I am a *rotten person* because I have a disability." These *irrational* beliefs can impact on the individual's emotion and behavior (e.g., chronic depression, anxiety, hostility). Thus, according to RET theory, external events (A) experienced by individuals may significantly contribute to, but do not cause, their response (C); rather their rational or irrational beliefs (B) determine how they feel and act.

To summarize, RET views *rational beliefs* as leading to appropriate emotional and behavioral responses to a negative experience. That is, regret, disappointment, sadness, grief, and their respective behavioral counterparts allow individuals to constructively express their emotion and to act more effectively in attempting to modify their situations. Conversely, *irrational beliefs* contribute to inappropriate or ineffective emotional and behavioral responses, resulting in increased and possibly ongoing emotional pain. It is important to note that RET theory does not hold that an emotionally healthy person never experiences pain or trauma (this would be irrational). Rather,

RET theory centers on why an individual *continues* to experience excessive feelings, and seeks to alleviate those symptoms (inelegant therapy) or to assist clients in restructuring their philosophical framework (elegant therapy). (Elegant and inelegant therapy will be discussed further in the Applications section of this chapter.)

Originally, Ellis (1962) hypothesized that there were 11 basic irrational beliefs. Since then, he has reduced these basic irrational beliefs into three major irrationalities, which Ellis feels all persons believe to some extent, but "which (emotionally) disturbed individuals hold more intensely, extensively, and rigidly" (Ellis, 1979b, p. 3). These are:

1. "I *must* be competent, adequate and achieving, and I *must* win the approval of virtually all the significant people in my life. It is *awful* when I don't. I *can't stand* failing in these all-important respects. I am a *rotten person.*"
2. "Others *must* treat me kindly, fairly, and properly when I want them to do so. It is *terrible* when they don't. I *can't bear* their acting obnoxiously toward me. They are damnable, worthless people when they don't do what they *must* do to treat me satisfactorily."
3. "I need and *must* have the things I really want. The conditions under which I live and the world around me *must* be well ordered, positive, certain, just the way I want them to be. I *must* gratify my desires easily and immediately, without having to deal with too many difficulties or hassles. It is *horrible* when conditions are not this way. . . The world is a rotten place and life is hardly worth living when things are not as they *should* be in this respect." (Ellis, 1979d, pp. 3–4)

RET hypothesizes that the individual who strongly believes in irrationality #1 (I *must* be competent . . .) may experience feelings of worthlessness, depression, inadequacy, or similar emotions. Irrational belief #2 (Others *must* treat me kindly . . .) may result in intense anger, vindictiveness, etc.; and #3 (I need and *must* have the things I really want . . .) contributes to depression, anger, and low frustration tolerance (Ellis, 1979b).

The above briefly outlines the basic concept of RET theory; the application of RET will be presented in the following section. Before proceeding, it may be helpful to consider the tenets of RET in the context of rehabilitation counseling with persons with disabilities. From a theoretical perspective, RET theory is egalitarian in its view of persons with disability. Disabilities (and their many aspects) are viewed as noxious events or problems experienced by the individual. There is no a priori assumption that any disability predisposes the individual to emotional disturbance. Rather, as Ellis explained at the

1979 National Rehabilitation Association convention in Chicago, the person experiencing a reaction (e.g., depression, anger, hostility) to a problem (disability) may create an emotional or psychological difficulty. Thus, a person with a disability is viewed no differently than any other individual experiencing a problem (loss of job, loss of loved one, alienation from family, sexual dysfunction, etc.). Further, persons with disabilities have the same capacity for rational and irrational thinking as others, and if they are experiencing ongoing emotional distress, it is likely they are intensely and extensively holding to an irrational belief. (Note: In the context of this chapter, emotional distress/disturbance/problem refers to an intense, persistent reaction which is causing the client ongoing emotional or behavioral difficulty. It would be *irrational* to assume that any individual, with or without disability, *never* experiences intense negative emotions, or *never* experiences persistent negative emotions. RET, as viewed by this author, is concerned with ongoing or recurring reactions that are disruptive to the individual.)

In its general form and approach, RET is similar to other cognitive learning therapies (Mahoney & Arnkoff, 1978). It shares commonalities with Cognitive Therapy (Beck, 1976), Multimodal Therapy (Lazarus, 1976), and Cognitive Behavior Modification (Mahoney, 1976; Meichenbaum, 1977a).

APPLICATIONS

Ellis (1979c) states that RET is an appropriate mode of therapy for a wide variety of problems, including moderate anxiety or maladjustment, marital and sexual difficulties, neuroticisms, character disorders, offenders of all ages, borderline psychosis and overt psychosis (if still somewhat in contact with reality), persons with mild mental retardation experiencing emotional difficulties, and psychosomatic disorders. However, Ellis feels that RET is not indicated for use with persons who are not in contact with reality, seriously brain-injured, autistic, highly manic, or with moderate to severe mental retardation (Ellis, 1979c). This suggests that RET may be appropriate with individuals who retain some ability to perceive reality accurately and who are able to understand the concept of the relationship between thoughts, feelings, and behavior (e.g., if I think this way, I end up feeling and acting in certain ways). Thus, it appears that RET may be useful in rehabilitation counseling with a wide variety of clientele. However, rehabilitation counselors should give careful consideration prior to initiating RET themselves or referring a client for RET (or any other type of counseling). To paraphrase Paul (1967): What treatment (therapy) given by which therapist will facilitate what result for this specific client with this specific problem?

The *major goal* of counseling in RET is "minimizing the client's central, self-defeating outlook and acquiring a more realistic, tolerant philosophy of life" (Ellis, 1979c, p. 205). As stated earlier, RET may be practiced in both an inelegant and elegant mode, each having different goals for the counselor. Inelegant RET may focus on symptom reduction as its goal, with the client increasing rational responses and decreasing irrational responses. The goal of elegant RET is the restructuring of the client's philosophical framework, disputing the client's irrational beliefs and having the client internalize this into his belief system. In counseling persons with disabilities (and persons without disabilities) elegant therapy is the preferred mode of treatment. While Ellis (1976) believes that humans are innately rational and irrational, he also hypothesizes that many irrational beliefs are held and/or generated by the person's social or cultural environment (e.g., we *must* be physically fit and attractive, successful, popular) (Ellis, 1962, 1973, 1977a, 1979d). Given the negative beliefs and attitudes toward persons with disabilities in society (English, 1971; Schneider & Anderson, 1980), elegant RET (disputing these irrational attitudes) may assist individuals with their psychosocial adjustment.

The relationship between counselor and client, and their respective roles in the counseling process, are well defined within RET. The counselor's role is one of a teacher in a rational problem-solving relationship. Further, the counselor strives for good rapport and accepts the client unconditionally. While counselors are warm and caring, they are not concerned with winning the client's approval, and assume a vigorous, active-directive and risk taking role (Ellis, 1973). Crucial to the client's role is a willingness to admit and to accept responsibility for irrational beliefs and a commitment to hard work and practice throughout the counseling process (Ellis, 1979c).

The sequence of the RET process begins with the counselor exploring and identifying, with the client, the irrational belief and the relationship of irrational ideas to emotional and behavioral response. Next, the counselor assists the client in understanding that by continuing to believe this irrationality, the client is perpetuating the emotional distress. Once the client understands and accepts this, the counselor focuses on having the client dispute or change the irrational belief. Finally, after the irrational beliefs are disputed, the counselor focuses on having the client generalize from this experience and develop a more rational philosophy of life (Patterson, 1973). Throughout this counseling process, RET utilizes a variety of cognitive, emotive, and behavioral techniques.

Cognitive Techniques

The cognitive techniques used in RET include disputing of irrational beliefs, cognitive homework, and many others. The process of disputing irrational beliefs generally begins with the counselor's educating the client in the basic A-B-Cs of RET as described earlier. Once the client understands that his irrational beliefs have an impact on feelings, the next step is to assist the client in disputing this irrationality. For example, consider a client who has interviewed for a job but was not employed, and experiences anxiety, depression, or worthlessness, which impacts on or interferes with further job-seeking behavior (too anxious to interview for other jobs, performs poorly in interviews due to anxiety, depression, or anger). In this case, where the client experiences intense, ongoing emotion that impacts on job-seeking behavior, it is likely that the individual is catastrophizing and holding irrational beliefs. Rational beliefs might include: "I wish I would have gotten the job," "I don't like getting rejected by employers," "It's annoying and unfortunate to have to keep looking for a job." These types of beliefs and self-statements may result in emotions such as regret, irritation, disappointment, or sorrow, and lead to positive behaviors (e.g., continuing the job search, increasing interview skills). However, the client who is experiencing anxiety, depression, etc., is not focusing on rational beliefs or self-statements but on irrational beliefs such as: "It's awful that I didn't get that job," "I can't stand being rejected by employers for a job," "I am a terrible worthless person because I didn't get the job." Once the client and counselor have identified the specific irrational belief which is contributing to the emotional reaction, they begin to systematically dispute the belief, by asking and answering questions about the belief. The client is led by the counselor to dispute the irrationality in the following fashion:

> "Why is it awful not to get that job? It's not. It's frustrating, unfortunate, and unpleasant, maybe even obnoxious. The more I say it's awful, the worse I feel. If I see it as inconvenient, it won't stop me from continuing to look for other jobs—unless I let it." "Where is the proof that I can't stand being rejected? There is none, I have stood it. I may not like it, but I can stand it." "Why am I a terrible, worthless person? I'm not. Maybe I didn't have the skills to get the job and I have some unfortunate traits, but that doesn't make me terrible!"

Thus, by systematically analyzing and disputing the irrationalities with the client, and by having the client practice systematically disputing them on a daily basis, the belief is rejected or at least weakened. In this fashion, the client then begins focusing on rational rather than irrational beliefs or self-statements.

Cognitive homework is used extensively in RET and ranges from the note taking of internal sentences during unpleasant events to using report forms which identify the experience, irrational sentences, negative emotions, disputing techniques, and outcomes. In the present example the client might be asked to write down all of the self-statements following the next job interview, or in a mock interview situation. These irrational beliefs can then be systematically disputed (Ellis, 1979a). Other cognitive techniques include bibliotherapy, using RET with others, and employing new self-statements.

Emotive Techniques

Emotive techniques in RET include unconditional acceptance, role playing, modeling, rational-emotive imagery, and shame-attacking exercises (Ellis, 1979a, c). Acceptance, role playing, and modeling are relatively common techniques and therefore will not be discussed here. However, rational-emotive imagery and shame-attacking exercises appear to be fairly unique to RET practice. Somewhat similar to imagery in other therapeutic interventions (e.g., systematic desensitization) rational-emotive imagery involves the client imagining the anxiety or anger producing situations, feeling the emotional consequence, and then systematically disputing the irrational belief precipitating the reaction. The client then focuses on the change of emotion brought about by disputing the belief and changing the self-statements. The client in the above example would be asked to imagine a job interview and, focusing on emotions and self-statements, dispute the irrational belief and notice any emotional change. In this fashion the client may learn the relationship between thoughts and emotions.

Shame-attacking exercises (Ellis & Abrahms, 1978) are also given as homework assignments to aid in the disputing of the client's irrational beliefs. Ellis believes that shame contributes to many emotional disturbances in that clients may feel humiliated or foolish when they act in a manner that others will not approve of (or that clients believe others won't approve of) and consequently believe they are worthless or foolish people. These assignments may be as simple as having the client refuse to tip a waiter or returning imperfect food in a restaurant. By completing these assignments clients learn (with the counselor's assistance) that others may not be as shocked or interested in these behaviors as had previously been supposed. It is important, however, that the shame-attacking not put the client at risk legally, physically, or psychologically, and that the rehabilitation counselor use common and professional sense prior to assigning a client an exercise.

Behavioral Techniques

RET also utilizes several behavioral techniques throughout the counseling process (Ellis, 1979a). RET frequently employs operant conditioning/self-reinforcement methods to aid the client in attempting a noxious task. Clients are instructed in self-reinforcement techniques prior to a homework assignment, and consequently reward their own behavior upon completion of the task. For example, a client experiencing anxiety in social situations may reward himself or herself with a pleasant or enjoyable experience they have identified previously, after initiating a conversation.

Another behavioral method used in RET is relaxation training. Ellis (1979a) views relaxation as "healthfully distracting" when clients wish to stop worrying. However, Ellis states that these techniques offer only temporary relief as they do not directly undermine the client's irrational belief system. Thus, within RET, relaxation is viewed as a positive skill for the client to obtain but not as a therapeutic end in itself.

Finally, RET includes skill training as a therapeutic method. The type of skill training employed in counseling relates directly to the client's deficit (e.g., social, assertiveness, vocational, sexual, marital). Through skill training, the client may be able to have some impact on A (the activating event) in the A-B-C structure. In the job example cited earlier, the client may benefit from job-seeking skills training, and thereby integrate that thinking and behaving rationally have a positive impact on emotions.

In summary, RET uses a wide variety of counseling techniques with the goal of assisting the client to dispute irrational beliefs and develop a more tolerant philosophy of living. The diversity may be viewed as a strength regarding the practice of RET, allowing the client and counselor to affect cognition, emotion, and behavior during the counseling process. However, this diversity of technique presents potential problems in validating the underlying theory of RET.

RESEARCH

Ellis (1979b) cites hundreds of studies in support of the theoretical principles and practical applications of RET. Further, in Gottman and Markham's (1978, p. 26) presentation of Glass and Smith's Meta-analysis, RET compared favorably to other counseling approaches in terms of client outcome. It would appear from the existing literature that RET is a relatively effective mode of counseling. However, a problem in validating the principles of RET, and possibly its treatment regime, results from the multiple methods used with the RET process. When clients are involved in disputing irrational beliefs, cognitive homework, bibliotherapy, unconditional acceptance, role play, modeling, imagery, self-reinforcement, skill training, and other counseling techniques, it is difficult to separate the effects of one technique versus another. Many of the methods used in RET are also included in other types of cognitive therapies (e.g., Bandura, 1977; Beck, 1976; Maultsby, 1984; Meichenbaum, 1977a). Recent research cited in Hoffman (1984), Kendall and Hollon (1979) and Reda and Mahoney (1984) provides empirical support for a variety of cognitive therapies. Thus, as a whole, cognitive therapy approaches, including RET appear to be useful and effective counseling modalities.

The following sources may be helpful to the rehabilitation counselor interested in RET and other cognitive approaches:

Beck, A. T. (1976). *Cognitive therapy and the emotional disorders.* New York: International Universities Press.

Ellis, A. & Greiger, R. (Eds.) (1977). *Handbook of rational-emotive therapy.* New York: Springer.

Ellis, A. & Abrahms, E. (1978). *Brief psychotherapy in medical and health practices.* New York: Springer.

Ellis, A. & Harper, R. (1979). *A new guide to rational living.* N. Hollywood, CA: Wilshire Book Co.

Ellis, A. & Whitely, J. (Eds.) (1979). *Theoretical and empirical foundations of rational-emotive therapy.* Monterey, CA: Brooks/Cole.

Mahoney, M. J. (1976). *Cognition and behavior modification.* Cambridge, MA: Ballinger.

Maultsby, M. C. (1984). *Rational behavior therapy.* Englewood Cliffs, NJ: Prentice Hall.

Meichenbaum, D. (1977). *Cognitive behavior modification: An integrative approach.* New York: Plenum Press.

18 Reality Therapy in Rehabilitation Counseling

Joseph N. Ososkie
Joseph O. Turpin

Equipped with the proper therapeutic tools, the rehabilitation counselor will be prepared to effectively encounter the problems associated with adjustment to severe disability. It is to this end that the principles of William Glasser's Reality Therapy are introduced. His concepts of commitment, responsiblity, and involvement (Glasser, 1965) are integral in the rehabilitation of clients who have disabilities. The forthcoming approach may be added to the counselor's existing repertoire of therapeutic techniques employed when working with clients regarding the facilitation of independence.

The strength of Reality Therapy lies in individual client goal attainment where personal self-worth is accomplished. Individual rather than normative successes are congruent with rehabilitation philosophy and outcome measurement. Responsibility, or the ability to fulfill needs without interfering with anmother person's ability to do the same, is a fundamental concept of Reality Therapy. "The crux of the theory is personal responsibility for one's own behavior, which is equated with mental health" (Glasser & Zunin, 1973, p. 287). Clients must learn in counseling that there are responsible alternatives in the fulfillment of needs. A person who is recently physically injured and has begun to depend upon alcohol as a means of adjusting to a new life with a disability would benefit from learning alternative ways of adjusting. The continued use of alcohol in this case would gradually isolate the client and reduce chances of involvement. The choice of alcohol may interfere with the need fulfillment of family members who have become straddled with financial and care responsibilities of the person who has a disability. These situations can be met by rehabilitation efforts and personal responsibility, not by introducing alcohol dependence.

PERSONALITY THEORY

Glasser is not concerned with the actual symptomatology employed by an individual. Whether a person has a problem of depression, drug addiction or resistance toward psychological adjustment to physical disability, the core problem is the same. "We believe that, regardless of how he [or she] expresses his [or her] problem, everyone who needs psychiatric treatment suffers from one basic inadequacy: he [or she] is unable to fulfill his [or her] essential needs" (Glasser, 1965, p. 5). The single, basic, psychological need required by all individuals is the establishment of an identity. An identity develops from being loved and loving, and from feeling worthwhile and being perceived as worthwhile by another. This idea may initially appear amorphous. However, the essential quality is involvement with others. Involvement reduces isolation and facilitates interaction with the environment as well as persons in the environment. A person who has a disability is faced with environmental factors that may hinder the ease with which involvement occurs. An example would be social prejudice toward the disabled. Stigma, an attribute that is deeply discrediting (Goffman, 1963), has personal and social implications for a person with a disability in establishing an identity. The reality of these circumstances must be recognized and confronted by the individual. Essentially, involvement reduces the isolation of the person with a failure identity and increases environmental interaction as in the person with a success identity.

Rehabilitation counselors encounter clients who have failure identities. They may either ignore or deny reality (Glasser & Zunin, 1973). A person who has epilepsy may ignore the symptomatological reality of this invisible disability. On the other hand, a person may deny reality in the form of emotional disturbance. Glasser (1965) contends that "therapy will be successful when they are able to give up denying the world and recognize that reality not only exists but that they must fulfill their needs within its framework" (p. 6). Clients must learn to face the reality of a disability and live within its framework. DeLoach and Greer (1981) explain the incorporation of stigma into the self-concept in similar terms. "Stigma isolation" (p. 219) keeps disability-related stress outside the individual. "Stigma recognition" (p. 219) incorporates the disability into the self-concept. A disability is thus evaluated in terms of its meaning in the person's life. Responsibility for dealing with stigma is in the hands of the client. Disabilities will not be used as excuses for dependence. This concept is in line with Glasser's rejection of a psychiatric diagnosis. Labeling promotes sick behavior, and responsibility is given up to the expert hands of the helping professional.

The goal of the individual in all cases is to reduce pain and to increase pleasure. People reduce pain in a positive way by giving and receiving love, giving and receiving worth and recognition, becoming self-disciplined, and having fun. Pain is reduced in a negative manner by giving up, denying failure, or finding pleasure in failure. Along a continuum with extremes of strength and weakness, individuals may be described by the following: a rational person, positively addicted; a security person, concerned with the base needs of the Maslow hierarchial conception; a give-up person, given up on themselves such as in regard to living effectively with multiple sclerosis; a symptom person, destructive acting out behavior such as physical abuse; and a negatively addicted person, addicted to alcohol, gambling, or food. Glasser (1976) describes the steps to positive and negative addictions. Positive addiction involves non-competitiveness, self-belief, persistence, and not being self-critical in an activity performed daily. Learning to be non-critical will be beneficial to a client with a disability who has experienced failure. Activities should be initially measured in terms of personal success in order to build a success identity. Being critical will reinforce failure. In contrast, steps to negative addiction usually start with giving up when failure is experienced regularly. Next, a person, according to Glasser, chooses a symptom such as back pain or hallucinations. These symptoms typically relieve the individual of personal responsibility. Finally, pain is reduced through negative addiction. Counseling needs to be directed at helping clients accept responsibility by teaching positive ways to succeed in pain reduction.

Rehabilitation efforts should be geared toward independence, requiring people who have disabilities to do what they are capable of doing. This should be implemented early in order that the client does not become dependent upon the rehabilitation setting. Leventhal and Hirschman (1982) define three levels of prevention that apply to Reality Therapy's impact on rehabilitation. Primary prevention is aimed at halting disease before it occurs. Secondary prevention is concerned with detecting early signs of a disease in order to stop the disease process. Typically, rehabilitation efforts are directed at tertiary prevention or restoration to optimal functioning. Employing Reality Therapy principles in primary and secondary prevention would help stop the spread of psychological problems related to physical disability. In a positive sense, treatment would be attempted with a psychologically healthy person who has a physical disability. Otherwise, clients are not usually identified until they are defined as symptom persons. Psychological prevention can be addressed along with physical rehabilitation for the psychologically healthy, physically disabled individual.

Compared to Other Perspectives

Reality Therapy differs from traditional insight oriented therapies. Transference is in contrast to involvement.

> Rather than reinforcing the development of transference phenomenon and then analyzing the so-called transference, the reality therapist attempts in every way possible to present himself [herself] as a genuine, concerned, real person, helping the patient face reality, understand reality and accept reality. (Glasser & Zunin, 1973, p. 293)

It is more critical in Reality Therapy that the counselor relates as a person and not as a transference figure. The more person-centered conditions of genuiness, respect, concreteness, and empathy (Egan, 1975) are important in conveying client self-worth through involvement with the therapist.

The difference between Reality Therapy and conventional therapy (psychodynamic) goes beyond an issue of transference. Mental illness is better described as irresponsibility. Since a very small percentage of it is related to a biochemical etiology. Past experiences and insights into the unconscious are dismissed as not being crucial to successful outcome. Value judgments about one's behavior and making plans and commitments to them are not part of conventional psychiatric treatment. In sum, "Traditional psychiatry reinforced maladaptive behavior by voyeuristically attending to the negative aspects of personality" (Leblanc, 1976, p. 15). Positive characteristics of the client are highlighted toward the goal of establishing a success identity in the Reality Therapy perspective.

Mowrer's Integrity Therapy is in line with the value judgement concept of Reality Therapy. He indicates that psychological problems do not result from attempts to live up to a moral code, but when individuals do not live up to their own moral convictions (Glasser & Zunin, 1973). Making a value judgment about one's behavior is considered to be critical by Glasser. Mainord held patients responsible for their behavior and found that "crazy" behavior was extinguished if it was not reinforced in therapy. Abraham Maslow (1954) believed, as did Glasser, in the self-actualizing potential of the individual. Belief in the client's ability to change is important in conveying worthiness and fostering a success identity.

The perspective of Reality Therapy has been called a blend of Trait and Factor Theory, Rational Emotive Therapy, and Existential Humanistic Psychology with an emphasis on client responsibility (Ivey & Simek-Downey, 1980). Glasser does not deny these similarities. Rozsnafszky (1974) proposes that "Adler is the unrecognized father of two important trends in current therapeutic thinking: the stress on appropriate, realistic behavior, rather than insight, as the criterion of mental health; and, a renewed belief in the patient's responsibility for his [or her] behavior" (p. 65). She compares Rational Emotive Therapy, Transactional Analysis, and Reality Therapy to an Adlerian approach. Adler does attend to goals, inferiority feelings, and social reality. These are similar to Reality Therapy's concepts of plans, failure identity, and reality.

EVOLUTION

Antecedents

Reality Therapy is a common sense set of principles with precursors interested in equality with patients and a philosophy that focused on health rather than disease. Notable personalities include Paul DuBois, a Swiss physician; Jules Dejerine; and Joseph Pratt, an American innovator of group psychotherapy (Glasser & Zunin, 1973). Abraham Low was also interested in low-cost common-sense treatment for those with psychiatric problems.

Development

Glasser developed Reality Therapy after dissatisfaction with conventional psychiatric treatment while a psychiatric resident in Los Angeles under Dr. G. L. Harrington. Harrington was supervised by Helmuth Kaiser who was interested in genuine communication. Harrington and Glasser implemented the concepts of Reality Therapy at the Veterans Administration Neuropsychiatric Hospital in West Los Angeles on a ward of patients diagnosed as chronically psychotic. Glasser became consulting psychiatrist at the Ventura School for Girls and obtained positive results similar to those experienced at the VA Hospital. Leonard Zunin employed the principles of Reality Therapy at Camp Pendleton Naval Hospital when working with Vietnam War widows. He stressed a focus on the present and the future and not the past. This may be likened to Logotherapy's emphasis on moving ahead after a significant and devastating life event.

Currently, training courses are available at the Institute for Reality Therapy and the Educator Training Center. Present interest is centered more on prevention than tertiary rehabilitation. Promotion of a success identity early in the life of a child in the schools where a failure identity is usually exacerbated (Glasser, 1969) will help alleviate some rehabilitation needs.

THERAPEUTIC PRINCIPLES/STEPS

Reality Therapy concentrates on individual strengths, attributes, and potentials (Glasser & Zunin, 1979). It links these traits with current behaviors and experiences in an effort to develop a success perspective in life. The eight principles contained within Reality Therapy are appropriate in a wide variety of rehabilitation settings and applicable to individuals with diverse disabilities.

Personal Involvement

The personal communication of a caring attitude by the counselor is essential to the client's ability to succeed. This focus permits a decrease of interest in the client's misery and an increase of interest in involvement with the client's success-identified activities (Glasser, 1965).

The rehabilitation counselor in a sheltered employment setting assisting the worker provides an excellent opportunity for fostering involvement. Within such a setting, the counselor can demonstrate the attitudes of warmth, understanding, and concern in the context of current work activities. It is not necessary to rely upon the worker's difficulties, but discussion can incorporate activities of interest to either the counselor or worker. Being personal implies that the rehabilitation counselor cares, follows through, and works hard to help the client achieve success in terms of mutually agreed upon goals.

Focus on Present Behavior Rather than Feelings

It is important to understand the theory's focus on present behavior. In the cycle of behavior, affect, and cognition, Glasser contends that people have most control over behavior. A person's cognition and affect are not ignored nor denied existence, but change will be more readily effected if counseling efforts are concentrated on behavior.

Glasser believes that it is easier to order oneself to do than to convince oneself to feel better.

Focus on the Present

It is the task of counseling to concentrate on current life behaviors with the idea that past events cannot be changed. In counseling, if the past is discussed it is always related to the present. Prior events may be used by the counselor and client to discuss alternative behaviors which may have led to more success. When the counselor discusses difficulties arising from the client's behavior, the focus is on why there were not more serious problems resulting from the behavior than actually occurred. The counselor assesses the positive skills and attributes currently available to the client. These positive traits are utilized in developing a successful plan of action.

The rehabilitation counselor generally is working with a series of goals. Primary among these goals is that of vocational re-entry. As a counselor utilizing the Reality Therapy process, the focus is on the client's current strengths and attributes which can be used to build a successful vocational re-entry plan.

Value Judgment

Glasser believes the client must evaluate behavior in relationship to its contribution to failure. No real behavior changes occur unless the individual realizes the behavior is irresponsible. Such a value judgment cannot be made from the client's standpoint alone but should include significant others (Bassin, 1976). The counselor does not make value judgments for the client, since this would deny responsibility for one's actions.

Planning

A major part of the rehabilitation counseling process utilizing Reality Therapy is helping the client formulate a detailed plan to change failure behavior into success behavior. In order for the plan to be successful, the counselor must have expertise in areas specific to the client's difficulties. Since each counselor's experience is limited, a Reality Therapy counselor guides the client to appropriate sources, making use of experts in specific areas as the needs of the client indicate. It is better to have a plan that is too simple than one that is too complex with the risk of failure. Putting the plan in writing, such as with a contract, reduces the possibility of misunderstanding.

Additionally, the plan is not viewed by the rehabilitation counselor as an absolute solution, but rather as demonstrating to the client the multiple approaches available in meeting life's problems. The written plan, like a marked travel route on a map, is the way that the client is going to proceed to the goal. It is clearly recognized that if the plan does not work, regardless of the roadblock, alternatives are available for reaching success.

Commitment

Commitment to a plan allows the client to assume responsibility for the outcome. This is most effective when the commitment is in front of others (Hoppe, 1976). For this reason the involvement of the counselor is critical as the client takes initial steps toward commitment in a non-punitive atmosphere.

No Excuses

The rehabilitation counselor using Reality Therapy is not concerned with why the plan failed since not all commitments an individual makes can be achieved. Glasser is more interested in assisting the client to develop a new plan or modify the old one. Such re-working is seen as beneficial when the objective is a new commitment to achieving a plan which stands a greater change of success. The counselor avoids blaming but does not accept excuses. Concern is not focused on why the plan did not work, but rather when the critical behavior targeted for change is going to be accomplished (Glasser, 1965).

Eliminate Punishment

Central to the accomplishment of success for the client is the belief that punishment as a method of changing behavior works poorly on the client with a failure identity (Glasser, 1965). The rehabilitation counselor is alert to utilizing non-punitive statements. Any negative statement by the counselor becomes punishment and further reinforces the existing failure identity of the client.

The four concepts of planning, commitment, accepting no excuses, and elimination of punishment are focal principles of Reality Therapy when counseling in rehabilitation settings. Although the rehabilitation counselor may ascribe to each principle separately, the value of Reality Therapy is that the principles must be used together for the process to have its full impact.

APPLICATIONS

The principles of planning, commitment, no excuses, and eliminating punishment can be most effectively illustrated in rehabilitation by considering the vocational rehabilitation counselor in the state-federal rehabilitation agency. The plan could be likened to the Individual Written Rehabilitation Plan (IWRP). The planning is flexible, but should be mutually agreed upon. The client's and counselor's commitment to working together enhances the client's self-worth. Commitment to the plan by the client is demonstrated by agreeing to the IWRP. Commitment of the counselor to the client may be tested as the client may fear giving up the dependent relationship when the counselor encourages responsibility, and as self-punishment due to perceived guilt over unworthiness of counselor commitment. The genuineness of the counselor cannot be overemphasized as being important in working with this client group.

The rehabilitation counselor accepts no excuses for why the client did not complete the plan. Instead the counselor's task is to alter the old plan which will lead to a successful change of behavior. Part of the Reality Therapy process is that the natural consequences of the client's actions are not interferred with by the counselor (Bassin, 1976). If the vocational rehabilitation counselor has set up an interview for the client with a prospective employer and the client fails to make the appointment, the reason why is not of significance to the counselor. The employer, however, may refuse to make a new appointment with the client, and a job may be lost.

The goal of counseling is individual responsibility. Regardless of prior experiences, clients are responsible for their actions now. The client is thus held responsible for behavior, and the counselor is not manipulated into accepting or making excuses for irresponsible behavior.

RESEARCH

Although there have been no longitudinal studies on the significance of the effectiveness of Reality Therapy, outcome research is not discouraged. Glasser and Zunin (1973) view the evaluation of therapeutic effectiveness as not meaningful due to the lack of criterion measurement sophistication. Glasser reports positive outcomes. He relates success in industrial settings, schools, and private individual therapy. Statistics from the Ventura School for Girls indicate that recidivism was significantly reduced following use of Reality Therapy. English reported that Reality Therapy was effective in reducing disciplinary problems, increasing academic performance, and enhancing teacher involvement with each other, with students, and with the school system (Glasser & Zunin, 1979).

Hawes (1971) noted the success of Reality Therapy on minority students' belief in self-responsibility versus powerlessness, self-concept, and classroom behavior. Third- and sixth-grade pupils from two schools were included in the study. Results indicated that the experimental school program utilizing Glasser's principles significantly affected the subjects' beliefs in internal locus of control for success and failure. Significant increases for the experimental group were found in on-task behavior, information seeking and processing behavior, behaviors related to personal interaction, teacher-child contacts, child-related interactions, and reduction in compliance behaviors of subjects (Glasser & Zunin, 1979).

Future research efforts using a Reality Therapy perspective might incorporate outcome measures related to independent living or competitive employment. It would be helpful to investigate the effectiveness of Reality Therapy principles used at a comprehensive rehabilitation facility where all staff are instructed in this type of treatment. And finally, future research may be directed at considering the success of this perspective on specific disability groups. This would be aimed at showing its effectiveness over other approaches rather than highlighting differences among individuals with disabilities.

RESOURCES

Bassin, A., Bratter, T. E., & Rachin, R. L. (1976). *The reality therapy reader.* New York: Harper & Row.

Glasser, W. (1961). *Mental health or mental illness?* New York: Harper & Row.

Glasser, W. (1972). *The identity society.* New York: Harper & Row.

Glasser, W. (1981). *Stations of the mind.* New York: Harper & Row.

Zunin, L. M., & Zunin, N. (1972). *Contact: The first four minutes.* Los Angeles: Nash Publishing.

19 Trait-Factor Approach to Counseling: Revisited and Reapplied

Patricia Schmitt and Bruce Growick

HISTORICAL PERSPECTIVE

At the beginning of this century, Frank Parsons (1909) proposed the first major theory of vocational counseling. His simplistic approach rested on the assumption that people have different traits and that occupations require a particular combination of worker characteristics. The objective of vocational guidance, according to Parsons, was to match a person's traits with these worker characteristics. Parsons provided the impetus for research and continued expansion of vocational counseling theory based on a trait-factor approach.

In the 1930s Donald Paterson (in Paterson, Gerken, & Hahn, 1941) expanded upon Parsons' work and began to develop psychometric instruments at the Minnesota Stabilization Research Institute that could evaluate both the person and the job. These instruments were designed to measure individual differences that could be used in an actuarial approach to counseling. The process yielded empirical, statistical relationships of client characteristics and job requirements so that probability statements could be formulated.

The overall popularization of the trait and factor approach (often referred to as the Minnesota point of view) to counseling can be credited to E. G. Williamson (1965). It was Williamson who followed up on Paterson's development of tests and continually worked to refine the conceptual base of counseling according to the trait-factor approach. Indeed, during the 1950s and 1960s Williamson was prolific in his contributions to counseling theory. Much of his work, along with the pioneering efforts of Parsons and Paterson, influenced the post–World War II theories of counseling. Holland, Roe, Super, Tiedeman, and others initiated efforts to build concepts dealing with the motivations behind vocational decisions, developmental stages of vocational counseling, and the processes and outcomes involved in the exploration and selection of a career or occupation (Bordin, 1968).

In its inception, the trait-factor approach was a useful theoretical base for vocational counseling. After the 1950s, however, there was a recognized need to expand this simple method of matching a person's traits with the factors of an occupation. Career and vocational counselors began to integrate developmental stages in the individual's life, and extraordinary or unusual conditions outside the normative dimension of traits and factors into their conceptual base, such as disability and multiple career moves. Investigation of individual motivation, drive, values, family, and occupational history was also taken into consideration and incorporated by those who expanded on the trait-factor approach.

As we near the end of this century, the trait-factor approach as originally defined by Parsons, Paterson, and Williamson appears to be no longer adequate to serve individuals in today's world of work. The purpose of this chapter, therefore, is to examine not only the origins of trait-factor rehabilitation counseling, but also the usefulness and limitations of this approach. Recommendations for the modification and expansion of this theoretical base will also be presented.

BASIC ASSUMPTIONS

Parsons (1909) laid the groundwork for vocational counseling in his identification of a trait-factor theory of obtaining a sound knowledge of one's personality, abilities, skills, and limitations combined with an understanding of the demands and rewards of various types of work. Under Williamson's direction, the Minnesota point of view was constantly evolving and expanding as new information and changes in counseling psychology and the world of work were occurring. In establishing his theoretical base, Williamson paid particular attention to the nature of human development, the dimensions and techniques of effective counseling relationships, as well as the characteristics and objectives of successful counselor/client relationships.

Williamson (1965) presented a rational, logical, and educational framework to vocational counseling which he called personalism, or a concern with the whole individual. Diagnosis represented the efforts of the counselor in determining whether a client was operating on misinformation in the decision-making process. Assessing a client's aptitudes and testing their degree of consonance with some contemplated choice of training and vocation was viewed as a primary role of the counselor (Bordin, 1968).

Trait-factor represents the psychology of individual differences (trait psychology, trait measurement, differential psychology, actuarial/factorial approach) in occupational choice. It is operationalized through the development of psychometric tests to measure human traits, or unique patterns of capabilities and potentialities as they are correlated with an explicit set of factors (qualities) that are needed for success in a given job category (Wright, 1980). The Minnesota point of view attempts to apply a scientific approach to counseling by its use of measurement and prediction. The process consists of gathering objective information about a client, synthesizing the data into a diagnosis, and predicting outcomes (prognosis) from that data through a program of action. Essentially this scientific model involves a three-step sequence—diagnosis, treatment (plan of action), and prognosis (prediction).

The essence of the trait-factor approach is matching of individual traits to occupational environments based on the belief that individuals differ along measurable but stable dimensions and that jobs differ along the same dimensions. In trait-factor counseling, clients generally have personal problems solved or under control, but they need specific information about themselves and about occupations. They expect the counselor to assist and guide in the appraisal of personal and occupational data for making a career or job choice. Counseling centers around "information-giving" and "information receiving."

The general assumptions of trait factor counseling are (a) each person is keyed to a few correct occupations; (b) without vocational assistance, the individual wastes not only time and motion but also risks selecting an inappropriate occupation; (c) correct occupations influence other personal decisions over a period of time; (d) occupation and subsidiary decisions remain constant; (e) trait-factor provides descriptive information about a variety of relevant aspects of life; (f) life is generally predictable; (g) trait-factor establishes a base for client action and provides a large number of useful comparisons (Paterson, 1973).

LIMITATIONS AND SHORTCOMINGS

As career and vocational counseling theories began to incorporate developmental and decision-making components in a more extensive consideration of personality and occupational variables, the trait and factor model drew criticism. In particular, developmental career theorists like Super, Roe, and Tiedeman judged the trait-factor approach as inadequate and limited. Attention to the shortcomings of the trait-factor approach helped establish a new philosophical base for vocational guidance. Simple applications of trait-factor also came under scrutiny and attack as information became more abundant and technology improved in response to the changing world of work. Limitations of trait-factor counseling are primarily due to the inability of instruments to measure all traits and all work factors. Assessment of a person's abilities and traits requires more than objective testing techniques. Indeed, the question arises as to who decides what is objective data.

Hershenson and Roth (1970) have postulated that it is impossible to identify all traits of individuals and all the requirements of jobs. Isolating and measuring or quantifying a match of traits with factors is impossible. They question how the trait-factor approach can describe a personality in all its dimensions, particularly when client motivation is not considered in the process. Non-testing techniques, such as client interview, questionnaire, anecdotal records and personnel records, also tend to be ignored. The overemphasis on testing also increases the tendency to neglect counseling. Finally, as Crites and Super (1962) point out, the specific validity of the tests must also be considered.

The overall usefulness of this approach is limited because trait-factor adherents haven't extended the theory beyond the simple match of people and jobs. The application of empirical methodology in the arbitrary selection of what constitutes an important variable ignores the possibility that personality traits may not always be measurable and stable (Carkhuff & Berenson, 1967). Objective data is not always objective; it doesn't take into account interactions of a social, economic or political nature that can alter the assumed prediction (Carkhuff & Berenson, 1967). There are problems in applying normative data to the individual and introducing new data at different life stages in extreme and unique situations, such as the newly disabled client. Trait-factor often ignores vocational patterns of late maturity, relationships among major work roles, and moves to other jobs. It can emphasize the analysis of worker attributes with a tendency to exclude systematic patterns of job changes and may not give sufficient attention to the counseling relationship, related attitudes and motives.

The trait-factor model is paradoxical in its attempt to handle personal occupational choices in an objective, impersonal manner. Trait-factor may place an overconfidence and emphasis on objective data while at the same time underestimating affective, emotional dimensions. Although Williamson cautions that counseling cannot be effective if it is based on an inaccurate diagnosis, Patterson (1973) expressed doubt that an adequate diagnosis can be made with the limited state of knowledge about the client, the complexity of the variables in both the person and job, and the obsolescence and useful application of many instruments of assessment. No general principles are available to guide the counselor in choice and use of techniques for ultimate rendering of a diagnosis. The absence of the affective and emotional domain of the client, an understanding of client motivation, and factors that influence a person's selection of an occupation, necessitates careful diagnosis with predictive capacity as an especially significant counseling objective.

APPLICATION TO REHABILITATION COUNSELING

The trait-factor approach is particularly useful in situations where little prospect for client change appears possible, and counseling strives to achieve optimal adjustment for the individual. The greatest contribution of the trait-factor model appears to be in counseling of those individuals who could not otherwise make necessary choices, i.e., mentally, emotionally, or physically disabled persons (Carkhuff & Berenson, 1967). These exceptional individuals most frequently find job selection a difficult and confusing process.

Williamson's identification of the assumptions and objectives of effective counseling can be easily applied to rehabilitation counseling. Patterson (1973) enumerates a list of these variables which are summarized below:

1. The goal of counseling is to help the individual grow in the direction of optimum development in all aspects of life.
2. Counseling assures the uniqueness of each individual.
3. A distinctive feature of counseling is its problem-solving and decision-making dimensions with respect to objective difficulties in the external world.
4. Counseling assures the respect for the worth and dignity of each client.

Williamson views counseling as a didactic, educational process in which the counselor acts as the teacher, and the curriculum, or subject matter, is the client.

The rehabilitation counselor must consider the long-range career implications of occupational choices or preparation for a client. The scientific nature of this model can aid the counselor and client in achieving sound vocational planning. Vocational objectives must be identified as specific, work-related, time-oriented statements in a client's rehabilitation program. These objectives are subject to ongoing modification and revision as needed, and they are set by the client with the counselor's concurrence (Wright, 1980).

Although it is often difficult for disabled clients to develop long-term career goals, it is the role of the rehabilitation counselor to develop the client's interpersonal skills; help establish long-range goals; give special consideration to the selection and administration of assessment instruments that provide normative data for the disabled client rather than having the disabled client normed with able-bodied; and provide educational and training programs for vocational placement (Zunker, 1981).

Hershenson (Hershenson & Roth, 1970) proposes a model of vocational development based on the assessment of the following constructs:

1. The client's physical and psychosocial background.
2. The client's work personality characteristics such as vocational self-image, motivation, etc.
3. The client's work competencies—behaviors, skills, interpersonal relations in the work setting.
4. The client's work choice—and the appropriateness and completeness of career plans.
5. Work adjustment (satisfaction and effectiveness on the job).

Disabilities most directly affect work competencies, and client adjustment to disability depends on the prior nature of these constructs and their interrelationships. Of special importance is the onset and impact of disability in the individual's life span.

BEYOND TRADITIONAL TRAIT-FACTOR COUNSELING

Vocational counseling has evolved over the years from the simple measurement and match of client traits and job requirements to a model encompassing developmental stages in an individual's life and career; acquisition of a vocational self-concept (Super, 1957); exploration and entry into the world of work resulting in job satisfaction, monetary reward, positive self-esteem and self image; and the degree of correspondence (worker satisfaction and job satisfactoriness) between an individual's vocational needs and the reinforcers provided by the job (Lofquist & Dawis, 1969).

The Minnesota point of view has incorporated the trait-factor theory into a larger, more expansive model that includes the recognition and importance of the individual's need to achieve and maintain correspondence with the environment. This reciprocal and complementary relationship between the individual and the work environment is manifested by the degree to which the individual is able to fulfill the requirements of the work environment as a satisfactory worker while the work environment fulfills the requirements of the individual as satisfied worker. The outcome of this essential component of the vocational counseling approach is indicated by tenure on the job (Dawis, 1973; Dawis & Lofquist, 1984; Lofquist & Dawis, 1969).

The complexity of factors impinging on a constantly changing world of work in the technologically advanced age of information and telecommunications requires the development and acquisition of decision-making skills as they relate to vocational rehabilitation. Hershenson and Roth (1970) propose a process of decision-making that requires a predictive system of assessment of possible alternative actions, outcomes and probabilities; a value system weighing the desirability associated with outcomes and a decision criterion to integrate and select appropriate action.

The role of the rehabilitation counselor is to assist the client in this process. Essential to this system is freedom of choice, and the selection and use of reliable and pertinent information for realistic decision-making. Counseling attempts to help the client make more immediate decisions for purposes of reality testing, developing a self-concept and influencing decisions about more long-term goals.

Throughout the decision-making phase, the rehabilitation counselor serves as a guide in a directive manner by organizing the process, examining the variables, such as risk taking, and in a nondirective manner by allowing the individual to select and move toward the actual choice/outcome. Successful decision making requires problem solving and anxiety management. The decision-making component in vocational choice is a continuous process of anticipation and implementation and adjustment. It involves exploration of all possible alternatives; compilation of information dealing with specific choices and possible alternatives to those choices; examination of selection outcomes; reality testing; information processing and further decision-making based on results of prior decisions (Hazler & Roberts, 1984).

The rehabilitation counselor's role expands to that of labor market analyst, placement director, business and industry liason, information and systems analyst, interpreter of computer-generated assessment data about both the client and the world of work. The complexity of the world of work and labor market realities must be understood by the rehabilitation counselor and translated to the client. This process of structuring the exploration of a large number of occupations and relevant occupational information is essential for appropriate vocational selection.

IN CONCLUSION

The variety and diversity of occupations in today's society offer greater opportunities for utilization of the skills of uniquely different individuals. The total number of available occupations has become too large and unwieldly, and the relationships among them too complex for individuals to identify easily those most likely to provide a sense of correspondence. The rehabilitation counselor must intervene to act as information broker, mediator, and interpreter, in addition to the role of counselor, to facilitate client placement and adjustment to work. Future vocational decisions will require a sophisticated occupational grouping and assessment model with labor market analysis, data information banks, predictive situational assessment and vocation evaluation systems, and other state-of-the-art information and communication networks.

A vocational choice represents a significant and important decision by a client. The rehabilitation counselor must help the client not only in the assessment process but also in decision-making in order to make an appropriate career choice. The rehabilitation counselor must be able to accumulate various kinds of client data (generated by biographical information, observation, testing, etc.), synthesize the data, apply it to a sophisticated technological evaluation, and guide the client in occupational selection. This process will require the counselor to conceptualize disability in psychological terms, adding vocationally pertinent information to the medical and physical data, and be able to translate and explain the assessment of these data in a way that utilizes computer technology as the most comprehensive, cost-effective, and efficient manner of data gathering and analysis.

As an epilogue, Dawis and Lofquist (1984) recommend the following steps in vocational rehabilitation counseling of the disabled:

1. Accumulation of relevant medical and personal data.
2. Psychometric assessment, data gathering for prediction of work personality and adjustment.
3. Evaluation of pre-trauma work personality and impact on treatment and counseling.
4. Evaluation of measured values, abilities, skills, aptitudes, and needs.

5. Determination of jobs, levels, areas of work, and correspondence to client's ability pattern.
6. Decision-making, selection and match of job/client.

Clearly, as recommended by Dawis and Lofquist (1984) and suggested by Hershenson and Roth (1970), the trait-factor approach is a component and a construct in a much more detailed and expansive process of vocational counseling. It is a variable that, together with a number of other variables, elicits sufficient information for an accurate diagnosis, prescription for a plan of action, and a prediction of outcome.

20 Rehabilitation Counseling: A Psychoeducational Perspective *

Rochelle V. Habeck
Thomas C. Fuller

In recent years, the practice of rehabilitation has been evolving from an individual, clinical service model to ecological approaches that reflect awareness of the impact of environment in creating and alleviating disability and handicaps. Rehabilitation efforts have become increasingly devoted to alteration of specific environments and societal attitudes as major modalities of rehabilitation intervention. The advent of developments such as electric wheelchairs, synthesized speech devices, barrier-free design, and legislative incentives and requirements for affirmative action in employment are examples of environmental and social interventions that have helped modify the effects of disability. New definitions distinguish between impairment (organ level), disability (functional level), and handicap (social role level), where handicaps result from specific environmental interactions. In addition, the disability rights movement has led to increased consumer participation in rehabilitation.

These changes have altered the paradigm within which we view the psychosocial impact of disability and appropriate models for intervention. The role of the counselor has been redefined in some contemporary models of rehabilitation from clinician to that of guide and advocate in a cooperative relationship with the client, addressing psychosocial problems that originate not only within the individual but often within the environment (Stubbins, 1982). We view the psychoeducational model as (a) consistent with these conceptual changes in our understanding of disability and the needs of disabled

* We wish to acknowledge the influence of our colleague William Hinds, whose work in life-style change for stress management introduced us to formal concept of psychoeducation. We also thank Hanoch Livneh, Greg Holmes, Don Anderson, and Steve Yelon, whose comments improved the manuscript.

people and (b) well suited to the skills, roles, and functions of rehabilitation counselors.

THE PSYCHOSOCIAL IMPACT OF DISABILITY

Many propositions have been advanced to explain individual response to disability. While some generalized responses have been observed, psychosocial responses to disability are heterogeneous and are not necessarily correlated with severity or type of impairment (Roessler & Bolton, 1978). This has led some theorists to shift away from intraindividual models to explanations that emphasize social and environmental factors. For example, Vash (1981) describes the psychology of disability as the study of normative responses from psychologically normal organisms to abnormal stimuli (i.e., biological, environmental, economic, and social). Similarly, DeLoach and Greer (1981) discuss the psychological impact of disability from a stress model, where disability places adjustive demands (e.g., physical, psychological, social) on the individual that require new beliefs, reactions, and skills for coping with the stressor.

In an elaboration of this interactive process from a learning perspective, Fordyce (1982) states that the subsequent behavior of a person who incurs disability is a function of the behavioral repertoire prior to onset of disability, the behaviors which remain available to the individual after the disability, the significance of the disability to the individual, and the immediate environmental response to the disability of the individual. Athelstan (1981) describes specific problems faced by newly disabled persons as those of coping with physical and psychological loss. Major losses include changes in body image, social status, earning capacity, anxiety and grief (which often accompany these changes), and the need to learn new behaviors to accommodate these changes in order to plan for the future.

These authors recognize the significance of life-style change, environmental response, and requirements for new learning and new behaviors in determining the psychological stress experienced by the disabled person. The impact of the disability is viewed as resulting from the loss of capacity to perform valued roles and behaviors that have been integral to the individual's identity. As disruption of previously valued personal characteristics and roles increases, the need for learning opportunities to restore or replace valued rewards increases (Athelstan, 1981).

From this interactive conceptualization of the impact of disability, follows an adjustment model that is based on learning. DeLoach and

Greer (1981) discount reliance on solely internal psychological processes as sufficient to accomplish adjustment. They also view practical information as to how to manage day-to-day living problems as a necessary component for competent handling of the adjustive demands created by a disability. Coping is seen as the development of new values and goals to replace those that have been lost to the disabled person and the ability to use task-oriented approaches effectively. Adjustment, as an outcome, is composed of self-acceptance, responsible behaviors, and social techniques as well as psychological mechanisms to cope with the behaviors of others (DeLoach and Greer, 1981, p. 25).

Vash (1981) advances the concept of "psychogogy" to describe psychosocial/vocational interventions that are directed toward meeting the unique learning needs presented by disability. Psychogogic approaches are based on an educational model which emphasizes teaching, prevention, strengthening, and guiding rather than correcting or during. Psychogogic approaches apply primarily to rehabilitation clients who are psychologically well but encounter situational problems severe enough to require help, whereas psychotherapeutic or correcting approaches may be emphasized when psychological symptoms constitute the major disabling effect. The psychogogic model utilizes training approaches to develop personal and interpersonal skills to realize life goals and to effectively meet functional and environmental challenges. The skills required in psychogogic approaches (i.e. counseling/coaching, teaching, consulting/advising, environmental intervention) are suitable to the roles and skills of rehabilitation counselors as well as peer counselors, consumer advocates, and independent living specialists (Vash, 1981).

COMPONENTS OF THE PSYCHOEDUCATIONAL MODEL

Ivey (1977) has defined psychoeducation as "a deliberate and planned effort to *teach* individuals or groups understandings, skills, or competencies in the area of human relations" (p. 23). The goal of psychoeducation is to provide people with the abilities that are necessary to manage their own lives in their own way (Ivey, 1977). The psychoeducational model of counseling utilizes explicit education to help clients understand psychological and social processes, identify psychological relationships, and develop specific psychosocial skills and competencies.

The basic assumptions that underlie the psychoeducational model are specified by Larson (1984) as follows:

1. The counselor is viewed as a teacher, rather than as a physician or healer.
2. The clients' problems are conceptualized as learning deficits rather than as symptoms of illness (or as learning needs, in the context of acquired disability, created by novel stimuli).
3. The client is seen as an active and self-responsible agent, capable of directing his/her own learning, rather than as a passive recipient of treatment.

The model has been contrasted with the medical model by Authier, Gustafson, Guerney, and Kasdorf (1975). In a medical model, the process begins with client abnormality (or illness → proceeds to diagnosis → to prescription → to therapy → and results in cure. In psychoeducation, the process is represented as beginning with client dissatisfaction (or ambition) → precedes to goal setting → to skill teaching → and results in satisfaction (or goal achievement).

The role of the counselor in the psychoeducational model is to help the client/student to objectively define problem areas, set realistic goals, acquire the necessary skills and competencies to pursue the goals, and evaluate his/her progress. As a teacher, the psychoeducational counselor takes an active role as a student advocate, bringing his/her psychological and educational expertise into the community to effect necessary environmental changes. Goldstein (1981) states that the psychoeducational orientation operates on the assumption that the client is deficient or lacking in effective skills, and the therapist is a teacher of new skills. The model views clients as having *functional* skill deficiencies that arise in attempting to cope with circumstances that exceed the limits of their current skill level or past learning opportunities or requirements. The client becomes an active agent in the learning process, with the corresponding expectations and responsibilities of the student role.

Psychoeducational methods are based upon principles of education and learning system design (Alschuler & Ivey, 1973; Davis, Alexander, & Yelon, 1974; Gagne, 1970) to facilitate acquisition, internalization, and transfer of learning. Alschuler and Ivey (1973) identified five principles that serve to maximize long-term internalization: (a) gaining the student's attention and interest, (b) providing an experience of the skill, (c) developing a clear conceptualization, (d) relating the learning to other areas of experience, and (e) providing the student with opportunities to practice the skill meaningfully. Larson (1984) has summarized the common themes in psychoeducational skill training programs. Psychoeducational programs strive to elicit active participation from clients in the learning process and, hence, minimize the mystification of psychological knowledge.

Psychoeducational designs are based upon established learning principles (observation, discrimination, reinforcement, and generalization) and consist of both didactic and experiential components. Psychoeducational programs are highly structured, goals are identified and specified, and progress is evaluated and reported to clients. The primary focus is on the mastery and maintenance of specific behaviors.

The principles of psychoeducation have been used to develop applied learning programs to teach specific psychosocial skills. These instructional programs make use of written manuals, audio and video technologies, experiential exercises, and feedback procedures to increase the client's awareness and develop instrumental skill competencies. Specific programs have been advanced for enhancing relationships (Guerney, 1984), increasing parent effectiveness (Anderson, Hogarty & Reiss, 1980; Gordon, 1984), facilitating decision making and vocational planning (Lucas, 1977; Tiedeman, 1979), problem solving (D'Zurilla & Goldfried, 1971), developing cognitive control (Ellis & Harper, 1974; Meichenbaum, 1977a), sexual competence (Masters & Johnson, 1970), enhancing social and moral development (Gazda, 1977; Mosher & Sprinthall, 1971), increasing assertiveness (Lange & Jakubowski, 1976), developing communication skills (Carkhuff, 1971b; Ivey, 1971; Kagan, 1972), and learning to relax (Bernstein & Borkovec, 1973), among others.

EVOLUTION OF THE PSYCHOEDUCATIONAL PERSPECTIVE

Psychoeducation is an emerging synthesis of several broad trends and developments in psychology, health care, and the American culture. Cole and Lacefield (1982) explain that psychoeducation emerged from the psychological and educational research in the early 1900s which attempted to explain and predict learning. Forerunners used general principles derived from the work of Gagne, Piaget, and others, in combination with specific content and skills to develop powerful approaches for specific groups and problems. Theories of learning, development, motivation, and personality were combined with counseling theory and practice to accomplish this desired merger of psychological education. Combinations of psychology and education were the basis for specialty areas such as rehabilitation counseling, developed to provide restorative intervention of individuals disabled during the war era and industrialization, in which the goal was to teach skill and attitudes to bring such groups to effective levels of coping (Cole & Lacefield, 1982).

In the arena of mental health, general dissatisfaction with medical model approaches to psychological problems has been a major impetus for the psychoeducation movement (Authier, 1977). Counselors recognized that many psychological problems are not best conceptualized as symptoms of illness or "trait diseases" (Thoreson, Kirmil-Gray, & Crosbie, 1977), but as failures to learn specific skills and competencies such as decision making, problem, solving, impulse control, or interpersonal sensitivity. Bernard Guerney (1977) has commented:

> . . . people's troubles, insofar as they are psychological at all (rather than problems of health or finances, for example) are due to learned reactions, attitudes, and expectations concerning others, oneself, and one's emotions. . . . If such troubles are generally learned, it must be true that theories, principles, technologies, analogies, and strategies related to attitude formation, learning, motivation, emotion, and behavior, are much more likely to be pertinent than those related to disease. (p. 10)

In addition, psychological counseling has had little success in obtaining generalization of treatment gains outside the therapy sessions into other problem areas. In response to these problems, the psychoeducation movement has developed to promote more responsible client involvement and to increase the generalization of therapeutic gain.

In the health care field, the shift from acute, contagious disease to an increase in chronic health problems has revealed limitations of the medical model. Lack of patient compliance or adherence to long-term medical treatment regimens has become a major obstacle in chronic disease management. In addition, health care professionals have recognized that many chronic diseases are, in fact, diseases of unhealthy life-styles and that further progress in the prevention and management of disease could not be achieved via traditional medical intervention alone. Psychoeducation in medical care has been applied to these problems in two ways. Educational psychologists have taken an active role in the development of curricula for physicians and other health care professionals that explicitly teach interpersonal skills to achieve effective relationships with patients (Cole & Lacefield, 1982). More recently, psychologists have contributed to the development of behavioral health management approaches to accomplish reeducation of patient groups. In this mode, psychological education has augmented earlier models of health management approaches to accomplish reeducation of patient groups. In this mode, psychological education has augmented earlier models of didactic patient education to motivate sustained lifestyle change and the development of healthy behavior.

In addition to a growing dissatisfaction with the medical model of service delivery, the 1960s and 1970s saw the popularization of psychology in the self-awareness and self-help movements as behavioral scientists sought to "give psychology away" (Hobbs, 1964; Larson, 1984). The distinctly American ethic of self-reliance has become "psychologized" with a growing emphasis on psychosocial competence, efficacy, and control. The wellness movement brought an increased awareness of mind-body and person-environment interactions, and resulted in the proliferation of programs for the development of life-skills (Adkins, 1984; Gazda, 1977). This popularization of psychology fostered the growth of paraprofessional training and the self-help movement by forcing professionals to operationalize their training methods. As psychological skills were taught to paraprofessionals, others argued that these same skills could and should be taught to the general public and to mental health clients as well (Authier, 1977). The case for prevention of mental health problems through life skills development had been made.

APPLICATION TO REHABILITATION COUNSELING

Athelstan (1981) has pointed out that counseling in rehabilitation settings is not directed primarily toward psychotherapeutic goals of increased insight, self-actualization or the restoration of personality. Rather, counseling in rehabilitation is provided in part for emotional support and to promote emotional growth but primarily to help clients solve practical problems of adjusting to life with a disability. Consequently, the tools of effective counseling in rehabilitation necessarily include teaching, consultation, advising, and environmental manipulation to assist clients in achieving independent, satisfying life-styles.

Rubin and Roessler (1981) point out that in face-to-face contacts most of the interview time that rehabilitation counselors spend with clients is devoted to information seeking and information giving. While counselors are reported to prefer counseling and guidance activity, their case loads and work demands are too large for this more traditional idealization of the counseling role (Rubin & Roessler, 1981). Techniques and methods are usually action oriented and goal directed, through a brief series of contacts. The nature of this counseling relationship can be seen as requiring skillful, time-limited intervention that leads to increases in client independence and self-acceptance. Such focused intervention requires specificity of objectives and concentration by the client and counselor on reaching goals (Rubin & Roessler, 1981).

Utilization of psychoeducational methods is not new to rehabilitation counseling. Several intervention programs have been developed over recent years that exemplify the principles of this approach. While these are often thought of as behavioral programs, they fall within the broader framework of psychoeducation presented here.

Recent developments in the rehabilitation of persons with chronic psychiatric disability have argued for the applicability of psychoeducational approaches. In this case, psychoeducation is not intended to replace medical or psychotherapeutic interventions but to complement symptom management in order to accomplish rehabilitation goals. Anthony (1978) explains that traditional psychiatric diagnosis and treatment have been unsuccessful in improving long term rehabilitation outcomes. Consequently, he has developed a rehabilitation approach to psychiatric disability with an emphasis on client skill development and the use of community settings to support client skills.

This psychiatric rehabilitation model illustrates the principles outlined in psychoeducation. The specific functional limitations that result from psychiatric impairments are addressed as learning needs in the individual's life skills. Psychiatric patients are viewed as having multiple areas of skill deficiencies (Gazda, 1984). This "reframing" of psychiatric illness into constellations of specific psychological and social skill deficits allows the counselor to set specific, attainable goals. The family of persons with schizophrenia can be treated in a similar psychoeducative manner and taught to simplify communication and clarify family boundaries (Anderson et al., 1980).

The approach begins with a rehabilitation diagnosis that includes the client's present level of skills, the skill demands of the eventual community setting, and the development of treatment plans to address skill deficits or to modify the environment to eliminate skill deficits. The goal in this approach is to assure that the psychiatrically disabled client has the physical, emotional, and intellectual skills needed to live, learn, and work in his or her own community setting. The process utilized in this approach involves teaching clients specific skills or modifying the environment to accommodate these specific skill deficits. The psychoeducational intervention is centered around direct client involvement and requires client concurrence with the diagnosis before proceding toward rehabilitation goals. Specific instructional programs have been utilized with severe psychiatric impairment and have been effective regardless of symptom severity (Anthony, 1978).

The personal quality of assertiveness has been identified as critical to the achievement of adjustment, autonomy, and effective management of environmental barriers and social stigma. Consequently, social skills training has become an important intervention offered in many rehabilitation programs, particularly in independent living centers and peer counseling programs. The Spain Rehabilitation Center has developed a psychoeducational program that addresses the concerns of persons with spinal cord injury and other wheelchair users (Parham, Richards, & Hobart, 1984). Results support the program's effect in teaching socially skilled responses and in increasing self-reported comfort in target situations (Parham, Richards, & Hobart, 1984).

A psychoeducational program for life-style change was designed to increase client awareness and control over the psychological, biological, and social components of stress (Hinds, 1983). The Personal Paradigm Shift is a counselor–mediated, self-discovery manual that assists the client in changing a life-style that aggravates his or her stress experience. The program has been applied to the rehabilitation of chronic pain patients to determine the effects of this explicit psychoeducational intervention on health care management behaviors and pain perceptions, within a comprehensive outpatient rehabilitation program (Hinds, Habeck, Jeney, & Hermanson, 1984).

In addition, psychoeducational principles have been applied to address vocational needs of various rehabilitation client groups. The effectiveness of programs to teach job seeking skills has been well supported (Azrin & Besalel, 1980). A more recent application is the supported work model described by Revell, Wehman, and Arnold (1984), in which counselors teach skills not only to clients but also assist employers and co-workers in achieving effective work relationships.

CONCLUSIONS

The major goal in rehabilitation counseling is to assist clients to become as independent as possible. However, some models of helping have been demonstrated to inadvertently result in dependency (Brickman et al., 1982). The psychoeducational approach uses methods of helping that actively involve clients in change and in learning attitudes, concepts, and skills for "students" to apply in their own efforts to achieve life satisfaction (Sanford, 1955). Psychoeducation, like rehabilitation, is based on a compensatory model of help which assumes that clients have responsibility in the solution of their life problems; a more "powerful" method of helping that reduces risks of inadvertently creating helplessness (Brickman et al, 1982).

Effective use of psychoeducation requires full use of the knowledge of psychological processes and defense mechanisms (Guerney, 1977). Particularly in early phases of disability impact, counselors must shift the content and methods of their intervention to sensitively respond to psychological needs of the individual at that particular point in the coping process. Livneh and Evans (1984) point out that interventions which are more specific, action-rational, and tailored to the individual (e.g., modeling specific skill teaching) may be more useful in later phases of the coping process and that more global strategies (e.g., supporting, reflecting) may be needed immediately following disablement.

It is clear from the work reported by Vash (1981) and DeLoach and Greer (1981) that optimal psychosocial adjustment to disability eventuates in a new definition of self and life meaning. These authors emphasize that the learning involved to achieve these new beliefs occurs gradually as the result of an ongoing learning process. No short-term educational program or therapeutic process can be sufficient to fully accomplish this outcome.

The main contribution of the psychoeducational model for rehabilitation counseling is that it broadens the counselor's scope from the prevailing medical/clinical model to include, in a meaningful way, concepts of learning, motivation, and development. We view the psychoeducational approach as a model that is consistent with the goals and skills of rehabilitation counselors and with a normalized, developmental approach to assisting the needs of disabled persons.

III

Rehabilitation Counseling: State of the Art with Specific Populations

The art and science of rehabilitation counseling continues to evolve as practice and research enumerate principles for efficient and effective service delivery. In this, the final section of this volume, the practice of rehabilitation counseling is described in its application to specific clientele. It is important to note that each client is an individual whose particular circumstance will dictate rehabilitation efforts. However, information regarding group characteristics can aid in effective and efficient rehabilitation counseling. The following information is provided to assist the rehabilitation counselor to better understand some of the more common specific populations our clients may be members of. The generalizations which are presented should be considered descriptive and, to the extent they are valid in working with a given client, helpful in prescriptive programming.

In developing this section each author was provided a Suggested Content Outline to promote consistency of coverage in each special population examined. This outline asked authors to address the following:

1. *Definition and Impact on Function.* That is, in addition to accepted definitions of the condition discussed, provide a functional translation of the condition enumerating the impact of the disability which may present issues relevant to the rehabilitation counselor.
2. *Psychosocial Aspects.* Based on functional limitations and residual capacities of the disabling condition, what

psychosocial issues generally present themselves when working with this population?

3. *Rehabilitation Planning.* What are the implications of the functional and psychosocial aspects of this condition in planning for independent living and vocational placement?
4. *Counseling Practice.* Based on experience and known information, provide a discussion of previous research and effective counseling strategies/orientations for the counselor working with this population.
5. *Bibliography and Resources.* Provide references which will aid the counselor wanting further information resources. Also include consumer organizations, clearinghouses, research institutes, and other sources of information which the reader should be made aware of.

With this outline in mind, we hope you find the following descriptions functional and informative.

21 Habilitation Services for Developmentally Disabled Persons

Robert W. Flexer

The field of developmental disabilities is perhaps unique in that its origins can be traced to an act of Congress. As the mental retardation legislation of the sixties was expiring, leaders and advocacy groups grasped the opportunity to expand the previous laws to benefit not only the mentally retarded but also disability groups whose impairments were developmental in nature and who had similar service needs. Consequently, PL 91–517, the Developmental Disabilities Services and Facilities Construction Act of 1970, was enacted and included with mentally retarded persons were those affected by cerebral palsy, epilepsy, and other neurological conditions found to be closely related to mental retardation or to require treatment similar to that required by mentally retarded individuals.[1]

Two important background factors were related to these changes. One was the desire to focus on the developmental aspects of these conditions. Developmental disabilities result in impairment to a broader range of functions which in turn affect the acquisition of basic life skills, while the developmental assignation also reduces the stigmatizing affect of the mental retardation label. The second factor concerned the chronicity of conditions considered to be developmental disabilities and the need for extended services. Clearly, the intent of the earlier laws was to serve those who have *substantial* unmet needs.

However, since many persons most in need were still not being served after passage of the 1975 act, PL 95–602 dropped the specification of categories of disability in favor of reference only to substantial impairment (Summers, 1981). Conversely, many served under the previous categories were not substantially impaired (e.g., some mildly retarded persons). PL 95–602 Rehabilitation, Comprehensive Services, and Developmental Disability Amendments of 1978,

[1] Autism and certain forms of dyslexia were included in PL 94–104.

the current law, therefore defines developmental disability as a severe, chronic disability of a person which:

(A) is attributable to a mental or physical impairment, or combination of mental and physical impairments;
(B) is manifested before the person attains age twenty-two;
(C) is likely to continue indefinitely;
(D) results in substantial functional limitations in three or more of the following areas of major life activity:
  (i) self-care,
  (ii) receptive and expressive language,
  (iii) learning,
  (iv) mobility,
  (v) self-direction,
  (vi) capacity for independent living, and
  (vii) economic self-sufficiency; and
(E) reflects the person's need for a combination and sequence of special, interdisciplinary, or generic care, treatment, or other services which are individually planned and coordinated.

As can be seen from the definition, five guidelines were utilized in framing the definition: etiology, age of onset, chronicity, need for extended services, and substantial impairment (Lubin et al., 1982). The duration and degree of impairment (both within and across major life activities) certainly suggests that developmental disabilities would meet most other definitions of severe handicap. Indeed, historically, developmental disability was designated as severe because this population is less vocal, subject to less visible improvement, and more expensive, which often leads to not being served in the rehabilitation system. Further implications of the definition are that comprehensive, coordinated, lifelong management of services will be required to meet the needs of the developmentally disabled person.

Unfortunately, the substantial impairment in life activities clause was not specified in the law in terms of functional skills or related objective criteria. As a result, the states have inconsistently implemented the law in terms of whom they serve and don't serve (Summers, 1981). One study (Lubin et al., 1982) found that mentally retarded, cerebral palsied, autistic, and epileptic persons, and those with combinations of those four diagnostic categories, met the New York state criteria of substantial impairment in 82% of the cases. The criteria for substantial impairment specified in New York's system, however, seem to be unduly restrictive.

New York state criteria for mobility specify that confinement to a wheelchair and inability to move about without assistance constitute a substantial impairment (Lubin et al., 1982). If specific environments and baseline skills of specific persons are taken into account, however, it seems that the delineation of substantial impairments in mobility could be expanded. For example, many mentally retarded individuals lack skills in independent travel which might preclude placement in a job. In cases in which travel skills could be trained specifically for employment (e.g., Rusch, 1979), lack of independent travel skills for other purposes, e.g., recreation/leisure, could still be viewed as a substantial impairment. Such narrowly defined criteria, as in New York state, seem to ignore other impairments which are substantial in their effect. Other criteria for other life activities also do not take into account the functional effect of a lack of skills. Perhaps substantialness should be gauged by the amount of resources required to assist developmentally disabled persons to gain access to normalized activities and settings.

Because substantial functional impairments are so pervasive in developmentally disabled populations, service needs take on vast importance relative to the number of parameters which must be considered in the habilitative process. The overriding consideration in looking at needs and impairments of developmentally disabled populations is the populations' apparent, pervasive, extensive level of incompetence or lack of skills valued by the society. Because of the centrality of this factor to all aspects of serving developmentally disabled persons, psychological aspects and rehabilitation services will be organized around it by specifying needs implied by the degree of disability and handicap. Specifically, psychosocial concerns are discussed both from a social-cultural perspective and from a social-emotional perspective. Following the exploration of these issues, services will be analyzed from the systems and habilitative levels.

PSYCHOSOCIAL ASPECTS

Social-Cultural Values and Attitudes

The most negative public attitudes and lowest professional expectations are experienced by mentally retarded and other developmentally disabled persons (Wolfensberger, 1980). Wolfensberger has written extensively on the historical social reactions to various forms of deviancy. In the case of the mentally retarded, role perceptions have been various, although their negative value may have been more or less virulent. The retarded person has been perceived by the larger social structure as subhuman, menacing or threatening, pitiable, charity-evoking, possessing religious power, childlike, and sickly. The importance of these social images is the part that they play in social role theory and subsequent treatment, care, and habilitation.

The sociological literature has had long standing interest in role perception (MacMillan, 1982). In the dynamic of this approach the perception of an identifiable group is communicated to group members by social agents. The individuals of the group in turn behave according to the view of others, and the expected behavior in turn reinforces the original perception of the social agent. In the case of deviant persons, like the mentally retarded, it is the negatively valued differentness that is the source of the altered perception (Wolfensberger, 1980). The power of the self-fulfilling prophecy is the greatest for groups like the developmentally disabled because their incompetence is so pervasive and obvious, and they are relatively powerless to alter perceptions.

That developmentally disabled persons are very negatively viewed is supported by attitudinal research as well. Tringo (1970) found that mental retardation and mental illness are the most negatively viewed of all handicapping conditions. This finding held for the attitudes of professionals and professionals in preparation as well (Harasymiw, Horne, & Lewis, 1976).

The power of expectations is well documented in the educational literature as well as special education (Ysseldyke & Algozzine, 1982). The dynamics of low expectations for the developmentally disabled population was a major force behind the unmet needs of this group and subsequent legislation. Historically, the public, the rehabilitation profession, and parents have expected little effect from habilitative efforts with developmentally disabled persons. To combat this, we must heed the observations of Gold (1973): only by allowing or developing the competence of persons belonging to this particular segment of the community, can we ever hope to offset the natural accentuation and influence of negatively valued differentness and deviance.

Social-Emotional Factors

The point of view taken in discussing social-emotional factors is an interactional one. Many studies have been conducted to determine the relationship between lowered cognitive functioning and social-personal deficiencies (see Rosen, Clark & Kivitz, 1977) and whether the incidence of significant psychological disturbance is greater in the mentally retarded population (see Robinson & Robinson, 1976). What remains unexplored, however, is the role of the ecology, and environment, and the way developmentally disabled persons are perceived and treated in fostering the development or continuation of these types of problems. Certainly, the developmentally disabled person has presented problems and behaviors which must be dealt with, but one should recognize the role of significant others and service systems in perpetuation or worsening them and the need to view intervention as more than treating the individual (Matson & Breuning, 1983).

Zigler (1966), early on, postulated that institutionalized mentally retarded persons were controlled by an outer-directedness orientation in learning situations, and that this contributed to even lower performance on problem-solving tasks than would be expected due to lowered cognitive functioning. Because the institutionalized retarded person was so deprived of social interaction, it was theorized he/she attended to social cues and/or to anticipated approval rather than to task cues for solutions to problems. In addition to Zigler's early work, several personality constructs have been studied to determine to what degree retardation may be associated with secondary personal-social handicaps which interfere with interpersonal relations and personality development (see MacMillan, 1982; Robinson & Robinson, 1976).

Perhaps that most systematic research which attempted to clarify the dynamics of personality development of mentally retarded persons is the work of Rosen et al. (1977). Drawing on and extending previous work in the social-personal development area, Rosen et al. delineated several behavioral predispositions in the personality realm, and developed a measurement and intervention methodology for dealing with the behaviors of each dimension when exhibited by mentally retarded individuals. According to Rosen et al., the behavior of many mentally retarded persons can be characterized as complaint and acquiescent—the acquiescent personality. There is some support for the construct of the acquiescent personality, and it appears to be related to the history of failure and rejection experienced by the mentally retarded as well as to expectancy of success and locus of control constructs previously explored in the literature. Behavior descriptions and methods of measurement and intervention for the concepts of helplessness, self-concept, and psycho-sexual adjustment of mentally retarded persons have also been developed. Although their original work was done with institutionalized samples, Rosen et al. have replicated the original studies and have demonstrated some generalizability of their constructs in studies of non-institutionalized persons.

The extent of social disadvantagement experienced by developmentally disabled persons and the secondary handicapping nature of development disabilities for the social-emotional developmental area has several implications for rehabilitation counseling:

1. When negative expectations exist on the part of significant others, professionals, or community members such as employers, how can the assets or behaviors amenable to intervention of the developmentally disabled person be brought to the forefront?
2. What social-emotional needs does the individual have and how can success and other experiences be used to enhance independence and self-reliance?
3. To what extent do inappropriate age and cultural designations and attributions contribute to non-habilitative role perceptions and treatment?

More specifically for developmentally disabled persons (from Wolfensberg, 1980):

1. Is a significant proportion of time spent and meaningful activities performed with non-handicapped persons?
2. Does personal appearance create a positive impression?
3. Are activities, routines, and rhythms of day, week, year as near the culturally-socially expected and valued as possible?
4. Are labels and forms of address appropriate to age and life activity and functions performed in habilitative settings?
5. Is there encouragement to act according to age and cultural expectations?
6. Are rights and autonomy respected?
7. Do programs and facilities foster competent images or deviant images?

REHABILITATION SERVICES

Normalization and least restrictive environment have been the philosophical cornerstones in attempts to develop effective service delivery systems for the developmentally disabled. Provision of as culturally normative services as possible to achieve as culturally normative behavior as possible (Wolfensberger, 1980) has become the major avenue to maximally, socially integrate the developmentally disabled. Even though there is great confusion and controversy in the field over the definition and implementation of normalization principles and the courts have become the last resort of advocates to get an interpretation of least restrictive environment, these two concepts will remain the foci around which services will be organized (e.g., Fiorelli, 1982). Establishment of organizational structures and service delivery systems which can realize the spirit of these concepts will provide the context in which an emerging habilitation technology can come to fruition.

Many service systems are necessary to meet the needs of developmentally disabled persons. That is why developmental disability legislation dictates that state programs plan and coordinate a comprehensive network of service systems to meet the lifelong programming and management needs of this population. Vocational services are discussed first, followed by a description of other necessary services systems. The final section concludes with an outline of counseling and habilitation methods, highlighting features unique to the complex needs of the developmentally disabled.

Vocational Services

Early vocational services were provided to the developmentally disabled through the efforts of parent and other advocacy groups like Associations for Retarded Citizens. As the developmentally disabled movement gained momentum and federal direction and funding increased services to this population, significant growth took place in programming options for the developmentally disabled persons. In fact, almost all of the phenomenal growth (400%) in sheltered work programs in the United States between 1968 and 1978 was in the establishment of work activity programs for developmentally disabled persons (Whitehead, 1979). Work activity programs are one kind of sheltered work programs covered under Department of Labor rules and regulations for subminimum wage programs.

However, average worker hourly earnings are very low in these programs—$.34 per hour on a national basis (Whitehead, 1979). While this gross indicator is convincing evidence that service systems frequently are not able to provide meaningful work opportunity, there are several other telling factors. There is often too little work available in these programs—again, in national studies it was found that work is provided to employees for less than half the hours they spend in programs. Moreover, the subcontracts are many times underbidded and require few worker skills to complete. Work activity programs have little incentive to obtain subcontracts that are profitable to both the worker and workshop while staff in most programs lack the training and supervision expertise with more severely handicapped workers to assure the level of performance necessary for the successful completion of most of their work (Pomerantz & Marholin, 1977). To compound the problem further, multiple funding and regulatory agencies at federal and state levels, including rehabilitation, developmental disabilities, social security, and labor, with differing orientations to the role of work, has resulted in a void in policy and direction.

A related concern is the failure of the flow-through model of sheltered vocational services. Work activity programs where inconsequential productivity is expected represent the first step in a series of programs which end for some in competitive job placement. However, almost no individual client or worker movement takes place from work activity programs to regular sheltered employment programs in which 50% of the minimum wage must be guaranteed (Bellamy, Sheehan, Horner, & Boles, 1980). These statistics would be depressing if not for the striking advances that have been made in vocational habilitation technology (e.g., Bellamy, Horner, & Inman, 1979; Gold, 1973) for behavior training and management. There are numerous illustrations in the literature on performance of complex vocational tasks at significant productivity levels by developmentally disabled persons.

Bellamy et al. (1980) proposed a structured employment model which holds promise as an alternative to the kinds of vocational services being offered to developmentally disabled persons presently. Based on several years research in their grant-supported Specialized Training Program, the model starts with the assumption, based on extensive literature, that meaningful wages and substantial productivity are possible for developmentally disabled populations. Their analysis then indicates that work opportunity is often denied because gains in social skills and independence are prerequisites for movement through the vocational continuum. Sheltered work programs, as they are presently constituted, do not represent real work opportunity, are not the least restrictive alternative possible for these persons, and do not measure up very well when evaluated against the principles of normalization (Flynn, 1980).

Conversely, there is growing optimism that the results of research and demonstration projects in which moderately and severely mentally retarded, as well as other developmentally disabled persons, are being successfully placed in competitive situations (e.g., Rusch & Mithaug, 1980; Wehman, Hill, & Koehler, 1979) will spur a greater effort in competitive placement in on-going programs. Possibilities for more normative sheltered employment, such as enclaves (Brolin, 1982) are also open up for developmentally disabled persons. Perhaps, if alternative placements are more vigorously developed, the pressure will be off sheltered work programs, and they will perform their function of providing adequate amounts of meaningful work to developmentally disabled persons.

Other Service Systems

The growth of work activity programs, previously discussed, resulted partly from the deinstitutionalization movement. A system of alternative living arrangements (ALA) to meet the need for supervised living for developmentally disabled persons was developed for those either released from institutions, in danger of being institutionalized, or living in the community and in need of such service (Novak & Heal, 1980). ALAs range in diversity from foster or family care to ICF/MRS (intermediate care facility for the mentally retarded) in which nursing services are required by Medicaid regulations. Group homes (usually averaging six to eight residents/home) are the most common group living situation in the community. ALAs are variously funded through Medicaid, state and local government funds, and private, family, and resident contributions, and may be operated by proprietorships, nonprofit organizations, or some governmental unit. The setting and routines of residence for developmentally disabled persons are supposed to approximate as best they can a home atmosphere. The ALA system is increasingly serving more severely handicapped persons while at the same time serving fewer residents from institutions (Bruininks, Hauber, & Kudla, 1979).

ALAs for developmentally disabled persons face many of the same problems as community-based vocational programs. Flynn (1980) found that although community residences were necessarily located in available housing in already existing neighborhoods, residential programs were not integrated into neighborhoods socially. Community support and attitudes are not always favorable toward the establishment and operation of ALAs, while a significant majority of the public is still questioning the desirability of having mentally retarded neighbors (Novak & Heal, 1980). Use of zoning regulations to prevent the opening of ALAs is not uncommon. As with work programs, there is movement toward Medicaid funding for residential services with the usual implications of a medical model orientation, larger facilities, and lack of community involvement (Fiorelli, 1982). In this examination of trends of the 1980s for community residential services for the developmentally disabled, Fiorelli also discussed problems of manpower development. Hopefully, he is correct in projecting increased professionalization and pre- and in-service training programs for management, habilitative, and direct service staff. If such changes take place, perhaps similar developments will occur to remedy the staff training problem in vocational services.

The logic of the comprehensive service system and community based programming for the developmentally disabled person is predicated on the accessibility and adequacy of generic services. The generic services system is relied upon to provide some educational and vocational, medical-dental, social/recreational, mental health, religious, and transportation services among others. Use of services available to other citizens is more normative, socially integrative, and lowers the cost of supporting a developmentally disabled person in the community. Flynn and Nitsch (1980) and Novak and Heal (1980) are recommended for extensive discussion of research and programmatic issues in deinstitutionalization, normalization, and least restrictive alternatives for community residential, vocational, and generic services for the developmentally disabled person.

COUNSELING AND HABILITATIVE INTERVENTIONS

As outlined in defining developmental disability, needs of persons with these conditions are pervasive and chronic, requiring a comprehensive, coordinated system of services. Especially difficult are the transitions required in going from the status of a dependent adolescent to an independent adult. The divisiveness of professionals and advocates over the definition of least restrictive environment, coupled with the lack of coordination typically found among agencies and programs, further compounds the complexity of service provision. Therefore, the process of habilitation for developmentally disabled persons will be described to convey the completeness with which services must be provided.

The chronic problems of the constituency and service system, notwithstanding, significant strides have been made in the development of principles and procedures for meeting the needs of this heterogeneous population. General principles of programming have evolved which have as their focus increasing participation by the consumer in the habilitation process. In the final section of this chapter is an overview of advances in procedural technology for exploiting the assets of developmentally disabled persons to assist them in participating in integrated environments.

Habilitation Process

In analyzing the role of the secondary teacher of the severely handicapped, Sailor and Guess (1983) observed that the professional in this setting is not only a classroom provider but also an integrator of services. If there is one key factor in the planning and provision of services for developmentally disabled persons, it is the facilitation of interactions among and between the varied alternate settings in which habilitation must take place—instruction and coordination are required in domestic, vocational, and community environments. With developmentally disabled persons, total habilitation planning is the necessary ingredient for positive, habilitative outcomes (e.g., Rusch & Mithaug, 1980).

Community-based instruction in alternate settings implies that the locus of interventions must not only be training or preparation environments (Brown et al., 1979). The focus of habilitative efforts must be preparation in functional skills in the settings where they are to be performed. Sailor and Guess (1983) provide an excellent delineation of skills required to function in alternate settings and a good review of the state-of-the-art in instructional technology. One example from this curriculum are behavioral domains required in community interaction skills. The domains included here are basic interaction skills like transportation and phone use, procurement of essential goods (e.g., shopping), participation in community activities like movies and restaurant eating, and procurement of essential services (e.g., banking). Fitting together all these teaching efforts in alternate settings demands very close coordination as well as extensive interagency cooperation.

The nature of total habilitation planning dictates a certain amount of aggressiveness in order for professionals to pursue adequate services. Some have argued that we need change agents operating programs (Wolfensberger, 1980) while others have put forth models for preparing professionals with advocacy skills (Rosenberg & Teslowski, 1980). Whatever the rationale, at least two functions not normally required in (re)habilitation of others, are critical to the success of total habilitation for developmentally disabled persons.

1. Alteration of the expectations, attitudes, and behavior of professionals, aides, tutors, parents, volunteers, and community members. The professional working with the developmentally disabled person must often change others in order to implement effective programs. When instruction in alternate settings is necessary, the performance

of other professionals is often crucial. For example, the services of the language therapist may be needed to teach appropriate conversation skills in the vocational setting. The coordinating professionals must either demonstrate for the therapist the requirements of that situation or teach the skills. In either case, alteration of typical performance will be required of the therapist. Another example of changing others stems from the often necessary one-on-one intervention required by developmentally disabled persons. Coordinating professionals in many cases are responsible for motivating, training, and monitoring the performance of tutors, aides, parents, volunteers, and others who are necessarily responsible for actual implementation of habilitation plans.

2. Development of interagency linkages with agencies like vocational rehabilitation, community residential services, generic services, social security, etc. These connections may require being effective with either individual professionals in those systems or with administrators and involve interagency solutions to problems. In rehabilitation counseling, the counseling function and expertise quite readily extends to intervening with the many and varied non-handicapped persons necessary for total habilitation planning and implementation.

Principles of Habilitative Intervention

Longitudinal chronological age-appropriate programming is a key concept in the provision of habilitation service to the developmentally disabled person (Brown et al., 1979). In planning long-term goals for developmentally disabled persons, present programming must project into future integrated environments in which functioning takes place and also reflect the present developmental stage of the developmentally disabled person. Brown et al. have outlined a sequential strategy to realize this goal. Phases include the following: delineate curriculum domains (e.g., vocational), delineate present and future *natural* environments, inventory subenvironments and functional skills required, teach those functional skills. Using this strategy, developmentally disabled persons are better prepared to make transitions from life stage to life stage and from environment to environment. Graduated, sequenced programming provides a framework for more independent functioning—ultimately in integrated settings.

Baumgart et al. (1982) have subsequently developed the principle of partial participation as a corollary. It asserts that developmentally disabled persons and other severely handicapped persons can acquire many skills that will allow them to function, at least in part, in a wide variety of least restrictive alternate environments through individualized adaptations. Brown et al. (1982) provide an example of a deaf-blind severely retarded man who opened and emptied boxes of bandages in a large hospital. However, personal assistance was required for location and setup of work materials—an adaptation that non-instructional persons were able and willing to assist with. Without these adaptations, work activity, at best, would have been the *final* placement for this person.

Because participation on the part of developmentally disabled consumers is usually difficult to foster, the directive approach in counseling is often the one of choice (Brolin, 1982). Language and communication problems make it difficult to reliably determine their opinions (Sigelman, Budd, Winer, Shoenrock, & Martin, 1982). However, inability to communicate with them does not mean that developmentally disabled persons do not have desires, wishes, preferences and opinions like any other person in the adult stage of development. Research findings and new approaches in habilitation are providing us the means to more fully involve the individual person in planning and counseling. These include

1. Methods to solicit the opinions (Bostwick & Ross, 1981; Sigelman et al., 1982) and job preferences (Becker, Schull & Campbell, 1981; Mithaug & Hagmeir, 1978) of the developmentally disabled person.
2. Advances in pragmatic communication research with the mentally retarded and other developmentally disabled persons (Rusch, Withers, Menchetti, & Schutz, 1980).
3. Techniques in teaching job seeking and interview skills to the moderately retarded person (Elias-Burger, Sigelman, Danley, & Burger, 1981; Hill, Wehman, & Pentecost, 1980).
4. Self-control interventions to allow developmentally disabled persons to self-reinforce and self-evaluate—to have control over the environment and themselves (Wehman, Renzaglia, & Schutz, 1977).
5. Increased focus on the role of exploration for decision making purposes in the assessment process (Brolin, 1982).

Evolving concepts in assessment and evaluation also have had an impact in increasing options, and, thereby, opportunity and choice for the developmentally disabled person. Contemporary assessment is one concept which has been recently articulated (Halpern, Lehman, Irvin, & Heiry, 1982). Contemporary assessment uses measures of targeted work and social behaviors. Unlike *traditional* assessment which attempts to measure traits for classifying individuals, contemporary assessment identifies the developmentally disabled person's training needs. Identification of specific training needs lends itself to easier selection of strategies for remediation and evaluation of effectiveness. Moreover, increased sophistication concerning ecological validity (Menchetti, Rusch, & Owens, 1983) has allowed us to more finely tune critical environments in which developmentally disabled persons function. Some of the burden has been removed from the recipient of services and placed back on the service system and professionals where it belongs. As Wolf (1978) pointed out, our interventions must meet more stringent tests than ever before—are important behaviors performed in meaningful contexts and to the satisfaction of consumers, the developmentally disabled person, significant others, and other important non-handicapped persons in the developmentally disabled person's environment?

This effort has reviewed many significant factors in the delivery of comprehensive, coordinated, lifelong services to meet the habilitative needs of the developmentally disabled person. Behaviors and impairments, systemic considerations, and principles of habilitation were presented. Not discussed in detail were principles of applied behavior analysis which are required instructionally to assist the developmentally disabled person to meet habilitative objectives. This omission should not be interpreted to mean that they are not important but that knowledge of their existing role in the habilitation process and to some extent the technology itself are known to most readers. In addition, excellent sources are available on the application of behavioral principles in sheltered employment settings (Bellamy et al., 1979), competitive employment settings (Rusch & Mithaug, 1980; Wehman, Hill, Goodall, Cleveland, Brooke, & Pentecost, 1982) and domestic and community settings (Sailor & Guess, 1982).

RESOURCE LIST

Accreditation Council for Services for Mentally Retarded and Other Developmentally Disabled Persons (AC/MRDD)
5101 Wisconsin Avenue, N.W.
Washington, DC 20016

Administration on Developmental Disabilities Office of Human Development Services Dept. Of Health and Human Services
330 Independence Avenue, S.W., Rm. 3194C
Washington, DC 20201

American Association of University Affiliated Programs for the Developmentally Disabled
1234 Massachusetts Ave., N.W., Ste. 813
Washington, DC 20005

American Association on Mental Deficiency (AAMD)
5101 Wisconsin Avenue, N.W.
Washington, DC 20016

Association for Retarded Citizens (ARC) National Headquarters
2501 Avenue J
Arlington, TX 76011

The Association for the Severely Handicapped (TASH)
7010 Roosevelt Way, N.E.
Seattle, WA 98115

Council for Exceptional Children
1920 Association Dr.
Reston, VA 22091

Development Disabilities Project on Residential Services and Community Adjustment
207 Pattee Hall, Univ., of Minnesota
150 Pillsbury Dr., S.E.
Minneapolis, MN 55455

Epilepsy Foundation of America
1928 L St., N.W.
Washington, DC 20036

National Easter Seal Society for Crippled Children and Adults
2023 W. Ogden Ave.
Chicago, IL 60612

National Industries for the Severely Handicapped
4350 East West Highway
Washington, DC 20014

People First International, Inc.
P.O. Box 12642
Salem, OR 97309

President's Committee on Mental Retardation (PCMR)
Washington, DC 20201

United Cerebral Palsy Associations
66 E. 34th St.
New York, NY 10016

University of Oregon Mental Retardation R & T Center
College of Education
212 Clinical Services Bldg.
Eugene, OR 97403

University of Wisconsin Mental Retardation R & T Center
Waisman Center on Mental Retardation and Human Development
1500 Highland Avenue
Madison, WI 53706

22 Rehabilitation Counseling with the Visually Impaired

Charles J. Vander Kolk

Visually impaired persons have traditionally received specialized rehabilitation services from staff with specific training or experience in the field of blindness. The rationale has been the unique needs and limitations of a population with a severe sensory impairment. Separate educational settings were first established for blind students because educators realized they could not meet the needs of visually impaired children in regular classrooms, given the state of the art and technology at that time. From residential schools for blind students emerged vocational workshops. As vocational rehabilitation agencies were established in the first half of the 20th century, separate services for blind persons were maintained. Even today nearly every rehabilitation agency maintains separate staff and separate facilities for their legally blind clientele. The following information is provided as basis for understanding the unique needs of those who are visually impaired, and the rehabilitation counseling practices required to best serve this population.

Although blindness is considered a low-incidence disability, a look at the prevalence and incidence figures reveals a substantial need for rehabilitation services. The National Society to Prevent Blindness estimates there are 46,600 new cases of legal blindness per year, most of whom would benefit from rehabilitation services. Estimates of prevalence vary according to the definition of blindness. Probably the most recognized figure, 1,700,000 in the United States, is given by the American Foundation for the Blind. Two-thirds of all blindness is related to old age (65 years or older); 21.1% of severely visually impaired persons are in the 45–64 age range, while only 9.2% are below age 45 (Kirchner & Lowman, 1978).

DEFINITION AND IMPACT ON FUNCTION

The most popular definition of legal blindness is "visual acuity for distance vision of 20/200 or less in the better eye with best correction, or visual acuity of more than 20/200 if the widest diameter of field of vision subtends an angle no greater than 20 degrees" (National Society to Prevent Blindness, 1980). A person, then, must have their vision corrected (e.g., with lenses), and the best eye must provide vision at less than 20/200 (can see no more at 20 feet than fully sighted person sees at 200 feet); or a person may have a severely restricted field of vision, found in conditions such as retinitis pigmentosa. When a person has a condition very likely leading to legal blindness in the near future, s/he may be eligible for rehabilitation services. The legal definition for blindness is not very acceptable to practitioners in the field because it says very little about a person's functional abilities and limitations. Even the notion that we can translate central visual acuity to percent of visual efficiency (e.g., 20/200 = 20% efficiency; 20/100 = 50% efficiency) does not help us a great deal. One reason is that individual visual acuity can vary from day to day and month to month depending on physical condition or disease state. Second, the immediate environment (e.g., lighting conditions) will affect vision. Third, two people with the same measured visual acuity will be able to use their vision at different levels. Two people with 20/200 vision may function very differently. One is able to read regular print, and is mobile using a cane occasionally. The second person must use a special lens to read newspaper print, has total loss of night vision, and is relatively immobile. Since 75% of legally blind people have some usable remaining vision, the variance in how it is utilized becomes a factor. Some are able to use low vision lenses, scopes, magnifiers, etc., to increase their functional capacity.

Levels of blindness are often referred to as partial vision, no useful vision and total blindness. In rehabilitation settings, partial blindness (or low vision) refers to the vision of those people with 20/200 to 20/500 acuity. The term partial vision can be confusing when the counselor works with a student, because educational settings begin the partial vision definition at 20/70. Although students between 20/70 and 20/200 qualify for educational services, they would not normally be eligible for vocational rehabilitation. People with vision of 20/500 up to total loss of vision are able to vaguely see objects, may be able to count fingers held near their eyes, or may have only light perception. Complicating the assessment vision, on occasion, is the person with hysterical blindness or those exaggerating vision loss for purposes of secondary gain. Functional vision is best determined through client observation in a number of circumstances requiring use of vision.

Persons with congenital total blindness or those losing vision before age 3 have not conceptualized information about their environment. They will be less able to understand concepts of size, distance, shape, and proportions, for example, and will not comprehend colors. These and other concepts emphasizing visual reference are necessary for adequate functioning in daily life and frequently in job settings. They can be taught through the use of tactile and hearing senses, or cognitive methods. One of the distinct disadvantages of many congenitally, totally blind persons is the lack of exposure to experiences with the environment, taken for granted by the sighted. The blind person must touch people or things to have an idea of size and shape. Directions and distances must be demonstrated concretely in order to comprehend their meaning. One cannot observe job duties to understand job requirements. Even the most simple tasks may never have been performed or observed by a congenitally blind person.

The tradeoff in terms of handicap, between the congenitally and adventitously blind person, is the difference in acceptance of disability. Generally, the congenitally blind people are more accepting of their disability because, as they often state it, "I haven't known any different." The newly blinded person typically must go through a readjustment stage, and often does not completely accept the modified self.

Adventitious blindness is most often caused by industrial or war accidents, being a secondary condition to pathologies such as diabetes, being part of the aging process (e.g., senile macular degeneration), biological changes such as a brain tumor, or infection. Congenital causes are also quite interesting; syphilis and albinism are two examples, the first due to disease during pregnancy and the second a genetic cause. The four major causes of blindness are macular degeneration, diabetic retinopathy, glaucoma, and cataracts. These are found primarily in the aged, but certainly loss of vision due to diabetes is found frequently with 45- to 65-year-olds in rehabilitation programs. Services to diabetics are difficult because the condition is unstable. One does not know when retinal blood vessels will break again or when there will be a retinal detachment. Functional vision will fluctuate, as will the emotional stability of the client. Vocational plans may be thwarted by the unsureness of where the physical condition will stabilize, or by the client who is alternately depressed and optimistic. The rate of diabetes is increasing by 6% a year, with 10 million Americans presently having diabetes.

The incidence of retinitis pigmentosa is 9,000 persons per year. This is a hereditary, progressive disease where the child begins to lose vision until becoming blind between ages 45 and 60. Peripheral vision becomes severely restricted, and there are problems with night vision. The counselors must deal with the psychological acceptance of a gradual loss of vision, restricted work or driving in low levels of light, and planning for a job that does not require vision even though the person may now have adequate central vision. Albinism is a metabolic deficiency that is associated with hypersensitivity to the sun, high refractive errors, and nystagmus. Most problems can be handled by adjusting lighting levels, prevention of glare, corrective lenses, and selective use of low lenses.

Rehabilitation counselors frequently work with clients who have a disability in addition to legal blindness. The rubella epidemic of about 20 years ago is bringing many deaf-blind persons into rehabilitation programs. The severe communication problems present a real challenge to rehabilitation counselors. The Helen Keller National Center for Deaf-Blind Youths and Adults, Long Island, New York, is one of the resources in this area. They have regional representatives covering all states. The organization has become increasingly active in vocational preparation and job placement.

Clearly, it is difficult to make generalizations about blindness due to the many causes, accompanying disabilities, and severity of vision loss. It has often been said, regarding functional limitation and capacities, that a blind person with no other disabilities is capable of complete independent living and has nearly the range of vocational opportunities found with the sighted population. Let us then look more specifically at the limitations presented by blindness and how each can be overcome.

OVERCOMING LIMITATIONS

Persons with severe vision loss may be confined to their homes or be very restricted in their travel due to poor mobility techniques. The two most frequently used techniques are cane travel or use of a guide dog, with strong proponents for the use of each. With either the cane or the dog and familiarization with the community and work location, the person is able to handle residential and commercial sections as well as public transportation. Since legally blind people are not allowed to drive (unless a special lens increases their vision), living arrangements should be made near public transportation whenever possible. Rural living is particularly difficult since public transportation and taxicabs are not available. Recent technology is assisting in the progress of meeting mobility needs. The sonic guide, for example, is a pair of glasses emitting sonic beams in several directions. The trained person can use the sound cues as information in locating objects in the path that must be avoided. Orientation and mobility specialists provide training so individuals can travel independently.

Communication barriers can exist when a person is not able to read printed matter. Inability to read due to low vision hinders academic progress, restricts knowledge about the environment, and reduces the number of job alternatives. All partially sighted persons should be evaluated by a low-vision specialist who determines specific deficits, and prescribes low-vision aids. Special lenses, scopes, reading lamps, and magnifiers are available. Other traditional devices such as tape-recorders and braille continue to be useful. The latest sensory-aid technology has opened things up dramatically in the area of communication. Jobs previously denied to blind persons are now available due to enhanced acquisition and reading of information (Scadden, 1983). Scadden reviews the tactile, auditory, and visual categories of information critical to a wide range of job types.

Tactile information can be communicated in several ways. Hard-copy braille can be produced by computer electrical signals as readily as it records print. This gives the blind person the same type of copy as the sighted person. A blind computer programmer can obtain permanent records of programs stored or being rewritten. Soft-copy braille (a temporary display of electromechanical pins) is more usable in jobs requiring sophisticated writing and editing capability. The retrieval capacity is especially attractive on jobs demanding editing and programming. The Optacon uses an electromechanical vibratory system, using a camera to transpose print and then sending the identical pattern to the index finger of the person by vibrations. It provides immediate and independent access to printed matter. It is being used by reservation clerks, telephone information expediters, word processor operators, stockroom clerks, and varied professionals.

Auditory displays of two types are now in use: speech output displays and coded tonal displays. Speech compression technology now allows a person to speed up a tape recording at least 2½ times and not only keep the pitch level tolerable, but speech is fully comprehensible. Thus, information by this means can be absorbed much more quickly and comfortably than ever. Also, new techniques to index information on tape through the use of tones will facilitate finding specific information needed on a tape. The use of speech synthesized by the computer and human speech stored on memory chips is becoming more sophisticated. For example, there are speech-output calculators, thermometers, voltmeters, and other measurement devices that assist a person on the job. Speech-output word processors can now be readily adapted to the display capability of most systems. Thus, the printout available to the sighted can be voiced to the blind person. Speech synthesizers are advancing rapidly. The Kurzweil Reading Machines use a camera to scan printed material line by line, which is then recognized by a computer that converts it to letters and a string of phonemic sounds. It brings unlimited speech output from virtually any printed material. Persons who are blind can now be competitive in jobs using word processors, computers, assembly and inspection jobs requiring the reading of digital equipment, and radio engineering positions. Coded tonal displays are used in measurement or detection jobs. Various tonal pitches communicate when an adjustment is too high or too low. They can be used in balances (e.g., in a parts department) to indicate proper weight. Tone can be used to detect light, as would be needed for a switchboard operator.

The final class of displays is useful with partially sighted persons. Closed circuit TV can be used to increase illumination, magnify material, and enhance the contrast. For example, a camera is directed at print material, enlarged up to 60 times, and displayed on a TV monitor. Computer printout and displays can be adapted to produce large print. Enlargement of print opens up jobs that require reading for partially sighted persons.

One of the abilities affected by visual impairment is manual dexterity. In certain work or daily living activities that require speed, the visually impaired person will not be able to perform the tasks as quickly (Vander Kolk, 1981). In some cases, the deficit can be remediated through training. Other times one must seek out occupations not requiring a specific type of manual speed. Verbal intelligence in legally blind individuals is at least equal to that of sighted persons (Vander Kolk, 1977); however, the counselor should be cognizant of a tendency in some congenitally blind clients to parrot what they have heard without a clear understanding of, or a referant for, what they have said. For example, a client may describe exactly how to get from the rehabilitation center to a drug store, but when asked to do so is unable. Translation of cognitive information into practice is not always carried out. Knowledge of the world of work may be limited not only because of isolation from the community, as we find with most disability groups, but also because the person has not seen people at work. What is sometimes diagnosed as lack of motivation or inability to carry out a task is actually a naive client who has never had a model for work behavior. Lack of persistence, poor organization, and lack of coordination is a result of limited experience and few demands placed on the person in the past. It is important for the counselor to give clients the experiences normally found in the sighted person's social, prevocational, and conceptual development. Rehabilitation may need to begin with work behaviors such as speed, accuracy, endurance, following directions, and productivity. Prevocational skills can be learned in an adjustment center or in the field (i.e., home, work site) under supervision.

Independent living is a challenge to the severely visually impaired person, yet training and adaptive devices make it a possibility for nearly everyone. Rehabilitation teachers are able to prepare a person to live in an apartment or a home independently, shop for food and clothing, handle finances, and lead a socially active life. For example, food, clothing and other items can be labeled in braille. Cooking devices and techniques allow the person to prepare his or her own meals. Severely visually impaired people go bowling, skiing, to movies and most other social activities. The American Foundation for the Blind has a booklet on adaptive devices for independent living.

PYSCHOSOCIAL ASPECTS

Socialization development varies a great deal across visually impaired children. We can say that blindness, in itself, does not play a significant role in the psychosocial development of the person. However, the reactions, feelings, and attitudes of significant people in the children's life affect personality development. Rather than duplicate the psychosocial dynamics (e.g., dependence) found with other disability groups, the focus will be on those unique to or having some unique effect on blind individuals.

The lack of vision or limited vision prevents the person from seeing the social behavior of others. We learn most of the social graces by watching our family and friends interact with one another. Facial expressions, gestures, posture, touching (and other forms of physical closeness) are not seen by the severely impaired young person. If the person is not taught these behaviors, they will either not be part of their repertoire, or the behaviors will be displayed in an unacceptable manner. For example, if mannerisms such as bobbing the head or flicking the hands rapidly occur and are distracting to others, the blind person may not know it is inappropriate. Another example is that of heterosexual relationships and information that is frequently poorly developed because of a lack of visual modeling. Acceptable times and forms of expressing affection must be explicitly taught. Our visual perception of the physical features of the opposite sex is not available to severely visually impaired persons. There is a need for sex education utilizing tactile models for body parts and function. Pre-marital counseling is invariably necessary to provide information on sexual intercourse, childbirth, and parenting. Tactual aides are important in communicating this information.

Certain psychosocial deficits may be found in visually impaired children and adults. The need for greater assertiveness when compared with the sighted was found by several researchers (Burlingham, 1965; Fraiberg, 1968; Sandler, 1966). Other studies show those with blindness to be more rigid as a group (McAndrew, 1950), and they have higher levels of anxiety and emotionality (Brieland, 1950). Most studies find no real differences in the blind population (Cowen, Underberg, Verillo, & Benham, 1961; Cross, 1947; Hastings, 1977). Most research data of value compare different types of blind subgroups. A higher level of anxiety in the partially sighted (Brieland, 1950; Cowen et al., 1961) can be related to two factors. First, the partially sighted person either tries or is expected to function very much like a sighted person. Second, many partially sighted people are unsure as to when and if they will lose more of their residual vision. Both factors can elicit anxiety in a person.

A classic and probably still valid study (Bauman, 1954) looked at differences among groups of blind persons employed and well adjusted, blind persons unemployed but well adjusted, and blind people unemployed and unadjusted persons. None of the demographic data differentiated between the groups, supporting the notion that blindness categories are not related to work and adjustment. Intelligence test scores and measures of personality differentiated between the groups. The adjusted, employed groups were brighter, more educated, like music and reading, and went to movies. They also showed more realistic acceptance of their blindness (with parents having the same attitude), were less willing to relinquish preblindness sources of pleasure, were more sure that people liked them, had fewer fears and petty annoyances, had greater confidence about getting what they wanted, were less depressed, and were not as hypersensitive. It is interesting to note the well-adjusted employed groups had more rehabilitation education experience than did the less well adjusted. Additionally, family attitudes of treating the person the same as others, and the ability to psychologically cope with the realities of visual impairment seemed to result in a happier, productive person.

Attitudes

Attitudes of the family and the community toward blind persons range from pity, dislike, and rejection, to curiosity, acceptance, and admiration (Finestone, Lowry, Whiteman, & Lukoff, 1968; Lukoff & Cohen, 1972; Monbeck, 1973). Negative family reactions also include guilt, overprotectiveness, and permissiveness. The young adult wishing to enter the work world is often unprepared because the family did not make normal demands. Furthermore, school personnel who have made exceptions, expected less of the blind student, and made high grades a "gift" promote nonadaptive behaviors in the disabled person. The rehabilitation counselor then must put together a program that will undo past incorrect learning and build coping skills and behaviors. Even rehabilitation agencies do not always offer programs in the best interests of the client who is blind (Scott, 1969); rather than be self-serving, agencies and programs must be geared to the unique needs of the visually impaired (Vander Kolk, 1982).

Beyond the usual variety of personality dynamics found in any group of people, there are modified features one can observe with *some* visually impaired persons.

1. Belief that sighted persons are watching them, particularly in public places.
2. Lack of awareness of sensitivity to socially appropriate behavior.
3. Wishing to associate primarily or exclusively with other blind persons.
4. Wanting to associate only with sighted persons in order to deny their disability and be accepted by the mainstream of society.
5. Attitude of learned helplessness and expecting the sighted to care for and give them extra breaks.
6. Denial of disability, seen in illegal driving, refusing a cane or dog for mobility, and rejection of suitable training.
7. Poor body image reflected in inadequate exercise, poor diet, and lack of knowledge concerning physical functioning.
8. Excessive fantasy life as a means of escaping or substituting for healthy interpersonal relationships.

Adventitiously blind persons are required to make a modification of self-perception as a result of physical changes and limitations in certain functional areas. The counselor should be aware of the usual mourning process. It is possible for an adventitiously blind person, however, to never be depressed; or, on the other hand, to be depressed beyond a normal period of mourning. Many newly blinded persons have made a fine adjustment to their disability, yet frequently wake up in the morning irritated with the fact of their disability. The counselor must have patience in helping newly blinded persons cope in spite of their limitations. Clients with an unstable visual condition will go through cycles of depression, irritation, self-pity, and disappointment, with anxiety an everpresent factor. An interesting study (Greenough, Keegan, & Ash, 1978) demonstrated how newly blinded persons who displayed lower levels of depression had personality characteristics before the loss that apparently better prepared them to cope: assertiveness, independence, stubbornness, and a venturesome experimenting attitude. The more depressed persons had been more staid, rule-bound, and conservative in their pre-loss personalities.

REHABILITATION ASSESSMENT AND PLANNING

Nothing can prepare the rehabilitation counselor better for work with the blind than knowledge of the psychosocial, family, physical, and vocational aspects related to rehabilitation. The cause, current condition, history, family dynamics, personality, and abilities of the person interact to form a person requiring an individualized program. Assessment is the critical first step in formulating a plan with the client. Perhaps the unique factor in assessing the visually impaired individual is the need for adaptive test techniques, adaption of instruments, or instruments specifically designed for the blind. Vander Kolk (1981), and Scholl and Schnur (1976) review the techniques and instruments now available.

The counselor needs to choose assessment instruments appropriate for visually impaired clients. Examples of these include the Wechsler verbal scales, Haptic, and Perkins-Binet for measures of intelligence. Separate norms are available for the Purdue Pegboard, and Valpar now has the CUBE to measure selected work-related skills and is normed on a sample of blind persons. Interest inventories can be administered orally. Bauman (1973) had devised an interest inventory specifically for persons who are blind. It can be purchased from the Nevil Interagency Referral Service. The Wide Range Achievement Test is available in large print, and the Stanford Achievement Test is available in braille. Most print personality inventories can be administered orally, with some threat to validity. The Emotional Factors

Inventory was normed on a sample of blind persons. It also is available from the Nevil agency.

Once a comprehensive assessment has been completed, the counselor factors in all data to come up with a plan for independent living and job placement. An advantage the counselor has in the field of blindness is that rehabilitation centers have a relatively long history of providing prevocational and independent living services for their clients. Mobility, communication skill, personal and home management, social skill, and work adjustment training are normally available. Vocational training and placement is much more of a challenge in view of the fact that historically many jobs have not been available to the blind, and employers have not viewed blind workers as capable. The challenge to rehabilitation counselors can be seen in the results of an employment survey by Kirchner and Peterson (1979). While three-fourths of the general adult population was employed, less than one-third of the visually impaired were in the work force, and the unemployment rate is at least double that of the country as a whole. Furthermore, a greater proportion of blind employees are at lower-level occupations.

Vocational planning needs to center of three elements necessary for success. The first is accurate assessment of the client to determine abilities, motivation, interests, etc. Second, the selection of alternatives suitable to the client and marketable in the labor market must be done. For example, sensory devices for the blind make them great candidates for jobs opening up in the technological field. Third, preparation of the client is important before the placement occurs. Lack of independent living skills, poor work behaviors, and emotional problems have prevented more visually impaired persons from obtaining or keeping a job than has the lack of job skills. Therefore, the counselor needs to attend to personal and work adjustment and independent living as much or more than the actual work skills. Another part of preparation needs to be the use of low-vision aids, sensory devices, and adaptation of the work site whenever called for. The rehabilitation counselor can be the key person shaping a successful rehabilitation plan.

COUNSELING PRACTICE

The rehabilitation counselor working with visually impaired clients usually is assigned either to a field office or to a facility. Let us look at the role of the field counselor first.

Field Counselor

Ideally, the field counselor spends a majority of time coordinating the case, providing guidance and counseling, and doing job development and placement. As part of the coordinating function, an assessment is the first significant step to take, whether it takes place in the field office or in a rehabilitation facility. Partially sighted clients should always have a low-vision examination if one has not been done recently. If the person was previously employed, the counselor needs to do a job analysis to see whether the person could return to the same job or to a similar one with adaptations.

Guidance and counseling will center around preparation for work and adjustment to independent living. Most clients who are blind need a great deal of vocational information, awareness of their own abilities and limitations, and skills for obtaining and holding a job. Counseling is critical to the client's selection of an appropriate occupation. Lack of readiness for future education or work has been a major reason for lack of success in the past. For example, many visually impaired persons are sent to college without the independent living skills necessary to live on campus. Additionally, a major field is often selected where job opportunities are limited. Many states have pre-college summer programs that should be mandatory for clients.

The most important function in the field is the one most neglected. Job development and placement is especially important with this disability group because of the apparent client limitations and employer attitudes. Five functions are critical to job success.

1. Prepare the client. This includes job interview skills developed through modeling and role-playing in groups. Work adjustment skills are obtained from the facility.
2. Educate employers. An allotted time each week should be set aside to meet with personnel managers and other employer staff to educate them concerning the ability of blind persons.
3. Form a job club with clients.
4. Placement. Assist the client in locating and going through the steps of seeking and landing a job. This will include adapting the work site and the use of sensory devices.
5. Follow-up. Meet with the employer and the client regularly, especially soon after the placement, to handle problems as they arise.

The field counselor, in order to carry out all of these roles, must work closely with the client, the family, and the employer. If one link is missing, the client will not receive adequate services.

Facility Counselor

The facility counselor sees the client more intensely, but for a shorter period of time than does the field counselor. Also, the facility counselor functions primarily in the areas of assessment and training. Normally the rehabilitation counselor coordinates the client's program while s/he is at the facility. In addition to working with the independent living staff, the counselor or counselors are involved in the following pre-vocational activities:

1. Social skill development. This may include communication skill training for lower functioning clients, interpersonal skill training, and assertiveness training. These are best carried out in a group.
2. Vocational counseling. Clients need information on their abilities and limitations, the world of work, vocational alternatives, and how to select an occupation.
3. Therapeutic counseling. Many clients need individual or group counseling to deal with their attitude toward their disability, acceptance of self, how to develop coping behaviors, and a genuine desire for independence.
4. Family counseling. With young clients, it is advisable to involve the family in short-term counseling to explore and confront how family dynamics are related to having a disabled family member.
5. Work adjustment and training. The counselor devises a program to include simulated work activities, and provides guidance in expected work behaviors. This may be part of a workshop or simulated work in a manual arts area.

Many techniques and approaches have been used successfully to carry out the various roles mentioned here. Wilson (1970) found counseling with visually impaired clients to be helpful in their behavioral reactions related to the disability. Transactional analysis was used successfully in group counseling by Thomson (1974). Other group techniques include para-analytic (Avery, 1968), and a time-limited, problem-oriented, "theragnostic" group (Manaster, 1971; Manaster & Kucharis, 1972). Counseling with families having a member who is blind has been tried in several ways. Telson (1965) reports group work with parents of visually impaired children. A heavily educational approach to working with families was employed by Schulz (1968). It has been suggested that special groups for diagnostic categories such as diabetics (Kantrow, 1967) and persons with a retinal detachment (Farley, 1973) would be beneficial. More recently a group counseling and educational program for young people with Usher's syndrome has been proposed (Vernon & Hicks, 1983).

In general, however, the counseling approaches utilized with sighted individuals are also appropriate with visually impaired persons. Emphasis on behavioral techniques that get clients to act out feelings, attitudes, and behavior would be especially useful because words alone will not have the same significance to a blind person. Thus, techniques such as modeling, role-playing, psychodrama, Gestalt techniques, behavioral rehearsal, and detailed feedback would be particularly effective.

Although guidelines to practice could be presented here, the reality is that we have little evidence as to what works well in rehabilitation counseling with blind clients. We know quite well what the needs are, and we have many agency and staff mechanisms to deliver service, but we have many questions as to the relative effectiveness of different methods of assessment, training and counseling. With only one research center (at Mississippi State University) and no rehabilitation counseling programs specializing in the area of blindness, the support to further our knowledge in the area of the visually impaired is highly inadequate.

ORGANIZATIONS INTERESTED IN VISUAL IMPAIRMENT

American Foundation for the Blind
15 West 16th St.
New York, NY 10011

Association for the Education of the Visually Handicapped
919 Walnut Street
Philadelphia, PA 19107

Library of Congress
Division for the Blind and Physically Handicapped
1291 Taylor Street, NW
Washington, DC 10542

Recordings for the Blind, Inc.
215 East 58th Street
New York, NY 10022

American Printing House for the Blind
1839 Frankort Ave.
Louisville, KY 40206

Howe Memorial Press
549 East Fourth Street
South Boston, MA

Nevil Interagency Referral Service, Inc.
Room 400, 919 Walnut Street
Philadelphia, PA 19107

Warwick Research Unit for the Blind
University of Warwick
Coventry CV4 7A1
England

American Association of Workers for the Blind

American Council for the Blind

National Federation of the Blind

National Society to Prevent Blindness

(all can be found in the local phone book)

23 Rehabilitation Counseling with Deaf Clients

Marita Danek

The term *hearing impairment* encompasses a continuum of severity from mildly hard-of-hearing to profoundly deaf. Although hearing impairment is one of the most prevalent forms of physically disabling conditions in the United States, deafness is not. Because deafness is a severe disability of relatively low incidence—only one or two persons per thousand are pre-vocationally deaf—the rehabilitation needs of deaf people are not, even among professionals, widely understood. This chapter will focus on the impact of deafness—particularly profound prelingual and pre-vocational deafness—upon an individual's psycho-social, intellectual, educational, and vocational functioning. It will also discuss current needs and practices in the field of deafness rehabilitation.

DEFINITIONS

The distinction between deafness and other hearing impairments frequently depends upon the perspective of the professional discipline making this distinction—education, medicine, or rehabilitation.

An educational definition is contained in PL 94–142 which describes deafness "as a hearing impairment which is so severe that the child's hearing is non-functional for purposes of educational performance."

Medically, deafness is defined in terms of type of loss (conductive or sensorineural) and decibel (dB) loss ranging from "nominal" (less than 25 dB) to "profound" (greater than 90 dB) (Hylbert & Hylbert, 1979).

The federal-state rehabilitation program uses a coding system for all hearing impairments which emphasizes the functional limitations of the hearing impairment upon communication and further defines it according to the age of onset and etiology. ("New disability coding," 1981, p. 3). Under this system, deafness is defined as a "hearing impairment of such severity that the individual must depend primarily on visual communication such as writing, lip reading, manual communication, and gesture." A hard-of-hearing individual has a "functional loss, but not to the extent that the individual must depend primarily upon visual communication."

Using these definitions, deafness is a severe disability; a hard-of-hearing individual is usually not severely disabled. However, RSA also recognizes a category known as "severely disabled hard-of-hearing" which is defined according to the unaided dB loss and speech reception threshold ("New disability coding," 1981, p. 3).

Two other important qualifiers of hearing impairment are considered crucial for rehabilitation planning: age of onset of the hearing loss and etiology. Age of onset is divided into three broad, but significant, age ranges: prelingual, pre-vocational, and post-vocational.

Prelingual hearing loss occurs prior to the acquisition of language (age 3 or before). *Pre-vocational* hearing loss occurs after the acquisition of language but before the individual enters the work force; *post-vocational* hearing loss occurs after the individual has started to work (approximately age 19) (Schein & Delk, 1974).

The cause of the hearing impairment is another important piece of information for rehabilitation planning purposes because whatever causes the deafness may also cause a secondary handicapping condition (Vernon, 1969). The causes of hearing impairment are divided by RSA into four categories:

1. "Congenital" refers to prenatal or perinatal factors present at birth, including heredity, RH incompatibility, maternal rubella, or prematurity. It does not necessarily relate to age of onset. For example, some genetic types of deafness do not appear until later in life.
2. "Disease" refers to degenerative, infectious, or neoplastic processes such as meningitis or a brain tumor.
3. "Accident/injury" refers to trauma, including noise-induced loss.
4. "Unknown" includes all ill-defined, unspecified, and unknown causes ("New disability coding," 1981).

Up to one-third of all deaf adults report one or more additional disabilities (Schein & Delk, 1974).

In a study of deaf rehabilitation clients (Danek & Lawrence, 1981), approximately 20% had a secondary handicap. This is at least partially due to the fact that many major causes of deafness—such as prematurity, RH complications, prenatal rubella, herpes II, meningitis, etc.—can also cause cerebral palsy, visual and cardiac problems, mental retardation, and learning disabilities (Jaffee, 1978; Vernon, 1969).

IMPACT ON FUNCTION

For the prelingually deaf individual (approximately 87% of the total deaf population), deafness is experienced as a developmental disability which limits the incidental learning normally acquired through everyday communication and results in psychosocial, educational, and vocational problems (Moore, 1978).

The functional limitation imposed by deafness is communication, much as the limitation imposed by blindness is mobility. Communication is not merely speech but the ability to understand and be understood by speech, pantomime, gestures, writing, or whatever. Language is the symbolic representation of our system of communication. For most prelingually deaf adults, a visual-gestural system known as American Sign Language (ASL)—*not* English (spoken or signed)—is the most natural form of language (Stokoe, 1978). Despite years of oral training, including endless speech and lip reading drills in various educational settings, most prelingually deaf people will use ASL to communicate (Mindel & Vernon, 1971).

Obviously, deaf individuals are the only disability group to use a separate language system. The system provides a unique means of identification available to no other group of disabled individuals. Just as a language is both the expression and result of a distinct culture, deafness is as much a culture as it is a disability (Glickman, 1983; Vernon, 1969). The "deaf community" is as culturally distinct as any other minority group (Baker & Cokely, 1980). It is important to maintain this perspective, because the great majority of *prelingually* and many *pre-vocationally* deaf rehabilitation clients will be members of this cohesive cultural group within the broader community.

Psychosocial Adjustment

Prelingual deafness in a child is frequently misdiagnosed or undiscovered until the child fails to develop spoken language. The shock of the diagnosis of deafness often results in parental guilt, overprotection, and/or rejection (Vernon & Mindel, 1971). The stress placed on the parents is frequently compounded by contradictory or misleading information regarding language development. It is the rare hearing parent who uses a visual system of language rather than a spoken one. The stress that the child experiences under these circumstances relates directly to the thwarting of a natural means—language—of expressing emotions, of labeling and processing experience, and, of course, of communicating with others. Lack of communication means that the young child's world can change drastically without apparent reason, that the older child is socially isolated and often rejected by peers. Such early social and cultural influences within the family setting can result in delayed or restricted emotional development and marginal coping behaviors (Levine, 1976; Vernon, 1971).

Mindel and Vernon (1971) note that the condition of deafness during an individual's early development markedly alters the perceived environment and leaves many deaf people unable to handle the complexities of daily living. In short, parental and societal responses to deafness can impose difficult and stressful conditions upon a developing individual who has limited opportunity to express feelings and comprehend the environment. Despite these difficulties, most deaf individuals lead exceedingly normal lives—they marry, raise children, work, and have active leisure and social pursuits.

Education

Although the educational *achievement* of most deaf people is comparable to that of hearing people, educational *attainment* is not. Over one-third of the deaf population has completed the 12th grade, but the average deaf person reads at about the 4th grade level (Schein & Delk, 1974). This discrepancy underscores the language and experiential deprivation resulting from early severe deafness. This discrepancy between achievement and attainment is *not* due to intellectual deficiency. Indeed, numerous studies have confirmed deaf subjects have similar scores, with the same range and variability on performance intelligence tests as the hearing population (Vernon, 1968).

Although the subject is beyond the scope of this chapter to explore in depth, rehabilitation workers should be aware of some of the major trends and controversies which have determined educational strategies for deaf children. "Oral versus manual"—basically an argument about whether deaf children should be educated through a visual system such as ASL or some variant of this such as SEE (Signing Exact English) or through an oral system—is the major controversy (Moores, 1978). Most educators today espouse "total communication"—the philosophy of using any and all methods of communication to assist the child to learn (Jordon, Gustason, & Rosen, 1976). However, many older deaf clients will recall hands that were stopped or tied to force them to use speech. These individuals will remember when using ASL was a stigma, an admission that you were failing to adapt to the hearing world. Rehabilitation counselors must be prepared to accept and cope with the ambivalence these individuals feel toward themselves and hearing people.

Another trend is the "mainstreaming" of deaf children under PL 94–142 into regular classrooms. Previously, almost all prelingually, profoundly deaf children were educated in residential or day programs only for deaf individuals (Moores, 1978). Although these programs were accused of "segregating" deaf children from the real world—and residential schools in particular were said to contribute to a narrow "institutionalized" approach to life—the educational approaches used were those demonstrated to be most effective with deaf children. Perhaps most important, the social environment was basically equalitarian with normal peer interaction. Mainstreaming is said to work well for some deaf children but not for others, particularly if special consideration is not made for the communication needs of deaf children and they are socially isolated (Moores, 1978). Rehabilitation workers will encounter more young deaf clients graduating from mainstreamed programs in the future. The ability of these clients to deal with vocational training goals will be a reflection of the relative and perhaps uneven quality of these programs.

Vocational Issues

The language handicap resulting from early deafness can lead to educational and experiential deficits. The vocational problems encountered by deaf persons can best be described as underemployment and lack of job mobility. Limited access to information about occupations, lack of self-awareness, and inadequate community resources often result in deaf individuals entering a restricted range of occupations, usually semi-skilled or unskilled (Lerman & Guilfoyle, 1973; Rosenstein & Lerman, 1963; Schein & Delk, 1974). Deaf persons are under-represented in professional and managerial occupations (Crammatte, 1962), and clerical and sales work, as well as service occupations. Overall, the pre-vocationally deaf worker earns only 72% as much as the general population average (Schein & Delk, 1974).

Although most employers express satisfaction with their work, deaf employees are usually the first to be laid off (Lerman & Guilfoyle, 1973). Unemployment will probably become more of a problem, particularly as the trend toward automation and the increase in service occupations continues, resulting in a lessened demand for workers in jobs traditionally held by many deaf people.

STEREOTYPES

The reality of deafness stands in stark contrast to some of the myths and stereotypes encountered in the lay and professional literature. Some of these myths which are particularly important for rehabilitation counselors to be aware of are as follows:

Most deaf people are good lip readers. The reality is that lipreading is a most difficult skill to master, even for those who become deaf post-vocationally. For prelingually deafened persons proficiency in speech reading is close to impossible because between forty and sixty percent of English words are formed identically on the lips (Vernon, 1971). The most natural form of communication for most prelingual and many pre-vocational deaf persons is ASL; even with post-vocationally deafened persons, reliance on speech and lipreading is fraught with imprecision.

Deafness implies "dumbness." Again, deaf people have the same range of intellectual abilities as the population as a whole (Vernon, 1968). However, the lack of opportunity to learn language by hearing it means that ability to use spoken and written English will be limited and this limitation will sometimes be confused with intellectual deficiencies.

Deaf people have a higher rate of emotional illness. The prevalence of mental and emotional illness among deaf people is roughly comparable to that of hearing people (Rainier & Altshuler, 1970).

REHABILITATION PLANNING AND SERVICES

Only 2 to 3% of all rehabilitation clients are deaf (RSA, 1981). Nonwhite deaf persons appear to be less frequently served by rehabilitation (Schein & Delk, 1971), perhaps because they are unaware of the services offered or believe these services would not meet their needs.

The rehabilitation process involves four major steps for the deaf client: assessment, goal setting, service delivery, and placement. The special needs of deaf clients in each of these steps will be discussed in turn.

Assessment

Assessment involves evaluating the individual's readiness to begin services and complete from a medical, educational, social, and vocational perspective.

Medical evaluation is usually the first step in rehabilitation assessment. The individual needs a general medical evaluation not only to substantiate the disability but also to determine any other physical or mental work limitations. Because almost one-third of all deaf people have a secondary disability, it is important for the counselor to be aware of this possibility and to note both the onset of deafness and etiology on the referral form to the physician. Any other health-related complaints or concerns about work stamina and functioning should be noted by the counselor on the referral form as well as a specific list of questions about work limitations that the physician can answer. Since most physicians are unable to use ASL and unwilling to spend their time pushing written notes across the desk, engaging the services of a certified interpreter to get a thorough medical evaluation is money well spent. Special attention should be paid to any visual problems of deaf clients since vision is so important for communication. Additionally, some visual problems can be related to deafness; for instance, Usher's syndrome (progressive deaf-blindness caused by a recessive gene) or maternal rubella (Vernon, Grieve, & Shaver, 1980).

Otological and audiologial evaluation (either or both) are also required by some states to establish the existence of deafness, describe its parameters, and specify any aural habilitation measures. Unfortunately, most prelingually deafened adults have had their hearing tested ad nauseam since early childhood and may resent or not understand the need for this testing. In some cases, recent audiological testing as contained in school records will suffice. At other times a new evaluation is warranted, particularly if the hearing loss is progressive. The purpose of all medical evaluations should be clearly communicated to the deaf client. An understanding of health care services is sorely lacking among the deaf population (Schein, 1981).

The use of standardized psychological test batteries for deaf clients should be approached with extreme caution. Ziezuila (1982) notes some caveats: (a) test items which rely on *verbal* or *language ability* will be invalid for most deaf people; (b) tests which rely on *verbal communication* between examiner and deaf client should not be used unless the examiner is proficient in interpreting directions into ASL; (c) certain items on some standardized tests may unintentionally discriminate against persons with a hearing impairment (e.g., the most obvious offender, on the MMPI, is the item "my hearing is apparently as good as that of most people"); (d) if hearing impaired individuals have not been included in the normative sample by the test developer, the counselor should interpret the results cautiously.

To obtain information which will be helpful to both the client and counselor, non-parametric data is frequently the best and easiest to obtain. This would include as assessment of individual's educational, social and work history, motivation to work or participate in rehabitation services and an assessment of the personal support systems available to the client. Since deaf individuals have a normal range of intelligence, the "average" deaf person can be considered to be of "averge" intelligence and therefore capable of performing a wide range of jobs. Unless some deviation in either direction is suspected, the counselor should probably not refer the client for intelligence testing. An individual who has completed around 12 years of schooling, most probably at a residential or day school for deaf students, would be considered "average;" only about 12% of all prelingually deaf people attend post-secondary institutions.

Positive factors, then, for predicting a deaf person's rehabilitation success include average ability, a consistent and uninterrupted employment history, and freedom from dependence on parents, spouse, or public sources of support such as SSI. Additionally, as a developmentally disabled person most prelingually deafened persons have a medically stable condition and have gradually adjusted to their disability, accepted their deafness, and function as contributing members of the deaf community through church, clubs, or other activities.

Indications that the deaf client might pose some rehabilitation challenges include a troubled school or work history, financial or interpersonal dependence upon parents past adulthood, social isolation and/or lack of meaningful relationships with other deaf people, obvious distrust of hearing people, a history of dependence upon SSI or other sources of support, and the existence of a secondary handicap.

For deaf clients with no work history and no interest in post-secondary training, a work evaluation is sometimes useful. The counselor should specify exactly what information is needed—a list of the client's abilities, a list of jobs that the client can do, or a list of the *potential* jobs a client could do after receiving services such as work adjustment training, vocational training, or even communication skills training (Sliger & Culpepper, 1979). The work evaluator should, of course, have adequate ASL skills or the evaluation is of questionable validity.

Goal Setting

Goal setting should take into account the client's assessed strengths as well as his/her level of self-awareness and knowledge of career options. Integrating this information requires considerable counselor skill in both communication and counseling. Unfortunately, many deaf clients have little understanding of work requirements and choose either unrealistic or stereotyped occupational goals. A cognitive-behavioral counseling approach works best with those clients who need some exposure to reality and the consequences of their choices.

One under-utilized technique with deaf clients which holds promise is structured group counseling. Another strategy which has been used successfully with deaf clients is the Job Club. An impediment to realistic goal setting is the lack of available community resources to meet vocational goals. The availability of training for deaf clients should be determined when considering a goal; it is a rare deaf person who can succeed in a vocational or post-secondary training program which is designed for hearing clients, even with the provision of interpreters, notetakers and other support services. Additionally, the local job market for certain job skills needs to be determined—for example, deaf people used to make good money as printers until automation decreased drastically the number of available jobs.

Service Delivery

The major concern in providing services for deaf clients is the availability and accessibility of appropriate resources. Because deafness is a low-incidence disability and the communication needs of deaf clients are unique, it is difficult to find training facilities—sheltered workshops through post-secondary programs—that use qualified staff and support services, including interpreters and notetakers. Similarly, mental and physical restoration services, if needed, must be chosen with great care. Frequently, because of a dearth of resources, the rehabilitation counselor will be required to provide services outside the usual purview of rehabilitation (Schein, 1977).

The Individualized Written Rehabilitation Plan (IWRP) potentially can involve the client more completely in the choice of goals and services to reach these goals. However, care must be taken to insure that the deaf client truly understands what is written in the IWRP and what client rights are assured through it. Otherwise, the time and effort involved in developing the IWRP is truly futile.

Placement

Placement considerations for the deaf client take into account the use of counselor intervention only when necessary. Counselor assistance may include all of the following or be limited to some of these strategies: contacting the employer, filling out application forms, modifying or waiving the use of verbally based employment tests, providing interpreters for the interview and for the job orientation after employment, informing employers of the training and communication needs of deaf employees, and suggesting communication aids and signaling devices. Other possible rehabilitation services include employer awareness programs regarding reasonable accommodation and environmental modification for deaf workers, including underemployment, job stereotyping, and lack of advancement.

RECENT TRENDS IN DEAFNESS REHABILITATION

Over the past decade, rehabilitation services for deaf clients have changed considerably due to new legislative emphasis, greater professional training and skill in working with deaf clients, more resources to meet a diversity of client needs, and greater consumer involvement. Each of these trends will be discussed.

Legislation

The Rehabilitation Act of 1973 (PL 93–112) has incorporated affirmative action and equal employment opportunity for all disabled persons under Title V, Sections 501–504 of the Act. Deaf persons can be provided reasonable accommodations in employment under this law, including, but not limited to, assistance with communication needs as noted previously. Under this law deafness qualifies as a severe disability, thus prioritizing the rehabilitation needs of deaf clients.

The Rehabilitation Amendments of 1978 (PL 95–602) further advance the possibility of expanded services to deaf clients in the area of information and referral, comprehensive rehabilitation centers, independent living, interpreting services, and the Individual Written Rehabilitation Plan (IWRP).

The sections which are particularly relevant to the needs of deaf clients are as follows:

Section 101(a)(7)c mandates hiring personnel, either counselors or interpreters, who can use the client's method of communication.

Section 102(b) requires that the annual review of the IWRP be performed in the client's method of communication either by the counselor or an interpreter.

Section 101(a)(22) provides equal access to information and referral programs for deaf clients.

Section 103(b) authorizes the purchase or rental of TDDs to assist deaf clients.

Section 304(d)(1) provides for interpreter training with specified standards of competency.

Section 305, which establishes Comprehensive Rehabilitation Centers, emphasizes the use of support personnel such as interpreters. Similarly, Centers for Independent Living are required to provide interpreter services as needed.

Professional Training

The number of rehabilitation counselors who have an understanding of deafness and are able to communicate in sign language has increased dramatically in the past decade, due primarily to the establishment of specialist rehabilitation education graduate programs and the recognition of the need for hiring RCDs (rehabilitation counselors for the deaf) and SCDs (state coordinators in deafness) within the state systems and legislation designed to make rehabilitation services accessible to deaf clients. There are seven graduate programs which specialize in deafness rehabilitation, two of which are accredited by the Commission on Rehabilitation Education (CORE). Most states have standards for and actively recruit RCDs; many have SCDs. Additionally, a state plan for services to deaf clients has been adopted by many states (Schein, 1979).

Resources

Deaf clients have available greater opportunities for post-secondary training due to new programs with full support services which have been established at over 52 colleges in the United States (Rawlings, Trybus, & Biser, 1981). To a lesser extent, rehabilitation and independent living centers and community service centers have expanded their services to deaf clients. A comprehensive listing of facilities and professionals serving deaf adults is updated yearly in the April issue of the *American Annals of the Deaf.*

Consumer Involvement

Deaf consumers, once quiescent, now actively advocate their rights through such organizations as the National Association of the Deaf (NAD), American Deafness and Rehabilitation Association (ADARA), and numerous local and state organizations. Many state rehabilitation agencies have deaf consumers on their Advisory Boards and on the screening committees which hire RCDs.

Future Concerns

Although many advances have been made in rehabilitation services to deaf clients, there remain some areas of concern:

1. As unemployment in general grows, there are increasing fears that the problem will become a greater problem for deaf workers particularly as the trend moves away from an industrial and toward a service-oriented economy.
2. Rehabilitation has always served the higher-functioning deaf client best. There still is a dearth of facilities designed to serve lower-functioning deaf clients (Danek & Lawrence, 1981; Peterson, 1981) particularly those with additional handicaps.
3. The number of young deaf adults who will be entering the labor force over the next decade is expected to double due to the 1963–65 maternal rubella epidemic. Many of these individuals will be multiply handicapped (rubella also causes mental retardation and orthopedic, visual, and cardiac problems) and will present rehabilitation challenges (Vernon, 1981). A doubling of RCDs to handle these clients is necessary but due to state and federal budget reductions, unlikely.

In summary, deaf clients have reaped the benefit of legislative and philosophical changes in rehabilitation services over the past decade. Concerns for the future include a projected increase in unemployment among deaf people, a doubling in the number of deaf individuals entering the job market over the short-term, and a lack of specialized or accessible facilities for clients who are unable to enter post-secondary programs.

SOURCES OF ADDITIONAL INFORMATION

National Association of the Deaf (NAD)
814 Thayer Avenue
Silver Spring, MD 20910

The official service organization for deaf people. Publication: *The Deaf American*

American Deafness and Rehabilitation Association (ADARA)
814 Thayer Avenue
Silver Spring, MD 20910
The professional deafness rehabilitation association. Publication: *Journal of Rehabilitation of the Deaf*

National Center on Employment of the Deaf
National Technical Institute for the Deaf
One Lomb Memorial Drive
Rochester, NY 14623
Has a nationwide Career Matching System.

24 Epilepsy Rehabilitation: Assessment and Counseling Concerns

Robert T. Fraser
David Clemmons

Epilepsy is a chronic disorder of the central nervous system. The word *epilepsy* comes from a Greek word meaning "to be seized" and is a generic term which refers to a wide variety of seizure conditions. A seizure, on the cellular level, involves a disruption of the normal electrical activity of the brain by a process in which the involved cells become unstable and discharge their electrical impulses simultaneously. A seizure may be confined to one area (partial seizures) or may take place throughout the entire brain (generalized seizures). The abnormal electrical discharges which cause seizures are phenomena which originate in the cerebral hemispheres, but may spread to other brain areas, such as the hypothalamus and the medulla. The extent to which seizures impair brain function depends both on their duration and their location in the brain. Thus, some seizures may impair normal functioning only slightly, while others involve a complete cessation of normal activities. The *recurring* nature of seizures is important to a definition of epilepsy. Many transient physical conditions may cause an isolated seizure, but a person is not said to have epilepsy unless seizures are recurring.

The incidence of epilepsy in the general population is between 1 and 3% and tends to vary with age group (Anderson, 1978, p. 148). Genetic causes in epilepsy are contributing but not major, and differ according to seizure type. Genetic diagnosis often involves family diagnosis to establish the rate of risk for having a child with the disability (Black, 1980). Major causes of epilepsy include head injury, birth trauma, infectious diseases in the mother, anoxia, brain tumors,

° Completion of this manuscript was partially supported by Grant No. NS-17111, awarded by the National Institute of Neurological, Communicative Disorders and Stroke and by Office of Special Education and Rehabilitation Services, Grant No. G0080C0025.

a high concentration of alcohol or street drugs, parasitic infections (e.g., meningitis), and vascular diseases affecting the brain's blood vessels. This is only a partial listing of epilepsy's causes, and it should be noted that in many cases the etiology of a persons' epilepsy is simply unknown.

SEIZURE TYPES

Seizures are classified according to the presence or absence of a local focus in the cerebral hemispheres, the effect on consciousness, and the clinical symptoms during the seizure. According to the International Classification of Seizure Types (Gastaut, 1970), the primary classifications of concern to the rehabilitation counselor would include

1. Partial seizure (seizures beginning locally, involving a part of one cerebral hemisphere) (a) without impairment of consciousness; (b) with impairment of consciousness.
2. Generalized seizures (involving impairment of both hemispheres).

Partial Seizures

Seizures that are considered partial can be further divided into partial elementary and partial complex seizures. Perhaps the most common category of seizures to be encountered by the rehabilitation counselor will be partial complex or partial seizures with complex symptoms. Psychomotor seizures of this type can involve both psychical changes (déjà vu experiences, other unusual sensory or emotional experiences, etc.) and sudden motor movements on the part of the individual. These motor movements can involve lip smacking, fumbling with one's hands, repetitive picking at clothing, and even removing articles of clothing. At times, an individual may be involved in aimless wandering around a room or other ambulatory movement. This seizure type can also be accompanied by humming, moaning, or nonsensical verbalization. There are other partial complex seizures without motor components, but these are less frequent. Partial complex seizures of this type usually involve impaired consciousness and complex symptoms, like sudden emotional or sensory changes.

Partial elementary seizures usually involve only one system such as the motor or sensory. Motor seizures, without impairment of consciousness, are particularly common. In some cases, the seizure will simply involve jerking movements of the thumb, toe, or some other part of the body. In other cases, there is actually a "march-like" movement in which the jerking begins in a hand and then seems to progressively involve the respective arm and shoulder (Jacksonian seizure).

Generalized Seizures

This seizure category involves aberrant electrical activity occurring in both cerebral hemispheres at the same time. Within this classification of seizures, the generalized tonic-clonic or "grand mal" seizure is the most common. Although not necessarily the most difficult to treat it is this seizure type with which the general public is most familiar. This type of seizure involves two stages: a tonic stage in which the body becomes rigid for about a 15-second period, and a clonic stage in which the person endures muscle contractions and jerking movements. This convulsive stage normally lasts less than a minute. The duration of the tonic-clonic or grand mal seizure is normally less than 2 or 3 minutes, although the person having the seizure may be disoriented or fatigued for some time. Some seizures begin as partial and generalize into "grand mal" seizures.

The other type of generalized seizure which is most common is the simple absence or "petit mal" seizure. This seizure takes only a few seconds and involves a blank staring, a brief disruption of consciousness, and frequently eyelid fluttering. Some absence seizures are more complex and involve automatic motor movements such as chewing. These distinguished from psychomotor or partial complex seizures by their distinctive 3-per-second spike and wave tracings on the electroencephalogram (EEG). *It should be emphasized that an individual can have any type of seizure and have been told by friends, family, or others that they have a petit mal condition* in order to minimize their concern about having seizures or due to a lack of seizure knowledge.

ANTICONVULSANTS

The general goal in using anticonvulsants is gaining maximum seizure control without causing undue harm to the body through the anticonvulsant's side effects. In some cases, an individual may be seizure-free but so toxic on medication(s) that school, work, and other life activities are precluded. The usual strategy in seeking seizure control is to use one primary anticonvulsant appropriate to the seizure type and monitor to maximum tolerable dosage. Adding a second drug can reduce the efficacy of both and result in cumulative side effects. Consequently, additional anticonvulsants are added only when necessary.

The maintenance of appropriate drug levels is a common problem in seizure management and is particularly difficult if an individual is taking several anticonvulsants. Periodic blood serum levels are helpful in ensuring that an individual is receiving maximum benefit from the anticonvulsant medication. Medication compliance is a real problem in epilepsy and a substantial segment of the population has poor seizure control due simply to poor compliance. It is common for people not to take their medication because of deficient memory, embarrassment, or side effect concerns. In other cases, the appropriate blood levels are not maintained due to changes in the person's metabolism, interactions with other medications such as aspirin and antabuse, or fever. In cases where an individual is taking other medications recommended by a psychiatrist, the first emphasis is on emotional stabilization—despite the fact that some psychiatric medications may reduce anticonvulsant effectiveness. Following the achievement of emotional stability (unless the seizure condition is life-threatening), the neurologist can work on the best anticonvulsant regimen. Women who are pregnant or considering pregnancy should consult their neurologist in regard to anticonvulsant regimen.

Dilantin and phenobarbital, introduced in the first half of the 20th century, have been commonly used in the treatment of epilepsy, but are not necessarily the medications of choice. More than a dozen anticonvulsants are now used in seizure management. If an individual has been on the same medical regimen for years with poor results, it is important that the anticonvulsants be re-evaluated by a neurologist who is currently versed in seizure management. Examples of anticonvulsants used in relation to seizure type include Tegretol, Dilantin, or Mesantoin as a primary anticonvulsant for generalized tonic-clonic or grand mal seizures. Absence or petit mal seizures are treated by Zarontin, or occasionally Clonopin. More recently, Depakene (valproic acid) has been used as a primary anticonvulsant for generalized tonic-clonic and absence seizures. For individuals with partial complex or psychomotor seizures, Tegretol and Dilantin are commonly used. To treat simple partial seizures, Dilantin is often used. Anticonvulsants that are utilized as secondary medications include Tranxene, Mysoline, phenobarbital, and Mesantoin.

The rehabilitation counselor must be cognizant of anticonvulsant side effects and relate this information to the neurologist in situations where this is not being done by the client. Side effects may include gum overgrowth, facial hair, clumsiness, double vision, drowsiness, inability to concentrate, nausea, or dizziness. Occasionally, more severe side effects such as disturbances in liver function or suppression of bone marrow have been observed. The above are presented only as examples and many individuals are primarily unaffected by anticonvulsant side effects in their daily functioning. Most individuals can gain sufficient seizure control (not necessarily freedom from seizures) to enter the work force. Estimates of those who will be seizure-free vary from 30 to 50% (Freeman, 1979; Reynolds, 1976), but medication compliance is a complicating factor in maintaining a seizure-free status. After 1 to 2 years of freedom from seizures, some neurologists will begin to take their patients off the medication.

MEDICATION STATUS: DEFINING FUNCTIONAL LIMITATIONS

In most cases, the rehabilitation counselor will have the benefit of the neurologist's examination and history-taking, in addition to the results of wake and/or sleep EEGs to confirm the seizure diagnosis. An ideal situation is working through a neurologist who specializes in epilepsy. Presently, the comprehensive epilepsy centers in this country are using prolonged (24-hour) EEG videotelemetry monitoring to aid in seizure diagnosis of the more difficult cases. It is of interest that prolonged monitoring of difficult cases often determines a case to be that of hysterical reaction in contrast to a true seizure condition. The computerized axial tomography (CAT) scan has been invaluable as a neuroradiologic device that identified abnormal structures and difficulties within the brain without invasive approaches and other more complicated techniques.

The rehabilitation counselor should begin vocational planning with the seizure client as soon as possible, despite the fact that optimal seizure control may not have been reached. Numerous clients perform well in school, in specialized training, and on the job while having grand mal and/or non-convulsive seizures on a monthly and sometimes weekly basis. The counselor does need to know very specific medical information for use in the vocational planning process. The following points need to be clarified in establishing functional limitations:

- Clear *description of seizure behavior* and frequency (i.e., does a person fall, have convulsions, or lose consciousness).
- Existence of a temporal or situational pattern to the seizures, (e.g., some have seizures only occurring at 5:00 A.M., when

dealing with specific family members, or when relaxing on a coffee break). Some individuals might be asked to keep a seizure log if they have no idea of a pattern.

- Do certain precipitants relate to seizure activity (e.g., stress, flickering lights, alcohol, fatigue, or menses)?
- Some individuals will *briefly* experience a seizure increase due to the stress of a new job.
- Does the individual have *consistent* warning sensation or aura related to a seizure's beginning and how much time does that provide in relation to taking safety precautions?
- How do people recover from seizures and what are the seizure consequences? Some people can return to work almost immediately following a seizure, while others will need to rest for some time. Certain individuals will be disoriented, unable to concentrate, and may need a few hours off the job.
- What are the client's specific medications and is compliance with anticonvulsants a problem? This area may need to be repeatedly addressed and medication efficacy monitored through blood levels.
- Will the client's anticonvulsant program change and are there any medication side effects?
- Can the individual drive? In some states a specific seizure-free period is required prior to licensing, while in other cases an individual determination is made by the neurologist, based upon comprehensive seizure information. Transportation concerns may need to be discussed in the majority of cases. For some clients, the inadvisability of their driving can become a counseling issue.

ASPECTS OF VOCATIONAL EVALUATION

In working to establish a vocational goal, most of the generally used aptitude, interest, and achievement tests are applicable for use with the epilepsy population. Some of the interest inventories can be more helpful than others. Since the vocational focus is often toward unskilled and semi-skilled jobs, or trades that require relatively short-term training, the Gordon Occupational Check List is particularly helpful. The Gordon directly lists several hundred work tasks in these areas and asks clients to indicate those activities in which they are most interested. The task-specific nature of these activities is particularly helpful. A section at the end of the inventory which asks the client to describe an ideal job and aspects of the job which they might like or dislike is also very assistive. This requires a client writing sample which serves as an initial screening procedure for learning disability.

It is of interest that a recent study using the Strong Campbell (Fraser, Trejo, Temkin, & Clemmons, 1982) suggests that early-onset males with grand mal seizures are particularly at risk in relation to having their band of interest narrowed and being less comfortable in academic settings than their male peers. Academic achievement tests such as the Differential Aptitude Test Battery are used as a rough gauge of academic achievement. It must be stressed, however, that those with an average level intelligence and above are often inappropriately placed in special education tracks during their elementary and high school years. These tests may be poor indicators of their academic capabilities due to the special education backgrounds and time loss from school due to seizures and anticonvulsant changes.

Standard vocational aptitude tests are often appropriately used in epilepsy rehabilitation because these tests ordinarily have norms developed more critically than would ordinarily be the case. While research in this area is not well developed, Clemmons (1983) has done some initial work with the General Aptitude Test Battery (GATB). Research with the battery indicated that it may not be an adequate predictor of success for jobs requiring manual abilities. In the Clemmons study, rehabilitation clients placed in jobs stressing manual dexterity and motor speed performed successfully, despite their GATB scores being substantially lower than the job's published cutting scores. These results underscore the importance of not using the GATB to screen out potential workers solely on the basis of lowered dexterity or motor speed scores. Employers often do not have uniform job aptitude demands. These individuals may also improve their motor and dexterity aptitudes given time, the modeling of co-workers, and the job's monetary or social reinforcement.

This same study indicated that the battery may be of utility as a rough screening device for lateralized cerebral dysfunction, a common pattern among neurologically disabled populations. The study implicated the scales for Verbal Ability (V) and for Spatial Perception (S) as being helpful in the early identification of persons with later confirmed impairment of the left and right hemispheres, respectively. When there was an observed discrepancy between the V and S scales in excess of one standard deviation, neuropsychological testing frequently demonstrated a corresponding discrepancy between language and visual-spatial skills. This finding has been used successfully in encouraging the state vocational rehabilitation agency to invest in more thorough evaluation of brain impairment using a neuropsychological battery. Although the Benton Visual Retention Test, the Trail Making Test, Wechsler Digit Symbol, and other tests have been used in screening for brain impairment, the GATB Verbal vs. Spatial differential and subtest scatter appears to be a better prognosticator of later findings using a complete neuropsychological battery. The GATB, of course, taps a wider range of abilities and consequently is more apt to be sensitive to brain impairment. Continuing study is ongoing in this area.

THE VALUE OF NEUROPSYCHOLOGICAL ASSESSMENT

Rodin, Shapiro, & Lennox (1977) studied the files of 369 patients seen at the Epilepsy Center of Michigan between 1970 and 1974. Results indicated that only 23% had *epilepsy only* without any associated difficulties. Among the remainder with associated problems, brain impairment was the largest presenting difficulty. There is no question that the counselor who works in the rehabilitation agency office or in a hospital setting will see a number of seizure clients with associated brain impairment. It must be emphasized that a psychological evaluation suggesting *organic brain damage* is simply not enough information. It is the neuropsychologist who can provide the counselor with more specific information on brain-behavior relationships and what neurological defects may have cost the client in relation to current performance abilities.

Typical referral to a neuropsychologist will involve evaluation on a comprehensive battery such as the Halstead-Reitan. Dodrill (1978) developed a comprehensive battery of 16 discriminative measures sensitive to brain impairment in epilepsy. The battery includes Halstead's Neuropsychological Battery for Adults, the Trail Making Test, the Aphasia Screening Test, the Logical Memory and Visual Reproduction parts of Wechsler Memory Scale, Form I, Sensory-Perceptual Examination, the Stroop Test, and Seashore Tonal Memory Test. These tests enable the evaluation of a broad range of functions that can relate to job performance, including motor performance, sensory-perceptual abilities, memory, ability to attend to a task, problem solving, language skills and visual-spatial abilities.

Before the widespread use of anticonvulsant medication following World War II, uncontrolled seizure conditions were often likely to overshadow other considerations. Today, most persons with epilepsy have attained at least partial seizure control and factors such as neuropsychological functioning and psychosocial adjustment are more likely to define the parameters of their vocational potential.

PSYCHOSOCIAL CONCERNS

Reviews of relevant literature indicate that no personality patterns have been established that are unique to the population with epilepsy (Epilepsy Foundation of America, 1975, p. 58). Bear and Fedio (1977) are representative of a number of individuals who have related temporal lobe epilepsy to changes in behavior (obsessionalism, hypergraphia), thought (consuming religious and philosophical interests), and sudden changes in affect (anger, emotional liability, and sadness). Much of the temporal lobe research remains controversial. Research, to date, on the psychosocial concerns of those with epilepsy may be nonrepresentative of the general population due to methodological problems (Fraser, 1983). It is likely, however, that those coming to rehabilitation agencies or hospital vocational units for services will have adjustment concerns relating to seizures (Dodrill & Batzel, 1981). Some individuals will feel *stigmatized* by having relatively few seizures, but below are the types of factors that can render the person with seizures at risk for psychosocial maladjustment:

- A substantial number of lifetime grand mal or psychomotor seizures
- Having several types of seizures
- Not understanding epilepsy and/or never having seen a seizure
- Lack of the disability's acceptance by significant others, parents, or teachers
- Member of lower socioeconomic group
- Limited range of life experience—social processing deficits
- Existence of significant neuropsychological impairment.

Among a number of clients, it is neuropsychological impairment that causes the greatest difficulties with adjustment (Dodrill, 1980). In assessing the need for psychosocial intervention, the 132-item Washington Psychosocial Seizure Inventory developed by Dodrill, Batzel, Queisser, and Temkin (1980) can serve as an excellent screening device. The critical item list can be particularly helpful as a starting point for counseling intervention. For a detailed discussion of psychosocial concerns and treatment issues in epilepsy, see the recent test by Sands (1982).

REHABILITATION PLANNING AND COUNSELING INTERVENTIONS

Following the collection of evaluation data, there are a number of planning issues that are important in epilepsy rehabilitation. An initial point is to ensure that the client's family and significant others are working in the same direction as counselor and client. Although parents identify independence and job finding as major concerns for a son or daughter (Sutton, Smith, & Fraser, 1979), they often detract from efforts in these areas by overprotecting and sheltering their offspring.

A key focus in counseling can be training parents and family to encourage risk-taking behavior on the part of the client (e.g., using public transportation alone). A complementary emphasis is to advise the job seeker with epilepsy to take all possible safety precautions when traveling or in new environs (e.g., being aware of hazardous objects in the environment or wearing a bracelet with identifying medical information). Family members often need assistance in identifying realistic expectations for the person with seizures. Those closest to the seizure client can be very helpful by encouraging medication compliance, adequate rest, and good diet.

Independent living efforts will often precede or directly follow the securing of a job. Some individuals will need to move to a group home situation or will profit from training by Developmental Disabilities and other community agency trainers in maintaining their own apartment, cooking, budgeting, and use of public transportation. It should be emphasized that the rehabilitation process should be a very active one for the seizure client. These individuals have spent much of their lives waiting for better seizure control, new anticonvulsants, or changes in their medication dosages. They can severely lack a sense of mastery over their lives. By being very active in the rehabilitative process, they can gain a feeling of control over their future and have greater faith in the process.

If immediate job search activity is not appropriate for a client, community work experiences on a volunteer basis can be very helpful. These types of experiences are often developed in any number of job slots (e.g., printing, custodial, secretarial, or food service) that exist within hospitals, universities, federal government, or non-profit agencies. A volunteer employee status can guarantee accident insurance coverage. These positions enable a client to explore interests, identify abilities, and learn to deal with seizure occurrences on a job site. After clients adjust to work activity, attention to a task and the motor movements involved in work often tend to raise the seizure threshold. Those with epilepsy who work will frequently have seizures while relaxing on break or at the end of the work day when fatigued.

In matching a client to a job functional limitations are frequently reduced due to job site modification or job restructuring. In the work setting, inexpensive plastic guards on hazardous machinery and rubber matting on a concrete floor area are examples of job site modification. In other cases, assigning driving tasks to a different worker or simply not requiring the person to do a specific task (e.g., operate a crane) are examples of job restructuring. Jobs in which client success have been demonstrated with modification or restructuring include those of luggage maker, foundry worker, or dental hygienist. Although working at heights or near molten liquid/hot ovens are common work environment restrictions, some individuals can work in these areas due to their specific seizure conditions or certain job accommodations.

Individual counseling sessions are often focused on acceptance of one's seizure condition and clarifying independence issues. Supportive, client-centered counseling approaches are helpful in enabling the client to explain what epilepsy is to them and its effect upon their lives. Some clients will need to be educated about the causes and nature of epilepsy. For those who experience this cyclic disability, it can be especially important that their counselor makes them feel understood and sensitively reflects their feelings. Feeling accepted and understood is particularly important for those who encounter few others within their family or community who really understand the disability. At the same time, however, the counselor can often establish a reasonable expectancy of vocational self-sufficiency for those experiencing even several seizures a month.

Since a substantial portion of the rehabilitation population with epilepsy will have some associated brain impairment, traditional psychodynamic counseling approaches are often ineffective. Paradoxical approaches as pioneered by Erickson (Haley, 1973) and other brief therapy approaches (Barten, 1971) have been useful with those having inflexible problem-solving styles. Behaviorally oriented counseling approaches, however, appear to be generally applicable. As a by-product of the disability, many individuals feel a loss of control in their lives, experience a considerable amount of self-defeating thoughts, and feel distress in social situations. Many become relative social isolates and present a mild to moderately depressed affect in the counseling interview.

A common approach with these clients is to assist them in identifying the life activities and situations which lead to negative, self-defeating thoughts and consequent anxiety or depression. Counselor and client might review the client's written record of specific activities, thoughts, and moods during a given week. The client, assisted by his counselor, will formulate new goals focused on positive behavior change and a hierarchy of tasks, simple to complex, designed to meet those goals. Clients might begin to complete simple tasks (e.g., getting a haircut) and reward themselves with previously identified reinforcers (e.g., scheduling a movie). The counselor will very often be a key reinforcer, being expansive in praise and further abet progress by assisting the client to begin to use more competence-engendering thoughts ("I'm doing more positive activities and moving towards my job goal"). Eventually, clients work toward more complex tasks to reach higher goals.

Skills have also been taught in a group format in a mood management class. For a complete discussion of this approach and other behaviorally oriented, skill training classes (problem-solving, conversational skills, or assertiveness), the reader is directed to a recent overview by Fraser and Smith (1982). The skill acquisition approach is often the most appropriate for the seizure client. Many have been developmentally sheltered and have not engaged in the risk-taking behavior that results in social learning and competency. A group format can be an efficient and equally effective intervention.

Group interactions among those with epilepsy can be of great value in their better understanding and accepting their seizure condition. This type of interaction is more important for individuals with an "invisible" disability. Job-finding clubs (Azrin, Flores, & Kaplan, 1977) are assistive not only for their behaviorally oriented approach to securing jobs, but also because the contact with others having seizures desensitizes clients to their personal condition. In the job club, job-seeking skills are modeled for the clients and rehearsed by them. Job-seeking behaviors are practiced and reinforced by counselors and group members. Since associated brain impairment can be prevalent, some behaviors will need to be almost "overtrained" with specific prepared scripts being used for some job search activity (e.g., telephone contacts with employers). Most clients with a seizure condition need to be counseled in regard to discussing their seizure condition with an employer. They may need to develop a personally comfortable statement that is understandable to the employer.

Post-employment counseling can be particularly helpful to assist those with epilepsy-associated difficulties, such as social processing skill deficits, emotional problems, or types of brain impairment, in adjusting to job task and environment demands. In a recent study, only 1 of 20 individuals actually lost a job due to seizures—counseling issues were prominent (Fraser, Clemmons, Trejo, & Temkin, 1983).

CONCLUSION

The present chapter has presented an overview of assessment concerns in the field of epilepsy rehabilitation. A perspective on rehabilitation planning and counseling intervention was also presented. It is emphasized that a thorough understanding of the client's disability early in the process can greatly facilitate positive placement outcome. The client with an active seizure condition can be highly employable. An emphasis on post-employment counseling can be especially helpful.

RESOURCES

1. Copies of the vocational intake form as used at the University of Washington Epilepsy Center can be received through requests to the authors. Epilepsy Center (ZA-50), 325 Ninth Avenue, Seattle, WA 98104.
2. The Washington Psychosocial Seizure Inventory, related materials, and cost sheet are available by writing to Carl Dodrill, Ph.D., at the same University of Washington Epilepsy Center address.
3. The Epilepsy Foundation of America frequently updates materials related to all aspects of epilepsy and epilepsy services. Computer searches are also available through its national library. National Headquarters address: 4351 Garden City Drive, Landover, MD 20785 (301) 459–3700.

25 Traumatic Head Injury: Implications for Rehabilitation Counseling

Ruth Torkelson Lynch

The complex physical, psychological, social, and vocational consequences of traumatic head injury have become a major concern for rehabilitation counselors. Each year, 400,000 to 600,000 persons incur a severe traumatic head injury. Each year, 100,000 of these people die, and between 30,000 and 50,000 others are left with disabilities severe enough to preclude a return to a normal life (U.S. Department of Education, 1981). Approximately one-half of all traumatic head injuries are caused by motor vehicle accidents; the incidence among males is almost twice that among females, and males 15 to 24 years of age incur more head injuries than any other age group (Anderson & McLaurin, 1980). Improved emergency medical care, advanced life support technology, sophisticated diagnostic equipment, and expanded patient management have greatly increased survival rates. With a higher incidence of traumatic head injury survivors, the rehabilitation community has been forced to examine services available for this client population. Consequently, there will be an ever-increasing concern for this group by rehabilitation counselors.

One aspect of the long-term consequences of head injury is the estimated economic expense associated with (a) direct care cost (the dollar value of real goods and services associated with health care), and (b) indirect cost (the monetary loss incurred by society when the productivity of the injured person has been interrupted). The total cost of head injury in the United States in 1974 was estimated at $2.4 billion ($3.9 billion in 1980). The largest average annual costs are with individuals from the 25- to 44-year-old age group who are in their prime wage-earning years and thus have higher indirect costs (Kalsbeek, McLaurin, Harris, & Miller, 1980). Since indirect costs make up two-thirds of the overall cost following head injury, there is crucial need for rehabilitation intervention.

From a rehabilitation standpoint, the traumatically head-injured have been a frustrating and often neglected group of clients since probability for "rehabilitation success" has been regarded negatively. Rusk, Block, and Lowman (1969) attributed this pessimistic attitude to the "profoundly critical nature of the initial neurologic picture, the multiplicity of concomitant complications, the long-time span of recovery, and the paucity of well-documented long-term clinical follow-up reports which might generate optimism" (p. 677). Within the past few years, however, there has been a significant increase in research investigating correlates of outcome and documenting positive rehabilitation gains (e.g., Ben-Yishay & Diller, 1981; Bond, 1976; Jellinek, Torkelson, & Harvey, 1982; Levin & Grossman, 1978; Najenson, Groswasser, Mendelson, & Hackett, 1980; Torkelson, Jellinek, Malec, & Harvey, 1983). Awareness of the complex rehabilitation needs of brain-injured individuals has stimulated the development of specialized rehabilitation programs, national and state organizations, and further research efforts. The topic has increasingly received attention by the public press (Lasden, 1982) and the federal government (National Institute of Handicapped Research, 1982; U.S. Department of Education, 1981).

DEFINITION AND IMPACT ON FUNCTION

Severe traumatic head injury occurs when there is either direct damage to the brain (e.g., caused by gunshot wounds or bone fragments), or severe concussion, which may lead to brain swelling, bruising or damage through an increase in intracranial fluid pressure (U.S. Department of Education, 1981). In contrast with the greater predictability of many other diseases of the brain which result in damage limited to local areas of the brain (e.g., stroke, brain tumor), traumatic head injury may result in diffuse brain damage. Since it is generally known that specific areas of the brain control various intellectual and physical functions (Reitan, 1975), each traumatic head injury can be expected to produce a unique set of resulting symptoms and functional deficits.

Several factors have been examined in relation to outcome following traumatic head injury. Age is one factor which strongly influences both the physical and mental consequences of injury, with young apes having the most favorable prognoses (Benton, 1979; Bond, 1976). Length of unconsciousness can occasionally be followed by a good recovery (e.g., returning to work) (Gilchrist & Wilkinson, 1979); most findings directly relate duration of unconsciousness to increasing psychological impairment (Bond, 1976; Klove & Cleeland, 1972). The extent of neurological damage can also provide valuable prognostic information. Cognitive impairment, interpersonal isolation, and motor slowing have been found to be directly related to the presence of EEG abnormalities and to abnormal CT findings (Levin & Grossman, 1978).

The functional impact of traumatic head injury can include physical, cognitive-intellectual, and personality-emotional components (Torkelson, 1982). Physical consequences can include hemiparesis; visual deficits; muscle spasticity; bowel and bladder dysfunction; seizures; sensory impairment related to touch, vision, pain, temperature, and position sense; aphasia; and/or deficits in spatial perception. Often both sides of the body are impaired to some extent even though one side may dominate (Anderson, 1981).

Cognitive-intellectual consequences can include impaired verbal associative processes such as naming and word production (Benton, 1979; Levin, Grossman, & Kelly, 1976a; Torkelson & Lynch, 1979); memory deficits (Brooks, 1975; Groher, 1977; Levin, Grossman & Kelly 1976b); decreased attention, reaction time, information processing, and speed of decision making (Gronwall, 1976; Levin & Grossman, 1978); impaired learning ability; decreased performance on verbal and mathematic intelligence tests; and/or alteration in cognitive processes such as concrete thinking and a decreased appreciation of subtleties (Wallhagen, 1979).

Personality-emotional consequences can be categorized as change of personality (i.e., change in reactions to events and to people) and changes of temperament. Change in personality may be evidenced by a lack of foresight, tact, and concern; inability to plan ahead or judge consequences of actions; loss of refinement; and/or lessened vitality (Lishman, 1973). Changes of temperament, which are likely to be based on specific brain pathology, include fluctuating depression and withdrawal; disinhibition and euphoria; morbid anxiety; obsessional traits; persistent irritability; perplexity, distractibility; and fatigue; and/or a lowered tolerance for frustration and noise (Lezak, 1978b; Lishman, 1973). Due to the multifaceted nature of brain functioning and the diffuse nature of traumatic injury, each individual will have a unique array of functional limitations and residual capacities.

PSYCHOSOCIAL ASPECTS

Although physical, cognitive-intellectual, and personality-emotional functioning are important determinants of the extent of life adjustment achieved by an individual with head injury, social and vocational functioning ultimately indicate how the individual is adapting. Jennett and Bond (1975) emphasized that the individual's post-traumatic cognitive and emotional status is at least as powerful a determinant of personal and socioeconomic adjustment as is physical and neurological status. Bond (1976) reported that family cohesion appeared to be resistant to physical disability but much less so to mental handicap, especially memory and personality impairment. Memory impairment and disorders of personality were the areas of mental function primarily responsible for poor social integration in terms of leisure, family, and work.

The immediate family's sense of isolation may be exacerbated by feelings of abandonment and lack of understanding from the extended family. Outside relatives are inclined to be critical because they do not experience the subtle changes in the brain-injured individual on a daily basis (Lezak, 1978b). Thomsen (1974) reported that the relationship between single patients and their mothers was generally better than between married patients and their spouses since very few spouses were able to accept such dramatic relationship changes. The persistence of denial by families (e.g., fantasies about patient recovery, inappropriate responses to the injured individual) typically leads to certain compromises in daily living (Romano, 1974). Families who allow themselves to recognize one area of limitation, usually involving physical function, meanwhile maintain denial of other limitations, typically those of mental functioning. In observations over a 4-year period following head injury, Romano (1974) observed that persistence of denial resulted in a family life centered around the injured family member, defending their normalcy to society, and accompanied by decreasing contact with non-family members.

Return to work has been the dominant theme in studies of social recovery after head injury. Factors having an adverse effect on return to work have been found to be age over 40; memory impairment; loss of concentration; impaired initiative, responsibility, intellect, and social sense; emotional liability; dysphasia; hemiplegia; sensory loss; and unrealistic goals (Bruckner & Randle, 1972; Lewinsohn & Graf, 1973). Cognitive limitations and disturbances in social behavior affect final employment results most negatively (Najenson, Grosswasser, Mendelson, & Hackett, 1980).

The "characterological alterations" (Lezak, 1978a) which are most likely to create adjustment problems for social, family, leisure, and vocational pursuits can be summarized in terms of deficits and psychosocial implications. An impaired capacity for social perceptiveness (deficit) results in self-centered behavior with greatly diminished empathy, self-reflective, and self-critical attitudes (implications). An impaired capacity for control and self-regulation (deficit) give rise to impulsivity, random restlessness, and impatience (implications). Stimulus-bound behavior (deficit) is evidenced as social dependency and difficulty in planning and organizing activities or projects (implications). Emotional alterations such as apathy, silliness, lability, irritability, and change in sexual interest (deficit) can seriously impinge on social and interpersonal relationships (implications). Inability to profit from experience (deficit) can compromise the individual's capacity for social learning (implication).

REHABILITATION PLANNING

Throughout the process of rehabilitation, goals and plans are set, modified, and put into action. The number of physical, social, psychological, and environmental problems which clients may experience can be confusing and overwhelming to rehabilitation professionals. This is particularly likely when dealing with complex cases of traumatic head injury. Merely identifying a person as having a closed head injury does not indicate whether the individual can speak, walk, handle perceptual tasks, or remember events from one hour to the next. The medical diagnosis itself does not provide any information about the person's ability to relate to other people, or about their vocational skills or environmental support system (Crewe & Athelstan, 1981). Thus, in order for goals to be meaningful, measurable, and manageable, it is helpful to utilize one of several functional descriptor measures (Indices, Inc., 1979). Rehabilitation planning which uses functional descriptors for physical and psychological variables can aid in recognizing specific components for rehabilitation intervention.

Understanding the typical course of recovery following head injury can facilitate rehabilitation planning. After head injury, an immediate precipitous decrease in the total breadth of functioning occurs (Fowler, 1981). Within approximately the first 6 months, there is spontaneous recovery of many abilities depending on factors such as age, length of unconsciousness, and extent of neurological damage and treatment. For several years after injury, recovery of function and abilities may occur, but the rate of recovery slows considerably after the initial, more rapid gains and is usually well stabilized at 12 months. The following generalizations by Fowler (1981) can be helpful.

> (a) the more closely the individual's abilities immediately following an injury resemble his premorbid abilities, the greater the probability that his future function will approximate his premorbid function; (b) the greater

> the loss immediately after injury, the lower the probability that even with time, the individual will come close to approximating the premorbid level; (c) the longer the period of time that the deficits persist, the greater the probability that they will be permanent. (p. 128)

Returning a person to work, school, and/or independent living demands a very careful evaluation of (a) the individual's job, school, or home setting; (b) the nature and extent of functional limitations present; and (c) the physical demands, complexity, interpersonal requirements and degree of new learning required for smooth transition to the community. It is important to consider stages of recovery, thereby enhancing the probabilities of success. If the client returns to a competitive work setting or independent living too early, the probability of failure increases. Early failure holds certain risks, including discouragement for client and family, employment termination, and damaged reputation which may prejudice future opportunities (Fowler, 1981).

Rehabilitation planning following head injury should allow time for spontaneous recovery; incorporate skill training/retraining to enhance functional recovery, improve the range of possible goals, and enhance goal attainment; and include serial assessment at various recovery points in conjunction with treatment (e.g., physical, medical, psychological, cognitive), retraining, and counseling. Flexibility in rehabilitation planning is of key importance considering ongoing changes in functional status.

COUNSELING PRACTICE

Counseling and assessment strategies following head injury are not easily separable. Assessment is ongoing and directs the counseling plan. Counseling practice could be conceptualized as incorporating three components: exploration/awareness, understanding/knowledge, action/skill building (Carkhuff, 1971a; Ponzo, 1976; Rubin & Roessler, 1978).

1. *Exploration/Awareness.* For each rehabilitation goal, the rehabilitation counselor should be willing to explore the experience of the injured person. By taking time to explore how and why each goal is important to the individual, barriers to goal attainment are more readily recognized and mutual compliance with rehabilitation planning is enhanced. This is equally applicable whether the goal is improved hygiene/grooming skills or vocational placement.

2. *Understanding/Knowledge.* Information and instructions should be communicated as clearly and explicitly as possible. For example, the injured person may find it difficult to understand how a particular cognitive retraining task, repeated over and over now, will relate to improved interpersonal skills and hence to increased social and vocational adjustment. Unless explanations are clear and repeated as often as necessary, progress toward functional goals may be hampered due to the individual's emotional reaction to a misunderstood task.

3. *Action/Skill Building.* This aspect of counseling can be essential for building skills and compensatory techniques which enhance functioning. Cognitive retraining using structured skill modules, memory retraining, language and communication exercises, adjustment counseling, and social skills exercises can be individualized to address vocational/independent living goals. Repetition of tasks and realistic discussion of functional limitations and assets are effective complements to skill building success. Since family involvement will likely enhance outcome significantly, family intervention via individual counseling, group support sessions, and educational discussions led by professionals is essential. Observations in environments and situations which are familiar to the injured individual can greatly aid the counselor's section of intervention strategies. Situation-appropriate behavior, problem-solving and planning ability, interactions with others, and behavior changes with environmental modifications can be assessed and incorporated into skill building.

RESOURCES

The rehabilitation counselor working with traumatic head-injured clients will soon realize that services needed by clients are often unavailable in the community. Existing services can frequently be adapted but in some cases they must be improvised (NIHR, 1982). Services need to be selected on a case-by-case basis since each individual's needs differ. Intensive services are especially crucial immediately after release from inpatient facilities. Community service providers, teachers, and employers will need education to help make appropriate accommodations. With multiple roles as advocate, educator, and case manager, the counselor should not hesitate to seek technical assistance, consultation from experts, and educational support.

Considering the sheer volume of head-trauma related disabilities and functional deficits, it is striking that efforts to initiate a national information network were not successful until 1980. At that time, the National Head Injury Foundation[1] was organized by family members and treatment professionals. Staffed by volunteers, the Foundation seeks to advocate for the needs of the head-injured person, and refers them and their families to local programs and services. State chapters and family emotional support groups have developed all over the country. The Foundation's quarterly newsletter, *Connection,* provides updated listings of support groups and specialized rehabilitation programs. Conferences specifically addressing head injury have also developed in various parts of the country sponsored by specialized rehabilitation centers. A Canadian counterpart is the Canadian Advocates for Rehabilitation of Head Trauma.[2]

For individuals seeking additional reading on the topic of traumatic head injury, professional journals in rehabilitation medicine, neurology, neuropsychology and disciplines offer numerous articles and research summaries. Federally funded research projects on severe head injury at New York University Medical Center and Santa Clara Valley Medical Center in San Jose, California, have published monographs and informational booklets, as have several other specialized rehabilitation centers around the country. A major effort at combining literature on head injury into one volume is exemplified by *Rehabilitation of the Head Injured Adult* (Rosenthal, Griffith, Bond, & Miller, 1983). For specific information regarding technical assistance, educational support, and specialized consultation, it is recommended that rehabilitation counselors contact the National Head Injury Foundation or a comprehensive rehabilitation center in their area.

CONCLUSIONS

Clearly, the best overall solution to the head injury problem is prevention. However, there will always be some incidence of head injury and thus a need for rehabilitation services. Traumatic head injury occurs msot frequently to young adult males in the prime of their career development and social independence. As such, the traumatically head-injured are a likely target for rehabilitation counseling services with respect to vocational and independent living goals. The rehabilitation counselor should first and foremost recognize the

[1] National Head Injury Foundation, Inc. (NHIF), 18A Vernon Street, Framingham, Massachusetts 01701, (617) 870-7473.

[2] Canadian Advocates for Rehabilitation of Head Trauma (CARHT), P. O. Box 8464, Dundas, Ontario L8H 5E7, Canada.

uniqueness of tramatic head injury. There has been sudden loss of "former self" which has implications for the injured individuals, their families, friends, teachers, and employers. Very often, head-injured individuals and their families exhibit a strong emotional reaction to any connotation of "brain damage." Although behaviors and functional limitations may be similar, the impact of traumatic head injury differs substantially from other disabilities (e.g., mental retardation, mental illness). Hence, efforts to arrange services in settings with other disabled persons are frequently met with resistance and may jeopardize the counselor/client/family relationship. An inability or resistance to recognize limitations may hinder cooperation with rehabilitation efforts. The mental/psychological limitations frequently increase over time even as physical problems decrease. Psychological distress of the head injured person and/or the family may be far more limiting than physical limitations. Flexibility, tenacity, creativity, and patience are key attributes for the rehabilitation professional serving this population.

Rehabilitation counselors have the opportunity to advocate and influence the future of specialized services for head-injured individuals. More and more, professionals with a conviction that treatment can be improved are developing aggressive programs designed to meet the complex needs of each patient. Various types of programs are taking shape, ranging from day treatment programs, which offer support services upon release from an intense rehabilitation program, to long-term care rehabilitation facilities for individuals who are best served in this way. An improved understanding of brain injury implications coupled with professional training in treatment techniques are a vital step toward improving rehabilitation outcomes. Returning the head-injured individual to a productive life with independence is certainly an exciting rehabilitation challenge.

26 Cancer and Chemotherapy: A Psychological Approach to Coping

John Dolan

Cancer is a complex disease that all too frequently causes prolonged and excruciating physical distress (Barckley, 1968; Bonica, 1978; Golden, 1975; Holland, 1976; Redd, 1980a, b; Rusk, 1971). In addition, the curative therapy for this condition is often accompanied by devastating side effects (Clark, Shapiro, & Friendly, 1981).

The Commission on Chronic Illness has defined chronic illness as "any impairment or deviation from normal that has one or more of the following characteristics: (1) is permanent; (2) leaves residual disability; (3) is caused by non-reversible pathological alteration; and (4) may be expected to require a long period of observation, supervision or care" (Mayo, 1956, p. 9). Cancer falls well within this definition as those who have this condition often manifest not just one, but all four of these characteristics.

The term *cancer* is a general one for a constellation of diseases that are characterized by a relatively rapid, abnormal, and uncontrolled growth of cells, the result of which is a tumor that has the capacity to invade and destroy surrounding normal tissues, thus interfering with the body's normal functioning. In addition, to further complicate matters, cancer cells possess the ability to metastasize or spread, invading any and all parts of the body (National Cancer Institute, 1981).

INCIDENCE

Bonica (1979) estimated that there are approximately 5 million deaths each year internationally due to cancer. Contrary to a widely held view, this condition may strike at any age, and though it is more frequent with advancing age, it is responsible for taking the lives of more children between the ages of 3 and 14 than any other disease.

Of every five deaths from all causes in the United States, one is the result of cancer. In 1979, 404,000 individuals died of cancer; in 1980, 412,000, and in 1981 the figure rose to 420,000. Based on the data from the National Cancer Institute's Third National Cancer Survey conducted during 1969 to 1971, the American Cancer Society in 1973 estimated that one of every four Americans then living would develop cancer. The recent SEER Report, *Incidence and Mortality Data,* 1973–1977 (National Cancer Institute, 1980b) indicates that the cumulative risk of developing cancer through age 74 has increased to 30.8%.

However, with more recent advances in medical science, wholly new kinds of treatments have been brought into the arsenal to help eradicate this condition. In particular, immunotherapy and chemotherapy have been demonstrated to be relatively effective in the treatment of cancer. As a result of these medical advances it has been estimated that the survival rate for all types of cancer has increased to 45% for white Americans and that between 50,000 and 60,000 people are now curable with chemotherapy as the primary means of treatment (National Cancer Institute, 1981).

IMPLICATIONS OF TREATMENT

This trend, while encouraging, is nevertheless mitigated by numerous factors, not the least of which is the fact that most of the chemotherapeutic agents used in treating the condition are toxic not only to cancer cells but also to normal cells. Consequently, many patients suffer agonizing side effects such as pain, nausea, insomnia, hair loss, diarrhea, loss of appetite, loss of weight, muscular tension, fear and anxiety (Barckley, 1968; Bonica, 1978; Golden, 1975; Holland, 1976; Redd, 1980a, b; Rusk, 1971). The ordeal can be so devastating that some patients literally choose to die rather than continue with the treatment. In fact, some actually die from the treatment before it can work. So serious a problem is this that at Duke University as many as 50% of the patients do not comply with the treatment regimen by either delaying or altogether missing treatment (Clark et al., 1961).

Physical Implications

Although the list of physical and psychological symptoms associated with the disease or as a side effect of treatment is a long one, two physical symptoms—pain and nausea—stand out as being the most pervasive, agonizing, and difficult to control (Oberst, 1978).

At present, the data suggest that severe pain is experienced by approximately 60 to 80% of hospitalized cancer patients. Swerdlow (1973) proposed that neoplastic disease is the most prevalent cause of intractable pain in patients with terminal diseases. Further, Bonica (1978) noted that the pain experienced by cancer patients is often improperly treated by both physicians and other health professionals. He suggested in addition that cancer pain has been especially neglected by teachers, investigators, oncologists, authorities, and national and regional cancer agencies. Even though there has been a great deal learned about pain in general during the last century, most of this information has not been applied to the population that may need it most. This, in spite of the fact that surgery, narcotic pain medications, sedatives and antidepressants which often have their own debilitating side effects are often ineffective in reducing or terminating pain (Black, 1979).

Surgery has been the traditional mode of treating chronic pain. However, even this extreme measure has not always proved effective in alleviating the pain experienced by cancer patients. Numerous researchers (Gottlieb et al., 1977; Mooney & Cairns, 1978; Newman, Painter, & Seres, 1978) concur that even multiple surgeries do not control all pain.

In a recent report, Toomey, Ghia, Mao, and Gregg (1977) noted that there is no known procedure that consistently and permanently relieves pain in all circumstances. Further, they noted that approximately 50% of chronic pain patients do not respond favorably to purely somatic methods of treatment.

Psychological Implications

There is general agreement among professionals that there is an integral relationship between emotional factors, illness, disability and how the patient responds to treatment and rehabilitation (Chapman, 1979; McGowan & Porter, 1967; Melzack, 1973; Turk, 1978; Weisenberg, 1977). Although the reports of specific psychotherapeutic techniques in the treatment of cancer are sparse, there is evidence that a variety of techniques could be helpful in the reduction of some of the negative experiences associated with cancer and its treatment (Burish & Lyles, 1979; Dolan, 1982; Dolan, Allen, & Sawyer, 1982; Redd, 1980a, b; Turk & Rennert, 1981).

In particular there are data to support the notion that one's emotional state, specifically anxiety about one's condition, may tend to increase the negative experiences. Following is an exploration of the relationship between anxiety and pain, and anxiety and nausea.

Anxiety and Pain

Evidence of the significance of emotional factors as they relate to the experience of pain was provided by Beecher (1959) who studied pain relief from placebo and morphine injections on 122 patients with post-operative wound pain. Interestingly, while 65% of the subjects experienced relief from the morphine injection, approximately 40% also experienced relief from the placebo. In a later report, Beecher (1960), summarizing 10 studies involving 831 patients experiencing pain from surgery, angina pectoris, headache, and even cancer, reported remarkable consistency with his findings of the previous study in that 35% of the subjects reported receiving satisfactory pain relief from placebos. The results of these clinical studies compare with only a 3% relief from pain in experimental pain studies (Sternbach, 1968). As a result of these findings, Beecher (1970) concluded that pain relief by placebo or morphine is at least partially a function of the degree of anxiety experienced by the individual.

Further, Byron and Yonemoto (1975) reported that 77% of patients with advanced cancer obtained complete relief from pain in 4 or more hours from placebo intervention. In an examination of this research, Melzack and Casey (1968) stated: "Pain can be treated not only by trying to cut down sensory input by anesthetic blocks, surgical intervention and the like, but also by influencing the motivational, affective and cognitive factors as well" (p. 435).

Finally, Freeman and Watts (1970) reported the effects of prefrontal lobotomies on pain. They stated: "Prefrontal lobotomy changes the attitude of the individual toward his pain, but does not alter the perception of pain. Patients report that the pain is still present, but that it is no longer bothersome to them" (p. 345).

From the evidence cited thus far, it would seem reasonable to conclude that there is a close relationship between anxiety and pain. Further, it should be evident that increasing anxiety results in a concomitant increase in the degree of pain experienced by the individual, and, conversely, decreasing anxiety results in a concomitant reduction in the intensity of pain experienced by the individual.

Anxiety and Nausea

In contrast to the number of empirical studies that confirm a positive relationship between anxiety and pain, few empirical studies exist for anxiety and nausea. However, some information has been provided by Redd (1980a, b) who used in vivo desensitization in the treatment of a 53-year-old female for chronic emesis following gastrointestinal surgery.

In another study, Burish and Lyles (1979) used progressive muscle relaxation training to reduce the conditioned negative responses of nausea and vomiting developed by a 30-year-old cancer patient receiving chemotherapy. Both studies are important in that they demonstrate a positive correlation between anxiety and regurgitation. In addition, the results of these studies tend to demonstrate that by decreasing anxiety that was associated with the condition, the patient's emesis could be controlled.

Finally, Dolan (1982) taught cancer patients a number of psychotherapeutic strategies to reduce the frequency, duration, and intensity of their pain, nausea, and sleep interruptions. Self-report data from patients plus social validation from the researcher and oncology team revealed that the program was effective in reducing negative side effects associated with the cancer experience and its invasive treatment.

The results of these studies, coupled with the fact that most antiemetics serve to act primarily as sedatives, suggest that anxiety over one's condition may be at least partially related to the degree of nausea cancer patients experience.

IMPLICATIONS FOR REHABILITATION COUNSELORS

In light of the evidence that has been presented, it seems reasonable to conclude that many factors are responsible for shaping the individual's experiences of and responses to the environment. To what degree each of these factors individually influence the individual's experiences and responses is not well defined or clearly understood. What is understood is that one's expectations, emotional state, and prior experiences all significantly affect the patient's experience of, and response to, cancer and its treatment.

These facts have significance for rehabilitation professionals and rehabilitation counselors in particular. As medical technology continues to advance, greater numbers of people who have cancer can be expected not only to live longer but also survive their ordeal. Because cancer and its curative therapy is so often a traumatic and devastating experience, many of its survivors may require rehabilitation services. As a result, rehabilitation counselors may be expected to render services to a population who until recently was not a significant part of the rehabilitation counselor's caseload.

In recognition of these facts, combined with the inception of the Rehabilitation Act of 1973, comprehensive rehabilitation and continuing care services for persons experiencing cancer have received increased attention (Lebow, Maisiak, Sanders, Soon, & Cain, 1982). Consequently, greater concern has been focused on those psychological implications of cancer which emphasize quality of survival (Diller et al., 1979; Lehmann et al., 1978). In this regard, the American Cancer Society (1979), Diller et al. (1979), and Lehmann et al. (1978) proposed that intervention by a single individual or program may be of assistance in the rehabilitation process. In addition, McAleer and Kluge (1978) recommended that rehabilitation counselors serving as liaison between the patient and the medical team may help reduce some of the anxiety the patient may be experiencing, and, therefore, facilitate the rehabilitation process.

With this in mind, rehabilitation counselors need to recognize the special needs of this disability population. Following are a number of vitally important factors rehabilitation counselors should be cognizant of in an effort to maximize their clients' potential for rehabilitation.

1. *A diagnosis of cancer does not necessarily lead to death.* While some forms of cancer are associated with higher survival rates, there is not a perfect relationship between types of cancer and survival. What is extremely important in addition to early diagnosis and appropriate treatment is the client's psychological perspective, i.e., clients who develop coping strategies are not only more likely to survive, but also better able to control the negative side effects of treatment (Dolan, 1982; Redd, 1980a, b). Rehabilitation counselors not only need to recognize this fact, but emphasize it to their clients in order to optimize the client's ability to cope with their condition.

2. *Persons experiencing cancer are individuals and need to be treated as such.* Although the statement would seem a foregone conclusion, many cancer patients report that once their diagnosis is known by others, they fail to be recognized and responded to as individuals. This behavior often extends beyond family and friends to professionals, including the oncology team, nurses, therapists, etc. Often patients are treated in stereotypic fashion which denies their individuality and human dignity. Of particular importance in this regard is that the side effects of treatment are highly individualized and diverse. Individuals experience a wide range of physical and emotional consequences that may not always be directly related to either the specific type of cancer or the therapeutic regimen. As noted, the patient's emotional state may significantly affect his/her response to treatment.

Rehabilitation counselors need to be sensitive to the individual needs of their patients and guard against treating their clients who have this disabling condition as though their experiences, perceptions and needs were identical.

3. *Persons experiencing cancer also experience heightened levels of anxiety.* As has been previously noted, anxiety may not only be debilitating in and of itself, but also appears to be directly related to the degree of physical discomfort, i.e., pain and nausea that the patient is experiencing. Therefore, any intervention that serves to decrease the patient's level of anxiety may also lead to a lessening of physical discomfort. In this regard, a number of anxiety-reduction techniques have been described (Dolan, Allen, & Sawyer, 1982) to assist rehabilitation counselors working with cancer patients.

4. *Cancer patients on occasion report feeling helpless, vulnerable, and "not in control."* In many cases, the individual who has been diagnosed as having cancer has been relatively healthy up to that time. From the moment of diagnosis, however, the individual is expected by the attending medical staff and family to assume the "sick role." This often takes the form of having things done to the patient with little or no explanation of why and how. Important information and explanation of what to expect are often withheld from the patient. Gradually, the patient abdicates all responsibility for his/her recovery in the hope that surgical and pharmacological therapies will lead to a "cure." Even though there may be little that patients can do to alter the course of their condition, there is much they can do to control their emotional state, quality of life, and degree to which they experience negative consequences of their condition. Rehabilitation counselors need to become aware of this destructive cycle. A number of intervention strategies (Burish & Lyles, 1979; Dolan, 1982; Dolan, Allen, & Sawyer, 1982; Redd, 1980a, b) have been demonstrated to be effective in allowing cancer patients to regain some control over their lives, allowing them to feel less vulnerable and helpless and more in control of their lives.

CONCLUSION

The author has attempted to provide individuals involved in the delivery of rehabilitation services with a current, broad overview of the medical and psychosocial implications of cancer and its treatment. In addition, a number of psychological approaches for coping with cancer and its treatment were examined and discussed. Finally, a number of crucial issues were highlighted in an effort to provide the rehabilitation counselor with a greater understanding of the cancer experience. It is hoped that this information will prove helpful to both rehabilitation counselors and the cancer patients who are in need of their services.

RESOURCES

Burish, T. G., & Lyles, J. N. Effectiveness of relaxation training in reducing the aversiveness of chemotherapy in the treatment of cancer. *Journal of Behavior Therapy and Experimental Psychiatry,* 1979, *10,* 357–362.

Diller, L., Gordon, W. A., Freidenbergs, I., Ruckdeschel-Hibbard, M., Levine, L. R., Wolf, C., Ezrachi, O., Lipkins, R., Lucido, D., & Francis, A. Demonstration of benefits of early intervention of psychosocial problems and early intervention toward rehabilitation cancer patients. *Final Report, New York University Medical Rehabilitation Research and Training Center* No. 1, New York, March, 1979.

Dolan, J. D. *The self-management of sleep interruptions, pain and nausea by adult oncology outpatients: An investigation.* Unpublished Doctoral Dissertation, Southern Illinois University, Carbondale, 1982.

Dolan, J., Allen, H. A., & Sawyer, H. W. Relaxation techniques in the reduction of pain, nausea, and sleep disturbances for oncology outpatients: A primer for rehabilitation counselors. *Journal of Applied Rehabilitation Counseling,* 1982, *13*(4), 35–39.

Holland, J. C. Coping with cancer: A challenge to the behavioral sciences. In J. W. Cullen, B. Fox, & R. Isom (Eds.), *Cancer: The behavioral dimensions.* New York: Raven Press, 1976.

National Cancer Institute. *The breast cancer digest: A guide to medical care, emotional support, educational programs and resources.* DHHS Publication No. (NIH) 81–1691. Bethesda, MD: National Cancer Institute, 1980.

National Cancer Institute. *Coping with cancer: A resource for the health professional.* DHHS Publication No. (NIH) 80–2080. Bethesda, MD: National Cancer Institute, 1980.

National Cancer Institute. *Chemotherapy and you: A guide to self help during treatment.* DHHS Publication No. (NIH) 81–1136. Bethesda, MD: National Cancer Institute, 1981.

Redd, W. H. In vivo desensitization in the treatment of chronic emesis following gastrointestinal surgery. *Behavior Therapy,* August 1980, 11(3), 42–427.
Sobel, H. J. *Behavior therapy in terminal care: A humanistic approach.* Cambridge, MA: Ballinger, 1981.
Swerdlow, M. Relieving pain in the terminally ill. *Geriatrics,* 1973, 100–103.

27 Alcoholism: A Pervasive Rehabilitation Counseling Issue

Fred Dickman
Elizabeth A. Phillips

Alcoholism has been universally recognized as *at least* the third leading health problem and disabling condition in the United States (National Center for Alcohol Education, 1978; U.S. Department of Health, Education, and Welfare, 1981). In addition to its status as the third most serious primary disabling condition, it is known to impact on and exacerbate many other disabling conditions, including some forms of heart disease and cancer, first and second in fatality causation respectively (American Medical Association, 1973; U.S. Department of Health, Education, and Welfare, 1981).

Conditions affected by alcohol abuse and alcoholism frequently encountered in public rehabilitation centers are the following:

1. *Mental illness.* It is estimated that up to 40% of persons diagnosed as mentally ill may be dually afflicted by alcoholism (Bachrach, 1976; Cotton, 1979; Leiber, 1982).
2. *Heart disease.* Researchers contend that alcohol has a detrimental effect on the heart muscle and is significantly correlated with cardiomyopathy (Hamby, 1970; Schwartz, Sample, & Wegle, 1975). Heart patients no longer are advised to have "a little glass of wine" (Schneider, 1980).
3. *Cancer.* While the research results on cancer are far from being conclusive, evidence is emerging to allow an inference of higher risk associated with alcoholism, alcohol abuse, and mere alcohol intake and some forms of cancer (Williams & Horn, 1977; Wynder, Bross, & Feldman, 1957).

The authors would like to thank William G. Emener, Ph.D., for his encouragement and invaluable editorial assistance.

4. *Orthopedic impairments and amputations.* Since 40 to 60% of all accidents are reported to be alcohol-related (U.S. Department of Health, Education, and Welfare, 1981), an as yet untested hypothesis is that alcoholism may impede the rehabilitation progress of the victim.
5. *Birth defects.* There is an abundance of new research available on fetal alcohol syndrome (FAS). FAS is the third leading cause of birth defective persons which adds significantly to the population of mentally retarded individuals (Clarren & Smith, 1978; Streissguth, Little, Herman, & Woodell, 1979).
6. *Other disorders.* Characteristic disorders or rehabilitation populations related to alcohol abuse and alcoholism are gastrointestinal disorders (Leiber, 1982), genitourinary disorders (Fort, 1973), liver problems and disease (Leiber, 1982), diabetes (Kissen & Begleiter, 1977), and central nervous system problems (Parsons & Farr, 1981; Smith, 1977).

While the above disabilities tend to be most frequently encountered in public rehabilitation programs (Wright, 1980), the private sector rehabilitation focuses on workers' compensation cases (Rasch, 1985). Many industrial accidents which are associated with a significant percent of these conditions are clearly alcohol related (Manello & Seaman, 1979; Woldenberg, Gold, & Tichauer, 1975). Other accidents covered by insurance, such as auto accidents and domestic falls (Haberman & Baden, 1978) are highly related to drinking alcohol.

When other rehabilitation issues and populations are addressed, i.e., divorse, spouse abuse, child abuse, runaways, school dropouts, suicide, and public offenders (Emerson, 1979; Hindman, 1977; Julian & Mohr, 1980; Kempe & Helfer, 1972), and the clear relationship these have to alcoholism is noted, the magnitude of the problem is brought into focus. These stress only alcohol-relatedness. When the identified alcoholic client population is considered, the problem for rehabilitation is formidable. Clearly, the rehabilitation counselor requires tools for diagnosis (early and late) and state-of-the-art methods of treatment.

ALCOHOLISM—A DEFINITION

In general, treatment experts and scholars vary only minimally in defining alcoholism. E. M. Jellinek (1960) defined alcoholism as any use of alcoholic beverages that causes any damage to the individual or to society or both.

The Alcoholism Subcommittee of the World Health Organization (1952) defined alcoholism as any form of drinking which in extent goes beyond the traditional and customary "dietary" use, or the ordinary compliance with the social drinking customs of the community concerned, irrespective of etiological factors leading to such behavior, and irrespective also of the extent to which such etiological factors are dependent upon heredity, constitution, or acquired physiopathological and metabolic influences.

The following definition is from the American Medical Association (1973):

> Alcoholism is an illness characterized by preoccupation with alcohol and loss of control over its consumption such as to lead usually to intoxication if drinking is begun; by chronicity; by progression; and by tendency toward relapse. It is typically associated with physical disability and impaired emotional, occupational, and/or social adjustment as a direct consequence of persistent and excessive use of alcohol. (p. 11)

The National Council on Alcoholism defined alcoholism as a chronic, progressive, and potentially fatal disease. It is characterized by tolerance and physical dependency, pathologic organ changes, or both, all of which are the direct consequences of the alcohol ingested.

Finally, Marty Mann, founder of the National Council on Alcoholism, defined the alcoholic as "a very sick person, victim of an insidious, progressive disease, which all too often ends fatally. An alcoholic can be recognized, diagnosed, and treated successfully" (Mann, 1958, p. 17).

The diagnostic criteria for alcohol abuse published by the American Psychiatric Association (1980, p. 169) specifically addresses

(a) pattern of pathological alcohol use;
(b) impairment in social or occupational functioning due to alcohol use; and,
(c) duration of disturbance of at least one month.

The diagnostic criteria for alcohol abuse published by the American Psychiatric Association (1980, p. 170) are

(a) either a pattern of pathological alcohol use or impairment in social or occupational functioning due to alcohol use; and
(b) either tolerance or withdrawal.

These definitions, a few among a myriad in the alcoholism literature, have a common theme which leads the authors to define alcoholism as a phenomenon with three criteria:

a. a drinking pattern;
b. a loss of control due to the drinking pattern;
c. a serious interference with one or more major areas of the drinking person's life, i.e., marriage and family, vocational, legal, financial, physical/medical, social, and intrapersonal areas.

ALCOHOLISM—THE DISEASE CONCEPT

In addition to a growing consensus on the definition of alcoholism, the rapidly growing alcoholism-treatment community is gaining agreement on the notion of alcoholism as a disease (American Medical Association, 1973; Blum & Blum, 1972; Forrest, 1978; Gitlow, 1973; Hunter, 1982; Jellenik, 1959; Johnson, 1980; King, Bissell, & O'Brien, 1979).

Inherent to the disease concept are the following:

1. *Chronicity.* Alcoholism once contracted is contracted unto death (Martin, 1972). This is the belief that alcoholism is incurable. This incurableness, however, has led many researchers (Armor, Polich, & Stambul, 1976; Sobell & Sobell, 1978) to hypothesize the opposite. Interestingly, to date no one has been able to prove that alcoholism recovery can be obtained with any treatment goal short of total abstinence (Fewell & Bissell, 1978; Gitlow, 1973; Johnson, 1980; Milam & Ketcham, 1981).

2. *Progressiveness.* Like any other disease, alcoholism has been thought of as having a "course" with definite, identifiable symptoms (Forrest, 1978; Jellinek, 1960; Johnson, 1980). This consideration is crucial to the rehabilitation counselor in that early identification is vital to successful intervention (Catanzaro, 1974; Johnson, 1980; Kinney & Leaton, 1978).

3. *Predictability.* Consequences of alcoholism are foreseeable, and as the progression of addiction continues, these consequences become more common and obvious in what is in the beginning a disparate and uniquely individual population (Catanzaro, 1974; Jellinek, 1960; Johnson, 1980).

4. *Primariness.* Alcoholism is a disease in and of itself and not a symptom of other more underlying disorders. In other words, alcoholism *causes* symptomatology; symptomatology does not cause alcoholism (American Medical Association, 1973; American Psychiatric Association, 1980; Estes, Smith-DeJulio, & Heinemann, 1980; Forrest, 1978; Johnson, 1980; Milam & Ketcham, 1981; Murphy, 1980).

5. *Fatality.* Undiagnosed, untreated alcoholism results in early fatality, estimated between 12 and 15 years off the average expected life span (American Medical Association, 1973; Kissen & Begleiter, 1972).

6. *Arrestableness.* Alcoholism is paradoxical in nature. It is the most destructive, pervasive, costly, and debilitative of the diseases; yet it is one of the most rehabilitative. Left alone, it is always fatal; diagnosed and successfully treated, the recovery is the most complete of all the diseases (Forrest, 1978; Glatt, 1974; Goldenson, Dunham, & Dunham, 1978; Milam & Ketcham, 1981).

Ironically, rehabilitation counselors, social workers, and other health professionals view the alcoholic as the least attractive, least acceptable client (Fewell & Bissell, 1978; Milam & Ketcham, 1981; Wechsler & Rohman, 1982).

A MODEL OF ALCOHOLISM: DIAGNOSIS, INTERVENTION, AND TREATMENT

Figure 27.1 illustrates a theory of the alcohol addictive progression and its predictable consequences, the intervention process, and signs of recovery. This model provides the counselor with state-of-the-art knowledge of alcoholism and its symptomatology with implications for intervention and rehabilitation planning. The model reproduces signs of alcoholism from early to late stages in that alcoholism, like most other diseases, is treatable in proportion to its early identification.

Symptoms Critical to Early Identification

The scope of this chapter precludes a thorough discussion of all symptoms depicted in Figure 27.1, but following are the more common ways the rehabilitation counselor can identify alcoholism early on in the progression.

1. *Has there been an increase in tolerance?* The concept of tolerance is considered a major indicator of addiction (American Psychiatric Association, 1980; Forrest, 1978; Jellenik, 1960; Kinney & Leaton, 1978). In the early stages, tolerance increases and often is a source of pride for the progressing alcoholic. Yet increasing tolerance is indicative of heavy consumption as the "budding" alcoholic is adding acquired and metabolic tolerance to innate individual capac-

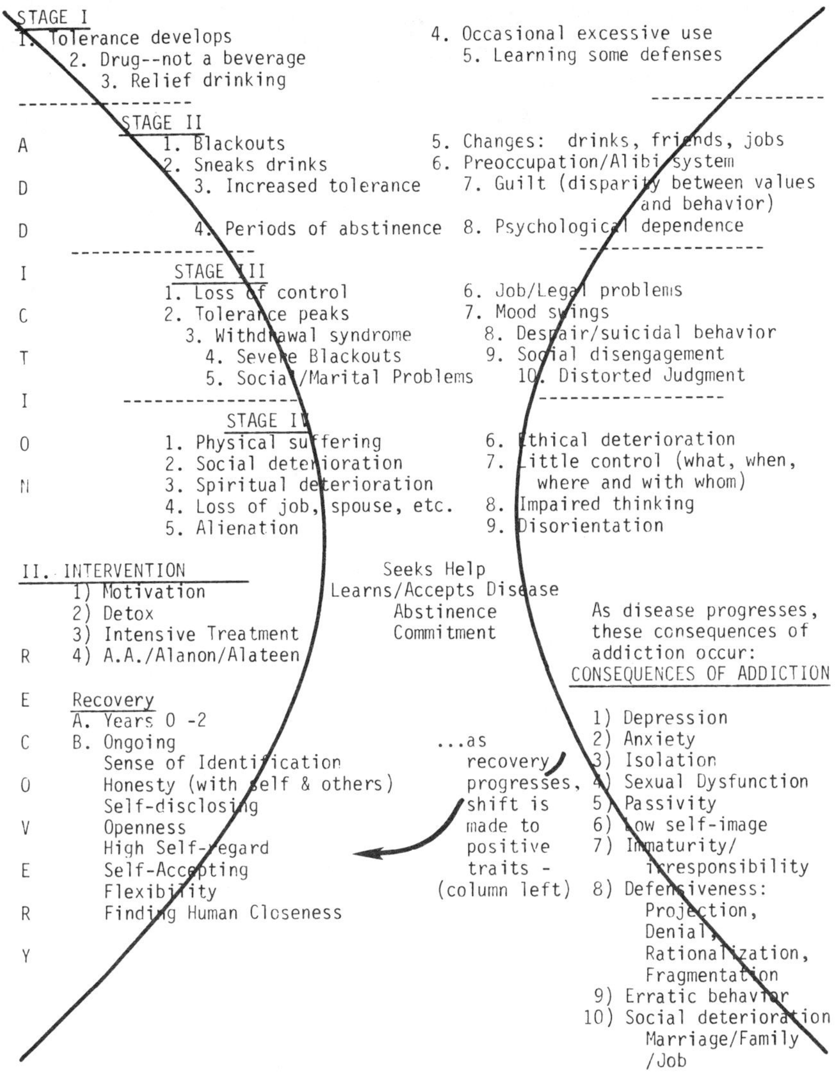

Figure 27.1. Hourglass Theory of Addiction and Recovery

ities. For example, a high blood alcohol content (BAC) has emerged from Driving While Intoxicated (DWI) Counterattack studies as a major early identifier.

2. *Has there been an arrest record, especially a DWI or driving while under the influence (DUI) charge?* U.S. Department of Transportation studies (1974) suggest that of those persons with one arrest,

60% are in some stage of alcoholism. Those with two or more arrests are within a 90% certainty of being alcoholic.

3. *Has the client experienced periods of forgetting events or blocks of time, even though not asleep, while drinking?* While blackouts occur all through many alcoholic individuals' drinking life, in varying degrees, they definitely are a sign of neurological disturbance due to alcohol ingestion (Fort, 1973; Kissen & Begleiter, 1972; Milam & Ketcham, 1981).

4. *Has the client experienced signs of physical withdrawal indicative of some phase of physical addiction?* Butterflies in the stomach, shakiness, insomnia, and irritability are all signs of alcohol withdrawal in some phase. Signs can be less severe to severe, such as delirium tremens, convulsions, hallucinations (Fort, 1973).

5. *Does the client become defensive when asked about his drinking pattern?* Treatment personnel agree alcoholic persons build a predictable wall of defenses to protect their drinking. They tend to rationalize, deny, project, and repress their drinking-involved behavior, probably to protect a declining self-image (Fewell & Bissell, 1978; Forest, 1978; Johnson, 1980; Murphy, 1980).

6. *What exists in the client's medical history with a probable relationship to an abusive drinking pattern?* Liver functioning, the gastrointestinal system, the pancreatic system (especially adult diabetes), and cardiomyopathy are particularly affected by alcohol abuse (Estes et al., 1980; Hamby, 1970; Schneider, 1980).

7. *What in the clients' marital and family history and present situation may point to alcoholism? Has there been child or spouse abuse reported? Is there alcoholism in their history? Have they been involved in frequent divorce?* Each of these has been correlated with alcohol abuse and alcoholism (Emerson, 1979; Filstead, 1977 Hindman, 1977; Krimmel, 1973).

8. *Is there any sign of loss-of-control drinking?* Progressing alcoholic persons cannot always predict how much they will drink, on which occasions they will drink, with whom they will drink, or what they will do when they drink. The insidiousness of this phenomenon is that often they can predict, but there are many times they cannot. This adds to their increasing fear which they attempt to build a defense against (Forrest, 1978; Jellinek, 1960; Johnson, 1980; Kissen & Begleiter, 1977).

9. *Do they project frequently rather than take responsibility for their behavior?* Progressing alcoholic persons quickly learn to defend a weakening ego by blaming their troubles on the outside world

(Fewell & Bissell, 1978). The skilled rehabilitation counselor can typically recognize this in the initial interview.

10. *Have any of the problems presented to the counselor been accompanied by drinking or other drug use?* Often an aware and sensitive intake counselor can identify a problem with drinking by asking the client or significant others the appropriate questions about presenting problems, i.e., a family fight, trouble with a child, marital problems, problems with an employer, etc. (Dalhauser, Dickman, Emener, & Lewis, 1984).

INTERVENTION STRATEGY

A myth exists that implies alcoholic individuals have to "hit bottom" before they will seek help or be receptive to treatment. Quite often, they are unable to do this. Their defense system simply is too strong. They must be confronted before they can perceive the need for treatment (Catanzaro, 1974; Fewell & Bissell, 1978; Forrest, 1978; Johnson, 1980).

Essential to an intervention strategy are (a) significant others, (b) caring confrontation, and (c) a treatment plan.

Significant Others

People close to defended alcoholic individuals can penetrate their defense systems so that they can see enough reality to enter treatment. Research indicates that well-trained confronters can increase the probability of entering treatment from 15% up to 70% (Dickman & Emener, 1982b; Emener & Dickman, 1983; Johnson, 1980). Also, research indicates that the best confronters are employers, spouse, other family members and friends, in that order (Johnson, 1980).

The counselor is invaluable in this process in that they train the interveners to make successful confrontations on the basis of proven principles.

Caring Confrontation

The following principles of caring confrontation are recommended by Johnson (1980, pp. 55–57):

1. Meaningful persons must present the facts or data.
2. The data presented should be *specific* and descriptive of events *which have happened* or conditions *which exist.*
3. The tone of the confrontation should not be judgmental.

4. The chief evidence should be tied directly into drinking wherever possible.
5. The evidence of behavior should be presented in some detail, and very explicitly, to give the alcoholic persons a panoramic view of themselves during a given period of time.
6. The goal of intervention, through the presentation of this material, is to have the alcoholic client see and accept enough reality so that, however grudgingly, the need for help can be accepted.
7. Now the available choices acceptable to interveners may be offered.

Treatment Plan

Treatment choice depends upon how far the addicted client has progressed. If they are clearly and well into Stages III or IV (see Figure 27.1), they probably need medical attention and should be referred to an intensive, inpatient (usually 28-day) program. For this purpose, the practicing rehabilitation counselor should have a directory of resources and treatment facilities. While the client is in this program, it is recommended that the rehabilitation counselor

1. Visit the client to secure the relationship as a caring one.
2. Arrange for outpatient follow-up.
3. Arrange for members of Alcoholics Anonymous to meet the client to secure a continuing program after inpatient treatment.
4. Arrange an appointment for weekly follow-up counseling with alcoholism specialists for the client and his/her family.
5. Continue frequent follow-up to check the progress of the client's recovery.

If intervention is early enough, inpatient treatment may not be necessary. For instance, it was found that a good employee assistance program intervenes early enough so that 7 out of 10 alcoholic employees can recover without inpatient treatment (Dickman & Emener, 1982a). If such is the case, all the above recommendations hold with the addition of (a) an immediate physical; (b) Antabuse treatment (if medically feasible); and (c) an intensive outpatient program to include individual, group, and family counseling.

SIGNS OF RECOVERY

Commensurate with the progression of the disease, the process of recovery offers predictable indicators for the rehabilitation counselor.

Although abstinence is critical to recovery (Gitlow, 1973; Milam & Ketcham, 1981), it must be considered as a first step on a journey of recovery along with other emotional and behavioral signs. Indeed, to get sober, the alcoholic individual cannot drink; to stay sober, alcoholic clients need to make changes in their lives. The process of recovery reverses the consequences of addiction (see Figure 27.1).

The following are signs to look for, and to counsel toward, in following up the recovery of an alcoholic individual:

1. *Hope replaces despair.* Does the client believe the circumstances can change? Do they believe their lives can become more meaningful? Are they willing to take steps to effect these changes?

2. *Acceptance of alcoholism.* Has the client stopped blaming others for the drinking behaviors? Do they understand it was not outside circumstances and people which caused them to drink? The clients grow to accept their alcoholism and incorporate it as part of their self-image.

3. *Attendance at Alcoholics Anonymous meetings.* Is client attending A.A. meetings regularly and willingly? This can be vital to recovery, increasing chances for a successful recovery by as much as 75% by attending A.A. meetings (Gellman, 1964). Does the client go to a particular group on a regular basis? Has the client obtained a sponsor?

4. *General appearance.* The rehabilitation counselor may notice early on in the alcoholic client's recovery a "glow" of health, i.e., improved personal appearance, with clients taking an interest in how they look. They begin to like the person they see in the mirror in the morning. For example, the rehabilitation counselor will notice improved eye contact and more open body language.

5. *Responsibility.* Are the clients taking responsibility for themselves in all areas of their lives? Are they going to work regularly and arriving on time? Are they fulfilling obligations and commitments to family and friends?

6. *Communication.* Is the client communicating more freely with significant persons, i.e., employer, family, counselor? Is the client more willing to share feelings and risk self-disclosure? In this sense, the rehabilitation counselor will note increasing congruency in what the client feels and says, with appropriate voice tone and cadence.

7. *New interests.* To replace the time spent drinking, the client will develop interests in leisure activities, i.e., sports, hobbies, and social situations that do not involve drinking alcohol. They will become less and less threatened by new experiences. Is the client experiencing increased socialization and integration in the community?

8. *Present-centeredness.* Is the client focusing on the here and now and on what is, rather than what has been or what might be? With increased self-worth and resultant self-acceptance, the recovering alcoholic client will experience "living in the here and now" more and more fully.

9. *Goal-directedness.* Has the client's life become purposeful? Does the client have short- and long-term goals that are realistic? With increasing self-worth, the client can function more freely and work in the direction of fulfilling personal potentials.

10. *Spirituality.* On a continuing journey of recovery, the alcoholic individual gains a sense of identification, of oneness, a feeling of being a part of, rather than apart from. A sense of alienation and loneliness is replaced with a sense of belonging and purposefulness; and the client grows to accept and believe in powers greater than self. Fears are replaced with a faith, and an attitude of trust develops that things will work out as they should, not necessarily as the client wants them to be.

The process of recovery is lifelong, beginning with abstinence, maintained by a support system of which Alcoholics Anonymous is crucial and of which the rehabilittion counselor can be a powerful part.

SUMMARY, CONCLUSIONS, AND RECOMMENDATIONS

The following conclusions and recommendations are offered.

1. Alcoholism is a hidden, serious factor in many other disabled populations and can easily sabotage the rehabilitation process, if not detected.
2. Alcoholism is one of the most treatable of the major rehabilitation disabilities.
3. The stigma surrounding alcoholism still is the major barrier to treatment and rehabilitation of alcoholic persons and their family. Rehabilitation counselors themselves need more alcoholism awareness training to make sure that their own attitudes are nonjudgmental. Alcoholism education and awareness help in this regard.
4. Alcoholism is a disease in the most practical sense of the concept. Whether alcoholic individuals can learn to drink again or not is a major research issue. However, state-of-the-art treatment practice would dictate a program aimed at cessation of drinking and a definite recovery program.

5. Family involvement in alcoholism counseling and treatment is critically important.
6. Rehabilitation counselor education programs need to offer more courses and training in alcoholism and alcoholism counseling.
7. Rehabilitation counselor education needs to focus more on family counseling theory and practice or at least help the rehabilitation counselor become aware of these services in the community.
8. Alcoholic individuals, fully recovering, are among the most productive workers in industry (Dickman & Emener, 1982b).

No one doubts that alcoholism is a major disabling condition. Nor is there doubt that alcoholism seriously affects the rehabilitation process in many cases involving other disabilities. Therefore, the profession of rehabilitation counseling should feel compelled to consider the pervasiveness of alcoholism and all of its ramifications.

RESOURCES FOR THE REHABILITATION COUNSELOR ON ALCOHOL(ISM) INFORMATION

Alcoholics Anonymous
PO Box 459, Grand Central Station
New York, NY 10017
(212) 686-1100

Al-Anon Family Groups
PO Box 182, Dept. G.
Madison Square Garden Station
New York, NY 10010
(212) 475-6110

National Council on Alcoholism
733 Third Avenue
New York, NY 10017

National Institute on Alcohol Abuse & Alcoholism
Division of Resource Development
5600 Fishers Lane
Rockville, MD 20857
(301) 443-2570

National Clearinghouse for Alcohol Information
PO Box 2345
Rockville, MD 20852
(301) 948-4450

The Clearinghouse is an information service of the National Institute of Alcohol Abuse and Alcoholism (NIAAA) and can furnish the rehabilitation counselor with listings of state alcoholism authorities and program directors, and public and private treatment facilities.

28 Rehabilitation Counseling for Older Disabled Persons: The State of the Art

Jane E. Myers

One-third of all functionally disabled persons are aged 65 or over (Rehabilitation Group, 1979), an age that represents 12% of our total population or "every ninth American" (Brotman, 1982). Those who reach their seventh decade are definitely survivors, and their potential for living actually increases! More specifically, while the average life expectancy of someone born today is 73.3 years, a person who is 65 today can expect to live an average of 16.3 more years, for a total of 81.3 (Brotman, 1982).

Since the inception of a formal state-federal rehabilitation program, the focus of services has been on persons "of working age." Rehabilitation counselors have been legislatively mandated to focus their efforts on younger persons. The passage of the Comprehensive Services, Developmental Disabilities, and Rehabilitation Services Amendments of 1978, especially the Title VII provisions for independent living rehabilitation (ILR), has raised the question of what to do about older people (Williams, 1981). Rehabilitation counselors are faced with an enormous and multifaceted challenge in regard to this population, for several reasons. First, their training, both in and preservice, has excluded attention to the needs of older people. Second, the underlying philosophy of *vocational* rehabilitation (not to mention the 26-closure "reward" system) has *naturally* excluded older people from service consideration. Third, social prejudice against older people, combined with the first three facts, has created a situation wherein rehabilitation counselors often view older people as having little or no rehabilitation potential (Benedict & Ganikos, 1981; Rasch, Crystal, & Thomas, 1977).

In order to meet this challenge effectively, rehabilitation counselors need a variety of information about older disabled people. This chapter provides a review of the state of the art in regard to rehabilitation counseling with this population. It begins with a definition of older disabled people, including medical conditions and functional limitations, followed by a discussion of psychosocial considerations. The implications for rehabilitation planning are discussed, followed by a review of counseling practice with regard to clientele. The chapter concludes with a list of available resources to assist counselors in learning about and working with older disabled people.

TOWARD A DEFINITION OF AGING AND DISABILITY

"Rehabilitation of the aged is a meaningless phrase. At best, it merely insinuates that all aged persons need to be rehabilitated" (Wolcott & Wheeler, 1971, p. 279). This quote exemplifies a major problem in rehabilitating older people, that of defining the eligible client population. Old age is not a disease. In fact, there are no specific diseases or illnesses characteristic of older people exclusively (Radzyminski, 1969; Rusk, 1977). Even senile dementia of the Alzheimer type (SDAT) is known to occur as early as age 40 (National Institute on Aging, 1981). It thus becomes necessary to examine the following factors: a definition of old age, a definition of aging, per se, common health problems of older people, disability among older people, and the impact of disabling conditions on functional limitations.

What is "old" depends on who is asked. For example, the Age Discrimination in Employment Act (PL 90–202) covers "older workers" between the ages of *40* and 70. Social Security benefits are available for "old" people at age 65 and *disabled old* people at age 62. The World Health Organization defines middle age as 45–59, elderly at 60–74, and aged 75 and over (in Puner, 1974), and the *old-old,* ages 75 and above (Youmans, 1977). Changes in mandatory retirement age legislation further complicate the issue.

An alternative approach is to consider a functional definition of old age, based on known facts about the aging process. Unfortunately, this process is not well understood. Wolcott and Wheeler (1971) distinguish between *primary aging,* which is due to the passage of time, and *secondary* aging, which results from declines in functional efficiency due to severe trauma or chronic debilitation. Jernigan (1981) notes that aging begins at conception, and the first signs of decline occur soon after puberty. Gradual and irreversible change occurs through out the life span, affecting all body systems adversely (Macione, 1979). True aging may thus be defined as incorporating four major characteristics: it is universal, progressive, decremental, and intrinsic (Strehler, 1962).

Biological aging, which occurs at varying rates in different people, is affected by genetic inheritance, life-style, disease, and psychological coping behaviors (Jernigan, 1981). Normal biological changes affect all aspects of life and result in decreased physical ability to adapt to change (Goldman, 1971), as well as predisposing the aged person to both acute and chronic illness (Macione, 1979). Normal aging changes may be insidious and develop so gradually that the aging individual either is unaware of them or progressively adapts with little need for outside intervention (Butler, 1975).

In regard to health problems, basically rehabilitation counselors will encounter two types of older clients (Jernigan, 1981). The first group is composed of individuals who led normal, healthy lives until the progressive decrements of aging resulted in physical limitations. The second group are those persons who became disabled sometime between conception and old age, and whose existing diseases and disabilities are further complicated by the normal processes of aging.

The primary conditions contributing to disability in old age are the same ones leading to death, since it may be presumed that physiological change and decline contribute to mortality (Blake, 1981). The 10 leading causes of death in old people, in descending order or prevalence, are diseases of the heart; malignant neoplasm; cerebrovascular disease; influenza and pneumonia; arteriosclerosis; diabetes mellitus; accidents; bronchitis, emphysema, and pneumonia; cirrhosis of the liver; and nephritis and nephrosis (Siegal, 1978). Three-fourths of all deaths among older people are attributed to the first three conditions (Brotman, 1982). Noninstitutionalized older persons, who comprise some 95% of the total elderly population, most frequently report having the following chronic conditions (Brotman, 1982): arthritis (44.3%), hypertension (38.5%), hearing impairments (28.2%), heart disease (27.4%), arteriosclerosis (12%), visual impairment (11.95%), and diabetes (8%).

It is obvious from the preceding discussion that many older people have multiple impairments. These both lead to and interact with additional diseases. Multiple pathology is the rule, and multiple conditions must be treated simultaneously (Cape, 1978). Accurate assessment of medical problems is essential, though complex (Jernigan, 1981; Schow, Christensen, Hutchinson, & Nervonne, 1978). It is important to recognize that *both* prevention and correction are possible and desirable, and depend to an extent on recognition that "although not preventable or reversible, aging is not disabling under normal conditions" (Gryfe, 1978, p. 238).

Generally, as compared to persons of younger age, old people tend to get sick more often, have more chronic illness, often have multiple health problems, and have both more and longer hospital stays (Blake, 1981; Harel, Scollod, & Bognar, 1982). Persons over age 65 have twice as much disability and four times as much activity limitation as those under 65 (Brotman, 1982). As estimated 86% of all older persons suffer from one or more chronic health problems that in some way restrict their activities of daily living (Brotman, 1976). Davis and Onyemelukwe (1977, p. 460) estimate that 35% of older persons "have some disability serious enough to limit their capacity to work, keep house, or engage in other major activities."

In addition to physical conditions, a large proportion of older persons suffer from some form of mental impairment. If detected and treated, these conditions often are reversible (Cohen, 1977).

Thus, virtually the entire gamut of possible disabling conditions may be seen in older clients. Functional limitations may vary based on severity of the disease or diseases involved, and the existence of multiple and interacting conditions. Most conditions of older people are chronic and progressive. Individual assessment is essential to identify residual capacities and functional limitations, which vary considerably across individuals and are complicated by the psychosocial factors discussed below.

PSYCHOSOCIAL ASPECTS

The population of older persons is both large and heterogeneous. Reactions to disability among older persons are basically the same as are encountered with persons of any age group, and it is difficult to describe psychosocial aspects that are unique to this population. However, it is important to recognize that, while the kinds of needs they have are the same needs experienced by all people, the degree or extent of need among older people varies (Ohio, 1960). In this section, some key psychosocial aspects to consider in working with older clients are discussed, with a focus on those sociological and psychological issues that are most intrinsic to this population.

The oldest and most widely researched topic in social gerontology is that of life satisfaction, or subjective well-being, and its relationship to mental health (Liang & Bollen, 1983). This feeling of contentment or morale is directly related to "successful aging." The major correlates of life satisfaction are socioeconomic status, education, income, age, marital status, formal participation in voluntary and church-related activities, visits with friends and neighbors, and perceived health (Chatfield, 1977; Edwards & Klemmack, 1973).

Factors affecting quality of life over the life span are similar for everyone, but some take on increased importance for old people. The five major components are as follows: first is the presence of a spouse; second and third for women are children and work, while for men the two are reversed; fourth is material well-being; and fifth, health (Flanagan, 1982). The basic environment that provides old people with happiness and a sense of security is the family unit (Townsend, 1957). Moreover, research has shown the presence of a single confidant to be the one essential factor that mitigates against the negative concomitants of aging and thus helps to maintain feelings of life satisfaction among older people (Lowenthal & Haven, 1968).

Many of the components of life satisfaction discussed above are not readily available to old people who also are disabled in some way. While a supportive social environment is essential for successful aging (Havighurst, 1968), many older people lack needed support because of the impact of factors such as ageism and loss, especially loss of social roles.

Ageism may be defined as bias against older persons (Butler, 1975) and is similar to sexism, racism, and handicapism. Negative attitudes are widespread and include perceptions of older persons by younger individuals as well as their own age peers (Cameron & Cromer, 1974; McTavish, 1971). Service providers, including rehabilitation counselors, also tend to have negative attitudes toward old people (Benedict & Ganikos, 1981).

Social role ambiguity contributes to ageist attitudes (Brine, 1979). Few norms or role expectations exist for older people (Bengston, 1977), whom Burgess (1960) described as being imprisoned in a "roleless role." Aged individuals are expected to accept, gracefully, the loss of social roles, whether or not replacements, such as leisure activities, are readily available. (Refer to the *Desiderata,* which states "gracefully surrender the things of youth.")

Older persons experience multiple losses, often simultaneously (Butler & Lewis, 1983), resulting in substantial coping needs resulting from "bereavement overload" (Kastenbaum, 1969). Social role loss is both inherent in and compounded by many of the losses that accompany old age (Bengston, 1977). Loss of the work role due to retirement may have deleterious effects on feelings of self-worth (Simpson & McKinney, 1966) as well as on perceived status in the community. Losses tend to lead to increased dependence (Brine, 1979), accompanied by drastic shifts in family relationships (Herr & Weakland, 1979).

The ways in which older persons cope with loss and disability are as varied as the individuals within this population (Neugarten, 1976).

Personality, developed over the life span, is a major determinant of characteristic coping styles. Personality in old age is determined primarily by personality before old age (Bengston, 1977). The major change appears to be an increase in introspection, accompanied by a shift in time perspective from time since birth to time left to live (Butler & Lewis, 1983; Neugarten, 1976).

A major study of personality and aging identified eight major personality types that are well established by middle age and continue into the later years (Neugarten, Havighurst, & Tobin, 1968). These have been related to successful aging, as well as to major theories of life span development and aging. A discussion of these theories is beyond the scope of this chapter; however, the interested reader may find numerous discussions in the literature, as well as a review of each theory in relationship to rehabilitation (Myers, 1983).

Reactions to loss, including physical losses, are not significantly different for older as compared to younger persons. These include denial and depression (Loyola, 1979; Pfeiffer & Busse, 1973) as well as anxiety and fear of death (Lawrence, 1981). Salmon (1981b) reviewed the interactive problems of health and disability for old people, and noted that limited personal resources combined with limited societal resources create massive problems for this population. He quotes Chown (in Salmon, 1981b, p. 48) as saying that "the old and ill or disabled may have almost too much to handle." Consequently, rehabilitation counselors, operating with a philosophy of maximizing independence, have much to offer older disabled persons. Some specific suggestions for how they might do this are discussed below.

REHABILITATION PLANNING

Considering the functional impact of disability among older persons and the fact that multiple problems are likely to be encountered, the application of the rehabilitation process can lead to effective interventions. This process in relation to older disabled persons is not remarkably different from its use with young disabled persons (Myers, 1980). Major differences appear in types of referral sources, available resources, and possible outcomes (Bozarth, 1981).

The process begins with a comprehensive and accurate assessment of the client's needs and resources, including attention to medical and psychosocial factors. Prognosis is complicated by a variety of interacting factors, but is important in determining treatment goals and potential for independent functioning. Either independent living or job placement may be the desired and most feasible outcome, or rehabilitation goal.

Comprehensive assessment of older disabled persons must be holistic in nature (Kobrynski, 1966), and must include consideration of historical factors. The pattern of disability often is established prior to old age and is helpful in predicting future patterns (Thomas, 1968). The ORS methodology for multidimensional functional assessment is a tool in common use that incorporates both medical and psychosocial evaluations (Pfeiffer, 1976).

Prognosis is dependent on extent of disability and handicap, available resources, and a variety of both tangible and intangible factors (Myers, 1983). Factors such as available transportation, income, and family or social supports will affect rehabilitation success (Butler & Lewis, 1982). It is important to consider both mental and physical faculties of the elderly client. Good communication, including vision, hearing, and speech, are important for interactions with service providers and counselors (Rosenbloom, 1974).

A major barrier affecting the prognosis for success is the prevalent negative attitudes among caregivers (Preston, 1979). These negative attitudes affect policymaking, service provisions, and the self-concept of older clients (Gaitz, 1974), and substantially inhibit the therapeutic process (Solomon & Vickers, 1979). Because the diseases of older persons so often are chronic and incurable, maintenance over the life span may be required (Butler, 1975). The prognosis for improvement of older disabled clients is good when attitudinal barriers are overcome (Hodgson & Quinn, 1980).

Rehabilitative treatment is based on the underlying goal of assisting disabled older persons to live independently as long as possible (Hunt, 1980). It is important to recognize that the needs and goals of older persons differ from those of younger people. Disease in young individuals often affects an otherwise healthy body, whereas disease in older persons may be superimposed on already existing degenerative conditions. For older disabled people, both restoration and rehabilitation always will require medical treatment (Sherman & Gingras, 1965). There are two primary objectives of this treatment: "(1) for the disabled aged, to increase the functional level and to decrease dependency on others, and (2) for the frail elderly, to prevent disablement which may lead to invalidism" (Kobrynski, 1966, p. 406). Treatment is aimed at either restoring the ability for self-care and ambulation, or at maintaining functioning and preventing decline.

Functional capacities of older disabled persons will determine whether rehabilitation goals are primarily in terms of full or part-time employment or independent living. It may be expected that many young-old persons, those aged 60 to 74, will be potentially employable, while many old-old individuals, those age 75+, will require independent living services.

Many older disabled persons both want to and are capable of working, but are unable to do so because of age discrimination in employment, mandatory retirement, and employer prejudice (Butler & Lewis, 1982), as well as low levels of education, skill obsolescence, and need for retraining (Sheppard, 1971). Dunn (1981) noted that many older workers are both disabled and working for several years. They could maintain employment if appropriate vocational rehabilitation services were provided (Jarvikowski & Lahelma, 1980). Barriers to employment of older persons have been described elsewhere (see Batten, 1980; Kasschau, 1976; Myers, 1980, 1983).

A variety of resources exist to provide assistance in job placement of older disabled workers (Myers, 1983). These include the U.S. Employment Service, federal ACTION programs such as Foster Grandparents, the Retired Senior Volunteer Program and the Senior Companion Program, the Senior Community Service Employment Program, and a variety of special older worker projects (see Dunn, 1981; Housman & Baumann, 1981).

Where vocational goals are impractical, the services required to achieve independent living among older persons are the same as those needed by other disabled people. Older persons, however, may need services for a longer period of time (Williams, 1981). The primary goals is to maintain the older disabled individual in a community setting, preferably in his/her own home (Goldstone, 1978). A variety of social, medical, and support services may be required to achieve independent living, including adapted housing, income maintenance, health care, transportation, shopping assistance, and so forth (Smith, 1978; see also Myers, 1983).

ILR settings for older people vary from totally independent housing to congregate living environments to nursing homes, depending on the extent of need for services. Within each setting, the goal is to achieve the maximum possible amount of independent functioning (Campbell, 1979). Such an emphasis on functioning can lead to gainful employment (Lobuts, 1977). In many cases, a critical ingredient in rehabilitation success is the intervention provided by a professional counselor.

COUNSELING PRACTICE

Counseling practice with older people is a relatively new area of professional involvement, both for counselors in general and for rehabilitation in particular. In this section, specific uses and techniques of conseling with older disabled clients are reviewed.

Odell stated that "counseling and individualized job development and placement methods can double or even triple the chances of middle aged and older workers for new jobs" (in Dunn, 1981, p. 79). Counselors help both to motivate and remotivate older disabled clients and to build their self-esteem (Organization for Economic Cooperation and Development, 1967). Dunn (1981) suggests that counselors may help older clients understand ways in which their experiences and training can contribute to new employment objectives, as well as how physical declines may be compensated by other abilities.

Counselors can intervene with employers to overcome a variety of barriers to hiring older workers, including the process of dispelling myths about older workers' abilities. Counselors can help older clients to maintain their existing jobs or obtain new jobs, and can assist employers in modifying or restructuring job sites to make either outcome possible (Dunn, 1981; Myers, 1980). Retraining for modified jobs will sometimes be needed (Barkin, 1970, in Dunn, 1981). The least desirable alternative is a change in jobs, because of the loss of status and earnings that result (Dunn, 1981). The counselor's job in this instance is much more difficult. Some attention to retirement preparation or *retention* preparation can ease the transition from a full-time to part-time or non-work role.

Counseling is an important service also in achieving independent living goals with older people. It is often most effective on a group basis (Williams, 1981), as it aids the process of peer identification, the sharing of common problems, and the recognition that one is not alone. By helping older persons meet their needs for social services such as housing and transportation, counselors help to satisfy their emotional needs as well (Myers & Loesch, 1981; Stickle, 1977).

In addition to service coordination, referral and assistance with tangible problem areas, several techniques have proved effective in helping older persons achieve a subjective state of well-being, or life satisfaction. The primary counseling technique used with older disabled persons is life review therapy, developed by Butler (1974). Older clients are encouraged to talk about their lives, and the counselor can use the information provided to enumerate the clients' strengths and coping abilities. The conclusion that each individual older person is a "survivor" cannot be ignored.

Building self-esteem is a major concern in counseling with older clients, and may be achieved in a variety of ways. Waters and Weaver (1981) describe ways to help older people, using life review therapy, strength bombardment activities, providing assistance in problem solving, and teaching assertiveness techniques. Salmon (1981a) adds techniques for building and using support networks to enhance the capabilities of older clients to meet their needs on a continuing basis.

For those older clients whose impairments are of such severity that institutional placement is needed, several milieu therapies have been developed and used successfully. These include reality orientation therapy, remotivation, and resocialization (Butler & Lewis, 1983; Weiner & Weinstock, 1979–1980). These approaches are potentially useful with clients who are confused and/or withdrawn.

Generic counseling techniques may and in fact should be applied in working with older disabled persons. Modifications can be made on an individual basis if counselors recognize the need to view all older persons as unique and distinct individuals. The potential for this to occur will increase in direct proportion to the knowledge counselors have of the characteristics, needs and concerns of older people in general and older disabled persons in particular. The following section includes some resources for further information about older people, their needs, and programs available to help them meet these needs. Rehabilitation counselors expecting to work effectively with older disabled clients can maximize their ability to do so by careful study of these resources.

RESOURCES

Federal Agencies That Coordinate or Provide Services for Older People

U.S. Administration on Aging (counterpart of RSA), 330 C St., S.W., Washington, DC 20201; ACTION, Washington, DC 20525.

Ganikos, M.L., Grady, K.P., Olsen, J.B., Blake, R., Fitzgerald, P., and Lawrence, P. *A handbook for conducting workshops on the counseling needs for older people.* Falls Church, VA: American Personnel and Guidance Association, 1979.

Myers, J.E., Finnerty-Fried, P.F., & Graves, C. (Eds.) *Counseling older persons, Volume I, Guidelines for a team approach to training.* Falls Church, VA: American Personnel and Guidance Association, 1981.

Rehabilitation Research and Training Centers Conducting Research on Handicapped Older Persons

University of Pennsylvania—RT-27, School of Medicine, Philadelphia, PA 19104; Rancho Los Amigos Hospital, University of Southern California, Los Angeles, CA.

Special Issues of Journals Dealing with Older People

Counseling over the lifespan. *Personnel and Guidance Journal,* 1976.

Work-life counseling for older people. *Journal of Employment Counseling,* March, 1980, 17(1).

Counseling the Elderly I, II, and III. *Counseling and values,* February, April & July 1980, 24 (2, 3, & 4).

Rehabilitation of older persons. *Journal of Rehabilitation,* October, November, December 1981, 47(4).

Aging education: Perspectives and techniques for school counselors. *The School Counselor,* March 1982.

Assessment of older persons. *Journal of Measurement and Evaluation in Guidance,* October 1982, 15(3).

29 Insurance Rehabilitation: Counseling the Industrially Injured Worker

Ralph E. Matkin

Rehabilitation counseling entered the 1980s with an identified movement toward private sector employment. The likelihood that rehabilitation counselors will continue entering into proprietary settings is made evident in recent literature. For example, rehabilitation manpower forecasts project an increase in private sector employment among counselors, vocational evaluators, and job placement specialists (Gutowski, 1979; Gutowski, Harder, & Koshel, 1980); membership growth in the National Association of Rehabilitation Professionals in the Private Sector is unparalleled at a time when other professional rehabilitation organizations are experiencing membership decline (Field, 1981); journal editorials are written to identify applicable rehabilitation services for a variety of non-traditional work settings (Hasbrook, 1981; Meyer, Rastatter, & Gannaway, 1979); employment patterns among graduates of rehabilitation counselor training programs indicate movement toward private sector employment as job availability in the public sector becomes less abundant (Crisler & Fowler, 1981; Geist & McMahon, 1981); changing work roles and functions among Certified Rehabilitation Counselors is requiring the Commission on Rehabilitation Counselor Certification to revise its examination item classification scheme (Rubin et al., 1984); and recommendations are being made to revise the current rehabilitation counselor training curriculum model of the Council on Rehabilitation Education to include private sector content (Matkin, 1982a; McMahon & Matkin, 1983). In view of such a movement toward private sector rehabilitation employment, it is necessary to identify and examine the context within which rehabilitation counselors will be providing their services.

The principal influencing element shaping the context within which rehabilitation counselors work in the private sector is the insurance industry. Indeed, its influence is reflected by the types of services offered and the skills and knowledge requirements of private rehabilitationists (Lynch & Martin, 1982; Matkin, 1982c). Clients referred for vocational rehabilitation services typically consist of industrially injured employees who are covered by workers' compensation insurance (Diamond & Petkas, 1979; Griswold & Scott, 1979; Lewin, Ramseur, & Sink, 1979; McMahon, 1979b; Organist, 1979; Sales, 1979; Shrey, 1979). Although the vast majority of these clients are referred by private insurance companies, the federal government also refers injured employees covered by such statutes as the Federal Employer's Liability Act, Federal Employees' Compensation Act, and the Longshore and Harbor Workers' Act (U.S. Department of Health and Human Services, 1982; U.S. Department of Labor, 1980). More recently, the Social Security Administration has initiated studies to assess the feasibility of referring recipients of Social Security Disability Insurance to private vocational rehabilitation practitioners (J. Jeffers, Assistant Director of the Social Security Administration, personal communication, April 6, 1983). The purpose of this chapter is to examine the special needs of the industrially injured worker when providing vocational rehabilitation services within an insurance context.

DEFINITION AND IMPACT ON FUNCTION

The System

Rehabilitation counselors who serve industrially injured clients work in a climate that brings together a variety of complex, diverse, and often unrelated systems; each with its own rules, regulations, procedures, regulatory bodies, and legal and philosophical foundations. For example, Workers' Compensation statutes and insurance requirements are not uniform across states, e.g., not all states have compulsory workers' compensation laws (elective coverage in New Jersey, South Carolina, and Texas); compulsory coverage may vary between private and public employment settings; and waiting periods for income benefits, as well as provisions for medical benefits differ from state to state (U.S. Chamber of Commerce, 1983). Similarly, special provisions for vocational rehabilitation benefits differ among jurisdictions in terms of disability payments, length of time services are provided, types of services authorized, and so forth (U.S. Chamber of Commerce, 1983).

The Workers' Compensation system, which covers the majority of industrially injured workers in this country, represents only one of many systems the rehabilitation counselor must learn in order to work effectively in the private sector. Others include (a) insurance coverage for personal injuries sustained in unrelated work activities that may cover the costs of rehabilitation services; (b) automobile no-fault insurance coverage for injuries sustained in traffic or car accidents; (c) coverage provided to disabled railroad workers by the Railroad Workers' Retirement Act; (d) medical and vocational rehabilitation benefits offered to disabled persons covered by the Occupational Health and Safety Act; and (e) benefit coverages offered to recipients of Social Security Disability Insurance, as well as persons eligible to receive benefits provided by the Veterans' Readjustment Act. Furthermore, rehabilitation counselors working in an insurance context need to be familiar with and possess a working knowledge of operating procedures associated with industrial accident boards and commissions or bureaus established to review rehabilitation plans, as well as hearings and appeals boards and courts which may require vocational testimony. Moreover, the state rehabilitation agency counselor assigned an industrially injured client caseload must learn how to integrate the state system's policies and procedures to those of the insurance systems mentioned above. Thus, the system(s) defines rehabilitation counselor activities by stipulating the parameters in which services can be provided in any given jurisdiction.

The Client Served

Industrially injured clients represent many types and degrees of disabling conditions including, but not limited to, alcoholism, cardiovascular disorders, cancer, hearing impairments, pulmonary dysfunctions, visual impairments, head injuries, spinal cord injuries, amputation, disorders of the bones and joints, and neuromuscular disorders. While the special needs required for each of these conditions is beyond the scope of this chapter, a common characteristic among industrially disabled employees is the presence of a work history that the rehabilitation counselor can explore to identify alternative methods for returning clients to gainful employment. Thus, vocational rehabilitation efforts generally begin with an assessment of the job duties performed by the client at the time of injury or disease in relation to the functional limitations imposed by the disabling condition, i.e., job analysis. In this manner, the rehabilitation counselor is able to inform the client and all involved parties of the nature and scope of rehabilitation services necessary to restore the injured worker to self-sufficiency in the shortest time.

PSYCHOSOCIAL ASPECTS

In spite of having acquired vocational skills and a demonstrated work history prior to occupational injury or disease, unemployment among Workers' Compensation claimants far exceeds what would be expected on the basis of degree of physical impairment alone (Lynch, 1979). Beyond labor market fluctuations, there are several psychosocial factors associated with the industrially injured worker that should be considered by the rehabilitation counselor. First, accidents are, by their very nature, sudden in onset. The injured worker is usually unprepared to handle the physical, social, psychological, vocational and financial implications imposed by such an event. As a result, the injured worker soon feels a loss of his/her ability for self-determination (Lynch, 1979).

Second, in our bureaucratic system(s) of business and human services, the injured worker often experiences a degree of confusion. Not only is he or she unprepared for the immediate life-style changes imposed, but there is uncertainty surrounding whom to turn to for assistance; what insurance and other legal forms are required to be filed; what the extent of coverage is when written in "legalese;" how long it will take to receive treatment and income assistance; and so forth. The industrially injured worker additionally may become confused and worried if a lack of communication among involved parties appears to exist and/or diagnostic inconsistencies begin to emerge. Such factors promote feelings of distrust, resentfulness, hostility, depression, fear, and uncooperativeness by clients (Beals & Hickman, 1972; Meichenbaum & Turk, 1976). Closely related to these behaviors is a third factor: pain. Meichenbaum and Turk (1976) note that as fear and anxiety increase, pain tolerance decreases which promotes a continuation of the disability process. Ironically, the reliance on medication and prosthetic devices to help manage pain often serve to maintain the disability process and reduce the likelihood of successful vocational rehabilitation (Lynch, 1979).

Fourth, vocational rehabilitation of industrially injured workers can be impeded by what psychologists term "secondary gain," which may consist of the financial compensation received for a disability and/or gratification of dependency yearnings or attention seeking (Hinsie & Campbell, 1973). According to Dollard and Miller (1950), secondary gains also may help to reinforce the symptoms of disability and reduce a client's motivation for treatment. Similarly, Weiss and Bergen (1968) observe that secondary gains, in the form of "sick role" behaviors, enables impaired persons to receive gratification for their dependency needs without loss of self-esteem. In the Worker's Compensation systems and other insurance programs, the degree of "sick" behavior demonstrated by claimants can be used to determine the final compensatory settlement (Lynch, 1979). Thus, the disability may become a source of positive reinforcement for the disabled worker and thereby delay a speedy recovery.

Finally, the number of surgical procedures and the length of time between onset of disability and rehabilitation efforts appear to have an inverse relationship with successful vocational rehabilitation. For example, Beals and Hickman (1972) report that no back-injured clients with three or more operations returned to work. Furthermore, these authors suggest that with the passage of time, injured workers increasingly elaborate their physical symptoms although they are less depressed (clinically speaking) by their current situation than at the time of onset. Therefore, when working with industrially injured clients, rehabilitation counselors need to consider not only clients' disabilities when planning services, but also the possible financial "rewards" disabilities may have.

REHABILITATION PLANNING

In 1973, legislation was enacted (PL 93–112) that mandated the Individualized Written Rehabilitation Program (IWRP) in the public rehabilitation system. Although the content of the IWRP generally follows the federal guidelines established in the 1973 Rehabilitation Act, its format is left to the discretion of the individual states' departments of rehabilitation. Within the insurance rehabilitation systems, the IWRP has its counterparts in the form of rehabilitation plans developed by insurance companies, state Workers' Compensation Boards, or bureaus responsible for overseeing Workers' Compensation rehabilitation services. Unlike the public sector IWRP, however, rehabilitation plans developed in the private sector are scrutinized by all parties involved in the rehabilitation process, e.g., insurance representatives, a designated individual from the administering state or federal agency, attorneys representing the client and the insurance carrier, and disabled client.

When developing a vocational rehabilitation plan *with* an industrially injured client, the rehabilitation counselor must be aware of four important criteria by which the proposed plan is evaluated: (a) the relationship between the proposed vocational goal and the functional limitations imposed by the client's injury, work history, identified abilities and skills, current labor market, and pre-injury earning level; (b) the relationship between the proposed services and what the referral source requests; (c) justification of the proposed plan, services, and goals, as well as the reasons other services or goals were considered to be inappropriate; and (d) justification of the proposed vocational goal in relation to expeditiously returning the disabled client to work. Since the first criterion is self-explanatory, attention is focused on the remaining three.

Referral sources frequently request rehabilitation services in order to assist in returning industrially injured clients to work. Sometimes the request is very general (e.g., "Do what is necessary to place this client into competitive employment"), but often the request is very specific (e.g., interview and make recommendations of vocational feasibility, perform job placement services only). The specificity of a request from referral sources can be for many reasons. For example, portions of the rehabilitation process may have been completed prior to the referral, the reliability and/or validity of another service provider's recommendations are being questioned, the veracity of the service provider's billing procedures may be suspect, or the service provider may be qualified to offer only a specific service. Regardless of the situation, however, the rehabilitation counselor is obligated to charge for only those services requested (i.e., authorized) by the referral source. On the other hand, if additional services are considered necessary, the rehabilitation counselor should discuss these recommendations and their relevance with involved parties and request additional authorization.

Effective vocational rehabilitation planning with industrially injured clients, as with other client populations, requires active participation and involvement by the client throughout the process (Lynch, 1979). Service recommendations and vocational goals should come from a sound data base taking into consideration such factors as the client's interests, needs, abilities, work history, educational and vocational training, transferable skills, and community job openings in the recommended occupation(s). As each of these areas is explored during the rehabilitation process, choices will be made concerning suitable alternatives and methods for their attainment. In the event that disagreement arises between the rehabilitation counselor and *any* of the involved parties regarding vocational recommendations, counselors must be prepared to justify their decisions and actions based on sound rationale.

Finally, vocational goals must be justifiable in relation to their speed for returning injured workers to gainful employment, as well as considering the long-range stability of targeted occupations. These criteria are important for three reasons: (a) the sooner clients return to work, the less will be the expense of rehabilitation and the quicker the client will be able to return to as near the pre-injury income level as possible; (b) the sooner clients return to work, the more likely successful vocational rehabilitation will be achieved with minimum disruption to disabled person's life-style; and (c) consideration of long-range occupational stability, not only in terms of the impact of the disability, but the job itself, maximizes the likelihood of successful vocational rehabilitation. In order to promote the most expeditious and stable return to work possible, rehabilitation counselors generally attempt job placement of industrially injured workers according to the following hierarchy: (a) same job, same employer; (b) modified job, same employer; (c) different job capitalizing on transferable skills, same employer; (d) same or modified job, different employer; (e) different job using transferable skills, different employer; (f) formal training leading to a change of occupation, same or different employer; and (g) self-employment (e.g., Matkin, 1981).

COUNSELING PRACTICE

The Counselor and the System

In the insurance rehabilitation system, counselors interact with a variety of professionals as mentioned earlier. Frequently, the credibility of recommendations made by rehabilitation counselors and/or the criteria used by referral sources for selecting service providers is influenced by the credentials possessed by rehabilitation providers. Indeed, the more evidence rehabilitation counselors can provide in terms of training and other recognized forms of credentialing in the field, the better the opportunity rehabilitation counselors have to work with industrially injured workers (International Association of Industrial Accident Boards and Commissions, 1982). Among the credentials available to rehabilitation counselors, and in some jurisdictions mandated for practitioners are certification and licensure.

Licensing. Licensure by definition refers to a statutory process designed to limit the practice of a given specialty to individuals who have met basic professional requirements. Similarly, it serves to limit, restrict, or regulate the use of a title with the ultimate goals of protecting the welfare of the public served and raising the standard of services rendered (Gianforte, 1976). While state-enacted and -regulated licensing laws are not widespread for rehabilitation counselors as yet, six states have such laws presently (i.e., Alabama,

Arkansas, Florida, Idaho, Texas, and Virginia) with similar bills before the legislatures of over 25 states focused on counselors working in the private sector (Brooks, 1981). In addition to these laws, other statutes exist in each of the 50 states and the District of Columbia regulating the practice of job placement services by people and/or companies who perform them for a fee. In a comprehensive investigation of state licensing requirements for employment agencies and employment counselors, Matkin (1982b) reports the different stipulations for each jurisdiction within the United States, noting that rehabilitation counselors in the private sector who are performing job placement services for a fee are *not* listed among the exempted groups from licensure. Therefore, because of the restrictive nature on practices imposed by licensing, the possible penalties assessed for failure to be licensed while performing a regulated practice, and the variety of definitions among jurisdictions for licenseable activities, the prudent private sector rehabilitation counselor should be aware of local requirements and be prepared to remediate areas of deficiency if necessary.

Certification. Unlike licensure, certification is a nonstatutory process by which an agency of government or association of peers grants recognition to an individual for having met agreed upon standards of competency and/or demonstrated knowledge in a particular field or profession (Fretz & Mills, 1980). Certification also differs from licensure in that certification generally has a single definition of what it constitutes which is applied nationally, rather than different definitions according to specific jurisdictions. On the other hand, certification and licensure share a common characteristic: title control. For example, a person is not entitled to use the designation of a "Certified Rehabilitation Counselor" or its designation (CRC) unless he or she has successfully passed the national examination of the Commission on Rehabilitation Counselor Certification. Among the values of certification for rehabilitation counselors in the private sector are: (a) improved professionalism; (b) improved services rendered to clients; and (c) improved acceptance by others (McAlees & Schumacher, 1975).

The Counselor and the Client

Rehabilitation counselors should involve industrially injured clients in the rehabilitation process as actively as possible. Active participation in the exploration of and planning for appropriate vocational goals by the client increases the likelihood of successful rehabilitation outcome for two reasons. First, the industrially injured worker will begin to develop a personal investment in the process and its identified goals. Second, active participation is among the many criteria used by insurance carriers as evidence of client motivation to return to work. Notwithstanding, a lack of active participation in the rehabilitation process may be interpreted by the insurance carrier as evidence to support its suspension of benefit payments. Regardless of the level of or reasons for the client's participation in the rehabilitation process, the counselor has an obligation to report the nature and ongoing progress of the case to all involved parties.

Case reporting is a critical concern in the rehabilitation process of industrially injured workers. Because of the number of people typically involved in a case and the monetary nature of the situation, written reports must reflect accurate and up-to-date information in a timely manner. Similarly, rehabilitation counselors have a professional responsibility to inform the disabled client of the limitation of their confidentiality as early in the counseling process as possible. By providing this disclosure to the client early in the relationship, the rehabilitation counselor can minimize his/her risk of malpractice suits on grounds of breach of confidentiality or invasion of privacy.

SUMMARY

Rehabilitation counseling applied to industrially injured clients does not involve developing new or different counseling skills, methods, or techniques. It does require, however, that the rehabilitation counselor be prepared to use his/her knowledge to the fullest in terms of the effects disability has on a person's life in relation to job, family, personality, and finances. Moreover, rehabilitation counselors must be prepared to provide their services within a legal framework consisting of regulations quite unlike those found in traditional workplaces such as the state-federal agency system or private non-profit rehabilitation facility serving clients primarily referred from state agencies. Typically, private sector rehabilitation counselors must be knowledgeable about specific insurance statutes such as state Workers' Compensation laws, federal Workers' Compensation laws, or any of the other forms of compensation programs under which disabled clients may be eligible to seek vocational rehabilitation services. Furthermore, knowledge of the insurance systems providing compensation coverage for disabled clients is necessary in order for rehabilitation counselors to plan and implement effective services.

Finally, rehabilitation counselors working in an insurance context within which they are applied, but must be prepared to demonstrate levels of professional competency demanded by consumers within their jurisdiction of practice.

Although this chapter has attempted to provide some of the more cogent aspects of dealing with industrially injured clients, it is, by its very nature, an overview. Therefore, in addition to the references cited, the interested reader is referred to any of the following sources for more in-depth discussions.

RESOURCES

Books and Journals

Deneen, L.J., & Hessellund, T.A. *Vocational rehabilitation of the injured worker.* San Francisco: Rehab Publications, 1981.

Matkin, R.E. *Insurance rehabilitation.* Austin, TX: Pro-Ed.

Sanchez, I., Workman, E.L., Morris, G.M., Miller, J., & Edlestein, M. *The California workers' compensation rehabilitation system.* New York: The Macmillan Co., 1981.

Silberman, L.J., Rothaus, B., Scharpnick, S., & Buie, L. *Rehabilitation: The California system 1982–1983.* Santa Ana, CA: Alliance of Vocational Educators, 1982.

Taylor, J., Golter, G., Golter, M., & Backer, T.E. (Eds.). *Handbook of private sector rehabilitation.* New York: Springer Publishing Co., 1985.

American Rehabilitation Counseling Association. Private sector rehabilitation. *Rehabilitation Counseling Bulletin,* 1983, *27,* special issue.

National Rehabilitation Association. Rehabilitation in the private sector. *Journal of Rehabilitation,* 1979, *45*(3), special issue.

Medi-Claims. Publication of State Farm Mutual Automobile Insurance Company. Bloomington, IL: One State Farm Plaza.

Rehabilitation Forum. Publication of International Rehabilitation Associates, Inc. Wayne, PA: 985 Old Eagle School Road.

Organizations and Government Agencies

Alliance of American Insurers
1501 Woodfield Rd.,
Suite 400 West
Schaumburg, IL 60195–4980

California Association of Rehabilitation Professionals
6819 Sepulveda Blvd., Suite 210
Van Nuys, CA 91405

Institute of Insurers of America
Providence and Sugartown Roads
Malvern, PA 19355

International Association of Industrial Accident Boards and Commissions
P.O. Box 480
Arkadelphia, AR 71923

Health Insurance Association of America
1850 K Street, N.W.
Washington, DC 20006

National Health and Welfare Mutual Life Insurance Association, Inc.
666 5th Avenue
New York, NY 10019

National Association of Rehabilitation Professionals in the Private Sector
P.O. Box 708
Twin Peaks, CA 92391

National Rehabilitation Association
633 South Washington Street
Alexandria, VA 22314

National Rehabilitation Counseling Association
633 South Washington Street
Alexandria, VA 22314

American Rehabilitation Counseling Association
5999 Stevenson Avenue
Alexandria, VA 22304

United States Chamber of Commerce
1615 H Street, N.W.
Washington, DC 20062

United States Department of Health and Human Services
Social Security Administration
3244 Pennsylvania Avenue, S.E.
Washington, DC 20005

United States Department of Labor
Employment Standards Administration
200 Constitution Avenue, N.W.
Washington, DC 20037

30 Rehabilitation and Learning Disabilities: A New Challenge for Counselors

Barbara J. Witten

Learning disabilities are a heterogeneous group of disorders characterized by disruption in the processes of learning, understanding, or expression. Individuals with learning disabilities are average or above average in intelligence, but have difficulty with one or more modes of learning/expression. Einstein, Newton, Churchill, DaVinci, and Nelson Rockefeller had learning disabilities. Learning disabilities need not be an impediment to achievement, if appropriate accommodations and compensations are made. The U.S. Department of Education estimates that 3% of the school age population, at any given time, are learning disabled. Other estimates range from 1% to 20% of the population. While a considerable number of research efforts have addressed the impact of learning disabilities on academic achievement in children and adolescents, impact on adults and implications for independent living skills and work has begun only recently (Anderson, 1972).

Defining learning disabilities was a problem for educators (Drake, 1981). The term meant anything and everything in different settings at different times. It became an all-inclusive term for poor academic performance from any cause. Determination of eligibility for special educational services, and plans for appropriate services, were often inconsistent; misdiagnosis occurred frequently. Bartlow (1981) reported a 73% misdiagnosis of learning disability as the primary disability in his sample.

Regulations in education changed when the implementation of PL 94–142 included the 1967 National Advisory Committee on Handicapped Children's (NACHC) definition:

> Specific learning disability means a disorder in one or more of the basic psychological processes involved in understanding or in using language, spoken or written, which may manifest itself in an imperfect ability to

> listen, think, speak, read, write, spell, or to do mathematical calculations. The term includes such conditions as perceptual handicaps, brain injury, minimal brain dysfunction, dyslexia, and developmental aphasia. The term does not include children who have learning problems which are primarily the result of visual, hearing, or motor handicaps, of mental retardation, or emotional disturbance, or of environmental, cultural, or economic disadvantage. (U.S. Department of Education, 1977, p. 65083)

The definition implies discrepancy between achievement and expected achievement. In fact, "discrepancy formulas" have been used as criteria for services in some school districts. Typically, a "learning quotient" (achievement ÷ expectation × 100) below 85 indicates "severe learning disability." Discrepancy may also exist in day to day behavior. Variability between performance and verbal subtests on the WISC/WAIS is common.

People with learning disabilities have average or above average intelligence, but are functioning at a lower achievement level. Prior to 1981, people with specific learning disabilities (SLD) were typically ineligible for services from vocational rehabilitation (VR), even though they were eligible for special services in education. VR regulations up to that time required a diagnosis of a physical or mental condition (RSA, 1981a). Most physicians could not identify the site of the neurological dysfunctions for a "physical" diagnosis, and SLD was not recognized as a mental condition. Recognition of SLD by the American Psychiatric Association in the *Diagnostic and Statistical Manual of Mental Disorders, Third Edition* (DSM-III)(1980) and by the World Health Organization in the *International Classification of Diseases* (1980) provided impetus for changing the VR eligibility regulations (Gerber, 1981; Scalia, 1983).

Proposed changes in the regulations were published in the *Federal Register* (November 29, 1979), with invitation to comment. A VR task force, the National Joint Committee for Learning Disabilities (NJCLD) was appointed in 1980 to study eligibility and assessment issues. The NJCLD recommended the following definition of SLD:

> Learning Disabilities is a generic term that refers to a heterogeneous group of disorders manifested by significant difficulties in the acquisition and use of listening, speaking, reading, writing, reasoning or mathematical abilities. These disorders are intrinsic to the individual and presumed to be due to central nervous system dysfunction. Even though a Learning Disability may occur concomitantly with other handicapping conditions (e.g., sensory impairment, mental retardation, social and emotional disturbance) or environmental influences (e.g. cultural differences, insufficient/inappropriate instruction, psychogenic factors), it is not the direct result of those conditions or influences (NJCLD, 1980, p. 45)

The NJCLD wording differs from 94–142 in that it (a) does not exclude multiply handicapped individuals, (b) focuses on adults, and (c) stresses the heterogeneous nature of the dysfunctions.

The eligibility criteria adopted by the Rehabilitation Services Administration (RSA) and disseminated to the field (RSA, 1981b) reads as follows:

> Learning Disability: Individuals who have a disorder in one or more of the psychological processes involved in understanding, perceiving, or expressing language or concepts (spoken or written)—a disorder which may manifest itself in problems related to listening, thinking, speaking, reading, writing, spelling, or doing mathematical calculations—would be eligible to receive vocational rehabilitation services if they satisfy the following criteria: (a) their psychological processing disorder is diagnosed by a licensed physician and/or a certified psychologist who is skilled in the diagnosis and treatment of such disorders; and (b) their disorder results in a substantial handicap to employment; and (c) there is a reasonable expectation that vocational rehabilitation services may benefit the individual in terms of employability. (p. 3)

During the summer of 1981, a national short-term training conference on SLD was held for representatives from each state VR agency. Each state then developed procedures for implementing the new regulations: some by forming interdisciplinary task forces, holding statewide in-service training, developing special linkages with the school systems to enhance the referral process.

Learning disabilities can be conceptualized as a dysfunction in one or more of the receptive, integrative (comprehension), or expressive processes related to any of the five senses. While hearing and visual processes are called upon most often for success in school and work in our culture, disruptions in other sensory modalities (touch, taste, and smell) can greatly affect daily living skills (e.g., smell and taste for cooking), and many vocational tasks.

Another useful concept in understanding SLD is "learning style." Each of us has a particular learning style that is our preferred mode of operation—visual, auditory, spatial, or kinesthetic. "Visuals" learn best by reading; they prefer printed to verbal instructions or schematic diagrams. The last time you assembled a Christmas toy, was it easier for you to read the instructions, or to eyeball the diagram to "see" how it fit together? Were you a visual or a spatial learner? Or could you follow the directions only when someone read them to you—an auditory style.

I'm a spatial type. I give directions to my house by drawing maps; many of my friends "need to" (it's easier) translate the map into narrative (e.g., take the third left after the light). If pressed, they could follow the map, and I could write out the directions. While most of us can learn to some degree in each way, we do have definite strengths and weaknesses. A person with SLD, however, will be less able or unable to learn/perform in a non-dominant style.

Learning to ride a bicycle is a kinesthetic task. Reading about it and watching someone else ride won't help much. Learning is based on feedback from the muscle groups. When the golf or tennis pro moves your hands to change your grip, that's kinesthetic learning—when you get the "feel" of it. The way we describe events gives cues to our learning style: the "feel" of it, "I see," "I hear what you're saying."

Multiple dysfunctions reduce the availability of alternative channels for learning/performing. It is important, then, to assess specifically the nature of the deficit(s), and to plan using the individual's residual strengths and styles.

A major strength of SLD adults is their ability to compensate for their disability. By adulthood, many have learned to capitalize on the remaining intact processes. They have learned to ask for written or verbal instructions. They have learned not to miss classes if they're auditory learners. People with SLD can be very creative in developing compensatory strategies. That creativity can be stifled, however, by a cycle of failure that typically occurs in academic settings. A helplessness may set in that impairs willingness to try new tasks or settings.

The following section is arranged according to categorization developed by Dale Brown (1980). A brief description of each of the manifestations is followed by examples, implications for vocational and daily living skills. Reference to the above-mentioned conceptual frameworks and potential compensatory strategies are presented, where appropriate. While each characteristic is treated separately, SLD can occur in any combination.

Academic difficulties: Dyscalculia (math), dysgraphia (writing), and dyslexia (reading) are the major labels used in educations settings. Causes can be receptive, integrative or expressive visual (reading), hearing (math and reading), or tactile (writing) processes.

Dyslexia would affect visual learning style, and "simple" tasks such as reading the newspaper, reading street signs, catching the right bus, identifying entrance and exit signs, etc. Teaching key word recognition, as opposed to general reading remediation, use of tape recorders and other techniques associated with adaptation for visually impaired individuals has been found to be useful.

Dysgraphia, a motoric problem, can often be bypassed through the use of typewriters, taped or oral responses. While dysgraphia may not directly affect on the job performance, it could make job seeking difficult. Filling out a job application form "on-the-spot" might result in a messy form; taking it home to type or carefully print would create a better impression on the employer.

Dyscalculia would create problems in personal budgeting, balancing the checkbook, making change (or checking the change returned by a cashier). Use of a calculator may help with arithmetic problems. The more serious difficulty is with conceptual mathematical principles. While jobs such as stock room clerk would seem inappropriate, a "counter," a small device held in the palm of the hand with a pushbutton that advances the counter once each time it is depressed, would be a simple modification to use.

Associated reactions: A result of uncontrolled motoric function, "one part of the body moves involuntarily because of movement in another part of the body" (Brown, 1980, p. 10). Most observers would interpret such movement as a nervous tic and consider it perhaps annoying but inconsequential. Difficulties for the individual arise, however, when eye-hand-foot coordination is required, as in driving a car or riding a bike. Turning the steering wheel might create a head turn or leg motion that could adversely affect driving performance. For individuals with this dysfunction, jobs requiring complex coordination (e.g., punch press drill operator) may prove to be unmasterable, or result in erratic performance.

Auditory perceptual problems: Three categories of dysfunction can occur. *Auditory discrimination* problems are characterized by an inability to distinguish between similar sounds and could result in an inability to correctly identify tone of voice as a message cue. *Figure-ground* problems relate to an inability to identify or attend to the important input in a noisy environment, such as listening to some one when the radio is on. *Auditory sequencing* manifests itself by reversed or out-of-order messages. Remembering phone numbers or street addresses would be a difficult task. Jobs dependent upon oral transmission of information, such as taking sales orders by phone or receptionist duties, would prove to be a great challenge. An individual could adapt to some degree by controlling or eliminating extraneous sources of noise, asking for a series of shorter messages, and requesting information in writing. In social situations, individuals may misinterpret what is said and respond inappropriately, or may be labeled as disinterested because they can't attend to the input.

Catastrophic response: Too many stimuli or too much intensity can cause inappropriate behavioral responses, such as "losing one's temper, becoming dazed or unaware of one's surroundings, or freezing for a short time" (Brown, 1980, p. 11). This response pattern would affect interpersonal relationships, and would hinder job performance if it occurred frequently.

Cognitive problems: Conceptual difficulties can occur in sequencing (logic) or *discrimination* (distinguishing between similar concepts). Sequencing errors typically result in ineffective, inefficient speaking or writing patterns (Blalock, 1982). Discrimination problems would result in misinterpretation of messages, especially in social situations where shades of meaning are critical.

Crossing the midline: Another motoric response, problems occur when a limb is moved across the center of the body, e.g., from left to right side. Many daily living activities require such movement (e.g., combing hair, ironing) and may be affected. Both fine and gross motor coordination are affected when the midline is crossed.

Directional problems: Individuals have difficulty distinguishing left from right without thinking, or north-south-east-west. Getting to and from work or shopping, negotiating through a large building or store, and giving or following directions would be a serious strain, and more than likely would result in getting lost.

Disinhibition: Akin in some ways to catastrophic response, behavior becomes inappropriate. While catastrophic response is due to overload, disinhibition results from the inability of the brain to suppress a behavior. Inappropriate laughter and interrupting a conversation are signs of this phenomenon.

Intersensory problems: Difficulty is encountered in attempting to attend to more than one sensory modality at a time. The proverbial "You can't chew gum and walk at the same time" is an example of an intersensory problem. Sequencing the tasks to eliminate overlap in time, if feasible, would avoid the problem. Again, social situations, which are less controllable, create the most problems.

Motor problems: The inability to control body movement may have three causes. *Perceptual motor problems* are characterized by clumsiness and lack of coordination. *Visual motor problems* result in an inability to coordinate what is seen with what the body is trying to do, such as tying shoes, folding a letter, putting a key into the keyhole. With auditory motor problems, the body cannot appropriately respond to aural input, easily demonstrated by playing "Simon Says." While most jobs do not require expertise in "Simon Says," many do require movement in response to oral instructions (e.g., "Take this over there.").

Proprioceptive perceptual problems: The individual is unable to correctly identify his/her position in space. While many of us can become disoriented if we are turned upside-down under water, losing the cue from gravitational pull, individuals with this dysfunction cannot tell what position their limbs are in without looking. Results can be body image distortion, decreased eye-hand coordination, bumping into things. Touch typing would be an almost impossible task, as would playing almost any musical instrument.

Tactile perceptual problems: Receptive and integrative dysfunctions cause discrimination problems. The individual cannot distinguish between similar shaped or textured items by touch, or cannot judge the correct pressure needed for a task (e.g., cracking an egg, tickling vs. pinching). Hypersensitivity to touch can also occur, resulting in negative affective response to such things as handshakes, pats on the back, a squeeze of the arm. The individual may withdraw from social situations to avoid the negative stimulation.

Vestibular perceptual problems: A poor sense of balance can create an appearance of clumsy, awkward movement. This would prove dangerous in occupations requiring climbing (construction) or other tasks requiring a good balance.

Visual Perceptual Problems: The stereotypic example of SLD is letter and word reversal, mistaking *b* for *d, was* for *saw. Visual sequencing* is one of a variety of receptive visual dysfunctions. *Figure-ground problems* are characterized by an ability to "see" an object in the midst of other visual stimuli, such as locating a friend in a crowded room. Deficits in *visual discrimination* results in failure to distinguish between similar visual cues *(e* and *c),* similar shapes or colors. *Depth perception* may also be affected. Disruptions in the visual modality would create problems in reading, writing, and math, and many daily living skills (e.g., following a recipe, cleaning).

PSYCHOSOCIAL IMPACT

Blalock (1982) recently reported that adults with SLD frequently considered social perception problems to be the most serious problems. Inappropriate use of space (standing too close to someone), understanding the subtleties of non-verbal cues, and making inappropriate comments (Blalock, 1982, p. 11) can hinder development of interpersonal relationships and interfere with job-related interactions.

Difficulty with social relationships is frequently cited as a major problem for people with SLD (Blalock, 1981, 1982; Brown, 1980, 1982a, 1983; Casey, 1982; Cruickshank, Morse, & Johns, 1980; Ziemond & Brownlee, 1980). While social skills are difficult to teach, learning to structure the social situation may be a more feasible goals. Exclude extraneous noise; face away from visual distractions; reduce body movements; rehearse for special situations.

Rejection by peers due to poor social skills adds to the failure syndrome common to adults with SLD. Individuals in their late twenties and older probably did not have appropriate diagnostic and educational services when they were younger. Some developed compensatory skills and "passed" as non-disabled, never letting anyone know of their deficits, yet keenly aware of their inabilities. Some adults have developed life-styles in which they can function perfectly well, and do not want to admit a problem or seek help. These people are sometimes prompt to seek assistance when their children become school age. As parents, they can't read the teacher's reports or help with homework.

Fear, guilt, and doubt characterize the self-blaming of many individuals. "If I had paid more attention in school . . . If I had studied harder . . . Why didn't I . . . What's wrong with me . . ." Receiving a diagnosis of SLD is a relief to many adults. They really weren't crazy or lazy; there really is something wrong, and they need no longer feel ashamed.

Some adults were labeled by their teachers, parents, siblings, or friends, or even labeled themselves, as lazy, stupid, or "retarded." Some may have been placed in inappropriate special education classes for the "educable mentally retarded." Repeated failure at school, peer pressure, and parental pressure reinforced the negative self-image that was forming (Brown, 1983). Acting-out behavior would not be uncommon, and might lead to a placement in a "behaviorally disordered" classroom. People expected you to function "normally" because you didn't look disabled.

The negative feedback cycle, low self-esteem, and helplessness often lead to delinquency and adult criminal behavior (Keilitz, Zaremba, & Broder, 1979). Platt, Tunick, and Wienke (1982) cited a report that 29.5% of the inmate population at the Oregon State Penitentiary were SLD. A 5-year study by the National Institute for Juvenile Justice and Delinquency on the relationship between SLD and delinquency (Dunivant, 1982) revealed differential rates of arrest and adjudication for the same illegal acts (SLD vs. non-disabled). Delinquents with SLD had cognitive and social skill deficiences. The poor verbal skills and abrasive behavior exacerbated interactions with the legal system. Banks (1982) reported that rehabilitation intervention was necessary in the court system for individuals with SLD, since they may not understand the charges, be able to give an accurate account of their activities, be able to read court documents before signing, or assist in their defense.

Dunivant (1982) reported that in a remediation training program for SLD delinquents, decreased recidivism was not related to increased academic performance. Platt et al. (1982) implemented a training program for handicapped inmates, including SLD, in West Virginia. Screening, vocational evaluation, vocational training site placement, vocational training intervention, work adjustment skill development, and follow-up are components of the project. Perhaps the larger focus of this project will yield more encouraging results.

Another possible behavior pattern in response to SLD is withdrawal and dependency. Individuals become afraid to try new settings, including jobs, or meet new friends (Brown, 1983). They are convinced that they can't function without assistance. They are unaware of their strengths and capacities for independence. Increasing independence becomes a major goal for rehabilitation planning, which can lead to enchanced self-concept.

REHABILITATION PLANNING

Many people with SLD are unemployed, have difficulty in finding and keeping a job, or are dissatisfied with their jobs. Szuhay and Newill (1980) reported that 76% of SLD adults interviewed in Pittsburgh were unemployed. Brown (1982b) indicated that unemployment rates for young adults with SLD were extremely high, even before unemployment affected the general population (p. 9). Brown (1982b) also hypothesized that many workers' compensation cases may be the result of people with SLD in inappropriate jobs, since awkwardness, clumsiness, and accident-proneness are typical manifestations.

A needs assessment conference on rehabilitation of people with SLD (Crystal & Brady, 1982) identified attitudes of the employer and self concept as the major employment problems for this client population. Employers are uninformed as to the nature and characteristics of SLD, and may view a special request, such as the need for oral versions of written memos, with skepticism. Employers are less likely, without intervention, to make accomodations for someone who "doesn't look disabled."

Accurate assessment and testing are essential for successful rehabilitation. A total assessment of SLD should include (a) personal and family interviews, to identify attitudes, goals, expectations; (b) a review of all prior academic records, including psychological assessments; (c) a review of all medical records; (d) formal testing to identify the SLD (neuro-psychological battery); (e) assessment of coping and compensatory behaviors, strengths, and weaknesses; and (f) level of client expectation (Goulet, 1981; McCollum, 1983). Testing situations will likely invoke anxiety, as they resemble prior failure situations. The lack of flexibility in standardized tests, client distractability (short attention span, disinhibition), and time pressure can lead to lowered performance. Working wiht the client to create a non-threatening environment for testing will result in more accurate diagnostic information.

In planning needed services, the debate over remediation vs. compensation will arise. Recent literature (Blalock, 1982; Casey, 1982; Dunivant, 1982; Dyer, 1982) indicates that remediation, trying to improve the deficient skills (e.g., increase reading level) is a lengthy, "painful" process that yields minimal improvement. The person is faced with trying one more time to attack their problem head-on. Remediation is appropriate when the skill to be remediated is of critical emotional importance to the individual, when even minimal improvement in skill level will greatly enhance self esteem. Teaching compensation strategies and environmental adaptations has proven to be more successful in improving overall performance, since it draws on the individual's residual strengths.

Developing/identifying the specific accommodations needed requires a twofold analysis (a) of the individual's learning style, strengths, and deficits, and (b) the specific task to be accomplished. The task analysis should determine the specific skills and behaviors needed for "success." Modifications may take the form of alternative instructional procedures, environmental changes, structural modifications, or personal strategies, in any combination (Goodman, 1981). This approach is useful in academic settings, in work and vocational training situations, and for daily living skills training.

Increasing numbers of people with SLD are enrolling in post-secondary programs. The number of institutions which admit and provide some special services for SLD students has rapidly increased (Karnes, 1981). A national survey to identify special services for SLD was conducted in 1980; a guide (Ridenour & Johnston, 1981) was published for use by SLD individuals and the professionals who serve them. Services ranged from specialized LD clinics with assessment, tutoring, and counseling, to generic "handicapped student services," to a "we'd try to work something out" response by administrators, to "no services available." Individuals considering post-secondary settings should carefully select a setting. Crystal, Witten, & Wingate (1982) proposed a diagnostic and rehabilitation model for college-bound SLD students that included special assessment, support services, and VR linkages.

Casey (1982) reported that individual tutoring was the service deemed most useful by SLD students. Technology for the blind will often be needed to assist students with visual perceptual problems. Some intervention with faculty to accommodate alternative testing and evaluation of students may be needed. An ideal post-secondary program would have support from the central administration and would include training of faculty, advisors, and admissions and financial aid staff, funding for special services, and a designated special service network (Dyer, 1982). Rehabilitation counselors can assist their clients in post-secondary settings by providing some of these interventions/training to the college, as they would to a potential employer.

COUNSELING THE SLD CLIENT

Job seeking skills are of critical importance for SLD clients. As mentioned earlier, dysgraphia can result in sloppy job application forms. Clients with disorientation and directional problems will have difficulty finding their way to and from interviews or work and may even get disoriented within a building going from one room to another. Auditory perceptual deficits can create miscommunication during a job interview. Low self-esteem, timidity, and fear of new situations will also affect job seeking and interviewing behavior. Modeling and rehearsal, and development of accommodation strategies will reduce the negative impact of these deficits.

Specific modifications in counseling techniques may be necessary for effective communication with some SLD clients. Individuals with auditory perceptual deficits or oral expressive problems are not well suited to the typical verbal interaction style of most counseling techniques. Several other manifestations of SLD, such as short attention span, cognitive sequencing, catastrophic response, disinhibition, and intersensory problems will also interfere with smooth flow of a counseling session.

As a general rule, reduce all extraneous stimuli: meet in a quiet room—no "humming" lights, no loud air conditioner, no other people talking. Hold all calls so the phone doesn't ring in the office. Sit so the client has minimal visual distraction when facing you. Don't let people come into the room and interrupt.

For those with auditory and cognitive deficits, keep sentences short and concrete. Write notes if you have to. Be patient with the difficulty in oral expression. Paraphrase their response to be sure that's what they meant to say. Perhaps they'll need to write you notes. Use visual clues, pictures, or "acting" as alternatives to verbal descriptions. Be creative; what would you do if the person didn't understand English very well? Ask them to fill out a form, instead of you asking a series of questions. Switch to closed and yes/no questions that require less complicated responses. Try using modeling and demonstration instead of verbal or written descriptions during evaluation and training. And most of all, ask the clients what is easiest for them! They will know.

Peer groups and support groups have been found to be very useful for sharing compensation strategies and enhancing self-esteem. Specific training in assertion and communication skills will provide additional opportunities for enhancing interpersonal skill levels.

CONCLUSIONS

The manifestations of SLD are specific to each individual. Any single deficit or any combination of deficits can occur. Further, each type of deficit can manifest itself along a continuum from mild to severe impairment. The implications from vocational placement and counseling are very client- and task-specific. Accurate assessment of the specific strengths and weaknesses is critical to successful planning. SLD truly requires a multidisciplinary approach toward assessment and service delivery. Educational, psychological, and neuropsychological assessments must be integrated with personal strengths and weaknesses and familial expectations to develop a feasible rehabilitation plan. Vocational evaluation and work adjustment techniques must be suitably altered to draw on and highlight client strengths.

A holistic approach that incorporates remediation, compensation, and accommodation to independent living skills, careers, and personal/social skills is necessary. Some individuals will need more counseling services and personal skill training to combat the cycle of failure that has occurred. Others will need minimal assistance in this area.

Early intervention and linkage with the school system is necessary to identify eligible adolescents, provide a smooth transition from school to the world of work, and "optimize vocational options and potential before they are lost" (Geist, 1982, p. 6). The justice system can serve as an additional major referral source for adolescents and adults with SLD.

SUMMARY

The development of VR involvement with SLD was overviewed, including current eligibility definitions. A framework for conceptualizing SLD and descriptions of a variety of manifestations of SLD were presented. Examples of implications for vocational and daily living skills have been offered as a stimulus to the reader; individual clients will identify more specifically their own arrays of "problem tasks."

Accurate diagnostics and assessment of the functional abilities of clients with SLD is crucial to the development and successful implementation of a rehabilitation plan. Rehabilitation counselors will need to work closely with professionals from psychology, education, neurology, and vocational evaluation to best serve this client population.

Reference to the criminal justice system was made, due to the disproportionate numbers of inmates with SLD and the potential for SLD adolescents to develop acting out behaviors in reaction to failure in school, daily living, and relationships with peers. Two specific correctional "treatment" programs were reviewed.

Suggestions for counseling strategies were presented as a reminder to counselors to attend closely to the individual learning styles of the client, and to adapt accordingly. Counselors should be especially aware of (a) the potential for low self-esteem or (b) attempts to "pass" as non-disabled by SLD clients. Resource materials and associations that focus on SLD are listed below.

RESOURCES

Association for Children with Learning Disabilities (ACLD), 4156 Liberty Rd., Pittsburgh, PA 15326. A group for individuals, parents, and professionals, ACLD hosts local and national conventions, answers inquiries.

Association for Learning Disabled Adults, a self-help group. PO Box 9/22, Friendship Station, Washington, DC 20016.

Closer Look, Parents Campaign for Handicapped Children and Youth, Box 1492, Washington, DC 20013, provides packets on learning disabilities with information on groups in each state. A free self-remediation handbook for learning disabled adults *(Steps to Independence for People with Learning Disabilities)* is available.

ERIC Clearinghouse on Handicapped and Gifted Children, 1920 Association Drive, Reston, VA 22091. Free fact sheets are available on learning disabilities, post-secondary opportunities, and vocational education for SLD.

HEATH Resource Center, 1 Dupont Circle, Suite 780, Washington, DC 20036. Material is available on post-secondary opportunities.

Launch, Dept. of Special Education, East Texas State University, Commerce, TX 75429.

National Network of Learning Disabled Adults, PO Box Z, East Texas State Station, Commerce, TX 75428, provides a national listing of self-help groups.

Time Out to Enjoy, Inc., 113 Garfield St., Oak Park, IL 60304, an association of learning-disabled adults, published the *Guide to Post-Secondary Educational Opportunities for Learning Disabled Adults,* the results of their national survey.

31 Rehabilitation Counseling with Disabled Hispanics

Orlando A. Rivera
Rosanita Cespedes

It is not a handicap to be Hispanic; however, rehabilitation counseling with disabled Hispanics may present special problems.

Cross-cultural rehabilitation counseling offers the exciting challenge to capture this important body of knowledge and to gain the necessary skills that will assist in the rehabilitation of disabled persons who are culturally different. It has implications for international rehabilitation, and since certain disability groups develop their own culture, it can apply to them as well. This chapter will address the issue of rehabilitation counseling with disabled Hispanics. The term *Hispanic* will be used generically to include all persons of Spanish-speaking descent in the United States.

Definitions and Impact on Function

Hispanics

There are 14 million Hispanics in the United States according to the 1980 federal census. This is considered to be a conservative count and does not include those without documents. Hispanics are the second largest minority in the United States and growing rapidly, comprising the fifth largest Hispanic population in the world. Hispanics are heterogeneous, with diversity among them due to background, level of acculturation, and differences in socioeconomic status. It is not possible to describe the Hispanic population as a homogeneous group; however, they speak the same language and have cultural similarities. It is useful to become acquainted with those cultural attributes that impact upon the rehabilitation counseling process.

Culture

Every person has a culture. Culture serves to pass on the collective wisdom of a group of people enabling them to survive in their environment and to give order to their society. Culture is acquired by individuals beginning at birth (possibly earlier) in complex subtle ways. It might be said that we learn our culture at our mother's knee. It is internalized and cannot be easily changed. Culture influences the way a person perceives the world, life, health and illness, and disabling conditions. Knowledge of a person's culture will help in the work of the rehabilitation counselor.

Hispanic Culture

The literature refers to several Hispanic cultural characteristics. The primary one is the Spanish language. There are many others, and a few will be used to illustrate the impact of culture on rehabilitation counseling. These include but are not limited to *la familia,* family roles, *machismo, dignidad, respeto, la palabra,* cooperativeness, and *curanderismo.* Traditional Hispanic culture refers to that culture that existed in Hispanic communities before being influenced by the dominant society.

Writers will stipulate that the Hispanic cultural characteristics presented are not necessarily empirically based and that there is a great need for research and study in this area. For the purpose of this chapter, these descriptions will be related to traditional Hispanic cultural characteristics as the baseline for discussion.

Acculturation

Persons of different cultures are gradually socialized into the dominant culture of the society in which they live. This process is called acculturation or enculturation by sociologists and anthropologists. Some people are bicultural as they retain the fullness of their own culture and learn the culture of the dominant society. Others retain parts of their culture as they acquire the culture of the dominant society and might be described as being somewhere along the acculturation continuum. Rehabilitation counselors may need to make a clinical decision as to the client's position on the continuum. There are acculturation scales available, but most have limited utility and validity. The positioning of the client on the scale does not require high levels of refinement, rather a general understanding as to their preferred language and their orientation to societal sanctions.

Etic/Emic

Pike (1954) and Berry (1969) labeled cultural universals *etics* and cultural specifics *emics.* The etic/emic dichotomy is useful for describing basic problems associated with cross-cultural counseling. The etic approach assumes that all people have similar human characteristics, i.e., needs, problems, and values. This orientation may lead a counselor to project his/her personal experiences and cultural attributes onto others and therefore ignore their cultural differences. The emic approach seeks to identify the impact of specific cultural characteristics on the counseling process. This is gaining wide support in recent literature on cross-cultural counseling (Draguns, 1981). A caution to observe when stressing the emic is that in an effort to understand the specific cultural variables of a group there may be a tendency to stereotype, or expect them all to be alike, and thus fail to recognize their individual differences.

Socioeconomic Status

Hispanics also range along the continuum of socioeconomic status (SES) although their distribution is skewed toward the lower end. Unfortunately, a disproportionate number of Hispanics are poor but their poverty is not necessarily culturally determined. Poverty has consequences, i.e., people in poverty may have limited experiences. It may be acceptable to introduce programs to compensate for deficiencies due to poverty, but it should not be assumed that the person's ethnic culture is dysfunctional. People have survived in their environment because of their culture, and since culture is dynamic, it can help them cope with changes. A Hispanic person may be poor but still have a strong and rich culture. The rehabilitation counselor needs to be sensitive to the implications of SES and its impact on disabled Hispanic clients.

External Conditions

Hispanics are defined as a protected minority whose place in this society is often described by sociologists as one of internal colonialism (Blauner, 1969, 1972). As a result of this condition, they are disenfranchised, powerless, and experience external administration and racism. They not only lack self-determination but are under-represented in the institutions of society. They are often not in the network of referral sources that enjoy linkages with rehabilitation (Zamora, 1982). There is a basis to assume an underutilization of rehabilitation services by disabled Hispanics not unlike that in health, mental health, and other social services (Karno & Edgerton, 1969; Keefe, 1978; Padilla, Ruiz, & Alvarez, 1975). In addition, there seems to be a lack of sensitivity to cultural implications in the rehabilitation of disabled Hispanics. This results in misunderstanding and allegations that disabled Hispanics lack motivation or are malingering and dependent and do not apply for or pursue rehabilitation services.

Cross-cultural counseling is the approach that attempts to investigate and capture the knowledge that will facilitate effective counseling for the culturally different. Without this, counselors have been warned that they may mislabel as pathological attitudes and behaviors that are unlike their own (Draguns, 1981).

PSYCHOSOCIAL ASPECTS

The manner in which certain Hispanic cultural characteristics impact upon the rehabilitation counseling process will be discussed in this section.

La Familia

A characteristic attributed to Hispanic culture is that of *la familia,* or what is often described as the extended family. To Hispanics, *la familia* is the primary source of support, i.e., an individual goes to the family first before seeking assistance elsewhere (Padilla, Carlos, & Keefe, 1976).

The concept of *la familia,* as inculcated into Hispanics by their culture, demands a certain loyalty to their family with individual aspiration and interest subsumed to its needs. In some cases this may seem to rehabilitation counselors as a disinterest in the rehabilitation program by the disabled individual. It may not be a case of disinterest; rather it may be that the individual's problems have a lower priority to the family than a crisis or a situational concern of the family that has to be attended to before the client can feel free to pursue his/her own rehabilitation program. In many cases the rehabilitation counselor may be very helpful in mobilizing resources that may solve these problems, such as paying the rent, having the lights turned on, or finding health care services for the acute medical problems of a child. After these are taken care of, the rehabilitation program of the client can go forward. Some counselors may not feel it to be their job to work with other family members, but it is often a reality that unless these problems are resolved little or no progress may be made in the rehabilitation program.

Traditional Family Roles

Father. The Hispanic male has been taught that it is his responsibility as a father to provide for his family and to account for their behavior in and out of the home. In a traditional culture this role is clearly defined. As such, the father knows the expectations that his culture, community, family, and self have for him. If he satisfactorily meets these expectations, he is considered to be a successful, respectable man and has high esteem. The title of "Don" is given to men who have earned that respect. On the other hand, he may see his life devastated if he cannot fulfill his role when he cannot work because of a handicap. Rather than admit that he needs help, a sign of weakness, he may unsuccessfully try to continue working. If he cannot work, the wife may be forced to leave her role as *la ama de las casa* (homemaker) to get a job. There are serious consequences to these displacements of traditional family roles. The father may see himself as a failure and turn to alcohol, or he may leave his family. Also, exacerbated generation gaps may occur with the children who, lacking respect for the father, who is not living up to his role, may not respond to the traditional cultural family sanctions and engage in behavior that leads them away from school, involves them in delinquency, and leads them into drug/alcohol abuse. The experience of a disabling condition may have greater impact on an Hispanic male self-image than it would on persons who perceive themselves and their roles less stringently.

Machismo. Sex role development of children in traditional Hispanic homes emphasized male-oriented activities for boys and female-oriented activities for girls. Boys are taught to be men, to do men's work, and to behave like men. *Machismo* means "maleness" and can have positive connotations. As it is often used in the American vernacular, it seems to imply the need for males to prove their manhood by various means, e.g., heavy drinking, fighting, or the conquest of women. This may be descriptive of the behavior of extreme cases but not the culturally sanctioned behavior of men in the Hispanic community. These persons would be called *sinverguenzas* (without shame). The traditional male role is a conservative one of responsibility (described above).

Dignidad (dignity). Dignity within the Hispanic community is highly valued. Dignity is an individual's self-respect, integrity, personal value. It must be guarded, honored, respected, and cannot be compromised. Not only must a person maintain his/her dignity but must respect the dignity of others. One cannot ask for, beg, or seek services at the expense of his/her dignity, nor should another be expected to, particularly if the need is obvious. If too many obstacles are placed in the way of a rehabilitation program to test motivation or for the sake of forms, etc., the individual may not pursue it as it is an affront, a lack of genuineness, and places the individual in a position of conflict between fulfilling his/her needs or maintaining his/her dignity.

Respeto. *Respeto* is emphasized in the Hispanic community. It means respect for others, and this includes everyone—the elderly, adults, children, and strangers. *Respeto* is shown to the elderly and persons in authority by the use of language, e.g., by addressing them with the formal *usted,* rather than the familiar *tu.* The dignity of others is honored; it is not openly questioned nor confronted, and problems may be discussed indirectly. To some, this may appear as disinterest, nonattendance, or lack of assertiveness. If not clear to the counselor, it may lead to misinterpretation or misunderstanding. Direct eye contact may or may not be a Hispanic trait; rather it may be one of socioeconomic class where the peon was not to look at his master, but this does not apply to children and parents or significant others.

Personalismo. Hispanics relate to institutions through persons or acquaintances rather than through the organizational hierarchy. That is, they may seek services in an agency where they know someone rather than to apply directly to the appropriate office in their area. Until recently, there have been few Hispanic rehabilitation counselors with whom the disabled Hispanic would identify or that they knew personally from their community and understood their work. Thus, they may lack a familiarity or understanding of rehabilitation and of its services and, consequently, do not apply for them.

La palabra. Hispanics are known to negotiate according to unwritten or verbal contacts, or *acuerdos.* A person's word *(la palabra)* is binding, and if he gives it, he is honor-bound. Thus, a Hispanic may be uncomfortable and unfamiliar with formal or written procedures, e.g., application forms that must be signed, the verification of information, information release permits, and other documents that are often perceived by Hispanics as lack of trust. These formal written approaches seem so distant and impersonal to the clients that they feel they will never qualify for or be selected for services. Rehabilitation workers conceivably could interpret the failure to return forms as disinterest or a decision not to apply for rehabilitation services.

Folk medicine. Many Hispanics are not accustomed to modern medical care. Often they may rely on folk medicine and resort to medical doctors or health clinics only in times of crisis (Kiev, 1968; Trotter & Chavira, 1981). Thus, Hispanics may not have family doctors, and they may misunderstand the agency's need for a general medical or specialist examination.

There are other circumstances with which Hispanics may be extremely uncomfortable, e.g., having to completely disrobe for an examination or being examined by a physician of the opposite sex. They may perceive medical doctors or health care clinics negatively as they associate these with their illnesses and often attribute their health problems to their visits to them.

The reaction to medical procedures may be considerably different among certain Hispanics due to past experiences, e.g., a physician may order routine tests for tuberculosis and may not understand the alarm it causes the patient who associates tuberculosis with the disappearance of friends or neighbors who were sent to sanitariums and were never heard from again. The need for these examinations may require special explanation.

Migrant and seasonal farmworkers. Many Hispanics follow migratory and seasonal farm work. There are significantly higher rates of certain illnesses, respiratory infections, gastrointestinal disorders, and dermatitis and skin infections among them than found in the general population. These are caused by poor housing and sanitation, poor nutrition, lack of education, limited accessibility and availability of medical services, language and cultural barriers, working conditions, exposure to pesticides, and a higher frequency of farm accidents (Olsen, 1982). It is often very difficult for the migrant who lives and works in the country to lose a day's work to go to town for a medical examination.

REHABILITATION PLANNING

Rehabilitation planning, the process of integrating and directing a variety of data about the client toward a rehabilitation goal, is one of the specialized skills of the rehabilitation counselor. The rehabilitation counselor's ability to make correct clinical inferences from these data gives validity to the rehabilitation plan. Effective rehabilitation planning with disabled Hispanics would take into account the cultural implications.

The Hispanic traditionally relates to institutions in a personal way. Rehabilitation planning with disabled Hispanics, not unlike that effectively done with others, should be participatory. This would include an explanation as to the need for signatures on application forms, verification slips, and information-release permits. These seem routine to those who experience them frequently in a protective society but are questioned by those who are oriented to a personal approach and who may be offended by inferences that question their *palabra* (word).

Rehabilitation planning also may require general and specialist examinations. The need for these and their implications for the Hispanic client's rehabilitation program also requires careful explanation, since many Hispanics do not frequently use these services and may have a certain distrust for them.

Psychological Evaluation of Hispanics

Psychological evaluations often provide the rehabilitation counselor with data that have value in developing a rehabilitation plan. The psychological evaluation of the Hispanic is a major concern, not because the task is difficult, rather because there is a lack of Spanish-speaking psychologists to evaluate monolingual Spanish-speaking or limited-English-speaking Hispanics or who understand the implications of language, culture, and the complexities of these.

Valid psychological evaluations of disabled Hispanics are important to the rehabilitation process, and it may be that without these many clients will be overlooked or misunderstood. Some factors to be considered are as follows.

Language. Hispanics in the United States range from monolingual Spanish to monolingual English. There are many who are bilingual/bicultural and as such can be assessed to be capable persons and do not present problems of evaluation. For those who are fluent in English, testing and evaluation need not be too different than for the general population. Interestingly enough, the same can generally be said about those who are monolingual Spanish, and what is needed is a Spanish-speaking psychologist using the Spanish version of the instrument.

The Hispanics who fall somewhere along the continuum of limited English/Spanish-speaking ability may need a psychologist who is bilingual/bicultural and aware of the various cultural implications, Hispanic/non-Hispanic, that impact on the testing and evaluation process. They need to assess, by clinical observation, the client's position on the acculturation continuum. This will determine when to use the English or Spanish version of the instruments and help to attend to other questions about their use. Many items on tests are culture-bound, but when using individual tests, such as the WAIS, these can be handled clinically (Quintana, 1982). On paper-and-pencil tests or group tests, there is less flexibility, and it is more difficult to assess their validity with the disabled Hispanic. Tests have value and can be of tremendous assistance in rehabilitation planning. There is a place for testing when used professionally and when their limitations with the culturally different are understood.

The psychologist needs to be sensitive and understand the reaction that clients may have to the testing activities that they are subjected to, given their cultural background and their expected roles and behavior. For example, a traditional Hispanic male might take offense when told that he needs to go in for an examination and is faced by the Picture Completion subtest (a series of cartoons), the Block Design subtest, or the Picture Arrangement subtest on the WAIS. He may see these as children's games, and he might consider it an affront to be asked to manipulate them, particularly if he is experiencing frustration with the testing and is not sure why he is there in the first place. It may not be strange to most of us if asked questions about religion, the Bible, or things about American government and taxes. Consider the Cuban refugee from Mariel who has lived his whole life under a system where he has not been taught or experienced these concepts, and it can be anticipated that his response will be different than the norm. Or, if given the MMPI, certain Hispanics may consider that some of the items reflect normal attitudes and experiences and not the superstitions they are regarded as in this country (Quintana, 1982).

Rehabilitation counseling requires a bold, creative, pragmatic, yet sensitive approach. The rehabilitation counselor is aware of the individual differences of all clients. The preceding discussion is intended to draw attention to some that relate to planning with the disabled Hispanic.

COUNSELING PRACTICE

The effectiveness of existing counseling approaches, directive, non-directive, and insightful with Hispanic clients seems to depend on counselors' level of understanding of the Hispanic culture and their ability to adapt a given theoretical framework to meet the cultural characteristics and personal needs of the client. In addition, counseling outcomes also depend on the client's perception of the counselor, client's perception of the treatment approach, and the client's expectations of treatment (Acosta & Sheehan, 1976; Bergland & Lundquist, 1975; Boulette, 1976; Cortese, 1979; LaCalla, 1974; Maher, 1978; Santa Cruz & Hepworth, 1975).

The state of the art with Hispanic clients in this area is not different than that of the general population. It seems that a given treatment modality is not equally effective with all clients and with all problems. Consequently, without the empirical foundations on which to base the argument that one treatment approach is more effective than another, it seems appropriate to concentrate the efforts in culturally adapting current counseling approaches to increase their effectiveness with Hispanic clients.

The modification of existing counseling service to assist Hispanic clients becomes necessary when the client in question strongly identifies with the Hispanic culture and whenever the nature of the problem to be addressed is related to Hispanic cultural values, norms, attitudes, or behaviors.

If the Hispanic client is concerned with academic matters or employment, or if the client has a strong identification with the dominant society and shares these cultural values and characteristics, the need of culturally sensitive counseling is less than if the client strongly identifies with the Hispanic culture or is concerned with personal issues which are likely to be emic or culturally bound. In this latter case, culturally sensitive counseling is highly recommended (Furlong, Atkinson, & Casas, 1979). Thus, it is recommended that a careful determination be made regarding the client's degree of acculturation, and the nature of the problem to be addressed before recommending a culturally sensitive counseling approach.

There are several indicators which can be utilized to determine the need for culturally sensitive counseling. These indicators are the client's use of the Spanish language, the client's life-style, the source of their support system, and the nature of the problem to be addressed in counseling.

There are also several instruments available to determine the client's degree of acculturation (Mercer, 1976; Olmedo, Martinez, & Martinez, 1978; Szapocznik, Scopetta, Kurtines, & Arnalde, in press). These instruments, however, have many limitations which must be observed. For example, the instruments were normed on specific age groups such as junior and senior high school students. In addition, they were normed on a specific geographic area, i.e., California. No norms are available for other age groups and other geographic locations. Furthermore, these instruments measure strong adherence to either the Hispanic or the Anglo culture but not the degree of interaction between the cultures. Therefore, the need for culturally sensitive counseling can be determined more effectively by a clinical judgment based on the client's characteristics and the nature of the problem to be addressed rather than by utilizing available measures of acculturation.

This chapter proposes a culturally sensitive counseling approach which differs from traditional approaches in that counselors must be bilingual/bicultural individuals, utilizing theoretical approaches and a service delivery model adapted to the Hispanic culture. Similar approaches have been recommended by Padilla et al. (1975), Ruiz (1981), Ruiz, Casas, and Padilla (1977), Ruiz, Padilla, and Alvarez (1978), Ruiz and Casas (1981), and Ruiz and Padilla (1977).

Culturally Sensitive Counseling Services

Outreach and Advocacy

The purpose of this component is to increase the Hispanic utilization of available services by reaching out to the individual and visiting the person in his/her cultural and personal environment. It also enhances the counselor/client relationship and increases the effectiveness of counseling services to Hispanics.

The counselor can identify prospective Hispanic clients by becoming acquainted with community organizations, community leaders, churches, and other systems involved with the Hispanic population. Once the prospective clients are identified, the counselor must reach out to these individuals by setting up a meeting to visit the prospective clients in their homes. This may be accomplished through a telephone call, through a person having a relationship with the prospective client who can arrange the meeting, or personally by the counselor.

By visiting the prospective clients in their homes, the counselor is not only verbalizing interest in the person but is behaviorally demonstrating that interest. This step greatly enhances the client/counselor relationship. In addition, it allows the counselor to personally experience the life-style of the prospective client as well as the reality conditions of that person, that is, family problems, availability of transportation, and distance from the office where services are to be provided. Furthermore, the familiar surrounding of the client's home will allow this person to feel comfortable and secure, therefore, more likely to be open and trusting. In addition, needed documentation from the client is more likely to be obtained in this setting.

During this home visit, the counselor can explain the goals of the rehabilitation process, the services available, the benefits to be obtained from these services. If the prospective client is likely to qualify and is interested in services, a meeting in the counselor's office should be set up to begin the rehabilitation process.

Client Education Session

The purpose of this session is to explain to the client the rehabilitation process in detail, to gather needed information about the client, and to determine the type of counseling and counselor most appropriate for the situation.

The explanation of the rehabilitation process includes providing a rationale for requesting physical and psychological examinations as well as signatures and documentation to substantiate the client's disability. In addition, the counselor should explore the client's feelings and perceptions regarding the services to be provided, should answer any questions the client may have regarding the procedures, and clarify misconceptions, doubts, and misinterpretations in the client's mind.

Bilingual/Bicultural Counseling

Once determined that culturally sensitive counseling is the preferred or needed treatment approach, a bilingual/bicultural counselor should provide the service to the Hispanic client.

The utilization of bilingual/bicultural counselors eliminates the differences between clients and counselors which have been described as possible obstacles to effective therapy (Calia, 1966; Mitchell, 1971; Sue & Sue, 1977; Vontress, 1969, 1974; Williams & Kirkland, 1971). Furthermore, language and cultural similarities between client and counselor enhance the process and outcome of therapy and ultimately the utilization of counseling services (Karno & Edgerton, 1969; Mitchell, 1971; Padilla & Ruiz, 1977; Ruiz & Padilla, 1977; Sue & Sue, 1977; Williams & Kirkland, 1971).

In addition, knowledge and understanding of the Hispanic culture assists the counselor in differentiating therapeutic problems and maladaptive behaviors from cultural conflicts and peculiar behaviors in a Hispanic client.

Failure to differentiate between these behaviors is likely to result in the creation of an additional problem for the client. For example, a Hispanic female client may be angry and frustrated because of her inability to accomplish career goals. A deeper exploration of the situation may reveal that her behavior is "passive" and that she is unable to behave assertively in order to achieve her goals. The counselor's understanding of her role in the Hispanic culture will facilitate the exploration of role conflicts between cultures. This exploration will help the client understand how a given behavior may be necessary and, in fact, enhance her existence in the Hispanic culture, while being a hindrance to her life in the dominant society.

Culturally Adaptive Counseling Theories

Counseling theories can be adapted to meet the idiosyncracies of the Hispanic culture and the needs of a given client.

Ruiz, Casas, and Padilla (1978) and Ruiz and Casas (1981) propose a behavioristic counseling approach relevant to Hispanics. This model utilizes cognitive restructuring principles to achieve positive behavioral change. It emphasizes the identification of overt behaviors which cause difficulties in the client's life. In addition, the model recommends that the counselor respond to the client in a directive manner and that a limit be set to the number of problems to be addressed. Furthermore, it advocates for a contractual agreement between client and counselor regarding counseling objectives. Contractual agreements, *acuerdos,* need not be in writing if the client accepts the binding nature of *la palabra.*

Nondirective counseling approaches can also be effective with Hispanics who show capacity and interest in self-knowledge and introspection.

The adaption of these theories to Hispanic clients consists in establishing the needed therapeutic conditions for client change to occur and applying the theoretical construct consistently with the Hispanic culture.

The adaption of the client-centered approach to the Hispanic culture will be discussed to illustrate how this theory may be effectively utilized with Hispanic clients.

The client-centered approach is based on the belief that humans will grow rational under optimal conditions. Also, that humans have a powerful tendency to grow, to mature, and to reach self-actualization. Personality problems are seen as a result of a self-concept incongruent with the organism and/or experiences (Rogers, 1957). To obtain positive personality change in clients, the counselors must experience and convey to the client genuineness, empathy, and positive regard (Rogers, 1957).

The counselor utilizing the client-centered approach with Hispanic clients must believe in the Hispanic client's tendency to develop, to mature, and to reach self-actualization. Thus, a counselor holding negative attitudes or prejudices toward Hispanics will be unable to provide the necessary conditions to allow change in the client's personality.

Empathy, genuineness, and positive regard are the needed conditions in the counselor's attitude to effect positive personality changes in the client.

To be empathic the counselor must be able to accurately perceive the Hispanic client's subjective world. This implies going beyond understanding the client's words and being able to perceive feelings and the subjective world "as if" the counselor were the Hispanic client. The counselor must be able to verbally and nonverbally reflect the client's felt meanings and through this process allow the client to broaden his/her understanding of self and to incorporate his/her experiences into the self-concept. For example, the counselor must be able to understand the feelings and experiences of a person experiencing cultural value conflicts and the world's perception from a Hispanic's perspective.

Positive regard—that is, the counselor's ability to care for and to accept the client without judgment and with a strong belief in the client's ability to utilize his/her inner resources to grow and mature—also needs to be conveyed verbally and nonverbally to the Hispanic client.

Genuineness, the relationship between counselor and client, must be honest and sincere. This condition requires the absence of fronts or facades on the part of the counselor as well as the counselor's ability to relate to the client as a person on an equal level. The counselor must be able to rely on his/her felt experiences and feelings and to convey them to the client.

Genuineness in the counselor gives the client the opportunity to grow by experiencing an honest reaction from another individual toward his/her behavior. In order to convey felt experiences and feelings in an appropriate manner, the counselor must be familiar with the client's cultural protocol. The lack of familiarity with cultural norms and behaviors is likely to decrease the counselor's ability to fully communicate genuineness. In addition, the counselor might utilize verbal and nonverbal behaviors which might be offensive or insulting to the client.

Existing counseling theories should be adapted to the Hispanic culture and the unique needs of a given client in order to be effective with members of that population. In addition, the counselor should also be familiar and sensitive to the Hispanic culture and must be able to utilize culturally appropriate behaviors in order to effect positive personality change in the client.

SUMMARY

The rehabilitation of disabled individuals is enhanced by the counselor's knowledge and understanding of the client's culture.

Familiarity with the Hispanic culture gives the counselor the opportunity to utilize specific Hispanic cultural attributes such as *la familia, la palabra, dignidad,* and the client's traditional role as strengths and support systems in the rehabilitation program of disabled Hispanics. Furthermore, knowledge of the Hispanic culture gives the counselor the ability to provide culturally sensitive rehabilitation services. That is, the counselor is able to accurately interpret the client's feelings and reactions toward the rehabilitation process as well as the client's performance and behaviors during physical and psychological evaluations, and during interviews and counseling sessions.

In addition, knowledge of the Hispanic culture assists the counselor in differentiating therapeutic problems and maladaptive behaviors from cultural conflicts and unique behaviors in a Hispanic client. The accurate identification of the client's problem is essential to the successful outcome of rehabilitation services. Furthermore, cultural sensitivity is necessary in order to exhibit culturally appropriate behaviors and to avoid inappropriate ones. Thus, knowledge and understanding of the Hispanic culture is essential in order to successfully apply culturally adapted counseling theories and to effectively rehabilitate disabled Hispanics.

References

Acosta, F. X., & Sheehan, J. G. (1976). Preference toward Mexican-American and Anglo-American psychotherapist. *Journal of Consulting and Clinical Psychology, 44,* 272–279.

Adkins, W. R. (1984). Life skills education: A video-based counseling/learning delivery system. In D. Larson (Ed.), *Teaching psychological skills.* Monterey, CA: Brooks/Cole.

Akridge, R., & Means, B. (1982). Psychosocial adjustment skills training. In B. Bolton (Ed.), *Vocational adjustment of disabled persons.* Baltimore: University Park Press.

Akridge, R. L., Means, B. L., Milligan, G. T., & Farley, R. C. (1978). *Interpersonal skill training: Basic helping skills for rehabilitation workers.* Fayetteville, AR: University of Arkansas.

Alexander, F. M. (1963) *Fundamentals of psychoanalysis.* New York: Norton.

Alexander, F., & French, T. M. (1946). *Psychoanalytic therapy: Principles and application.* New York: Ronald Press.

Allen, H. A., & Falvo, D. (1983). *The principles and practices of vocational rehabilitation with persons with hidden disabilities: A critical analysis of the literature with annotated bibliography.* Washington, DC: National Institute of Handicapped Research.

Allen, T. W. (1971). The individual psychology of Alfred Adler: An item of history and a promise of a revolution. *The Counseling Psychologist, 3*(1), 3–24.

Alschuler, A. S., & Ivey, A. E. (1973). Internalization: The outcome of psychological education. *Personnel and Guidance Journal, 51*(9), 607–610.

American Cancer Society. (1979). *Report on the social, economic and psychological needs of cancer patients in California: Major findings and implications.* San Francisco: Author.

American Medical Association. (1973). *Manual on Alcoholism* (rev. ed.). Chicago: Author.

American Personnel and Guidance Association. (1971). Ethical standards. In H. A. Moses & C. H. Patterson (Eds.), Readings in rehabilitation counseling (2nd ed.). Champaign, IL: Stipes.

American Personnel and Guidance Association. (1971). A state policy. In H. A. Moses & C. H. Patterson (Eds.), *Readings in rehabilitation counseling* (2nd ed.). Champaign, IL: Stipes.

American Psychiatric Association. (1980). *Diagnostic and statistical manual of mental disorders* (3rd ed.). Washington, DC: APA.

Amerikaner, M. J. (1981). Continuing theoretical convergence: A general systems theory perspective on personal growth and development. *Journal of Individual Psychology, 37,* 31–53.

Andersen, R. H. (1979). Vocational expert testimony: The new frontier for the rehabilitation professional. *Journal of Rehabilitation, 45*(3), 39–40, 74.

Anderson, C. M. (1974). The brain injured adult: An overlooked problem. In R. E. Weber (Ed.), *Handbook on learning disabilities,* pp. 217–241. Englewood Cliffs, NJ: Prentice-Hall.

Anderson, C., Hogarty, G. E., & Reiss, D. J. (1980). Family treatment of adult schizophrenic patients: A psycho-educational approach. *Schizophrenia Bulletin, 6*(3), 490–505.

Anderson, D., & McLaurin, R. (Eds.). (1980). *Report on the national head and spinal cord injury survey. Journal of Neurosurgery* (Suppl.)

Anderson, J. (1976, October) *Basic concepts in the approach to adjustment services.* Paper presented at the meeting of the Region IV Counsel of Facility Specialists. West Palm Beach, FL.

Anderson, J. K., & Parente, F. R. (1982). Rehabilitation counselors forecast their future. *Journal of Rehabilitation, 48*(1), 36–42.

Anderson, T. P. (1981). Stroke and cerebral trauma: Medical aspects. In W. C. Stolov & M. R. Clowers (Eds.), *Handbook on severe disability.* Washington, DC: U.S. Department of Education, Rehabilitation Services Administration.

Anderson, V. (1978). Elving genetic counseling for epilepsy. In *Plan for Nationwide Action on Epilepsy* (Vol. 2). Washington, DC: Commission for the Control of Epilepsy and Its Consequences, USDHEW, PHS, NIH.

Andrews, H. (1981). Holistic approach to rehabilitation. *Journal of Rehabilitation, 47*(2), 28–31.

Ansbacher, H. L., & Ansbacher, R. R. (Eds.). (1956). *The individual psychology of Alfred Adler.* New York: Basic Books.

Anthony, W. (1978). Human relations skills and training: Implications for rehabilitation counseling. In B. Bolton & M. E. Jaques (Eds.), *Rehabilitation counseling: Theory and practice.* Baltimore: University Park Press.

Anthony, W. (1980). A rehabilitation model for rehabilitating the psychiatrically disabled. *Rehabilitation Counseling Bulletin, 24,* 6–21.

Anthony, W. A., Pierce, R. M., Cohen, M. R., & Cannon, J. R. (1980). *The skills of diagnostic planning: Psychiatric rehabilitation practice* (Books 1–6). Baltimore: University Park Press.

Appelbaum, S. A. (1982). Challenges to traditional psychotherapy from the "new therapies." *American Psychologist, 37*(9), 1002–1008.

Armor, D. J., Polich, J. M., & Stambul, H. B. (1976). *Alcoholism and treatment.* Report R-1739-NIAAA. Santa Monica, CA: Rand Corporation.

Asch, A. (1984). The experience of disability. *American Psychologist, 39*(5), 529–536.

Ashton, P. C. (1979). Rehabilitation in a major corporate setting. *Journal of Rehabilitation, 45*(3), 26–29.

Aspy, D. N., & Roebuck, F. N. (1974). From humane ideas to humane technology and back again many times. *Education, 95,* 163–171.

Aspy, D. N., & Roebuck, F. N. (1977). *Kids don't learn from people they don't like.* Amherst, MA: Human Resource Development Press.

Athelstan, G. (1981). Psychosocial adjustment to chronic disease and disability. In W. Stolov & M. Clowers (Eds.), *Handbook of severe disability,* (pp. 13–18). Washington, DC: U.S. Government Printing Office.

Atkins, B., Lynch, R., & Pullo, R. (1982). A definition of psychosocial aspects of disability. *Vocational Evaluation & Work Adjustment Bulletin, 15*(3), 55–61.

Authier, J. (1977). The psychoeducation model: Definition, contemporary roots and content. *Canadian Counselor, 12,* 15–22.

Authier, J., Gustafson, K., Guerney, B., & Kasdorf, J. (1975). The psychological practitioner as a teacher: A theoretical-historical and practical review. *Counseling Psychologist, 5*(2), 31–50.

Avery, C. (1968). Para-analytic group therapy with adolescent multi-handicapped blind. *New Outlook for the Blind, 62,* 65–72.

Azrin, N. H., & Besalel, V. A. (1980). *Job club counselor's manual. A behavioral approach to vocational counseling.* Baltimore: University Park Press.

Azrin, N. H., Flores, T., & Kaplan, S. J. (1975). Job-finding club: A group-assisted program for obtaining employment. *Behavior Research and Therapy, 13,* 17–27.

Azrin, N. H., & Phillip, R. A. (1979). The job club method for the job handicapped: A comparative outcome study. *Rehabilitation Counseling Bulletin, 23,* 144–155.

Bacharach, L. (1976). Characteristics of diagnosed and missed alcoholic male admissions to State and County mental hospitals in 1972. *Mental Health Statistical Note No. 124.* Bethesda, MD: National Institute of Mental Health.

Baker, E. (1985). Psychoanalysis and psychoanalytic psychotherapy. In S. Lynn & J. Garske (Eds.), *Contemporary psychotherapies: Models and methods.* Columbus, OH: Charles Merrill.

Baker, R., & Mercer, F. (1973). *Region IV Conference on Adjustment Services.* Auburn, AL: Auburn University, Rehabilitation Services Education.

Baker, R., & Sawyer, H. (1973). *Adjustment services: Emphasis on human change.* Auburn, AL: Auburn University, Rehabilitation Services Education.

Bandura, A. (1977). *Social learning theory.* Englewood Cliffs, NJ: Prentice-Hall.

Banks, J. (December 19, 1981). Personal Correspondence.

Barckley, V. (1968). Grief, a part of living. *Ohio's Health, 20,* 34–38.

Barrett, W. (1958). *Irrational man: A study in existential philosophy.* Garden City, NY: Doubleday.

Barten, H. H. (Ed.). (1971). *Brief therapies.* New York: Behavioral Publications.

Bartlow, C. (1981). *A clinical appraisal of secondary learning disabled work study students in the state of Oklahoma.* Unpublished doctoral dissertation, California Western University.

Baruth, L. G., & Huber, C. H. (1985). *Counseling and psychotherapy: Theoretical analyses and skills applications.* Columbus, OH: Bell and Howell.

Bassin, A. (1976). The reality therapy paradigm. In A. Bassin, T. E. Bratter, & R. L. Rachin (Eds.), *The reality therapy reader* (pp. 265–280). New York: Harper & Row.

Batten, M. D. (1980, May). Assessing older worker policy in the U.S. *Generations,* pp. 45ff.

Bauman, M. (1954). *Adjustment to blindness.* Commonwealth of Pennsylvania: Pennsylvania State Council for the Blind.

Bauman, M. (1973). Psychological and educational assessment. In B. Lowenfeld (Ed.), *The visually handicapped child in school.* New York: John Day.

Baumgart, D., Brown, L., Pumpian, I., Nisbet, J., Ford, A., Sweet, M., Messina, R., & Schroeder, J. (1982). Principle of partial participation and individualized adaptations in education programs for severely handicapped students. *The Journal of the Association for the Severely Handicapped, 7,* 17–27.

Beals, R., & Hickman, N. (1972). Industrial injuries to the back and extremities. *Journal of Bone and Joint Disorders, 54,* 1593–1611.

Bear, D. M., & Fedio, P. (1977). Quantitative analysis of interictal behavior in temporal lobe epilepsy. *Archives of Neurology, 34,* 454–476.

Beck, A. T. (1976). *Cognitive therapy and the emotional disorders.* New York: International Universities Press.

Becker, R. L., Schull, C., & Campbell, K. (1981). Vocational interest evaluation of TMR adults. *American Journal of Mental Deficiency, 85,* 350–357.

Beecher, H. K. (1959). Generalization from pain of various types and diverse origins. *Science, 161,* 267–268.

Beecher, H. K. (1960). Increased stress and effectiveness of placebos and "active" drugs. *Science, 132,* 91–92.

Bellamy, G. T., Horner, R. H., & Inman, D. P. (1979). *Vocational habilitation of severely retarded adults: A direct service technology.* Baltimore: University Park Press.

Bellamy, G. T., Sheehan, M. R., Horner, R. H., & Boles, S. M. (1980). Community programs for severely handicapped adults: An analysis of vocational opportunities. *Journal of the Association for the Severely Handicapped, 5,* 307–324.

Benedict, R., & Ganikos, M. L. (1981). Coming to terms with ageism in rehabilitation. *Journal of Rehabilitation, 47,*(4), 10–18.

Bengston, V. L. (1977). *The social psychology of aging.* Indianapolis: Bobbs Merrill.

Benjamin, A. (1981). *The helping interview* (3rd ed.). Boston: Houghton Mifflin.

Benton, A. (1979). Behavioral consequences of closed head injury. In G. Odom (Ed.), *Central nervous system trauma research status report.* Washington, DC: National Institute of Neurological and Communicative Disorders and Stroke.

Ben-Yishay, Y., & Diller, L. (1981). Rehabilitation of cognitive and perceptual defects in people with traumatic brain damage. *International Journal of Rehabilitation Research, 4*(2), 208–210.

Bergland, W. B., & Lundquist, G. W. (1975). The vocational exploration group and minority youth: An experimental outcome study. *Journal of Vocational Behavior, 1,* 289–296.

Berkowitz, M. (1981). Disincentives and the rehabilitation of disabled persons. In E. L. Pan, T. E. Backer, & C. L. Vash (Eds.), *Annual review of rehabilitation* (Vol. 2). New York: Springer Publishing Co.

Bernstein, D. A., & Borkovec, T. D. (1973). *Progressive relaxation training.* Champaign, IL: Research Press.

Berry, J. W. (1969). On cross-cultural comparability. *International Journal of Psychology, 4,* 119–224.

Berven, N. L. (1980). Psychometric assessment in rehabilitation. In B. Bolton & D. W. Cook (Eds.), *Rehabilitation client assessment* (pp. 46–64). Baltimore: University Park Press.

Berven, N. L. (1983). *Client vocational assessment.* (Rehabilitation Research Review Monograph 2). Washington, DC: National Rehabilitation Information Center.

Berven, N. L., & Scofield, M. E. (1980a). Evaluation of clinical problem-solving skills through standardized case management simulations. *Journal of Counseling Psychology, 27,* 199–208.

Berven, N. L., & Scofield, M. E. (1980b). Evaluation of professional competence through standardized simulations: A review. *Rehabilitation Counseling Bulletin, 24,* 178–202.

Bitter, J. (1979). *Introduction to rehabilitation.* St. Louis: C. V. Mosby.

Black, P. (1979). Management of cancer pain: An overview. *Neurosurgery, 5,* 507–518.

Black, R. B. (1980). Genetic counseling and epilepsy. In B. P. Hermann (Ed.), *A multidisciplinary handbook of epilepsy.* Springfield, IL: Charles C. Thomas.

Blake, R. (1981). Disabled older persons: A demographic analysis. *Journal of Rehabilitation, 47*(4), 19–27.

Blalock, J. (1981). Persistent problems and concerns of young adults with learning disabilities. In W. Cruikshank & A. Silver (Eds.), *Bridges to tomorrow: Vol. 2. The best of ACLD.* Syracuse, NY: Syracuse University Press.

Blalock, J. (1982). Residual learning disabilities in young adults: Implications for rehabilitation. *Journal of Applied Rehabilitation Counseling, 13*(2), 9–13.

Blauner, R. (1969). Internal colonialism and ghetto revolt. *Social Problems, 14,* 398–408.

Blauner, R. (1977). Colonized and immigrant minorities: Nation of nations. In P. I. Ross (Ed.), *The ethnic experience and racial crisis,* pp. 243–258. New York: Random House.

Blum, E., & Blum, R. (1972). *Alcoholism: Modern psychological approaches to treatment.* San Francisco: Jossey-Bass.

Bolton, B. (1974) *Introduction to rehabilitation research.* Springfield, IL: Charles C. Thomas.

Bolton, B. (1979). *Rehabilitation counseling research.* Baltimore: University Park Press.

Bolton, B. (1980). Preparing rehabilitation counselors to be research consumers. *Journal of Applied Rehabilitation Counseling, 11*(2), 70–73.

Bolton, B., Butler, A. J., & Wright, G. N. (1968). *Clinical vs. statistical prediction of client feasibility* (Wisconsin Studies in Vocational Rehabilitation, Monograph 7). Madison, WI: University of Wisconsin–Madison, Regional Rehabilitation Research Institute.

Bond, M. R. (1976). Assessment of the psychosocial outcome of severe head injury. *Acta Neurologica, 34,* 57–70.

Bonica, J. J. (1978). Cancer pain: A major national health problem. *Cancer Nursing, 1*(4), 313–316.

Bonica, J. J. (1979). Importance of the problem. In J. Bonica & V. Ventafridda (Eds.), *Advances in pain research and therapy* (Vol. 2). New York: Raven Press.

Bordin, E. (1968). *Psychological counseling.* New York: Appleton-Century-Crofts.

Bordin, G. S. (1955). *Psychological counseling.* New York: Appelton-Century-Crofts.

Bostwick, D. H., & Foss, G. (1981). Obtaining consumer input: Two strategies for identifying and ranking the problems of mentally retarded young adults. *Education and Training of the Mentally Retarded, 16,* 207–212.

Botterbusch, K. F. (1976). *The use of psychological tests with individuals who are severely disabled.* Menominee, WI: University of Wisconsin–Stout, Stout Vocational Rehabilitation Institute, Materials Development Center.

Botterbusch, K. F. (1978). *Psychological testing in vocational evaluation.* Menominee, WI: University of Wisconsin–Stout, Stout Vocational Rehabilitation Institute, Materials Development Center.

Botterbusch, K. F. (1982). *A comparison of commercial vocational evaluation systems* (2nd ed.). Menominee, WI: University of Wisconsin–Stout, Stout Vocational Rehabilitation Institute, Materials Development Center.

Boulette, T. R. (1976). *Determining needs and appropriate counseling approaches for Mexican-American women: A comparison of therapeutic listening and behavioral rehearsal.* San Francisco: Rand E. Research Associates.

Bozarth, J. D. (1981). The rehabilitation process and older people. *Journal of Rehabilitation, 47*(4), 28–32.

Bozarth, J. D., & Rubin, S. E. (1978). Empirical observations of rehabilitation counselor performance and outcome: Some implications. In B. Bolton & M. E. Jaques (Eds.), *Rehabilitation counseling: Theory and practice.* Baltimore: University Park Press.

Brickman, P., Rabinowitz, V. C., Karuza, J., Coates, D., Cohn, E., & Kidder, L. (1982). Models of helping and coping. *American Pyschologist, 37*(4), 368–384.

Bridges, C. D. (1946). *Job placement of the physically handicapped.* New York: McGraw-Hill.

Brieland, D. (1950). A comparative study of the speech of blind and sighted children. *Speech Monographs, 17,* 99–103.

Brine, J. M. (1979). Psycho-social aspects of aging: An overview. In M. L. Gainikos (Ed.), *Counseling the aged: A training syllabus for educators,* (pp. 65–81). Falls Church, VA: American Personnel and Guidance Association.

Britton, J. O., & Thomas, K. R. (1973). Rearing the disabled child: A framework for future research. *Journal of School Psychology, 11,* 105–109.

Brolin, D. E. (1982). *Vocational preparation of persons with handicaps.* Columbus, OH: Charles Merrill.

Brooks, D. K. (1981). Brooks examines "guts" of licensure laws. *Guidepost, 24*(8), 1, 3.

Brooks, D. N. (1975). Long and short term memory in head injured patients. *Cortex, 11,* 329–340.

Brotman, H. B. (1982). *Every ninth American: An analysis for the Chairman of the Select Committee of Aging, House of Representatives.* Washington, DC: U.S. Government Printing Office (Comm. Pub. No. 97–332).

Brown, D. (1980). *Steps to independence for people with learning disabilities.* Washington, DC: Parents' Campaign for Handicapped Children and Youth.

Brown, D. (1982a). Definitions and characteristics of learning disabilities. In P. Patton (Ed.), *Vocational rehabilitation of the learning disabled client.* San Diego, CA: San Diego State University.

Brown, D. (1982b). Rehabilitating the learning disabled adult. *American Rehabilitation,* 3–11.

Brown, D. (1983). Learning disability: An autobiography. *American Rehabilitation, 9*(1), 3–7.

Brown, L., Branston-McClean, M. B., Baumgart, D., Vincent, L., Falvey, M., & Schroeder, J. (1979). Using the characteristics of current and subsequent least restrictive environments in the development of curricular content for severely handicapped students. *AAESPH Review, 4*(4), 407–424.

Brown, M., Diller, L., Fordyce, W., Jacobs, D., & Gordon, W. (1980). Rehabilitation indicators: Their nature and uses for assessment. In B. Bolton & D. W. Cook (Eds.), *Rehabilitation client assessment* (pp. 102–117). Baltimore: University Park Press.

Brown, M., Gordon, W. A., & Diller, L. (1983). Functional assessment and outcome measurement: An integrative review. In E. L. Pan, T. E. Backer, & C. L. Vash (Eds.), *Annual review of rehabilitation* (Vol. 3, pp. 93–120). New York: Springer Publishing Co.

Bruckner, F. E., & Randle, A. P. H. (1972). Return to work after severe head injuries. *Rheumatology and Physical Medicine, 11,* 344–348.

Bruininks, R. H., Hauber, F. A., & Kudla, M. J. (1980). National survey of community residential facilities and residents in 1977. *American Journal of Mental Deficiency, 84*(5), 470–478.

Bugenthal, J. F. T. (1965). *The search for authenticity.* New York: Holt, Rinehart, and Winston.

Burgess, E. W. (1960). *Aging in western societies.* Chicago: University of Chicago Press.

Burish, T. G., & Lyles, J. N. (1979). Effectiveness of relaxation training in reducing the aversiveness of chemotherapy in the treatment of cancer. *Journal of Behavior Therapy and Experimental Psychiatry, 10,* 357–362.

Burlingham, D. (1965). Some problems of ego development in blind children. *Psychoanalytic Study of Children, 20*(b), 194–208.

Busch, E. J., Jr. (1981). Developing an employee assistance program. *Personnel Journal, 60,* 708–711.

Butcher, E., & Scofield, M. E. (1984). The use of a standardized simulation and process tracing for studying clinical problem solving competence. *Counselor Education and Supervision, 24,* 70–84.

Butcher, E., Scofield, M. E., & Baker, S. B. (1984). Validation of a standardization simulation for the assessment of competence in mental health counselors. *American Mental Health Counselors Association Journal, 6,* 162–172.

Butcher, E., Scofield, M. E., & Baker, S. B. (1985). Clinical judgment and mental health treatment planning: An empirical investigation. *American Mental Health Counselors Association Journal, 7,* 116–126.

Butler, R. N. (1974). Successful aging and the role of the life review. *Geriatrics.*

Butler, R. N. (1975). *Why survive? Being old in America.* St. Louis: C. V. Mosby.

Butler, R. N., & Lewis, M. I. (1983). *Aging and mental health: Positive psychosocial approaches.* St. Louis: C. V. Mosby.

Byron, R., & Yonemoto, R. (1975). Pain associated with malignancy. In B. Crue (Ed.), *Pain research and treatment.* New York: Academic Press.

Calia, V. F. (1966). The culturally deprived client: A re-formulation of the counselor's role. *Journal of counseling Psychology, 13,* 100–105.

Cameron, P., & Cromer, A. (1974). Generational homophyly. *Journal of Gerontology, 29*(2), 232–261.

Campbell, J. A. (1979). A behavioral approach to the maintenance and rehabilitation of independent functioning with the institutionalized elderly. *Dissertation Abstracts International, 39*(12-B), 6111–6112.

Cantrell, D. (1958). Training the rehabilitation counselor. *Personnel and Guidance Journal, 36,* 246–248.

Cape, R. (1978). Physical aspects in aging. In R. Cape (Ed.), *Aging: Its complex management* (13–38). Hagerstown, MD: Harper & Row.

Carkhuff, R. R. (1969). *Helping and human relationships* (Vols. 1–2). New York: Holt, Rinehart & Winston.

Carkhuff, R. R. (1971a). *The development of human services.* New York: Holt, Rinehart, & Winston.

Carkhuff, R. R. (1971b). Training as a preferred mode of treatment. *Journal of Counseling Psychology, 18*(2), 123–131.

Carkhuff, R. R. (1983). *IPS—interpersonal skills and human productivity.* Amherst, MA: Human Resource Development Press.

Carkhuff, R. R., & Anthony, W. A. (1979). *The skills of helping: An introduction to counseling.* Amherst, MA: Human Resource Development Press.

Carkhuff, R. R., & Bersenson, B. G. (1967). *Beyond counseling and therapy* (2nd ed.). New York: Holt, Rinehart and Winston.

Carkhuff, R. R., Pierce, R. M., & Cannon, J. R. (1980). *The art of helping IV.* Amherst, MA: Human Resources Development Press.

Carkhuff, R. R., & Truax, C. B. (1966). Toward explaining success and failure in interpersonal learning experiences. *Personnel and Guidance Journal, 44,* 723–728.

Carpenter, W. L., Fishel, A., George, S., & Gould, P. (1977). *Health instruction packages: Humanistic nursing—nurse/patient relations.* Los Angeles: League for Innovation in the Community Colleges.

Carter, R. (1978). Medical adjustment service for the severely handicapped. *Journal of Rehabilitation, 44*(1), 20–23.

Casey, A. (1983). Developing a dialogue between rehabilitation practitioners and researchers: A research dissemination approach. *Rehabilitation Literature, 44*(3-4), 76–79.

Casey, E. (1982). Environmental adaptation. In P. Patton (Ed.), *Vocational rehabilitation of the learning disabled client.* San Diego, CA: San Diego State University.

Castelnuovo-Tedesco, P. (1981). Psychological consequences of physical defects: A psychoanalytic perspective. *International Review of Psychoanalysis, 8,* 145–153.

Catania, A. C. (1984). *Learning.* Englewood Cliffs, NJ: Prentice-Hall.

Catanzaro, R. J. (1974). The disease: Alcoholism. In R. J. Catanzaro (Ed.), *Alcoholism: The total treatment approach. Springfield, IL: Charles C. Thomas.*

Cates, C. (1981). A comparison of three mailing approaches to solicit job opportunities for handicapped persons. Rehabilitation Counseling Bulletin, 24, 362–365.

Chapman, C. (1979). Psychologic and behavioral aspects of pain. In J. Bonica & V. Ventagridda (Eds.), *Advances in pain research and therapy.* New York: Raven Press.

Chatfield, W. F. (1977). Economic and sociological factors influencing life satisfaction of the aged. *Journal of Gerontology, 32*(5), 593–599.

Clark, M., Shapiro, D., & Friendly, D. (1981, November 2). Cancer—A progress report. *Newsweek,* p. 94–100.

Clarren, S. K., & Smith, D. W. (1978). The fetal alcohol syndrome. *New England Journal of Medicine, 298,* 1063–1067.

Clemmons, D. (1983). Relationship of GATB scores to successful employment for epileptics in a rehabilitation setting. *Epilepsia, 2,* 232–237.

Coffey, D. (1978). *Vocational evaluator competencies and their relative importance as perceived by practitioners and educator in vocational evaluation.* Unpublished doctoral dissertation, Auburn University.

Coffey, D., & Ellien, V. (1979). *Work adjustment curriculum development workshops.* Menominee, WI: University of Wisconsin-Stout.

Cohen, G. D. (1977). Mental health services and the elderly: Needs and options. In S. Steury & M. L. Blank (Eds.), *Readings in pyschotherapy with old people* (pp. 68–73). Rockville, MD: National Institute of Mental Health.

Coker, C. C., Currie, L., Menz, F., Andrew, J., & Dunn, D. (1976). *Rehabilitation facilities referrals: Step I—Determining client eligibiltiy.* Menomonie, WI: University of Wisconsin–Stout, Rehabilitaiton Research & Training Center.

Cole, H. P., & Lacefield, W. E. (1982). Theories of learning, development and psychoeducational design: Origins and applications in nonschool settings. *Journal of Allied Health, 58,* 6–16.

Connolly, S. C. (1974). The effects of human relations training using Gestalt therapy techniques upon selected personality variables in rehabilitation clients. *Dissertation Abstracts International, 35,* 7644–7645. (University Microfilms No. 75-11, 915)

Conte, L. E. (1983). Vocational development theories and the disabled person: Oversight or deliberate omission? *Rehabilitation Counseling Bulletin, 26,* 316–328.

Cook, D. W. (1980). Clinical vs. statistical prediction revised: Issues in building rehabililitation diagnostic capability. *Rehabilitation Counseling Bulletin, 24,* 151–160.

Cook, D. (1983). Disability, psychopathology, and vocational adjustment. *Rehabilitation Psychology, 28*(3), 177–182.

Cooper, P. G. & Davis, S. (1979). Case flow modeling: A program management innovation for planning services to the severely disabled. *Journal of Rehabilitation Administration 3*(1), 22–30.

Corey, G. (1982). *Theory and practice of counseling and psychotherapy* (2nd ed.). Monterey, CA: Brooks/Cole.

Cortese, M. (1979). Intervention research with Hispanic Americans: A review. *Hispanic Journal of Behavioral Science, 1*(1), 4–20.

Cosgrove, S. (1977). Permission to be O.K.: An essential component in adjustment services. *Vocational Evaluation & Work Adjustment Bulletin, 9*(2), 8–14.

Cotton, N. S. (1979). The familial incidence of alcoholism: A review. *Journal of Studies on Alcohol, 40*(1), 89–116.

Couch, R. (1979). Curriculum development in work adjustment. In D. Coffey & V. Ellien (Eds.), *Work Adjustment.* Menominee, WI: University of Wisconsin–Stout.

Couch, R., & Allen, C. (1973). Behavior modification in rehabilitation facilities: A review. *Journal of Applied Rehabilitation Counseling, 4,* 88–95.

Coven, A. B. (1977). The Gestalt approach to rehabilitation counseling. *Rehabilitation Counseling Bulletin, 20*(3), 167–174.

Coven, A. B. (1979). The Gestalt approach to rehabilitation of the whole person. *Journal of Applied Rehabilitation Counseling, 9*(4), 144–147.

Cowen, E., Underberg, R., Vertillo, R., & Benham, F. (1961). *Adjustment to visual disability in adolescence.* New York: American Foundation for the Blind.

Cramatte, A. (1968). *Deaf persons in professional employment.* Springfield, IL: Charles C. Thomas.

Crewe, N. M., & Athelstan, G. T. (1981). Functional assessment in vocational rehabilitation: A systematic approach to diagnosis and goal setting. *Archives of Physical Medicine and Rehabilitation* 62, 299–305.

Crewe, N. M., Athelstan, G. T., & Meadows, G. K. (1975). Vocational diagnosis through assessment of functional limitations. *Archives of Physical Medicine and Rehabilitation, 56,* 513–516.

Crimando, W., & Godley, S. (1984). *Use of computers in expanding the employment opportunities.* (Rehabilitation Research Review Monograph). Washington, DC: National Rehabilitation Information Center.

Crimando, W., & Sawyer, H. (1983). Microcomputer application in adjustment services programming. *Vocational Evaluation & Work Adjustment Bulletin, 16*(1), 7–12.

Crimando, W., Sawyer, H. W., & Poppen, G. (1984). Teaching self-management skills through cognitive behavior modification. *Vocational Evaluation & Work Adjustment Bulletin, 17,* 108–112.

Crisler, J. R. & Barney, O. R. (1976). A comparison of rehabilitation counselor effectiveness to caseload production supervisory and peer evaluations. *Journal of Applied Rehabilitation Counseling, 7*(2), 114–118.

Crisler, J. R. & Eaton, M. W. (1975). A ten year followup of graduates of a rehabilitation counselor training program. *Journal of Applied Rehabilitation Counseling, 6*(1), 35–41.

Crisler, J. R. & Fowler, N. L. (1981). Employment outcome of graduates of a rehabilitation counselor training program: A comparison of graduate employment between 1965–1974 and 1975–1979. *Journal of Rehabilitation, 47*(3), 28–32.

Criteria for CRE eligibility effective July 1, 1985. Undated memorandum. Board for Rehabilitation Certification, Chicago.

Crites, J., & Super, D. (1962). *Appraising vocational fitness* (rev. ed.). New York: Harper and Row.

Cronbach, L. J. (1970). *Essentials of psychological testing* (3rd ed.). New York: Harper & Row.

Cross, O. (1947). Brailled edition of the Minnesota Multiphastic Personality Inventory for use with the blind. *Journal of Applied Psychology, 31,* 189–198.

Cruickshank, W., Morse, W., & Johns, J. (1980). *Learning disabilities: The struggle from adolescence toward adulthood.* Syracuse, NY: Syracuse University Press.

Crystal, R. M. (1981). Counselors' perceptions of clients' needs. *Rehabilitation Counseling Bulletin, 24*(3), 212–218.

Crystal, R. M., & Brady, S. (1982). *Learning disabilities: Implications for rehabilitation research, teaching, and service.* Lexington, KY: University of Kentucky, College of Education.

Crystal, R. M., Witten, B. J., & Wingate, J. A. (1982). A diagnostic and rehabilitation model for learning disabled clients. *Journal of Applied Rehabilitation Counseling, 13*(2), 34–37.

Currie, L. E. (1977). Simulated casework: Some training and research aspects. *Rehabilitation Counseling Bulletin, 20,* 254–259.

Dahlhauser, H. F., Dickman, F., Emener, W. G., & Lewis, B. Y. (1984). Alcohol and drug abuse awareness: Implications for intake interviewing. *Journal of Applied Rehabilitation Counseling, 15*(4), 31–34.

Danek, M., & Lawrence, R. (1981). The multiply disabled hearing impaired client: Implications for rehabilitation practice. *Journal of Rehabilitation of the Deaf, 15*(3), 1–9.

Daniel, R. W. & Weikel, W. J. (1983). Trends in counseling: A delphi study. *Personnel and Guidance Journal, 61,* 327–331.

Davenport, D. W. (1984). Outplacement counseling: Whither the counselor? *Vocational Guidance Quarterly, 3,* 185–191.

Davis, D. A. & Onymelukwe, O. I. (1977). Unique problems of the handicapped aging. In *The White House Conference on Handicapped Individuals: Vol. 1. Awareness papers,* Washington, DC: U.S. Government Printing Office.

Davis, R. H., Alexander, L. T., & Yelon, S. L. (1974). *Learning system design.* New York: McGraw-Hill.

Dawis, R. (1973). A theory of work adjustment. In J. Cull & R. Hardy (Eds.), *Adjustment to work.* Springfield, IL: Charles C. Thomas.

Dawis, R., & Lofquist, L. (1984). *A psychological theory of work adjustment: An individual-differences model and its applications.* Minneapolis, MN: University of Minnesota Press.

DeLoach, C. & Greer, B. G. (1981). *Adjustment to severe physical disability: A metamorphosis.* New York: McGraw-Hill.

Dembo, T. (1974). The paths to useful knowledge. *Rehabilitation Psychology, 21*(4), 124–128.

Diamond, C. R., & Petkas, E. J. (1979). A state agency's view of private-for-profit rehabilitation. *Journal of Rehabilitation, 45*(3), 30–31.

Dickman, F., & Emener, W. G. (1982a). Employee assistance programs: An emergency vista for rehabilitation counseling. *Journal of Applied Rehabilitation Counseling, 13*(3), 18–20.

Dickman, F., & Emener, W. G. (1982b). Employee assistance programs: Basic concepts, attributes, and an evaluation. *Personnel Administrator, 27*(8), 55–62.

Diller, L. (1959). Psychological theory in rehabilitation counseling. *Journal of Counseling Psychology, 6*(3), 189–193.

Diller, L., Fordyce, W., Jacobs, D., Brown, M., Gordon, W., Simmens, S., Orazem, J., & Barret, L. (1983). *Final report: Rehabilitation indicators project* (R&D Project G008003039). Washington, DC: National Institute of Handicapped Research.

Diller, L., Gordon, W. A., Friedenbergs, I., Ruchdeschel-Hibbard, M., Levine, L. R., Wolf, C., Ezrachi, O., Lipkins, R., Lucido, D., & Francis, A. (1979). Demonstration of benefits of early intervention toward rehabilitation of cancer patients. *Final Report, New York University Medical Rehabilitation Research and Training Center,* No. 1. New York: New York University Medical Rehabilitation Research and Training Center.

Dodrill, C. B. (1978). A neuropsychological battery for epilepsy. *Epilepsia, 19,* 611–623.

Dodrill, C. B. (1980). Interrelationships between neuropsychological data and social problems in epilepsy. In R. Canger, F. Angleri, & J. K. Penry, *Advances in epileptology: XIth Epilepsy International Symposium.* New York: Raven Press.

Dodrill, C. B. & Batzel, L. W. (1981). Patterns of psychosocial problems in chronic epilepsy. M. Dam, L. Gram, & J. K. Penry (Eds.), *Advances in epileptology: XIIth epilepsy international symposium.* New York: Raven Press.

Dodrill, C. B., Batzel, L. W., Queisser, H. R. & Temkin, N. R. (1980). An objective method for the assessment of psychological and social problems among epileptics. *Epilepsia, 21,* 123–135.

Dohanian, J. (1981). Self marketing tactics for rehabilitation counselors. *Journal of Applied Rehabilitation Counseling, 12,* 160–163.

Dolan, J. D. *The self-management of sleep interruptions, pain and nausea by adult oncology outpatients: An investigation.* Unpublished doctoral dissertation, Southern Illinois University, Carbondale, 1982.

Dolan, J., Allen, H. A., & Sawyer, H. W. (1982). Relaxation techniques in the reduction of pain, nausea, and sleep disturbances for oncology outpatients: A primer for rehabilitation counselors. *Journal of Applied Rehabilitation Counseling, 13*(4), 35–39.

Dollard, J., & Miller, N. E. (1950). *Personality and psychotherapy.* New York: McGraw-Hill.

Draguns, J. G. (1981). Counseling across cultures: Common themes and district approaches. In P. P. Pedersen, J. G. Dragons, W. J. Lonner, & J. E. Trimble, *Counseling across Cultures* (pp. 1–21). Honolulu, HI: East-West Center, University of Hawaii.

Drake, G. (1981). *Definitions of learning disabilities.* Pater presented at Rehabilitation Strategies with LD Adults Workshop, Lexington, KY.

Dreikurs, R. (1967). *Psychodynamics, psychotherapy, and counseling.* Chicago: Alfred Adler Institute.

Driessenack, C. H. (1978). Outplacement: A benefit for both employee and company. *Personnel Administration, 23,* 24–26.

Drucker, P. F. (1980). Planning for redundant workers. *Personnel Administrator, 25,* 23–25.

Dunham, J. R., & Dunham, C. S. (1978). Psychosocial aspects of disability. In R. Goldenson, J. Dunham, & C. Dunham (Eds.), *Disability and rehabilitation handbook.* New York: McGraw-Hill.

Dunivant, N. (Fall, 1982). Learning disabilities and juvenile delinquency: A summary report. *State Court Journal.*

Dunn, D. (1974) *Placement services in the vocational rehabilitation program.* Menomonie, WI: University of Wisconsin–Stout, Research and Training Center.

Dunn, D. (1981a). Current placement trends. In E. L. Pan, T. E. Backer, & C. L. Vash (Eds.), *Annual review of rehabilitation* (Vol. 2) (pp. 113–146). New York: Springer Publishing Co.

Dunn, D. J. (1981b). Vocational rehabilitation of the older disabled worker. *Journal of Rehabilitation, 47*(4), 76–81.

Duvan, R. J. (1982). Psychological theories of physical disability: New perspectives. In M. Eisenberg, C. Griggins, & R. J. Duval, (Eds.), *Disabled people as second class citizens* (pp. 173–192). New York: Springer Publishing Co.

Dyer, E. (1982). Post-secondary program. In P. L. Patton (Ed.), *Vocational rehabilitation of the learning disabled client.* San Diego, CA: San Diego State University.

D'Zurilla, T., & Goldfried, M. (1971). Problem-solving and behavior modification. *Journal of Abnormal Psychology, 78,* 107–126.

Edwards, J. J., & Klemmack, D. L. (1973). Correlates of life satisfaction: A reexamination. *Journal of Gerontology, 28*(4), 497–502.

Egan, G. (1975). *The skilled helper: A model for systematic helping and interpersonal relating.* Monterey, CA: Brooks/Cole.

Elias-Burger, S. F., Sigelman, C. K., Danley, W. E., & Burger, D. L. (1981). Teaching interview skills to mentally retarded persons. *American Journal of Mental Deficiency, 85,* 655–657.

Ellis, A. (1962). *Reason and emotion in psychotherapy.* Secaucus, NJ: Lyle Stuart.

Ellis, A. (1973). *Humanistic psychotherapy.* New York: McGraw-Hill.

Ellis, A. (1976). The biological basis of human irrationality. *Journal of Individual Psychology, 32,* 145–168.

Ellis, A. (1977a). The basic clinical theory of rational-emotive therapy. In A. Ellis and R. Greiger (Eds.), *Handbook of rational-emotive therapy* (pp. 3–34). New York: Springer Publishing Co.

Ellis, A. (1977b). Rational-emotive therapy: Research data that support the clinical and personality hypotheses of RET and other modes of cognitive-behavior therapy. *The Counseling Psychologist, 7,* 2–42.

Ellis, A. (1979a). The practice of rational-emotive therapy. In A. Ellis and J. Whitely (Eds.), *Theoretical and empirical foundations of rational-emotive.* Monterey, CA: Brooks/Cole.

Ellis, A. (1979b). Rational-emotive therapy. In A. Ellis and J. Whitely (Eds.), *Theoretical and empirical foundations of rational-emotive therapy.* Monterey, CA: Brooks/Cole.

Ellis, A. (1979c). Rational-emotive therapy. In R. Corsini (Ed.), *Current psychotherapies* (2nd ed.). Itasca, IL: F. E. Peacock.

Ellis, A. (1979d). The theory of rational-emotive therapy. In A. Ellis and J. Whiteley (Eds.), *Theoretical and empirical foundations of rational-emotive therapy.* Monterey, CA: Brooks/Cole.

Ellis, A., & Abrahms, E. (1978). *Brief psychotherapy in medical and health practices.* New York: Springer Publishing Co.

Ellis, A., & Harper, R. A. (1974). *A guide to rational living.* Hollywood, CA: Wilshire Book Co.

Elstien, A. S., Sprafka, S. A., & Shulman, L. S. (1978). *Medical problem solving: An analysis of clinical reasoning.* Cambridge, MA: Harvard University Press.

Emener, W. (1981). *The role(s) of research in the professionalism of rehabilitation counseling.* Paper presented at APGA Annual Conference, St. Louis.

Emener, W. G., & Dickman, F. (1983). Corporate caring. *Management World, 12*(1), 36–38.

Emener, W., & Rubin, S. E. (1980). Rehabilitation counselor roles and functions and sources of role strain. *Journal of Applied Rehabilitation Counseling, 11,* 57–69.

Emerson, C. D. (1979). Family violence: A study by the Los Angeles County Sheriff's Department. *Police Chief, 46,* 48–50.

Engel, G. L. (1975). Psychoanalysis: Alive and well at 80. *Journal of the American Medical Association, 231*(6), 579–582.

English, R. W. (1971). Correlates of stigma towards physically disabled persons. *Rehabilitation Research and Practice Review, 2,* 1–17.

English, R. W. (1974). The application of personality theory to explain psychological reactions to physical disability. In J. Cull & R. Hardy (Eds.), *Rehabilitation techniques in severe disability.* Springfield, IL: Charles C. Thomas.

Epilepsy Foundation of America (1975). *Basic statistics of the epilepsies.* Philadelphia: F. A. Davis.

Esser, T. J. (1975). Client rating instruments for use in vocational rehabilitation agencies. Menomonie, WI: University of Wisconsin–Stout, Stout Vocational Rehabilitation Institute, Materials Development Center.

Esser, T. J. (1980). *Gathering information for evaluation planning.* Menomonie, WI: University of Wisconsin–Stout, Stout Vocational Rehabilitation Institute, Materials Development Center.

Esser, T., & Botterbusch, C. (1975). *Token economics in rehabilitation.* Menomonie, WI: University of Wisconsin–Stout.

Estes, N. J., Smith-DeJulio, K., & Heinemann, M. E. (1980). *Nursing diagnosis of the alcoholic person.* St. Louis: C. V. Mosby.

Evans, J. (1983). The treatment specialist: An emerging role for counselors within the criminal court system. *Personnel and Guidance Journal, 61,* 349–351.

Evans, R. L. (1984). The resource manager in physical rehabilitation. *Rehabilitation Literature, 45*(1–2), 16–18.

Eysenck, H. J. (1960). The effects of psychotherapy. In H. J. Eysenck (Ed.), *The handbook of abnormal psychology.* New York: Basic Books.

Eysenck, H. J. (1965). The effects of psychotherapy. *International Journal of Psychiatry, 1,* 99–178.

Falvo, D., Allen, H. A., & Maki, D. (1982). Psychosocial aspects of invisible disability. *Rehabilitation Literature, 43*(1–2), 2–6.

Farley, R. C., & Rubin, S. E. (1982). The intake interview. In R. T. Roessler & S. E. Rubin (Eds.), *Case management and rehabilitation counseling: Procedures and techniques* (pp. 39–58). Baltimore: University Park Press.

Farley, W. (1973, Fall). Counseling retinal detachment patients. *Sight-Saving Review,* pp. 157–175.

Fasel, G. (1983, Summer). Life after termination. *Advantage,* pp. 8–11.

Fechter, A. E., & Thorpe, C. O. (1977). *Labor market discrimination against the handicapped: An initial inquiry.* Washington, DC: The Urban Institute.

Feinberg, L. B. & McFarlane, F. R. (1979). Setting-based factors in rehabilitation counselor role variability. *Journal of Applied Rehabilitation Counseling, 10,* 95–101.

Fenderson, D. A. (1984). Opportunities for psychologists in disability research. *American Psychologist, 39*(5), 524–527.

Fewll, C. H., & Bissell, L. (1978). The alcoholic denial syndrome: An alcohol-focused approach. *Social Casework, 59*(1), 6–13.

Field, T. F. (1981). The consolidation of the rehabilitation professional associations: Pros and cons. *Journal of Applied Rehabilitation Counseling, 12,* 65–68.

Field, T. F., & Sink, J. M. (1981). *The vocational expert.* Athens, GA: VSB, Inc.

Fiedler, F. E. (1950). The concept of an ideal therapeutic relationship. *Journal of Consulting Psychology, 14,* 239–245.

Filstead, W. (1977). The family, alcohol misuse and alcoholism: Priorities and proposals for intervention. *Journal of Studies on Alcohol, 38*(7), 1447–1454.

Finestone, S., Lowry, F., Whiteman, M., & Lukoff, I. (1968). *Social casework and blindness.* New York: American Foundation for the Blind.

Finley, M. H., & Lee, A. T. (1981). The terminated executive: It's like dying. *Personnel and Guidance Journal, 59,* 382–384.

Fiorelli, J. S. (1982). Community residential services during the 1980's: Challenges and future trends. *The Journal of the Association for the Severely Handicapped, 7*(4), 14–18.

Flanagan, J. C. (1982). *New insights to improve the quality of life at age 70.* Bethesda, MD: National Institute on Aging.

Flannagan, T. (1974). Whatever happened to job placement. *Vocational Guidance Quarterly, 22*(3), 209–213.

Flannagan, T. W. (1977). Placement: Beyond the obvious. *Rehabilitation Counseling Bulletin, 21*(2), 116–120.

Flynn, R. J. (1980). Normalization, PASS, and service quality assessment. In R. J. Flynn & K. E. Nitsch (Eds.), *Normalization, social integration, and community services.* Baltimore: University Park Press.

Flynn, R. J., & Nitsch, K. E. (Eds.). (1980). *Normalization, social integration, and community services.* Baltimore: University Park Press.

Ford, D. H., & Urban, H. B. (1963). *Systems of psychotherapy.* New York: John Wiley.

Fordyce, W. (1982). Psychological assessment and management. In F. Kottke, G. Stillwell, & J. Lehman (Eds.), *Krusen's handbook of physical medicine and rehabilitation* (3rd ed.) (pp. 124–150). Philadelphia: W. B. Saunders.

Forer, L. (1976). *The birth order factor.* New York: McKay.

Foreyt, J. P., & Rathjen, D. J. (Eds.). (1978). *Cognitive behavior therapy: Research and applications.* New York: Plenum Press.

Forrest, G. C. (1978). *The diagnosis and treatment of alcoholism* (2nd ed.). Springfield, IL: Charles C. Thomas.

Fort, J. (1973). *Alcohol: Our biggest drug problem.* New York: McGraw-Hill.

Fowler, R. S., Jr. (1981). Stroke and cerebral trauma: Psychosocial and vocational aspects. In W. C. Stolov & M. R. Clowers (Eds.), *Handbook on severe disability.* Washington, DC: U.S. Department of Education, Rehabilitation Services Administration.

Fraiberg, S. (1968). Parallel and divergent patterns in blind and sighted infants. *Psychoanalytic Study of Children, 23* 264–300.

Frank, J. (1979). The present status of outcome studies. *Journal of Consulting and Clinical Psychology, 47,* 310–316.

Frank, V. E. (1955). *The doctor and the soul.* New York: Alfred A. Knopf.

Frankl, V. E. (1963). *Man's search for meaning: An introduction to logotherapy.* New York: Washington Square Press.

Frankl, V. E. (1967). *Psychotherapy and existentialism.* New York: Washington Square Press.

Fraser, R. T. (1978). Rehabilitation job placement research. *Rehabilitation Literature, 39*(9), 258–264.

Fraser, R. A. (1983). A needs review in epilepsy rehabilitation: Toward solutions in the 1980's. *Rehabilitation Literature, 44*(9–10), 264–269.

Fraser, R. T., & Clowers, M. R. (1978). Rehabilitation counselor functions: Perceptions of time spent and complexity. *Journal of Applied Rehabilitation Counseling, 9*(2), 32–35.

Fraser, R., & Smith, W. (1982). Adjustment to daily living. In H. Sands (Ed.), *Epilepsy: A handbook for the mental health professional.* New York: Brunner/Mazel.

Fraser, R. A., Clemmons, D., Trejo, W., & Temkin, N. R. (1983). Program evaluation in epilepsy rehabilitation. *Epilepsia, 24*(6), 734–746.

Fraser, R. A., Trejo, W., Temkin, N., & Clemmons, D. (1982, November). *Assessing the vocational interests of those with epilepsy.* Paper presented at a meeting of the American Epilepsy Society, Phoenix, AZ.

Freeman, S. (1979). *The epileptic in home, school and society.* Springfield, IL: Charles C. Thomas.

Freeman, W., & Watts, J. (1970). *Psychosurgery in the treatment of mental disorders and intractable pain* (2nd ed.). Springfield, IL: Charles C. Thomas.

Fretz, B. R., & Mills, D. H. (1980). *Licensure and certification of psychologists and counselors.* San Francisco: Jossey-Bass.

Freud, S. (1949). Mourning and melancholia. In J. Strachey (Ed. and Trans.), *The standard edition of the complete psychological works of Sigmund Freud* (Vol. 14). London: Hogarth Press.

Furlong, M. J., Atkinson, D. R., & Casas, L. M. (1979). Effects of counselor ethnicity and attitudinal similarity on Chicano student's perception of counselor credibility and attractiveness. *Hispanic Journal of Behavioral Science, 1*(1), 41–53.

Gagne, R. M. (1970). *The conditions of learning* (2nd ed.). New York: Holt, Rinehart, & Winston.

Gaines, T. F. (1979). Caseload management revisited. *Journal of Rehabilitation Administration, 3*(3), 112–118.

Gaitz, C. M. (1974). Barriers to the delivery of psychiatric services to the elderly. *The Gerontologist, 14*(3), 210–214.

Garfield, S. L. (1981). Psychotherapy: A 40 year appraisal. *American Psychologist,* 36(2), 174–183.

Garett, J. (1969). The current scene. In D. Malekin & H. Rusalem (Eds.). *Vocational rehabilitation of the disabled: An overview.* New York: New York University Press.

Garvin, R. E. (1983). Industrial relations: A service-oriented approach to job development. *Journal of Applied Rehabilitation Counseling,* 14(2), 44–46, 50.

Gastaut, H. (1970). Clinical and electroencephalographical classification of epileptic seizures. *Epilepsia, 11,* 102–113.

Gazda, G. M. (1977). Developmental education: A conceptual framework for a comprehensive counseling and guidance program. *Canadian Counselor, 12,* 36–40.

Gazda, G. M. (1984). Multiple impact training: A life skills approach. In D. Larson (Ed.), *Teaching psychological skills.* Monterey, CA: Brooks/Cole.

Geist, C. (1982). Rehabilitation and learning disabilities. *ARCA News, 10*(1), 6.

Geist, C. S., & Calzaretta, W. A. (1982). *Placement handbook for counseling disabled persons.* Springfield, IL: Charles C. Thomas.

Geist, G. O., & McMahon, B. T. (1981). Pre-service rehabilitation education: Where graduates are employed. *Journal of Rehabilitation, 47*(3), 45–47.

Gellman, I. P. (1964). *The sober alcoholic: An organizational analysis of Alcoholics Anonymous.* New Haven, CT: College and University Press.

Gellman, W. (1961). The vocational adjustment shop. *Personnel and Guidance Journal, 39*(8), 630–633.

Gellman, W., & Friedman, S. (1965). The workshop as a clinical rehabilitation tool. *Rehabilitation Literature, 26*(2), 34–38.

Gendlin, E. T. (1973). Experimental psychotherapy. In R. Corsini (Ed.), *Current psychotherapies* (pp. 317–352). Itasca, IL: F. E. Peacock.

George, R., & Cristiani, T. (1981). *Theory methods and procedures of counseling and psychotherapy.* Englewood Cliffs, NJ: Prentice Hall.

Gerber, P. J. (1981). Learning disabilities and eligibility for vocational rehabilitation services: A chronology of events. *Learning Disabilities Quarterly, 4,* 422–425.

Gianforte, G. (1976). Certification: A challenge and a choice. *Journal of Rehabilitation, 42*(5), 15–17, 39.

Gilchrist, E., & Wilkinson, M. (1979). Some factors determining prognosis in young people with severe head injuries. *Archives of Neurology, 36,* 355–359.

Gilliland, B., James, R., Roberts, G., & Bowman, J. (1984). *Theories and strategies in counseling and psychotherapy.* Englewood Cliffs, NJ: Prentice Hall.

Ginzberg, E., Ginsberg, S. W., Axelrad, S., & Herma, J. L. (1951). *Occupational choice: An approach to a general theory.* New York: Columbia University Press.

Gitlow, S. E. (1973). Alcoholism: A disease. In P. G. Bourne & R. Fox (Eds.), *Alcoholism progress in research and treatment.* New York: Academic Press.

Glasser, W. (1965). *Reality therapy.* New York: Harper & Row.

Glasser, W. (1969). *Schools without failure.* New York: Harper & Row.

Glasser, W. (1976). *Positive addiction.* New York: Harper & Row.

Glasser, W., & Zunin, L. M. (1973). Reality therapy. In R. Corsini (Ed.), *Current psychotherapies* (pp. 287–315). Itasca, IL: F. E. Peacock.

Glasser, W., & Zunin, L. M. (1979). Reality therapy. In R. Corsini (Ed.), *Current psychotherapies* (pp. 302–339). Itasca, IL: F. E. Peacock.

Glatt, M. M. (1974). *A guide to addiction and its treatment.* New York: John Wiley & Sons.

Glickman, N. (1983). A cross-cultural view of counseling with deaf clients. *Journal of Rehabilitation of the Deaf, 16*(3), 4–15.

Godley, S. (1979). Teaching job interview skills. *Vocational Evaluation & Work Adjustment Bulletin, 12*(3), 27–29.

Goffman, E. (1963). *Stigma: Notes on the management of spoiled identity.* Englewood Cliffs, NJ: Prentice-Hall.

Gold, M. W. (1973). Research on the vocational habilitation of the retarded: The present, the future. In N. R. Ellis (Ed.), *International review of research in mental retardation* (Vol. 6). New York: Academic Press.

Golden, S. (1975). Cancer chemotherapy and management of patient problems. *Nursing Forum, 14,* 216–221.

Goldenson, R. M., Dunham, J. R., & Dunham, C. S. (Eds.). (1978). *Disability and rehabilitation handbook.* New York: McGraw-Hill.

Goldiamond, I. (1976). Coping and adaptive behaviors of the disabled. In G. L. Albrecht (Ed.), *The sociology of physical disability and rehabilitation.* Pittsburgh, PA: University of Pittsburgh Press.

Goldman, L. (1971). *Using tests in counseling* (2nd ed.). Pacific Palisades, CA: Goodyear.

Goldman, L. (1977). Toward more meaningful research. *Personnel and Guidance Journal, 55*(6), 363–368.

Goldman, R. (1971). Decline in organ function with aging. In L. Rossman (Ed.), *Clinical geriatrics.* Philadelphia: J. P. Lippincott.

Goldstein, A. (1973). Behavior therapy. In R. Corsini (Ed.), *Current psychotherapies* (pp. 207–249). Itasca, IL: Peacock.

Goldstein, A. (1981). *Psychological skills training: Structured learning technique.* New York: Pergamon Press.

Goldstone, H. (1973). Helping old people to continue living at home. Stop, look, and listen. *Review of Social Health, 98*(1), 15–18.

Goodman, L. (1981). *Learning capacities approach.* Paper presented at Rehabilitation Strategies with LD Adults Workshop, Lexington, KY.

Gordon, J. (1979). Empirically based technologies for job development. In D. Vandergoot & J. D. Worrall (Eds.), *Placement in rehabilitation.* Baltimore: University Park Press.

Gordon, T. (1970). *Parent effectiveness training: The "no-lose" program for raising responsible children.* New York: Peter H. Wyden.

Gordon, T. (1984). Three decades of democratizing relationships through training. In D. Larson (Ed.), *Teaching psychological skills.* Monterey, CA: Brooks/Cole.

Gottlieb, H., Strite, L., Koller, R., Madorsky, A., Hockersmith, V., Kleeman, M., & Wagner, J. (1977). Comprehensive rehabilitation of patients having chronic low back pain. *Archives of Physical Medicine and Rehabilitation. 58,* 101–108.

Gottman, J., & Markham, H. J. (1978). Experimental designs in psychotherapy research. In S. Garfield & A. Bergin (Eds.), *Handbook of psychotherapy and behavior change: An empirical analysis.* New York: John Wiley & Sons.

Goulet, M. W. (1981). *Assessment of learning disabled adolescents and adults.* Paper presented at Rehabilitation Strategies with LD Adults Workshop, Lexington, KY.

Granovetter, M. (1979). Placement as brokerage-information problems in the labor market for rehabilitation workers. In D. Vandergoot & J. Worrall (Eds.), *Placement in rehabilitation.* Baltimore: University Park Press.

Graves, W. H., & Brown, J. T. (1976). *Placement services and techniques.* Champaign, IL: Stipes.

Greenleigh Study of Sheltered Workshops. (1976). Washington, DC: U.S. Department of Education, Rehabilitation Services Administration.

Greenough, T., Keegan, D., & Ash, D. (1978). Psychological and social adjustment of blind subjects on the 16PF. *Journal of Clinical Psychology, 34*(1), 84–87.

Greenstein, B., & Baum, K. (1981). On becoming a successful employee. *Vocational Evaluation & Work Adjustment Bulletin, 14*(2), 74–79.

Greenwood, R. (1982). Systematic management. In R. J. Roessler & S. E. Rubin (Eds.), *Case management and rehabilitation counseling* (chap. 10) Baltimore: University Park Press.

Gregg, C. H., Miller, L. A., & Roberts, R. R. (1976). A study of help seeking among rehabilitation clients. *Rehabilitation Counseling Bulletin,* 19(3), 496–499.

Gregory, R., Whitlow, C., Levin, M., & Wasmuth, W. (1982). The techniques of work adjustment. *vocational Evaluation & Work Adjustment Bulletin, 15*(1), 5–10.

Griswold, P. P., & Scott, J. W. (1979). The state rehabilitation agency and private rehabilitation: A partnership long overdue. *Journal of Rehabilitation, 45*(3), 32–33, 70.

Groher, M. (1977). Language and memory disorders following closed head trauma. *Journal of Speech and Hearing Research, 20,* 212–223.

Gronwall, D. (1976). Performance changes during recovery from closed head injury. *Proceedings of the Australian Association of Neurologists, 13,* 143–147.

Grummon, D. L. (1979). Client-centered theory. In H. M. Burks & B. Stefflre (Eds.), *Theories of counseling.* New York: McGraw-Hill.

Gryfe, C. I. (1979). Reasonable expectations in geriatric rehabilitation. *Journal of the American Geriatrics Society, 27*(5), 237–238.

Guerney, B. G. (1977). Should teachers treat illiteracy, hypocalligraphy, and dysmathematica? *Canadian Counselor, 12,* 9–14.

Guerney, B. G. (1984). Relationship enhancement therapy and training. In D. Larson (Ed.), *Teaching psychological skills.* Monterey, CA: Brooks/Cole.

Guerney, B., Guerney, L., & Stollak, G. (1971/72). The potential advantages of changing from a medical to an educational model in practicing psychology. *Interpersonal Development, 2,* 238–245.

Guerney, B., Stollak, G., & Guerney, L. (1971). The practicing psychologist as educator—an alternative to the medical practitioner model. *Professional Psychology, 2,* 276–282.

Gutowski, M. (1979). *Rehabilitation in the private sector: Changing the structure of the rehabilitation industry.* Washington, DC: The Urban Institute.

Gutowski, M., Harden, P., & Koshel, J. (1980). *Forecasting manpower needs in the rehabilitation industry.* Washington, DC: The Urban Institute.

Haberman, P. W., & Baden, M. M. (1978). *Alcohol, other drugs, and violent death.* New York: Oxford University Press.

Hahn, J. (1984). Understanding psychosocial adjustment to disability through scientific research and "the laboratory within." *Rehab Brief, 7* (10), 1–4.

Hahn, M. E. (1954). The training of rehabilitation counselors. *Journal of Counseling Psychology, 1,* 246–248.

Haley, J. (1973). *Uncommon therapy: The psychiatric techniques of Milton J. Erikson, M.D.* New York: W. W. Norton.

Hallenbeck, P., & Campbell, J. (1966). A conceptual framework for work adjustment training. *Journal of Counseling Psychology, 13*(4), 405–415.

Halpern, A. S., Lehman, J. P., Irvin, L. K., & Heiry, T. J. (1982). *Contemporary assessment for mentally retarded adolescents and adults.* Baltimore: University Park Press.

Hamby, R. I. (1970). Primary myocardial disease. *Medicine, 49,* 55–78.

Hamilton, K. (1950). *Counseling the handicapped in the rehabilitation process.* New York: Ronald Press.

Hanna, C., Mullinax, J., & Sadler, V. (1983). Rehabilitation nurse or vocational rehabilitation counselor: Competency based selection. *Journal of Rehabilitation, 49*(4), 75–78.

Harasymiw, S. J., Horne, M. D., & Lewis, S. C. (1976). A longitudinal study of disability group acceptance. *Rehabilitation Literature, 37*(4), 98–102.

Harel, Z., Scollod, R. N., & Bognar, B. J. (1982). Predictors of mental health among semi-rural aged. *The Gerontologist, 22*(6), 499–504.

Harrick, E. J., Hansel, J., & Schutzius, R. E. (1982). Outplacement training: Process, content, and attitude. *Training and Development Journal, 36,* 78–85.

Harrison, D. K., Garnett, J. M., & Watson, A. L. (1981). *Client assessment measures in rehabilitation* (Michigan Studies in Rehabilitation. Utilization Series: 5). Ann Arbor, MI: University of Michigan, Rehabilitation Research Institute.

Harrison, D. K., & Lee, C. C. (1979). Rehabilitation counseling competencies. *Journal of Applied Rehabilitation Counseling, 10*(3), 135–141.

Hasbrook, R. F. (1981). Editorial: If you have it—flaunt it. *Journal of Applied Rehabilitation Counseling, 12,* 143–145.

Hastings, H. (1977). An investigation of some aspects of the personality of the blind. In D. Warren (Ed.), *Blindness and early childhood development.* New York: American Foundation for the Blind.

Havighurst, R. J. (1968). A social-psychological perspective on aging. *The Gerontologist, 8,* 67–71.

Hawes, R. M. (1971). Reality therapy in the classroom, *Dissertation abstracts international,* (Doctoral dissertation, University of the Pacific). 32.

Hazler, R. & Roberts, G. (1984). Decision making in vocational theory: Evolution and implication. *Personnel and Guidance Journal, 62*(7), 408–410.

Henke, R. O., Connolly, S. G., & Cox, J. G. (1975). Caseload management: The key to effectiveness. *Journal of Applied Rehabilitation Counseling, 6,* 217–227.

Henriksen, D. (1982). Outplacement: Program guidelines that ensure success. *Personnel Journal, 61,* 583–589.

Herr, J. J., & Weakland, J. H. (1979). *Counseling elders and their families.* New York: Springer Publishing Co.

Hershenson, D. B. (1974). Vocational guidance and the handicapped. In E. L. Herr (Ed.), *Vocational guidance and human development.* Boston: Houghton Mifflin.

Hershenson, D., & Roth, R. (1970). A decisional process model for vocational development. In R. Roth, D. Hershenson, & T. Hilliard (Eds.), *The psychology of vocational development: Readings in theory and research.* Boston: Allyn and Bacon.

Hill, J. W., Wehman, P., & Pentecost, J. (1980). Developing job interview skills in mentally retarded adults. *Education and Training of the Mentally Retarded, 15,* 179–187.

Hindman, M. (1977). Child abuse and neglect. The alcohol connection. *Alcohol Health and Research World,* 2–7.

Hinds, W. (1983). *Personal paradigm shift: A lifestyle intervention approach to health care management.* East Lansing, MI: Michigan State University.

Hinds, W., Habeck, R., Jeney, J., & Hermanson, G. (1984, August). *A lifestyle intervention approach to health care in pain management.* Poster presented to the American Psychological Association, Toronto.

Hinsie, L. E., & Campbell, R. J. (1973). *Psychiatric dictionary* (4th ed.). New York: Oxford University Press.

Hobbs, N. (1964). Mental health's third revolution. *American Journal of Orthopsychiatry, 34,* 822–833.

Hodgson, J. H., & Quinn, J. L. (1980). The impact of the triage health care delivery system upon client morale, independent living, and the cost of care. *The Gerontologist, 20*(3), 364–371.

Hoffman, N. (Ed.) (1984). *Foundations of cognitive therapy: Theoretical methods and practical applications.* New York: Plenum Press.

Holland, J., Magoon, T., & Spokane, A. (1981). Counseling psychology: Career interventions, research, and theory. *Annual review of psychology, 32,* 279–305.

Holland, J. L. (1966). *The psychology of vocational choice.* Waltham, MA: Blaisdell.

Holland, J. L. (1973). *Making vocational choices: A theory of careers.* Englewood Cliffs, NJ: Prentice-Hall.

Holland, J. L. (1976). Coping with cancer. A challenge to the behavioral sciences. In J. W. Cullen, B. Fox, & R. Isom (Eds.), *Cancer: The behavioral dimensions.* New York: Raven Press.

Hoppe, B. (1976). An anti-failure approach. In A. Bassin, T. E. Bratter, & R. L. Rachin, (Eds.), *The reality therapy reader* (pp. 253–264). New York: Harper & Row.

Horowitz, L. (1976). New perspectives for psychoanalytic psychotherapy. *Bulletin of the Menninger Clinic, 40,* 263–271.

Hourcade, J. J., & Parette, H. P., Jr. (1985). Acquisition of a vocational assembly skill by severely retarded learners as a function of type of response prompt. *Journal of Rehabilitation, 51,* 46–48, 77.

Housman, R. Y., & Bauman, N. J. (1981). Employment and older disabled persons. *Journal of Rehabilitation, 47*(4), 82–83.

Human Interaction Research Institute. (1976). *Putting knowledge to use: A distillation of the literature regarding knowledge transfer and change.* Los Angeles: Author.

Hunt, T. E. (1980). Practical considerations in the rehabilitation of the aged. *Journal of the American Geriatrics Society, 28*(2), 59–64.

Hunter, C. W., Jr. (1982). Freestanding alcohol treatment centers—a new approach to an old problem. *Psychiatric Annals, 12*(4), 396–408.

Hutchinson, J., & Cogan, F. (1974). Rehabilitation manpower specialist: A job description of placement personnel. *Journal of Rehabilitation, 40*(2), 31–33.

Hylbert, K., & Hylbert, R. (1979). *Medical information for human service workers.* State College, PA: Counselor Education Press.

Indices, Inc. (1978). *Functional limitations: A state of the art review.* (Grant No. 13-p-59220/3-01). Washington, DC: U.S. Department of Health, Education, & Welfare, Rehabilitation Services Administration.

Indices, Inc. (1979). *Functional limitations: A state of the art review.* Falls Church, VA: Author.

International Association of Industrial Accident Boards and Commissions. (1982). *Report of the rehabilitation committee.* Presentation at the annual conference, San Juan, Puerto Rico.

Ivey, A. (1971). *Microcounseling: Innovations in interviewing training.* Springfield, IL: Charles C. Thomas.

Ivey, A. E. (1977). Cultural expertise: If the counselor is to become a teacher, toward what should that teaching be directed? *Canadian Counsellor, 12,* 23–29.

Ivey, A. E., & Simek-Downing, L. (1980). *Counseling and psychotherapy: Skills, theories, and practice.* Englewood Cliffs, NJ: Prentice-Hall.

Jacobs, H. E., Kardashian, S., Kreinbring, R. K., Powder, R., & Simpson, A. R. (1984). A skills-oriented model for facilitating employment among psychiatrically disabled person. *Rehabilitation Counseling Bulletin, 28*(2), 87–96.

Jacobson, E. (1938). *Progressive relaxation.* Chicago: University of Chicago Press.

Jacques, M. (1970). *Rehabilitation counseling: Scope and services.* Boston: Houghton Mifflin.

Jaffee, B. F. (1978). Viral causes of sudden inner ear deafness. *The Otolaryngologic Clinics of North America, 2*(1), 63–69.

Jarvikowski, A., & Lahelma, E. (1980). *Early rehabilitation at the work place.* New York: World Rehabilitation Fund.

Jellinek, E. M. (1959). Recent trends in alcoholism and in alcohol consumption. *Quarterly Journal Studies on Alcoholism, 20,* 261–269.

Jellinek, E. M. (1960). *The disease concept of alcoholism.* New Haven, CT: Hill House Press.

Jellinek, H. M., & Harvey, R. F. (1982). Vocational/educational services in a medical rehabilitation facility: Outcomes in spinal cord and brain injured patients. *Archives of Physical Medicine and Rehabilitation, 63,* 87–88.

Jellinek, H. M., Torkelson, R. M., & Harvey, R. F. (1982). Functional abilities and distress levels in brain injured patients at long-term follow-up. *Archives of Physical medicine and Rehabilitation, 63*(4), 160–162.

Jennett, B., & Bond, M. (1975). Assessment of outcome after severe brain damage: A practical scale. *Lancet, 1,* 480–484.

Jernigan, J. A. (1981). Loss of physical function and disability: Health problems of older persons. *Journal of Rehabilitation, 47*(4), 34–47.

Johnson, V. W. (1980). *I'll quit tomorrow* (rev. ed.). San Francisco: Harper & Row.

Joint Commission on Accreditation of Hospitals. (1983). *Accreditation manual for hospitals—1984.* Chicago: Author.

Jordon, I. K., Gustason, G., & Rosen, R. (1976). Current communication trends at programs for deaf. *American Annals of the Deaf, 121,* 527–532.

Julian V., & Mohr, C. (1980). Father-daughter incest—profile of the offender. *Denver national Study on Child Neglect & Abuse Reporting.*

Jung, H. (1978). Gestalt therapy in rehabilitation counseling. Psychosocial Rehabilitation Journal, 2(3), 26–34.

Kagan, N. (1972). *Influencing human relations: Interpersonal process recall.* East Lansing, MI: Michigan State University.

Kallsen, P. (1982). *PK's ten commandments on how to keep evaluators honest and influence administrators with your honesty.* Paper presented at Region V Program Evaluation Conference, Milwaukee, WI.

Kalsbeek, W. D., McLaurin, R. L., Harris, B. S. H., & Miller, J. D. (1980). The national head and spinal cord injury survey: Major findings. In D. W. Anderson & R. L. McLauring (Eds.), *Report on the national head and spinal cord injury survey. Journal of Neurosurgery* (Suppl.).

Kantrow, A. (1967). Counseling services for diabetics. *Sight-Saving Review, 37,* 73–77.

Karnes, J. (1981). *Accommodations in higher education for LD adults.* Paper presented at Rehabilitation Strategies with LD Adults Workshop, Lexington, KY.

Karno, M. & Edgerton, R. B. (1969). Perception of mental illness in a Mexican-American community. *Archives of General Psychiatry, 20,* 233–238.

Kasschau, P. L. (1976). Perceived age discrimination in a sample of aerospace employees. *The Gerontologist, 16*(2), 166–173.

Kastenbaum, R. (1969). Death and bereavement in later life. In A. H. Kutscher (Ed.), *Death and bereavement.* Springfield, IL: Charles C. Thomas.

Kazdin, A. E. (1977). Assessing the clinical or applied significance of behavior change through social validation. *Behavior Modification, 1,* 427–452.

Kazdin, A. E. (1978). *History of behavior modification: Experimental foundations of contemporary research.* Baltimore: University Park Press.

Kazdin, A. E. (1980). *Behavior modification in applied settings.* Homewood, IL: Dorsey.

Keefe, S. E. (1978). Why Mexican-Americans underutilize mental health clinics: Facts and fallacy. In J. M. Casas & S. E. Keefe (Eds.), *Family and mental health in the Mexican-American community.* Los Angeles: University of California (Los Angeles), Spanish-Speaking Mental Health Research Center. (Monograph No. 7)

Keilitz, I., Zaremba, B. A., & Broder, P. K. (1979). The link between learning difficulties and juvenile delinquency: Some issues and awareness. *Learning Disabilities Quarterly, 2,* 2–11.

Keith, R. D., Engelkes, J. R., & Winborn, B. B. (1977). Employment seeking preparation and activity: An experimental job-placement training model for rehabilitation clients. *Rehabilitation Counseling Bulletin, 21*(2), 159–165.

Kemp, C. G. (1971). Existential counseling. *Counseling Psychologist, 2*(3), 2–30.

Kempe, H., & Heller, R. E. (1972). *Helping the battered child and his family.* New York: Lippincott.

Kempler, W. (1973). Gestalt therapy. In R. J. Corsini (Ed.), *Current psychotherapies.* Itasca, IL: F. E. Peacock.

Kendall, P. C., & Hollon, S. D. (Eds.). (1979). *Cognitive-behavioral interventions: Theory, research and procedures.* New York: Academic Press.

Kern, R. M., Matheny, K. B., & Patterson, D. (1978). *A case for Adlerian counseling: Theory, techniques, and research evidence.* Chicago: Alfred Adler Institute.

Kernberg, O. (1975). *Borderline conditions and pathological narcissism.* New York: Jason Aronson.

Kiesler, C., Cummings, N., & Vanden Bos, G. (1979). *Psychology and national health insurance: A sourcebook.* Washington, DC: American Psychological Association.

Kiev, A. (1968). *Curanderismo: Mexico-American folk psychiatry.* New York: Free Press.

King, B. L., Bissell, L. & O'Brien, P. (1974). A.A., alcoholism counseling and social work treatment. *Health and Social Work, 4*(4), 181–198.

Kinney, J., & Leaton, G. (1978). *Loosening the grip: A handbook of alcohol information.* St. Louis: C. V. Mosby.

Kirchner, C., & Lowman, C. (1978). Sources of variation in the estimated prevalence of visual loss. *Journal of Visual Impairment and Blindness, 72,* 329–333.

Kirchner, C., & Peterson, R. (1979). Employment: Selected characteristics. *Journal of Visual Impairment and Blindness, 73*(b), 239–242.

Kissen, B., & Begleiter, H. (1972). *The biology of alcoholism.* New York: Plenum Press.

Kissen, B., & Begleiter, H. (Eds.). (1977). *The treatment and rehabilitation of the chronic alcoholic.* New York: Plenum Press.

Klove, H., & Cleeland, C. S. (1972). The relationship of neuropsychological impairment to other indices of severity of head injury. *Scandinavian Journal of Rehabilitation Medicine, 4,* 55–60.

Kneipp, S. A., Vandergoot, D., & Lawrence, R. E. (1980). An evaluation of two job-search skills training programs in a vocational rehabilitation agency. *Rehabilitation Counseling Bulletin, 23*(3), 202–207.

Kobrynski, B. (1966). Rehabilitation of the elderly patient. *Journal of the American Geriatric Society, 14*(4), 400–406.

Koestenbaum, P. (1977). *The new image of the person: The theory and practice of clinical philosophy.* Unpublished manuscript.

Kogan, J. (1976). The genesis of Gestalt therapy. In C. Hatcher & P. Himelstein (Eds.), *The handbook of Gestalt therapy.* New York: Jason Aronson.

Kohn, A. (1984, Summer). Existentialism here and now. *The Georgia Review.*

Kohut, H. (1971). *The analysis of the self.* New York: International Universities Press.

Kravetz, S. P., & Thomas, K. R. (1978). A learning theory approach to counseling indecisive clients. In B. Bolton and M. E. Jaques (Eds.), *Rehabilitation counseling: Theory and practice* (pp. 60–68). Baltimore: University Park Press.

Krimmel, H. E. (1973). The alcoholic and his family. In P. G. Bourne & R. Fox (Eds.), *Alcoholism progress in research and treatment.* New York: Academic Press.

Krumboltz, J. D. (1965). Behavioral counseling: Rationale and research. *Personnel and Guidance Journal, 44,* 383–387.

Krumboltz, J. D. (1966). *Revolution in counseling.* Boston: Houghton Mifflin.

Krumboltz, J. D., & Schroeder, W. W. (1965). Promoting career planning through reinforcement. *Personnel and Guidance Journal, 44,* 19–26.

Krumboltz, J. D., & Sheppard, L. E. (1969). Vocational problem solving experiments. In J. D. Krumboltz & C. E. Thoresen (Eds.), *Behavioral counseling: Cases and techniques.* New York: Holt, Rinehart & Winston.

Kubler-Ross, E. (1969). *On death and dying.* New York: Macmillan.

LaCalla, J. J. (1974). Group psychotherapy with Mexican-American drug addicts (Doctoral dissertation, United States International University, 1973). *Dissertation Abstracts International, 34,* 1753B. (University Microfilms No. 73-22, 675)

Landesman-Dwyer, S. (1981). Living in the community. *American Journal of Mental Deficiency, 86,* 223–234.

Lange, A., & Jakubowski, P. (1976). *Responsible assertive behavior.* Champaign, IL: Research Press.

Larson, D. (1984). *Teaching psychological skills: Models of giving psychology away.* Monterey, CA: Brooks/Cole.

Lasden, M. (1982, June 27). Coming out of coma. *The New York Times Magazine,* pp. 29–35, 38–40, 54.

Lauterback, J. R. (1982, April 5). Coaching the disabled back to work. *Industry Week,* pp. 52–55.

Lawrence, P. (1981). Applying skills with special populations. In J. E. Myers (Ed.), *Counseling older persons; Vol. 3, Trainer's manual for basic helping skills.* Falls Church, VA: American Personnel and Guidance Association.

Lazarus, A. A. (1976). *Multimodal behavior therapy.* New York: Springer Publishing Co.

Leblanc, A. F. (1976). About reality therapy. In A. Bassin, T. E. Bratter, & R. L. Rachin (Eds.), *The reality therapy reader* (pp. 14–22). New York: Harper & Row.

Lebow, J., Maisiak, R., Sanders, E., Soong, S-J., & Cain, M. (1982). Rehabilitation counseling needs of cancer patients. *Rehabilitation Counseling Bulletin, 25*(4), 231–234.

Lehmann, J. F., Delisa, J. A., Warren, C. G., DeLateur, B. J., Bryant, P. L. L., & Nicholson, C. G. (1978). Cancer rehabilitation assessment of need, development, and evaluation of a model of care. *Archives of Physical Medicine and Rehabilitation, 59,* 410–419.

Leiber, C. S. (1982). Medical issues: The disease of alcoholism. In E. L. Gomber, H. R. White, & J. A. Carpenter (Eds.), *Alcohol, science, & society revisited.* New Brunswick, NJ: Rutgers Center of Alcohol Studies; Ann Arbor, MI: University Press of Michigan.

Lerman, A., & Guilfoyle, G. (1973). *The evaluation of vocational development of deaf young adults.* New York: Lexington School for the Deaf. (ERIC Document Reproduction Service No. Ed. 090 741)

Lerman, A. M., & Guilfoyle, G. R. (1970). *The development of pre-vocational behavior in deaf adolescents.* New York: Columbia University Press.

Leslie, J. (1984). Interview: The impact of rehabilitation research. *NARRTC Reports.*

Leventhal, H., & Hirschman, R. S. (1982). Social psychology and prevention. In G. S. Sanders and J. Suls (Eds.), *Social psychology of health and illness* (pp. 183–226). Hillsdale, NJ: Erlbaum.

Levin, H. S., & Grossman, R. G. (1978). Behavioral sequelae of closed head injury: A quantitative study. *Archives of Neurology, 35,* 720–727.

Leven, H. S., Grossman, R. G., & Kelly, P. J. (1976a). Aphasic disorder in patients with closed head injury. *Journal of Neurology, Neurosurgery and Psychiatry, 39,* 1062–1070.

Levin, H. S., Grossman, R. G., & Kelly, P. J. (1976b). Short-term recognition memory in relation to severity of head injury. *Cortex, 12,* 175–182.

Levine, E. S. (1976). Psycho-cultural determinants in personality development. *The Volta Review, 73,* 258–267.

Levine, E. S. (1981). *The ecology of early deafness: Guides to fashioning environments and psychological assessments.* New York: Columbia University Press.

Levine, L. S., & Pence, J. W. (1953). A training program for rehabilitation counselors. *Journal of Rehabilitation, 19*(1), 16–20.

Levitsky, A., & Perls, F. (1970). The rules and games of Gestalt therapy. In J. Fagon & I. Shepard (Eds.), *Gestalt therapy now.* New York: Harper Colophon.

Levitt, E. E. (1963). Psychotherapy with children: A further evaluation. *Behavior Research and Therapy, 1,* 45–51.

Lewin, S. S., Ramseur, J. H., & Sink, J. M. (1979). The role of private rehabilitation: Founder, catalyst, competitor. *Journal of Rehabilitation, 45*(3), 16–19.

Lewinsohn, P. M., & Graf, M. A. (1973). A follow-up study of persons referred for vocational rehabilitation who have suffered brain injury. *Journal of Community Psychology, 1,* 57–62.

Lezak, M. D. (1978a). Living with the characterologically altered brain injury patient. *Journal of Clinical Psychiatry, 39*(7), 592–598.

Lezak, M. D. (1978b). Subtle sequelae of brain damage: Perplexity, distractibility, and fatigue. *American Journal of Physical Medicine, 57*(1), 9–15.

Liang, J., & Bollen, K. A. (1983). The structure of the Philadelphis Geriatric Center Morale Scale: A reinterpretation. *Journal of Gerontology, 38*(2), 181–189.

Lindeman, E. (1945). Symptomatology and management of acute grief. *American Journal of Psychiatry, 100,* 141–148.

Lishman, W. A. (1973). The psychiatric sequelae of head injury: A review. *Psychological Medicine, 3,* 304–318.

Livneh, H., & Evans, J. (1984). Adjusting to disability: Behavioral correlated and intervention strategies. *Personnel and Guidance Journal, 62,* 363–365.

Lobuts, J. E. (1977). *A project to demonstrate the role of a rehabilitation team in providing comprehensive services to the older legally blind on an itinerant basis. Final Report.* Charleston, WV: West Virginia Department of Education.

Lofquist, L. H., & Dawis, R. V. (1969). *Adjustment to work: A psychological view of man's problems in a work-oriented society.* New York: Appleton-Century-Crofts.

Lofquist, L. H., & Dawis, R. V. (1972). Application of the theory of work adjustment to rehabilitation and counseling. *Minnesota Studies in Vocational Rehabilitation, 30.*

Lofquist, L. H., Dawis, R. V., & Hendel, D. D. (1971, June). Application of the theory of work adjustment to rehabilitation and counseling. *Minnesota Studies in Vocational Rehabilitation* (Bulletin No. 58). Minneapolis: University of Minnesota, Industrial Relations Center.

Lombardi, D. N. (1973). Eight avenues of life style consistency. *The Individual Psychologist, 10*(2), 5–9.

Lowenthal, M. F., & Haven, C. (1968). Interaction and adaptation: Intimacy as a critical variable. In B. L. Neugarten (Ed.), *Middle age and aging.* Chicago: University of Chicago Press.

Loyola, U. (1979). Educative/psychotherapeutic rehabilitation groups following myocardial infarction: A study of denial and depression in the post infarct patient. *Dissertation Abstracts International, 38*(11-B), 5566.

Lubin, R., Jacobson, J. W., & Kiely, M. (1982). Projected impact of the functional definition of developmental disabilities: The categorically disabled population and service eligibility. *American Journal of Mental Deficiency, 87,* 73–79.

Luborsky, L., Singer, B., & Luborsky, L. (1975). Comparative studies of psychotherapies: Is it true that "Everybody has won and all must have prizes"? *Archives of General Psychiatry, 32,* 995–1021.

Lucas, D. (1977). The counselor as teacher in career development. *Canadian Counselor, 12,* 59–61.

Lukoff, I., & Cohen, O. (1972). *Attitudes toward blind persons.* New York: American Foundation for the Blind.

Lutzker, J. R., & Martin, J. A. (1981). *Behavior change.* Monterey, CA: Brooks/Cole.

Lutzker, J. R., Martin, J. A., & Rice, J. M. (1981). Behavior therapy in rehabilitation. In M. Hersen, R. M. Eisler, & P. M. Miller (Eds.), *Progress in behavior modification* (Vol. 12). New York: Academic Press.

Lynch, R. K. (1979). Vocational rehabilitation of worker's compensation clients. *Journal of Applied Rehabilitation Counseling, 9,* 164–167.

Lynch, R. K. (1983). The vocational expert. *Rehabilitation Counseling Bulletin, 27,* 18–25.

Lynch, R. K., & Martin, T. (1982). Rehabilitation counseling in the private sector: A training needs survey. *Journal of Rehabilitation, 48*(3), 51–53; 73.

Macione, A. (1979). Physiological changes and common health problems of aging. In M. L. Ganikos (Ed.), *Counseling the aged: A training syllabus for educators.* Falls Church, VA: American Personnel and Guidance Association.

MacMillan, D. L. (1982). *Mental retardation in school and society.* Boston: Little, Brown.

Maher, B. A. (1978). Stimulus sampling in clinical research: Representative design review. *Journal of Consulting and Clinical Psychology, 46,* 643–647.
Mahler, M. (1968). *On human symbiosis.* New York: International Universities Press.
Mahoney, M. J. (1976). *Cognitive and behavior modifications.* Cambridge, MA: Ballinger.
Mahoney, M. J., & Arnkoff, D. B. (1978). Cognitive and self-control therapies. In S. Garfield & A. Bergin (Eds.), *Handbook of psychotherapy and behavior change: An empirical analysis* (2nd ed.). New York: John Wiley.
Maki, D., McCracken, N., Pape, D., & Scofield, M. (1978). The theoretical model of vocational rehabilitation. *Journal of Rehabilitation, 44*(4), 26–28.
Maki, D. R., McCracken, N., Pape, D. A., & Scofield, M. E. (1979). A systems approach to vocational assessment. *Journal of Rehabilitation, 45*(1), 48–51.
Malcom, J. (1981). *The impossible profession.* New York: Alfred A. Knopf.
Mallik, K., & Yuspeh, S. (1979). Job development and enhanced productivity for severely disabled persons. (Final Report, RSA Grant No. 16-p-56803/3). Washington, DC: George Washington University, Job Development Laboratory.
Manaster, A. (1971). The therognostic group in a rehabilitation center for family visually handicapped persons. *New Outlook for the Blind, 65,* 261–264.
Manaster, A., & Kicharis, S. (1972). Experimental methods in a group counseling program with blind children. *New Outlook for the Blind, 66,* 15–19, 25.
Manello, T. A., & Seaman, F. J. (1979). Prevalence, costs, and handling of drinking problems on seven railroads. *U.S. Department of Transportation Federal Railroad Administration.* Washington, DC: University Research Corporation.
Mann, M. (1958). *New primer on alcoholism; how people drink, how to recognize alcoholics and what to do about them.* New York: Holt, Rinehart and Winston.
Marmor, J. (1979). Short-term dynamic psychotherapy. *The American Journal of Psychiatry,* 136(2).
Martin, D. G. (1983). *Counseling and therapy skills.* Monterey, CA: Brooks/Cole.
Martin, J. (1972). *Chalk talk on alcoholism.* National Audiovisual Center. Washington, DC: General Services Administration.
Maslow, A. (1954). *Motivation and personality.* New York: Harper & Row.
Masters, W. H., & Johnson, V. E. (1970). *Human sexual inadequacy.* Boston: Little, Brown.
Mathews, R. M., & Fawcett, S. B. (1985). Assisting in the job search: A behavioral assessment and training strategy. *Journal of Rehabilitation, 51,* 31–35, 69.
Matkin, R. E. (1980). The rehabilitation counselor in private practice: Perspective for education and preparation. *Journal of Rehabilitation, 46*(4), 60–62.

Matkin, R. E. (1981). Program evaluation: Searching for accountability in private rehabilitation. *Journal of Rehabilitation, 47*(11), 65–68.

Matkin, R. E. (1982a). Preparing rehabilitation counselors to perform supervisory and administrative responsibilities. *Journal of Applied Rehabilitation Counseling, 13*(3), 21–24.

Matkin, R. E. (1982b). Rehabilitation placement services: Unlicensed employment agencies or something else? *Journal of Applied Rehabilitation Counseling, 13*(1), 24–33.

Matkin, R. E. (1982c). Rehabilitation services offered in the private sector: A pilot investigation. *Journal of Rehabilitation, 48*(4), 31–33.

Matkin, R. E. (1983). The roles and functions of rehabilitation specialist in the private sector. *Journal of Applied Rehabilitation Counseling, 14*(1), 14–27.

Matkin, R. E., Sawyer, H. W., Lorenz, J. R., & Rubin, S. E. (1982). Rehabilitation administrators and supervisors: Their work assignments, training needs, and suggestions for preparation. *Journal of Rehabilitation Administration, 6*(4), 170–183.

Matkin, R. E., & Wallace, W. C. (1985). Disability management. In R. E. Matkin (Ed.), *Insurance rehabilitation* (Chap. 6). Austin, TX: Pro-Ed.

Matson, J. L., & Breuning, S. E. (Eds.). (1983). *Assessing the mentally retarded.* New York: Grune and Stratton.

Maultsby, M. C. (1984). *Rational behavior therapy.* Englewood Cliffs, NJ: Prentice-Hall.

May, R. (Ed.). (1961). *Existential psychology.* New York: Random House.

May, R. (1967). *Psychology and the human dilemma.* Princeton, NJ: Van Nostrand.

May, R., Angel, E., & Ellenberger, H. P. (Eds.). (1958). *Existence: A new dimension in psychiatry and psychology.* New York: Basic Books.

May, V. R., & Vieceli, L. (1983). Barriers to placement: Strategies and resolution. *Journal of Rehabilitation, 49*(3), 43–46.

McAleer, C. A., & Kluge, C. A. (1978). Counseling needs and approaches for working with a cancer patient. *Rehabilitation Counseling Bulletin, 21,* 238–245.

McAlees, D. C., & Schumacher, B. (1975). Toward a new professionalism: Certification and accreditation. *Rehabilitation Counseling Bulletin, 18,* 161–165.

McAndrew, H. (1950). The use of projective techniques in the personality evaluation of the blind. *American Psychologist, 5,* 340.

McArthur, C. (1954). Analyzing the clinical process. *Journal of Counseling Psychology, 1,* 203–208.

McCarron, L., & Dial, J. (1976). *McCarron-Dial Work Evaluation System: Evaluation of the mentally disabled—a systematic approach.* Dallas, TX: Common Market Press.

McClure, D. (1972). Placement through improvement of clients' job-seeking skills. *Journal of Applied Rehabilitation Counseling, 3*(3), 188–196.

McCollum, P. S. (1983). *Assessment of adults with learning disabilities.* Paper presented at American Personnel and Guidance Association Convention, Washington.

McDonald, D. J. (1974). The rehabilitation counselor: A resource person to industry: A revitalized approach to selective placement. *Journal of Applied Rehabilitation Counseling, 5,*(1), 3–7.

McFarlane, F. R. (1973, October). *A study of the region IX task force on graduate preparation in rehabilitation counseling.* San Diego, CA: San Diego State University.

McFarlane, F. R., & Di Paola, S. M. (1979). Rehabilitation counselor, vocational evaluator and work adjustment specialist: Are these professionals different? *Journal of Applied Rehabilitation Counseling, 10*(3), 148–153.

McFarlane, F., & Sullivan, M. (1979). Educational and training needs of rehabilitation counselors: Implications for training. *Journal of Applied Rehabilitation Counseling, 10,* 41–43.

McGowan, J., & Porter, T. (1967). *An introduction to the vocational rehabilitation process.* U.S. Department of Health, Education & Welfare.

McGraw, M. J., & Bitter, J. A. (1974). Perceptions of client vocational needs. *Rehabilitation Counseling Bulletin,* 18(2), 83–89.

McMahon, B. T. (1979a). A model of vocational redevelopment for the mid-career physically disabled. *Rehabilitation Counseling Bulletin, 23,* 35–47.

McMahon, B. T. (1979b). Private sector rehabilitation: Benefits, dangers, and implications for education. *Journal of Rehabilitation, 45*(3), 56–58.

McMahon, B. T., & Matkin, R. E. (1983). Preservice graduate training needs for private rehabilitation counselors. *Rehabilitation Counseling Bulletin, 27,* 54–60.

McMahon, B. T., Matkin, R. E., Growick, B., Mahaffey, D., & Gianforte, G. (1983). Recent trends in private sector rehabilitation. *Rehabilitation Counseling Bulletin, 27,* 32–47.

McTavish, D. G. (1971). Perceptions of old people: A review of research methodologies and findings. *The Gerontologist, 11*(4), 90–101.

Meadow, K. P. (1968). Parental responses to the medical ambiguities of deafness. *Journal of Health and Social Behavior, 9,* 299–309.

Meadow, L. (1964). New approaches to job placement. *Rehabilitation Record, 5*(1), 29–31.

Means, R., & Akridge, R. (1978). Psychosocial and behavioral adjustment: A model of healthy personing. *Journal of Rehabilitation, 44*(1), 24–29.

Means, R., & Roessler, R. (1976). *Personal achievement skills training.* Fayetteville, AR: University of Arkansas, Rehabilitation Research & Training Center.

Meehl, P. E. (1954). *Clinical vs. statistical prediction.* Minneapolis: University of Minnesota Press.

Meichenbaum, D. (1977a). *Cognitive behavior modification: An integrative approach.* New York: Plenum Press.

Meichenbaum, D. (1977b). Dr. Ellis, please stand up. *The Counseling Psychologist,* (1), 43–44.

Meichenbaum, D., & Turk, D. (1976). The cognitive-behavioral management of anxiety, anger and pain. In P. O. Bavidson (Ed.), *The behavioral management of anxiety, depression, and pain.* New York: Brunner/Mazel.

Melia, R. (1984). Job development and placement research. *American Rehabilitation,* 10(1), 23–26, cover 3.

Melzack, R. (1973). *The puzzle of pain.* New York: Basic Books.

Melzak, R., & Casey, K. (1968). Sensory, motivational and central control determinants of pain: A new conceptual model. In D. Kenshalo (Ed.), *The skill senses.* Springfield, IL: Charles C. Thomas.

Menchetti, B. M., Rusch, R. R., & Owens, D. M. (1983). Assessing vocational training needs of mentally retarded adults. In J. L. Matson & S. E. Breuning (Eds.), *Assessing the mentally retarded.* New York: Grune & Stratton.

Mercer, J. R. (1976). Pluralistic diagnosis in the evaluation of Black and Chicano children: A procedure for taking socio-cultural variables into account in clinical assessment. In C. Hernandez, M. Huag, & N. Wagner (Eds.), *Chicanos: Social and psychological perspectives* (2nd ed.). St. Louis: C. V. Mosby.

Meyer, H. E. (1977, May). The flourishing new business of recycling executives. *Fortune,* 328–338.

Meyer, P. S., Rastatter, C. J., & Gannaway, T. W. (1979). Editorial: Rehabilitation in the private sector. *Journal of Rehabilitation, 45*(3), 3, 71.

Michael, J. (1970). Rehabilitation. In. C. Neuringer & J. Michael (Eds.), *Behavior modification in clinical psychology.* New York: Appleton-Century-Crofts.

Milam, J. R., & Ketcham, K. (1981). *Under the influence.* Seattle: Madrona Publishers.

Mindel, E., & Vernon, M. (1972). *They grow in silence.* Silver Spring, MD: National Association of the Deaf.

Minton, E. B. (1977). Job placement: Strategies and techniques. *Rehabilitation Counseling Bulletin, 21*(2), 141–149.

Misiak, H., & Sexton, V. S. (1966). Existentialism and psychology. In H. Misiak and V. S. Sexton, *History of psychology: An overview* (pp. 432–459). New York: Grune & Stratton.

Mitchell, H. (1971). Counseling black students: A model in response to the need for relevant counseling training programs. *The Counseling Psychologist, 2,* 117–122.

Mitchell, K. M., Bozarth, J. D., & Krauft, C. C. (1977). A reappraisal of the therapeutic effectiveness of accurate empathy, nonpossessive warmth, and genuineness. In A. S. Gurman & A. M. Razin (Eds.), *Effective psychotherapy: A handbook of research.* Oxford: Pergamon Press.

Mitchell, M. E., & Sink, J. M. (1983). *Process, issues, and needs, in private for-profit rehabilitation.* Washington, DC: The National Rehabilitation Information Center.

Mithaug, D. E., & Hagmier, L. D. (1978). The development of procedures to assess prevocational competencies of severely handicapped young

adults. *American Association for the Education of the Severely/Profoundly Handicapped Review, 3*(2), 94–115.
Monbeck, M. (1973). *The meaning of blindness.* Bloomington, IN: Indiana University Press.
Mooney, V., & Cairns, D. (1978). Management of the patient with chronic low back pain. *Orthopedic Clinics of North America, 9,* 43–47.
Mooney, W. L. (1966). *An experiment in the use of two vocational placement techniques with a population of hard-to-place rehabilitation clients.* (NTIS No. PB197525).
Moores, D. (1978). *Educating the deaf: Psychology, principles, and practices.* Boston: Houghton Mifflin.
Morgan, C. A. (1980). The piration twins of placement: Inspiration and perspiration. In *Louis P. Ortale Memorial Lectures on Placement.* Washington, DC: National Rehabilitation Association, Job Placement Division.
Morin, W. J., & Yorks, L. (1982). *Outplacement techniques: A positive approach to terminating employees.* New York: AMACON.
Morris, K. (1973). Welfare reform 1973: The social services dimension. *Science, 181,* 515–522.
Morris, K. T., & Kanitz, H. M. (1975). *Rational-emotive therapy.* Boston: Houghton Mifflin.
Mozak, H. H. (1954). The psychological attitude in rehabilitation. *American Archives of Rehabilitation Therapy, 2,* 9–10.
Mosak, H. H. (1958). Early recollections as a projective technique. *Journal of Projective Techniques, 22* (3), 302–311.
Mosak, H. H. (1977a). Lifestyle. In A. Nikelly (Ed.), *Techniques for behavior change.* Springfield, IL: Charles C. Thomas.
Mosak, H. H. (1977b). *On purpose.* Chicago: Alfred Adler Institute.
Mosak, H. H. (1979). Mosak's typology: An update. *Journal of Individual Psychology, 35* (2), 192–195.
Mosak, H. H. (1984). Adlerian psychotherapy. In R. J. Corsini (Ed.), *Current psychotherapies* (3rd ed.). Itasca, IL: Peacock.
Mosak, H. H., & Mosak, B. (1975). *A bibliography for Adlerian psychology.* Washington, DC: Hemisphere.
Mosher, R. L., & Sprinthall, N. A. (1971). Psychological education: A means to promote personal development during adolescence. *Counseling Psychologist, 2,* 3–82.
Moses, H. A., & Patterson, C. H. (1971). *Readings in rehabilitation counseling* (2nd ed.). Champaign, IL: Stipes.
Murphy, H. B. M. (1980). Hidden barriers to the diagnosis and treatment of alcoholism and other alcohol misuse. *Journal of Studies on Alcohol, 41*(5), 417–428.
Murphy, T. (1973). Cancer pain. *Postgraduate Medicine, 53,* 187–194.
Muthard, J. E. (Ed.). (1965). *Third Institute on rehabilitation services: Training guides in case load management for vocational rehabilitation staff.* Final report, Committee on Case Load Management. Washington, DC: U.S. Department of Health, Education and Welfare, Vocational Rehabilitation Administration.

Muthard, J. E., & Salamone, P. R. (1969). The role and functions of the rehabilitation counselor. *Rehabilitation Counseling Bulletin, 13,* 81–168.

Myers, J. E. (1980). Counseling the disabled older person for the world of work. *Journal of Employment Counseling, 17*(1), 37–48.

Myers, J. E. (1985). Rehabilitation of older persons: The state of the art. In E. L. Pan, S. S. Newman, T. E. Backer, & C. L. Vash, *Annual review of rehabilitation* (Vol. 5) (pp. 1–54). New York: Springer Publishing Co.

Myers, J. E., & Loesch, L. C. (1981). The counseling needs of older persons. *The Humanist Educator, 20*(1), 21–35.

Nadler, L. (1979). *Developing human resources.* Austin, TX: Learning Concepts.

Najenson, T., Grosswasser, Z., Mendelson, L., & Hackett, P. (1980). Rehabilitation outcome of brain damaged patients after severe head injury. *International Journal of Rehabilitation Medicine, 2,* 17–22.

Nathanson, R. (1979). Counseling persons with disabilities: Are the feelings, thoughts, and behaviors of helping professionals helpful? *Personnel and Guidance Journal, 58,* 233–237.

National Cancer Institute. (1980a). *The breast cancer digest: A guide to medical care, emotional support, educational programs and resources.* DHHS Publication No. (NIH) 81–1691. Bethesda, MD: National Cancer Institute.

National Cancer Institute. (1980b). *Incidence and Mortality Data: 1973–1977.* SEER Report. Bethesda, MD: Author.

National Cancer Institute. (1981). *Chemotherapy and you: A guide to self help during treatment.* DHHS Publication No. (NIH) 81–1136. Bethesda, MD: National Cancer Institute.

National Center for Alcohol Education. (1978). *The community health nurse and alcohol-related problems.* Rockville, MD: National Institute on Alcohol Abuse and Alcoholism.

National Council on Rehabilitation Education (1984). *Membership directory.* Emporia, KS: Emporia State University.

National Institute on Aging. (1981). *Progress report on Senile Dementia of the Alzheimer's Type.* Bethesda, MD: National Institute of Health.

National Institute of Handicapped Research. (1982). Working with brain injured clients. *Rehabilitation Brief, 5*(5).

National Joint Committee for Learning Disability. (1982). Learning disabilities: Issues on definition. In P. L. Patton (Ed.), *Vocational rehabilitation of the learning disabled client: Proceedings and resource guide.* San Diego, CA: San Diego State University Rehabilitation Center.

National Society to Prevent Blindness. (1980). *Vision problems in the U.S.* New York: Author.

Neff, W. S. (1966). Problems of work evaluation. *Personnel and Guidance Journal, 44,* 682–688.

Neff, W. S. (1977). *Work and human behavior* (2nd ed.). New York: Atherton Press.

Nemiah, J. C. (1975). Classical psychoanalysis. In S. Arieti (Ed.), *American handbook of psychiatry* (2nd ed.) (Vol. 5). New York: Basic Books.

Neugarten, B. L. (1976). *Psychology of aging.* Washington, DC: American Psychological Association.

Neugarten, B., Havighurst, R., & Tobin, S. (1968). Personality and patterns of aging. In. B. Neugarten (Ed.), *Middle age and aging.* Chicago: University of Chicago Press.

New disability coding system for hearing impairments. (1981). *Journal of Rehabilitation of the Deaf, 15*(2), 1–4.

Newman, R., Painter, J., & Seres, J. (1978). A therapeutic milieu for chronic pain patients. *Journal of Human Stress, 4,* 8–12.

Ninth Institute on Rehab Services. (1971). *Placement and follow-up in the vocational rehabilitation process.* DHEW publication No. (SRS) 72–25007. Washington, DC: Rehabilitation Services Administration.

Novak, A. R., & Heal, L. W. (Eds.). (1980). *Integration of developmentally disabled individuals into the community.* Baltimore: Paul H. Brooks.

Obermann, C. E. (1965). *A history of vocational rehabilitation in America.* Minneapolis: T. S. Denison.

Oberst, M. T. (1978). Priorities in cancer nursing research. *Cancer Nursing, 1*(4), 281–290.

Occupational outlook handbook. (1985). Washington, DC: U.S. Department of Labor, Bureau of Labor Statistics.

Ohio, Governor's Commission on Aging. (1960). *Ohio's senior citizens.* Columbus: State of Ohio.

Olmedo, E. L., Martinez, J. L., & Martinez, S. R. (1978). Measure of acculturation for Chicano adolescents. *Psychological Reports, 42,* 1959–1970.

Olsen, D. (1982). Health problems and disabilities related to environmental and occupational hazards of the emigrant life-style. In O. Rivera & R. Cespedes (Eds.), *Rehabilitation of handicapped emigrant and seasonal farmworkers,* pp. 65–86. Salt Lake City, UT: Institute of Human Resource Development.

Olson, G. (1979). *Early recollections: Their use in diagnosis and psychotherapy.* Springfield, IL: Charles C. Thomas.

Organist, J. (1979). Private sector rehabilitation practioners—organize within the NRA. *Journal of Rehabilitation, 45*(3), 52–55.

Organization for Economic Cooperation and Development. (1967). *Promoting the placement of older workers.* Paris: Author.

Orlinsky, D. E., & Howard, K. I. (1978). The relation of process to outcome in psychotherapy. In S. L. Garfield & A. E. Bergin (Eds.), *Handbook of psychotherapy and behavior change: An empirical analysis* (2nd ed.). New York: John Wiley.

Orne, M. T. (1975). Psychotherapy in contemporary America: Its development and context. In S. Arieti (Ed.), *American handbook of psychiatry* (2nd ed.) (Vol. 5). New York: Basic Books.

Ortale, L. (undated). *The challenge of placement as a real professional service.* Unpublished manuscript.

Oseas, L. (1963). A model for establishing therapeutic work conditions. *Journal of Counseling Psychology, 10*(4), 368–372.

Osipow, S. H. (1976). Vocational development problems of the handicapped. In H. Rusalem & D. Malikin (Eds.), *Contemporary vocational rehabilitation.* New York: New York University Press.

Overs, R. P., & Trotter, A. B. (Eds.). (1969). *Counseling theories: A handbook for practicum.* Milwaukee, WI: Curative Workshop of Milwaukee, Research Department.

Padden, C. A., & Markowitz, H. (1976). Cultural conflicts between hearing and deaf communities. In Crammatte, Crammette, & Markowitz (Eds.), *VII World Congress of the World Federation of the Deaf* (pp. 407–413). Silver Spring, MD: National Association of the Deaf.

Padilla, A. M., Carlos, M. L., & Keefe, S. E. (1976). Mental health service utilization by Mexican-Americans. In M. R. Miranda (Ed.), *Psychotherapy with the Spanish-Speaking: Issues in research and service delivery.* Los Angeles: Spanish-Speaking Mental Health Research Center. (Monograph No. 3).

Padilla, A., & Ruiz, R. (1977, March). Prejudice and discrimination. *Personnel and Guidance Journal,* pp. 110–120.

Padilla, A. M., Ruiz, R. A., & Alvarez, R. (1975). Community mental health services for the Spanish-speaking/surnamed population. *American Psychologist, 30,* 892–905.

Papalia, A. S., & Kaminski, W. (1981). Counseling and counseling skills in the industrial environment. *Vocational Guidance Quarterly, 30,* 37–42.

Pape, D. A. (1983). *Case management techniques.* (Rehabilitation Research Review Monograph 13). Washington, DC: National Rehabilitation Information Center.

Pape, D. A., & Berven, N. L. (1983). Effects on training on intake interview skills in rehabilitation counseling. *Rehabilitation Counseling Bulletin, 26,* 164–173.

Parham, J., Richards, J., & Hobart, S. (1984). *Social skills for the physically disabled: Dealing with people who can't deal with your disability.* (Medical Research and Training Center). Birmingham, AL: University of Alabama at Birmingham.

Parker, R. M., & Hansen, C. E. (1981). *Rehabilitation counseling.* Boston: Allyn & Bacon.

Parloff, M. B. (1961). Therapist-patient relationships and outcome of psychotherapy. *Journal of Consulting Psychology, 25*(2), 9–38.

Parson, O. A., & Farr, S. P. (1981). The neuropsychology of alcohol and drug use. In S. B. Filkov & T. J. Boll (Eds.), *Handbook of clinical neuropsychology.* New York: John Wiley.

Parsons, F. (1909). *Choosing a vocation.* Boston: Houghton-Mifflin.

Passons, W. R. (1975). *Gestalt approaches in counseling.* New York: Rinehart & Winston.

Patterson, C. H. (1960). *Readings in rehabilitation counseling.* Champaign, IL: Stipes.

Patterson, C. H. (1969). *Rehabilitation counseling: Collected papers.* Champaign, IL: Stipes.

Patterson, C. H. (1973). *Theories of counseling and psychotherapy* (2nd ed.). New York: Harper & Row.

Patterson, C. (1974). *Relationships counseling and psychotherapy.* New York: Harper & Row.

Patterson, C. H. (1985). *The therapeutic relationship: Foundations for an eclectic psychotherapy.* Montery, CA: Brooks/Cole.

Patterson, D. (1973). *Theories of counseling and psychotherapy.* New York: Harper & Row.

Patterson, D., Gerken, C. d'A., & Hahn, M. (1941). *The Minnesota occupational rating scales.* Chicago: Science Research Associates.

Paul, G. L. (1967). Strategy of outcome research in psychotherapy. *Journal of Consulting and Clinical Psychology, 31,* 109–118.

Pelletier, K. R. (1983). *Healthy people in unhealthy places: Stress and fitness at work.* San Francisco: Delacorte Press.

Perdue, F. B., & Minton, E. B. (1983). *Functional assessment.* (Tenth Institute Rehabilitation Issues). Dunbar, WV: West Virginia Research & Training Center.

Perlman, L. G. (1977). *The persons with epilepsy: Lifestyle, needs, expectations.* Chicago: National Epilepsy League.

Perls, F. (1969). *Gestalt therapy verbatim.* Moab, UT: Real People Press.

Perls, F. (1973). *The Gestalt approach and eye witness to therapy.* Palo Alto, CA: Science and Behavior Books.

Perls, F., Hefferline, R. F., & Goodmon, P. (1951). *Gestalt therapy.* New York: Julian Press.

Peterson, E. (1980). The process and the professional in vocational evaluation: An appeal for integration. In B. Clarke (Ed.), *Help wanted: Jobs for deaf and hearing impaired people.*

Pfeiffer, E. (1976). *Multidimensional functional assessment. The DARS methodology. A manual.* Durham, NC: Duke University Center for the Study of Aging and Human Development.

Pfeiffer, E., & Busse, E. (1973). Mental disorders in late life—affective disorders: Paranoid, neurotic, and situational reactions. In E. Busse & E. Pfeiffer (Eds.), *Mental illness in later life.* Washington, DC: American Psychiatric Association.

Pike, K. L. (1954). *Language in relation to a unified theory of the structures of human behavior* (Part I: Preliminary edition). Glendale, CA: Summer Institute of Linguistics.

Platt, J. S., Tunick, R. H., & Wienke, W. D. (1982, February). Developing the work and life skills of handicapped inmates. *Corrections Today,* pp. 66–73.

Pomerantz, D., & Marholin, D. (1977). Vocational habilitation: A time for change. In E. Sontag (Ed.), *Educational programming for the severely and profoundly handicapped.* Reston, VA: The Council for Exceptional Children, Division on Mental Retardation.

Ponzo, A. (1976). Integrating techniques from five counseling theories. *Personnel and Guidance Journal, 54*(8), 415–419.

Porter, T., Rubin, S., & Sink, J. (1979). Essential rehabilitation counselor diagnostic, counseling, and placement competencies. *Journal of Applied Rehabilitation Counseling, 10,* 158–162.

Preston, R. P. (1979). *The dilemmas of care: Social and nursing adaptations to the deformed, the disabled and the aged.* New York: Elsevier North Holland.

Pruitt, W. (1973). Work adjustment: A report on a national opinion survey. *Vocational Evaluation & Work Adjustment Bulletin, 6*(2), 19–28.

Puner, M. (1974). *To the good long life: What we know about growing old.* New York: Universe Books.

Quintana, L. (1982). Psychological evaluation and their use with migrant and seasonal farmworkers. In O. A. Rivera & R. Cespedes (Eds.), *Rehabilitation of handicapped migrant and seasonal farmworkers* (pp. 93–115). Salt Lake City, UT: Institute of Human Resource Development.

Radzyminski, S. F. (1969). Symposium on care and rehabilitation of the geriatric patient. Part 1: Introduction and general considerations. *Journal of the American Geriatrics Society, 17*(12), 1134–1165.

Rainier, J. D., & Altshuler, K. Z. (1970). *Expanded mental health care for the deaf: Rehabilitation and prevention.* New York: Research Foundation for Mental Hygiene, Rockland State Hospital and New York State Psychiatric Institute.

Rank, O. (1945). *Will therapy and truth and reality.* New York: Alfred A. Knopf.

Rasch, J. D. (1985). *Rehabilitation of workers' compensation and other insurance claimants: Case management, forensic and business aspects.* Springfield, IL: Charles C. Thomas.

Rasch, J. D., Crystal, R. M., & Thomas, K. R. (1977). The perception of the older adult: A study of trainee attitudes. *Journal of Applied Rehabilitation Counseling, 8,*(2), 121–127.

Rasch, J. D., Hollingsworth, D. F., Saxon, J. P., & Thomas, K. R. (1984). Student recruitment issues in the 1980's. *Rehabilitation Counseling Bulletin, 28*(1), 46–49.

Rawlings, B. W., Trybus, R. J., & Biser, J. (Eds.). (1978). *A guide to college/career programs for deaf students.* Gallaudet College, Office of Demographic Studies.

Reagles, K. W. (1980). Rehabilitation counseling a profession. *ARCA News, 8*(2), 8.

Reagles, K. W. (1983). Rehabilitation in a multiprogram private sector company. *Rehabilitation Counseling Bulletin, 27,* 48–53.

Reda, M. A., & Mahoney, M. J. (Eds.). (1984). *Cognitive psychotherapies: Recent developments in theory, research and practice.* Cambridge, MA: Ballinger.

Redd, W. H. (1980, October 3). *Behavior therapy with cancer patients.* Professional Seminar presented at Southern Illinois University-Carbondale, Illinois.

Redd, W. H. (1980). In vivo desensitization in the treatment of chronic emesis following gastrointestinal surgery. *Behavior Therapy, 11*(3), 421–427.

Redd, W., Anderson, G. V., & Minagawa, R. Y. (1982). Hypnotic control of anticipatory emesis in patients receiving cancer chemotherapy. *Journal of Consulting and Clinical Psychology, 50,* 14–19.

Rehabilitation Group, Inc. (1979). *Digest of data on persons with disabilities.* Washington, DC: U.S. Government Printing Office. (Stock No. 017–090–00050–0).

Rehabilitation Services Administration. (1978). Transitional employment enhances job placement for epileptic clients. *Rehabilitation Brief, 1*(4), 1–2.

Rehabilitation Services Administration. (1981b, July 14). *Memorandum from the task force on learning disabilities.* Information Memorandum RSA–IM–81–37. Washington, DC: Author.

Rehabilitation Services Administration. (1981a, July 27). *Acceptance of specific learning disability as a medically recognizable disability.* Program Instruction Memorandum RSA–PI–81–22. Washington, DC: Author.

Reitan, R. M. (1975). Assessment of brain-behavior relationships. In P. McReynolds (Ed.), *Advances in psychological assessment* (Vol. 3). San Francisco: Jossey-Boss.

Revell, W., Jr., Wehman, P., & Arnold, S. (1984). Supported work model of competitive employment for persons with mental retardation: Implications for rehabilitative services. *Journal of Rehabilitation, 50,* 33–38.

Reynolds, E. H. (1976). Unsatisfactory aspects of the drug treatment of epilepsy. *Epilepsia, 17,* xiii–xv.

Ridenour, D. M., & Johnston, J. (1981). *A guide to post-secondary educational opportunities for the learning disabled.* Oak Park, IL: Time Out to Enjoy, Inc.

Riggar, T. F., Godley, S. H., & Hafer, M. (1984). Burnout and job satisfaction in rehabilitation administrators and direct service providers. *Rehabilitation Counseling Bulletin, 27*(3), 151–160.

Riggar, T. F., & Matkin, R. E. (1984). Rehabilitation counselors working as administrators: A pilot investigation. *Journal of Applied Rehabilitation Counseling, 15*(1), 9–13.

Riggar, T. F., & Riggar, S. W. (1978). The rehabilitation counselor in an educational setting. *Personnel and Guidance Journal, 56,* 58–60.

Robinson, N. M., & Robinson, H. B. (1976). *The mentally retarded child.* New York: McGraw-Hill.

Rodin, E. A., Shapiro, H. L., & Lenox, K. (1977). Epilepsy and life performance. *Rehabilitation Literature, 38,* 34–38.

Roe, A. (1957). Early determinants of vocational choice. *Journal of Counseling Psychology, 4,* 212–217.

Roessler, R., & Bolton, B. (1978). *Psychosocial adjustment to disability.* Baltimore: University Park Press.

Roessler, R., & Bolton, B. (1983). Assessment and enhancement of functional vocational capabilities: A five year research strategy [Richard J. Baker

Memorial Monograph, Series No. 1]. *Vocational Evaluation & Work Adjustment Bulletin.*

Roessler, R. T., & Hiett, A. (1983). Strategies for increasing employer response to job development surveys. *Rehabilitation Counseling Bulletin, 26*(5), 368–370.

Roessler, R. T., & Rubin, S. E. (1982). *Case management and rehabilitation counseling.* Baltimore: University Park Press.

Rogers, C. R. (1942). *Counseling and psychotherapy.* Boston: Houghton Mifflin.

Rogers, C. R. (1951). *Client-centered therapy.* Boston: Houghton Mifflin.

Rogers, C. R. (1957). The necessary and sufficient conditions of therapeutic personality change. *Journal of Consulting Psychology, 21,* 95–103.

Rogers, C. R. (1959). A theory of therapy, personality, and interpersonal relationships, as developed in the client centered framework. In S. Koch (Ed.), *Psychology: A study of science. Study 1. Conceptual and systematic: Vol. 3. Formulations of the person and the social context* (pp. 184–256). New York: McGraw-Hill.

Rogers, C. R. (1961). *On becoming a person.* Boston: Houghton Mifflin.

Rogers, C. R. (1975). Empathic: An appreciated way of being. *Counseling Psychologist, 5,* 2–10.

Rogers, C. R. (1980). *A way of being.* Boston: Houghton Mifflin.

Rogers, C. R., Gendlin, E., Keisler, D., & Truax, C. (1967). *The therapeutic relationship and its impact.* Westport, CT: Greenwood Press.

Roman, P. (1981, March–April). Latest corporate EAP statistics: Corporate pacesetters making EAP progress. *Alcoholism,* pp. 37–41.

Romano, M. D. (1974). Family response to traumatic head injury. *Scandinavian Journal of Rehabilitation Medicine, 6,* 1–4.

Rosen, M., Clark, G. R., & Kivitz, M. S. (1977). *Habilitation of the handicapped: New dimensions in programs for the developmentally disabled.* Baltimore: University Park Press.

Rosenberg, H., & Tesolowski, D. G. (1980). Teacher education: Preparing professional educators to be advocates for vocationally oriented special needs students. *Education and Training of the Mentally Retarded, 15,* 132–138.

Rosenbloom, A. A. (1974). Prognostic factors in the visual rehabilitation of aging patients. *New Outlook for the Blind, 68*(3), 124–127.

Rosenstein, J., & Lerman, A. (1963). *Vocational status and adjustment of deaf women.* New York: Lexington Scool for the Deaf.

Rosenthal, M., Griffith, E., Bond, M., & Miller, J. D. (Eds.). (1983). *Rehabilitation of the head injured adult.* Philadelphia: F. A. Davis.

Rossi, P. H. (1969). Evaluating educational programs. *The Urban Review, 3,* 17–18.

Roth, R. (1981, March–April). The EAP works: A profitable new tool for the private sector. *Alcoholism,* pp. 24–27.

Rozsnafsky, J. (1974). The impact of Alfred Adler on three "free-will" therapies of the 1960's. *Journal of Individual Psychology, 3,* 65–80.

Rubin, S., & Emener, W. (1979). Recent rehabilitation counselor role changes and role strain—a pilot investigation. *Journal of Applied Rehabilitation Counseling, 10,* 142–147.

Rubin, S. E., & Farley, R. C. (1980). *Intake interview skills for rehabilitation counselors.* (Advanced Facilitative Case Management Series, Training Package I). Fayetteville, AR: University of Arkansas/Arkansas Rehabilitation Services, Arkansas Rehabilitation Research & Training Center.

Rubin, S., Matkin, R., Ashley, J., Beardsley, M., May, V., Onsott, K., & Puckett, F. D. (1984). Roles and functions of certified rehabilitation counselors. *Rehabilitation Counseling Bulletin, 27*(4), 199–224.

Rubin, S. E., Means, B. L., Rice, B. D., Bozarth, J. D., & Milligan, G. T. (1974). *Facilitative case management: Instructor's manual.* Fayetteville, AR: University of Arkansas.

Rubin, S. E., & Rice, J. M. (1986). Rehabilitation research: An analysis of a problem and suggestions for remedition. *Rehabilitation Counseling Bulletin,* in press.

Rubin, S. E., & Roessler, R. T. (1978). *Foundation of the vocational rehabilitation process.* Baltimore: University Park Press.

Rubin, S. E., & Roessler, R. T. (1983). *Foundations of the vocational rehabilitation process* (2nd ed.). Austin, TX: Pro-Ed.

Rudrud, E. H., Rice, J. M. Robertson, J. M., & Olson, N. M. (1984). The use of self-monitoring to increase and maintain work production rates. *Vocational Evaluation & Work Adjustment Bulletin, 17,* 14–17.

Ruffin, J. E. (1984). The anxiety of meaninglessness. *Journal of Counseling and Development, 63*(1), 40–42.

Ruiz, R. A. (1981). Hispanic history and culture as background for the counseling of Chicanos. In D. W. Sue (Ed.), *Cultural perspectives in counseling.* New York: John Wiley.

Ruiz, R. A., & Casas, M. L. (1981). Culturally relevant and behavioristic counseling for Chicano college students. In *Counseling across cultures,* (pp. 181–202). Honolulu: The University Press of Hawaii.

Ruiz, R. A., Casas, J. M., & Padilla, A. M. (1977). *Culturally relevant behavioristic counseling.* Los Angeles: University of California (Los Angeles), Spanish-Speaking Mental Health Research Center. (Occasional Paper No. 5)

Ruiz, R. A., Casas, M. L., & Padilla, A. M. (1978). Culturally relevant behavioristic counseling. *Personnel and Guidance Journal.*

Ruiz, R. A., & Padilla, A. M. (1977). Counseling Latinos. *Personnel and Guidance Journal, 55*(7), 401–408.

Ruiz, R. A., Padilla, A. M., & Alvarez, R. (1978). Issues in the counseling of Spanish-speaking/surnamed clients: Recommendations for therapeutic services. In G. R. Walz & L. Benjamin (Eds.), *Transcultural counseling needs, programs, and techniques.* New York: Human Science Press.

Rule, W. (1977). Corrective reactions to client negativism using a combined facilitative and Adlerian-based approach. *Corrective and Social Psychiatry and Journal of Behavior Technology Methods and Therapy, 23,* 7–10.

Rule, W. (1982). Lifestyle interpretation using imagination of the ideal social self. *Individual Psychology: The Journal of Adlerian Theory, Research and Practices, 38*(4), 339–342.

Rule, W. (Ed.). (1984). *Lifestyle counseling for adjustment to disability.* Rockville, MD: Aspen Systems Corp.

Rusch, F. R. (1979). Toward the validation of social-vocational survival skills. *Mental Retardation, 17*(3), 143–145.

Rusch, F. R., & Mithaug, D. E. (1980). *Vocational training for mentally retarded adults: A behavior analytic approach.* Champaign, IL: Research Press.

Rusch, F. R., Withers, J. A., Menchetti, B. M., & Schutz, R. A. (1980). Social validation of a program to reduce topic repetition in a nonsheltered setting. *Education and Training of the Mentally Retarded, 15,* 208–216.

Rusk, H. A. (1971). Rehabilitation of patients with cancer related disability. *Rehabilitation medicine* (4th ed.). St. Louis: C. V. Mosby.

Rusk, H. A. (1977). *Rehabilitation medicine.* St. Louis: C. V. Mosby.

Rusk, H. A., Block, J. M., & Lowman, E. W. (1969). Rehabilitation following traumatic brain damage. *Medical Clinics of North America, 53*(3), 677–684.

Ryan, T. A., & Krumboltz, J. D. (1964). Effect of planned reinforcement counseling on client decision-making behavior. *Journal of Counseling Psychology, 11,* 315–323.

Sailor, W., & Guess, D. (1983). *Severely handicapped students: An instructional design.* Boston: Houghton Mifflin.

Salamone, P. R. (1971). A client-centered approach to job placement. *Vocational Guidance Quarterly, 19*(4), 266–270.

Salamone, P. R., & Usdane, W. M. (1977). Client-centered placement revisited: A dialog on placement philosophy. *Rehabilitation Counseling Bulletin, 21*(2), 85–91, 176.

Sales, A. (1979). Rehabilitation counseling in the private sector: Implications for graduate education. *Journal of Rehabilitation, 45*(3), 59–61; 72.

Salmon, H. E. (1981a). How can I make the best use of support networks. In J. E. Myers (Ed.), *Counseling older persons; Volume 3. A trainer's manual for basic helping skills.* Falls Chruch, VA: American Personnel and Guidance Association.

Salmon, H. E. (1981b). Theories of aging, disability and loss. *Journal of Rehabilitation, 47*(4), 44–50.

Sampson, J. P., Jr. (1983a). An integrated approach to computer applications in counseling psychology. *Counseling Psychologist, 11*(4), 65–74.

Sampson, J. P., Jr. (1983b). Computer-assisted testing and assessment: Current status and implications for the future. *Measurement and Evaluation in Guidance, 15,* 293–299.

Sandler, A. (1966). Aspects of passivity and ego development in the blind infant. *Psychoanalytic Study of Children, 18,* 343–361.

Sands, H. (Ed.). (1982). *Epilepsy: A handbook for the mental health professional.* New York: Brunner/Mazel.

Sanford, F. (1955). Creative mental health and the principle of habeus mentem. *American Psychologist, 10,* 829–835.

Santa Cruz, L. A., & Hepworth, D. H. (1975). Effects of cultural orientations on casework. *Social Casework, 56,* 52–57.

Sawyer, H. (1983). Progress tracking and program evaluation: A dynamic duo for accountability in adjustment services. *Vocational Evaluation & Work Adjustment Bulletin, 16*(2), 50–55.

Sawyer, J. (1966). Measurement and prediction, clinical and statistical. *Psychological Bulletin, 66,* 178–200.

Scadden, L. A. (1983). Technology and the labor market, implications for blind and visually impaired persons. *Blindness,* 17–24.

Scalia, V. (1983). *LD and rehabilitation: A historical perspective.* Paper presented at the American Personnel and Guidance Association Convention, Washington, DC.

Schein, J. (1977). *Model state plan for vocational rehabilitation of deaf clients* (rev. ed.). New York: New York University, Deafness Research and Training Center.

Schein, J., & Delk, M. (1974). *The deaf population of the United States.* Silver Spring, MD: National Association of the Deaf.

Schein, J. R., & Delk, M. (1980). Survey of health care for deaf people. *Deaf America, 32,* 5–6.

Schiffman, A., Cohen, S., Nowick, R., & Selinger D. (1978). Initial diagnostic hypotheses: Factors which may distort physicians' judgements. *Organizational Behavior and Human Performance, 21,* 305–315.

Schlenoff, D. (1975). A theory of career development for the quadraplegic. *Journal of Applied Rehabilitation Counseling, 6,* 3–11.

Schlenoff, D. (1978). Considerations in the development of the job placement specialist. *Rehabilitation Literature, 39*(6–7), 190–191.

Schloss, P., & Schloss, C. (1982). Social skills training in the vocational rehabilitation of mentally retarded individuals. *Vocational Evaluation & Work Adjustment Bulletin, 15*(4), 142–147.

Schneider, C. R., & Anderson, W. (1980). Attitudes toward the stigmatized: Some insights from recent research. *Rehabilitation Counseling Bulletin, 23,* 299–313.

Schneider, H. C. & Dunaway, H. L. (1977). The relationship of case-service expenditures and severity of disability of rehabilitation success. *Journal of Rehabilitation Administration, 1*(3), 17–24.

Schneider, M. A. (1980). Some medical aspects of alcohol and other drugs of abuse. (Film narrative), Rev.

Scholl, G. & Schnur, R. (1976). *Measures of psychological, vocational, and educational functioning in the blind and visually handicapped.* New York: American Foundation for the Blind.

Schow, R. L., Christensen, J. M. Hutchinson, J. M., & Nerbonne, M. A. (1978). *Communication disorders of the aged: A guide for health professionals.* Baltimore: University Park Press.

Schultz, J. H., & Luthe, W. (1969). *Autogenic therapy* (Vol. 1). New York: Grune & Stratton.

Schultz, P. (1968). A group approach to working with families of the blind. *New Outlook for the Blind, 62*(3), 82–86.

Schumacher, B. (1977). Rehabilitation counseling. In P. J. Valletutti & F. Christopher (Eds.), *Interdisciplinary approaches to human service,* Baltimore: University Park Press.

Schwartz, L., Sample, K. A., & Wegle, E. D. (1975). Severe alcoholic cardiomyopathy reversed with abstention from alcohol. *American Journal of Cardiology, 36*(12), 963–966.

Schofield, M. E. (1983). *Rehabilitation Education and Training.* (Rehabilitation Research Review Monograph 1). Washington, DC: National Rehabilitation Information Center.

Scott, R. (1969). *The making of blind men.* New York: Russell Sage Foundation.

Sheils, J. (1980). Work samples and normative data: Are deaf norms really needed? *Journal of Rehabilitation of the Deaf, 14*(1), 14–21.

Shepard, I. L. (1970). Limitations and cautions in the Gestalt approach. In J. Fagon & I. L. Shepard (Eds.), *Gestalt therapy now.* Palo Alto, CA: Science & Behavior Books.

Sheppard, H. L. (1971). *New perspectives on older workers.* Washington, DC: The W. E. Upjohn Institute for Employment Research.

Sherman, E. D., & Gingras, G. (1965). Rehabilitation of the aged. *Canadian Medical Association Journal, 93*(15), 797–800.

Sherman, S. W., & Robinson, N. M. (Eds.). (1982). *Ability testing of handicapped people: Dilemma for government, science, and the public.* Washington, DC: National Academy Press.

Shontz, F. C. (1975). *The psychological aspects of physical illness and disability.* New York: Macmillan.

Shrey, D. E. (1979). The rehabilittion counselor in industry: A new frontier. *Journal of Applied Rehabilitation Counseling, 9,* 168–172.

Shrey, D. E. (1982). *Conference proceedings rehabilitation in industry: State of the art.* Boston: Boston University, Department of Rehabilitation Counseling, Sargent College of Allied Health Professionals.

Shulman, B. H. (1972). Confrontation techniques. *Journal of Individual Psychology, 28,* 177–183.

Shulman, B. H. (1973). *Contributions to individual psychology.* Chicago: Alfred Adler Institute.

Shulman, B. H. (1977). Encouraging the pessimist: A confronting technique. *The Individual Psychologist, 14,* 7–9.

Siegel, J. S. (1978). *Prospective trends in the size and structure of the elderly population, impact of mortality trends, and some implications.* Statement before the Select Committee for Aging and the Select Commission on Population, U.S. House of Representatives, May 24, 1978. Washington, DC: Superintendent of Documents. (Y4. P81:95/9)

Sigelman, C. K., Budd, E. C., Winer, J. L., Schoenrock, C. J., & Martin, P. W. (1982). Evaluation alternative techniques of questioning mentally retarded persons. *American Journal of Mental Deficiency, 86,* 511–518.

Silverman, E. B., & Sass, S. D. (1982). Applying the outplacement concept. *Training and Development Journal, 36,* 70–77.

Simkin, J. (1979). Gestalt therapy. In R. J. Corsini (Ed.), *Current Psychotherapies* (2nd ed.). Itasca, IL: F. E. Peacock.

Simpson, I. H., & McKinney, J. C. (Eds.) (1966). *Social aspects of aging.* Durham, NC: Duke University Press.

Sinick, D. (1977). Vocational counseling trends in rehabilitation settings. *Journal of Rehabilitation, 43*(3), 19–21, 35.

Skinner, B. F. (1953). *Science and human behavior.* New York: Free Press.

Skinner, B. F. (1969). *Contingencies of reinforcement: A theoretical analysis.* New York: Appleton-Century-Crofts.

Slany, R. B. (1977). "Real" therapy and the rehabilitation counseling student. *Rehabilitation Counseling Bulletin, 20,* 202–205.

Smith, E. (1978). Helping old people to continue living at home: Development of new methods. *Review of Social Health, 98*(1), 11–14.

Smith, J. W. (1977). Neurological disorders in alcoholism. In N. J. Estes & M. E. Heinemann (Eds.), *Alcoholism.* St. Louis: C. V. Mosby.

Smith, M., Glass, G., & Miller, T. (1980). *The benefits of psychotherapy.* Baltimore: Johns Hopkins University Press.

Sobell, M. B., & Sobell, L. C. (1978). *Behavioral treatment of alcohol problems: Individualized therapy and controlled drinking.* New York: Plenum.

Soloff, A. (1972). The utilization of research. *Rehabilitation Literature, 33*(3), 66–72.

Solomon, K., & Vickers, R. (1979). Attitudes of health workers toward old people. *Journal of the American Geriatrics Society, 27*(4), 186–191.

Space, L. G. (1981). The computer as psychometrician. *Behavior Research Methods and Instrumentation, 13,* 545–606.

Stein, L., Mindel, E., & Jobaley, T. (Eds.). (1981). *Deafness and mental health.* New York: Grune & Stratton.

Sterman, P. S. (1983). Transcendence or tranquilization: An existential perspective on chemical dependency (Doctoral dissertation, United States International University, 1983). *Dissertation Abstracts International, 44,* 1582 B.

Sternback, R. (1968). *Pain, a psychophysiological analysis.* New York: Academic Press.

Stewart, L. (1976). The role of vocational rehabilitation in the delivery of services to deaf people. In V. Glenn (Ed.), *National Conference on Rehabilitation Services for the Deaf.* Arkansas Rehabilitation Research and Training Center.

Stickle, F. (1977). Satisfying the emotional needs of the elderly: A call for counselors. *Counseling and Values, 21*(3), 180–184.

Stokes, T. F., & Baer, D. M. (1977). An implicit technology of generalization. *Journal of Applied Behavior Analysis, 10,* 349–367.

Stokoe, W. C. (1978). *Sign language structures.* Silver Spring, MD: Linstock Press.

Strehler, B. L. (1962, 1977). *Time, cells, and aging.* New York: Academic Press.

Streissguth, A. P., Little, R. E., Herman, C. S., & Woodell, S. (1979). IQ in children of recovered alcoholic mothers compared to matched controls. *Alcoholism: Clinical and Experimental Research, 3*(2), 197.

Struthers, R. (1982). *A conceptual outline for evaluating and improving rehabilitation programs.* Michigan Department of Education, Michigan Rehabilitation Services. (Monograph)

Stubbins, J. (1982). *The clinical attitudes in rehabilitation: A cross cultural view.* World Rehabilitation Fund Monograph #16. New York: World Rehabilitation Fund.

Sturm, T. E., Otto, N. R., & Bakeman, M. (1972). *Vocational diagnostic interviewing.* Minneapolis: Minneapolis Rehabilitation Center.

Sue, D. W., & Sue, D. (1977). Barriers to effective cross-cultural counseling. *Journal of Counseling Psychology, 24,* 420–429.

Summers, J. A. (1981). The definition of developmental disabilities: A concept in transition. *Mental Retardation, 19,* 259–265.

Sundberg, N. D. (1977). *Assessment of persons.* Englewood Cliffs, NJ: Prentice-Hall.

Sundberg, N. D., & Tyler, L. E. (1962). *Clinical psychology.* New York: Appleton-Century-Crofts.

Super, D. E. (1953). A theory of vocational development. *American Psychologist, 8,* 185–190.

Super, D. (1957). *The psychology of careers.* New York: Harper & Row.

Super, D. (1974). *Measuring vocational maturity for counseling and evaluation.* National Vocational Guidance Association. (Monograph).

Super, D. E., & Overstreet, P. L. (1960). *The vocational maturity of ninth grade boys.* New York: Teachers College Bureau of Publications.

Sussman, M. B. (1970). *From student to practitioner: Professionalization and de-professionalization in rehabilitation counseling.* (Working Paper #7), Cleveland, OH: Case Western Reserve University.

Sutton, D., Smith, W. R., & Fraser, R. T. (1979, March). *A comparative study of parent counseling approaches.* Paper presented at the Thirtieth Annual Western Institute on Epilepsy, Portland, OR.

Sutton-Smith, B., & Rosenberg, B. G. (1970). *The sibling.* New York: Holt, Rinehart & Winston.

Swerdlow, M. (1973). Relieving pain in the terminally ill. *Geriatrics, 28*(7), pp. 100–103.

Switzer, M. E. (1956). Role of the federal government in vocational rehabilitation. *Archives of Physical Medicine and Rehabilitation, 37,* 542–546.

Szapocznik, J., Scopetta, M. H., Kurtines, W., & Arnalde, M. A. (in press). Theory and measurement of acculturation. *Interamerican Journal of Psychology.*

Szasz, T. (1961). *The myth of mental illness: A foundation of a theory of personal conduct.* New York: Harper & Row.

Szuhay, J. A., & Newill, B. (1980). *Field investigation and evaluation of learning disabilities (Vols. 1–6).* Scranton, PA: University of Scranton Press.

Taylor, J. (1975). Early recollections as a projective technique: A review of some recent validation studies. *Journal of Individual Psychology, 31*(2), 213–218.

Taylor, L. J. (1980). Toward a humanistic-existential rehabilitation psychology: A study of the congruence of the principle of rehabilitation psychology with the tenets of the humanistic-existential approach in psychology (Doctoral dissertation, University of Southern California, 1980). *Dissertation Abstracts International, 41,* 678 B.

Telson, S. (1965). Parent counseling. *New Outlook for the Blind, 59,* 127–129.

Tenth Institute on Rehabilitation Studies. (1972). Washington, DC: Department of Health, Education and Welfare, Rehabilitation Services Administration.

Thomas, K. R., & Butler, A. J. (1981). Counseling for personal adjustment. In R. M. Parker and C. E. Hansen (Eds.), *Rehabilitation counseling: Foundations-consumers-service delivery* (pp. 227–260). Boston, MA: Allyn & Bacon.

Thomas, K., & Parker, R. (1981). Promoting counseling in rehabilitation settings. *Journal of Applied Rehabilitation Counseling, 12,* 101–103.

Thomas, K. R., & Parker, R. M. (1984). Counseling interventions. *Journal of Applied Rehabilitation Counseling, 15,* 15–19.

Thomas, P. (1968). Experiences of two preventive clinics for the elderly. *British Medical Journal, 2*(601), 357–360.

Thompson, J. K., Kite, J. L. & Bruyere, S. M. (1979). *Caseload management: Content and training perspective.* Paper presented at the American Personnel and Guidance Association Annual Convention, Dallas, TX.

Thomsen, I. V. (1974). The patient with severe head injury and his family. *Scandinavian Journal of Rehabilitation Medicine, 6,* 180–183.

Thomson, S. (1974). Insight for the sightless: A TA group for the blind. *Transactional Analysis, 4*(1), 13–17.

Thoreson, C. E., Kirmil-Gray, K., & Crosbie, P. (1977). Processes and procedures of self-control: A working model. *Canadian Counselor, 12,* 66–75.

Thorne, F. C. (1968). *Psychological case handling: Vol. 1. Establishing the conditions necessary for counseling and psychotherapy.* Brandon, VT: Clinical Psychology.

Tichenor, D. F., Thomas, K. R., & Kravetz, S. P. (1975). Client-counselor congruence in perceiving handicapped problems. *Rehabilitation Counseling Bulletin, 19*(1), 299–304.

Tiedeman, D. V. (1979). *Career development: Designing our career machines.* New York: Character Research Press & Carroll Press.

Tiedeman, D. V., & O'Hara, R. P. (1963). *Career development: Choice and adjustment.* New York: College Entrance Examination Board.

Time. (1979, April 2). Psychiatry on the couch. pp. 74–82.

Tindall, L. W., Gugerty, J. J., & Dougherty, B. (1984). *Utilizing the Job Training Partnership Act funds for the vocational education, training, and employment of special needs students.* Madison, WI: University of Wisconsin, The Vocational Studies Center.

Toomer, J. E. (1982). Counseling psychologists in business and industry. *Counseling Psychologist, 10,* 9–18.

Toomey, T., Ghia, J., Mao, W., & Gregg, J. (1977). Acupuncture and chronic pain mechanisms: The moderating effects of affect, personality, and stress on response to treatment. *Pain, 3,* 137–145.

Torkelson, R. M. (1982). *The relationship of psychological factors to adaptive physical functioning following severe traumatic brain injury.* Unpublished doctoral dissertation, University of Wisconsin–Madison.

Torkelson, R. M., Jellinek, H. M., Malec, J., & Harvey, R. F. (1983). Traumatic brain injury: Psychological and medical factors related to rehabilitation outcome. *Rehabilitation Psychology, 28*(3), 31–37.

Torkelson, R. M., & Lynch, R. K. (1979). Rehabilitation considerations with the communicatively handicapped individual. *Journal of Rehabilitation, 45*(4), 48–51.

Townsend, P. (1957). *The family life of old people.* Boston: Routledge & Kegan Paul.

Tringo, J. L. (1970). The hierarchy of preferences toward disability groups. *The Journal of Special Education, 4,* 295–305.

Trotter, R. T., & Chavira, J. A. (1981). *Curaderismo: Mexican American folk healing.* Athens, GA: University of Georgia Press.

Truax, C. B. (1966). Reinforcement and nonreinforcement in Rogerian psychotherapy. *Journal of Abnormal Psychology, 71,* 1–9.

Truax, C. B., & Carkhuff, R. R. (1967). *Toward effective counseling and psycho-therapy.* Chicgo: Aldine.

Truitt, C. P., & Vandergrift, J. B. (1980). A comparison of bureaucratic and professional expectations for casework accountability. *Journal of Rehabilitation Administration, 4*(2), 64–70, 80.

Turk, D. (1978). Cognitive-behavioral techniques in the management of pain. In J. Foreyt & D. Rathjen (Eds.), *Cognitive behavior therapy: Research and application.* New York: Plenum.

Turk, D. C., & Rennert, K. (1981). Pain and the terminally ill cancer patient: A cognitive-social learning perspective. In H. J. Sobel (Ed.), *Behavior therapy in terminal care: A humanistic approach.* Cambridge, MA: Ballinger.

Tuthill, M. (1982, June). Joining the war on drug abuse. *Nation's Business,* pp. 65–66.

U.S. Bureau of the Census, Current Population Reports. (1980). *Persons of Spanish Origin in the United States.* (March, 1979. Series P. 20, No. 354). Washington, DC: U.S. Government Printing Office.

U.S. Chamber of Commerce. (1983). *Analysis of workers' compensation laws 1983.* Washington, DC: Author.

U.S. Department of Education. (1977). Regulations. *Federal Register,* p. 65083.

U.S. Department of Education, Office of Special Education and Rehabilitation Services. (1981). Head injury: The problem, the need. *Programs for the Handicapped, 6,* 1–3.

U.S. Department of Health, Education and Welfare. (1978, 1979). *Annual report of the U.S. Department of Health, Education, and Welfare to the President and the Congress on federal activities related to the administration of the Rehabilitation Act of 1973 as amended.* Washington, DC: Author.

U.S. Department of Health, Education and Welfare. (1980). *Study of state vocational rehabilitation agency use of post-employment services.* Information Memorandum, Rehabilitation Services (IM–80–15). Washington, DC: Author.

U.S. Department of Health, Education and Welfare. (1981). *Fourth special report to the U.S. Congress on alcohol and health from the Secretary of Health and Human Services, January, 1981.* Washington, DC: National Institute on Alcohol Abuse and Alcoholism.

U.S. Department of Health and Human Services, Social Security Administration. (1982). *Disability insurance vocational rehabilitation demonstrations: Project statement.* Washington, DC: Author.

U.S. Department of Labor, Employment Standards Administration. (1980). *Guidelines for rehabilitation services from private rehabilitation agencies.* Washington, DC: Author.

U.S. Department of Transportation. (1974). *Alcohol safety action projects: Evaluation of 1972 operations.* Vol. 1, NHTSA Technical Report. Washington, DC: Author.

Urban Institute. (1980). *Forecasting manpower requirements in the rehabilitation industry.* Washington, DC: Author.

Usdane, W. M. (1974). Placement personnel—a graduate program concept. *Journal of Rehabilitation, 40*(2), 12–13.

Usdane, W. M., & Salamone, P. R. (1977). Reconceptualization of the placement process: A dialog. *Rehabilitation Counseling Bulletin, 21*(2), 92–102.

Vale, C. D. (1981). Design and implementation of a micro-computer based adaptive testing system. *Behavior Research Methods and Instrumentation, 13,* 399–406.

Vander Kolk, C. (1977). Demographic, etiological, and functional variables related to intelligence in the visually impaired. *Journal of Clinical Psychology, 33*(3), 782–786.

Vander Kolk, C. (1981). *Assessment and planning with the visually impaired.* Baltimore: University Park Press.

Vander Kolk, C. (1982). Rehabilitation and visual impairment: A human system. *Journal of Visual Impairment and Blindness, 76*(9), 346–350.

Vandergoot, D. (1976). A comparison of two mailing approaches attempting to generate the participation of businessmen in rehabilitation. *Rehabilitation Counseling Bulletin, 20,* 73–75.

Vandergoot, D. (1982). A job description for an employment services specialist. *Rehabilitation Counseling Bulletin, 26*(2), 114–118.

Vandergoot, D., Swirsky, J., & Rice, K. (1982). Using occupational information in rehabilittion counseling. *Rehabilitation Counseling Bulletin, 26*(2), 94–100.

Vandergoot, D., & Worrall, J. D. (1979). *Placement in rehabilitation: A career development perspective.* Baltimore: University Park Press.

Vandergoot, D., Worrall, J. D., & Jacobsen. (1979). New directions for placement practice in vocational rehabilitation. In D. Vandergoot & J. D. Worrall (Eds.), *Placement in rehabilitation: A career development perspective.* Baltimore, MD: University Park Press.

Vash, C. L. (1981). *The psychology of disability.* New York: Springer Publishing Co.

Veglahn, P. A. (1976). Job search patterns of paraplegics. *Rehabilitation Counseling Bulletin, 20*(2), 129–135.

Vernon, M. (1968). Fifty years of research on the intelligence of deaf and hard of hearing children: A review of literature and discussion of implications. *Journal of Rehabilitation of the Deaf, 1*(4), 1–12.

Vernon, M. (1969). *Multiple handicapped deaf children: Medical, educational and psychological aspects.* Washington, DC: Council of Exceptional Children.

Vernon, M. (1971). Psychological evaluation of the severely handicapped deaf client. In L. Stewart (Ed.), *Toward more effective rehabilitation services for the severely handicapped deaf adult* (pp. 6–30). Hot Springs, AR: Arkansas Rehabilitation Research and Training Center.

Vernon, M. (1981). The decade of the eighties: Significant trends and developments for hearing impaired individuals. *Rehabilitation Literature, 42*(1–2), 1–9.

Vernon, M., Grieve, B., & Shaver, K. (1980). Handicapping conditions associated with the congenital rubella syndrome. *American Annals of the Deaf, 125*(8), 993–997.

Vernon, M., & Hicks, W. (1983). A group counseling and educational program for students with Usher's Syndrome. *Journal of Visual Impairment and Blindness, 77*(2), 64–66.

Vocational Evaluation and Work Adjustment Association. (1975). Vocational evaluation project final report. *Vocational Evaluation & Work Adjustment Bulletin, 8* (Special Edition).

Vontress, C. E. (1969). Cultural barriers in the counseling relationship. *Personnel and Guidance Journal, 48,* 11–17.

Vontress, C. E. (1974). Racial and ethnic barriers in counseling. *Counseling across cultures.* Honolulu: The University Press of Hawaii.

Wainwright, C., & Couch, R. (1978). Work adjustment: Potential and practice. *Journal of Rehabilitation, 44*(1), 39–42.

Walker, C. E., Hedberg, A. G., Clement, P. W., & Wright, L. (1981). *Clinical procedures for behavior therapy.* Englewood Cliffs, NJ: Prentice-Hall.

Wallhagen, M. I. (1979). The split brain: Implications for care and rehabilitation. *American Journal of Nursing, 79*(12), 2118–2125.

Walls, D. A. (1983). Placement: Rehabilitation's assets to industry. *Journal of Applied Rehabilitation Counseling, 14*(2), 47–50.

Walls, R., Werner, T., & Bacon, A. (1976). *Behavior checklists.* Institute, WV: West Virginia Rehabilitation Research & Training Center.

Waters, E., & Weaver, A. L. (1981). Specialized techniques to help older people. In J. E. Meyers (Ed.), *Counseling older persons: Vol. 3. A trainer's manual for basic helping skills.* Falls Church, VA: American Personnel and Guidance Association.

Watkins, C. G. (1983). Transference phenomena in the counseling situation. *Personnel and Guidance Journal, 62,* 206–210.

Watson, D. (Ed.). (1976). *Deaf evaluation and adjustment feasibility.* New York: New York University, Deafness Research and Training Center.

Wechsler, H., & Rohaman, M. (1982). Future caregivers' views on alcoholism treatment—a poor prognosis. *Journal of Studies on Alcohol, 43*(9), 939–955.

Wehman, P. (1976). Experimental rigor in rehabilitation research: Fact or fantasy. *Journal of Rehabilitation, 42*(3), 39.

Wehman, P., Hill, M., Goodall, P., Cleveland, P., Brooke, V., & Pentecost, J. H. (1982). Job placement and follow-up of moderately and severely handicapped individuals after three years. *The Journal of the Association for the Severely Handicapped, 7,* 5–16.

Wehman, P., Hill, J. W., & Koehler, F. (1979). Placement of developmentally disabled individuals into competitive employment: Three case studies. *Education and Training of the Mentally Retarded, 14,* 268–276.

Wehman, P., Renzaglia, A., & Schutz, R. (1977). Behavioral training strategies in sheltered workshops for the severely developmentally disabled. *AAESPH Review, 2,* 24–36.

Weiner, M. B., & Weinstock, C. S. (1979–80). Group progress of community elderly as measured by tape recording, group tempo and group evaluations. *International Journal of Aging Human Development, 10*(2), 177–185.

Weisenberg, M. (1977). Pain and pain control. *Psychological Bulletin, 84,* 1008–1044.

Weiss, C. (1979). The many meanings of research utilization. *Public Administration Review, 29*(5), 426–431.

Weiss, R. J., & Bergen, B. J. (1968). Social supports and the reduction of psychiatric disability *Psychiatry, 31,* 107–115.

Whitehead, C. (1979). Sheltered workshops in decade ahead. In G. T. Bellamy, G. O'Connor, & O. C. Karan (Eds.), *Vocational rehabilitation of severely handicapped persons.* Baltimore: University Park Press.

Whitehouse, F. (1975). Rehabilitation clinician. *Journal of Rehabilitation, 41*(3), 24–26.

Wiggins, J. S. (1973). *Personality and prediction: Principles of personality assessment.* Reading, MA: Addison-Wesley.

Wiig, E. H. (1972). The emerging learning disability crisis. *Journal of Rehabilitation, 38,* 15–17.

Will, M. (1984, March–April). Bridges from school to working life. *Programs for the handicapped,* pp. 1–5. Washington, DC: Department of Education, Office of Special Education and Rehabilitative Services, Office of Information and Resources for the Handicapped.

Willey, D. A. (1978). Caseload management for the vocational rehabilitation counselor in a state agency. *Journal of Applied Rehabilitation Counseling, 9*(4), 156–158.

Williams, M. G. (1981). Independent living and older people. *Journal of Rehabilitation, 47*(4), 69–71.

Williams, R. L., & Kirkland, J. (1971). The white counselor and the black client. *Counseling Psychologist, 2,* 114–116.

Williams, R. R., & Horn, J. W. (1977). Association of cancer sites with tobacco and alcohol consumption and socioeconomic status of patients: Interview study from the Third National Cancer Survey. *Journal of National Cancer Institute, 58*(3), 525–547.

Williamson, E. G. (1965). *Vocational counseling: Some historical, philosophical, and theoretical perspectives.* New York: McGraw-Hill.

Wilson, E. (1970). Group therapy in a rehabilitation program. *New Outlook for the Blind, 64*(7), 237–239.

Wolcott, L. E., & Wheeler, P. C. (1971). Rehabilitation and the aged. In A. B.Chirn (Ed.), *Working with older people: Vol. 4. Clinical aspects of aging.* Washington, DC: USDHEW, PHS.

Wolf, A. (1963). The psychoanalysis of groups. In M. B. Rosenbaum and M. Berger (Eds.), *Group psychotherapy and group function.* New York: Basic Books.

Wolf, M. M. (1978). Social validity: The case for subjective measurement or how applied behavior analysis is finding its heart. *Journal of Applied Behavior Analysis, 11*(2), 203–214.

Wolfensberger, W. (1980). A brief overview of normalization. In R. Flynn & K. E. Nitsch (Eds.), *Normalization, social integration, and community services.* Baltimore: University Park Press.

Wolkenberg, R. C., Gold, C., & Tichauer, E. R. (1975). Delayed effects of acute alcoholic intoxication of performance with reference to work safety. *Journal of Safety Research, 7,* 104.

World Health Organization. Expert Committee on Mental Health. (1952). *Alcohol Subcommittee second report.* W.H.O. Technical Report Series, No. 48. Geneva: Author.

World Health Organization. (1980). *International classification of diseases.* Ann Arbor, MI: Edwards Brothers.

Wren, C. G., & Darley, J. G. (1979). An appraisal on the professional status of personnel work. In E. G. Williamson (Ed.), *Trends in student personal work.* Minneapolis: University of Minnesota Press.

Wright, G. N. (Ed.). (1975). *Epilepsy rehabilitation.* Boston: Little, Brown.

Wright, G. N. (1980). *Total rehabilitation.* Boston: Little, Brown.

Wright, G. N. (1983). *Private sector: Role of rehabilitation professionals.* Washington, DC: The National Rehabilitation Information Center.

Wynder, E. L. (1978). Epidemiology of cancers of the upper alimentary and upper respiratory tracts. *Laryngoscope, 88*(1), 50–51.

Wynder, E. L., Bross, I. J., & Feldman, R. M. (1957). A study of the etiological factors in cancer of the mouth. *Cancer, 10,* 1300–1323.

Yates, A. J. (1980). *Biofeedback and the modification of behavior.* New York: Plenum Press.

Yontef, G. M. (1971). *A review of the practice of Gestalt therapy.* Los Angeles: Tirdent Shop, California State University.

Youmans, E. G. (1977). Attitudes: Young-old and old-old. *The Gerontologist, 17*(2), 178–188.

Ysseldyke, J. E., & Algozzive, R. (1982). *Critical issues in special and remedial education.* Boston: Houghton Mifflin.

Zadny, J. J., & James, L. F. (1976). *Another view of placement: State of the art, 1976.* Portland, OR: Portland State University, School of Social Work, Regional Rehabilitation Research Institute.

Zadny, J. J., & James, L. F. (1977). Time spent on placement. *Rehabilitation Counseling Bulletin, 21*(1), 31–38.

Zadny, J. J., & James, L. F. (1979a). Job placement in state vocational rehabilitation agencies: A survey of technique. *Rehabilitation Counseling Bulletin, 22*(4), 361–378.

Zadny, J. J., & James, L. F. (1979b). The problem with placement. *Rehabilitation Counseling Bulletin, 22*(5), 439–442.

Zamora, A. (1982). Where are we now and where are we going: A federal perspective. In O. Rivera & R. Cespedes (Eds.), *Rehabilitation of handicapped migrant and seasonal farmworkers* (pp. 163–172). Salt Lake City, UT: Institute of Human Resource Development.

Zieziula, F. R. (Ed.). (1982). *Assessment of hearing impaired people: A guide for selecting psychological, educational and vocational tests.* Washington, DC: Gallaudet College Press.

Zigler, E. (1966). Motivational determinants in performance of retarded children.*American Journal of Orthopsychiatry, 36,* 848–856.

Zigmond, N., & Brownlee, J. (1980). Social skills training for adolescents with learning disabilities. *Exceptional Children Quarterly, 1,* 77–83.

Zimmerman, J., Stuckey, T. E., Garlick, B. J., & Miller, M. (1969). Effects of token reinforcement on productivity in multiply handicapped clients in a sheltered workshop. *Rehabilitation Literature, 30,* 34–41.

Zohn, C. J., & Bornstein, P. H. (1980). Self-monitoring of work performance with mentally retarded adults: Effects on work productivity, work quality and on-task behavior. *Mental Retardation, 18,* 19–25.

Zunker, G. (1981). *Career counseling: Applied concepts of life planning.* Monterey, CA: Brooks/Cole.

Index